Jeffrey Aven

Sams **Teach Yourself**

Hadoop

in **24 Hours**

SAMS   800 East 96th Street, Indianapolis, Indiana, 46240 USA

Sams Teach Yourself Hadoop™ in 24 Hours

Copyright © 2017 by Pearson Education, Inc.

ISBN-13: 978-0-672-33852-6

ISBN-10: 0-672-33852-1

Library of Congress Control Number: 2017935714

Printed in the United States of America

1 17

Trademarks

Warning and Disclaimer

Special Sales

For information about buying this title in bulk quantities, or for special sales opportunities (which may include electronic versions; custom cover designs; and content particular to your business, training goals, marketing focus, or branding interests), please contact our corporate sales department at corpsales@pearsoned.com or (800) 382-3419.

For government sales inquiries, please contact governmentsales@pearsoned.com.

For questions about sales outside the U.S., please contact intlcs@pearsoned.com.

Editor in Chief
Greg Wiegand

Acquisitions Editor
Trina MacDonald

Development Editor
Chris Zahn

Technical Editor
Adam Shook

Managing Editor
Sandra Schroeder

Project Editor
Lori Lyons

Project Manager
Dhayanidhi

Copy Editor
Abigail Manheim

Indexer
Cheryl Lenser

Proofreader
Sathya Ravi

Editorial Assistant
Olivia Basegio

Cover Designer
Chuti Prasertsith

Compositor
codeMantra

Contents at a Glance

Table of Contents

Part III: Managing Hadoop

Preface

Hadoop is synonymous with Big Data, and the two are inexorably linked together. Although there have been many books written about Hadoop before this one, many of these books have been focused on one particular area of Hadoop, or required some prior experience with Hadoop. This book is different as it explores all areas of Hadoop and the Hadoop ecosystem, as well as providing an understanding and background to the genesis of Hadoop and the big data movement.

This book is also useful if you have had some exposure to Hadoop as it explores adjacent technologies such as Spark, HBase, Cassandra, and more. The book includes many diagrams, code snippets, hands-on exercises, quizzes, and Q&As, which will help you in distilling key concepts.

I have dedicated the past several years of my career to this subject area, teaching courses and consulting to clients on analytics and big data. I have seen the emergence and maturity of the big data and open source movements, and been part of its assimilation into the enterprise. I have tried to synthesize my personal learning journey over this time into this book.

I hope this book launches or assists in your journey to becoming a big data practitioner.

How This Book Is Organized

This book starts by establishing some of the basic concepts behind Hadoop, which are covered in **Part I, "Getting Started with Hadoop."** I also cover deployment of Hadoop both locally and in the cloud in Part I.

Part II, "Using Hadoop," is focused on the programming and data interfaces available with Hadoop, which include MapReduce, Pig, Hive, Spark, and more, as well as introductions to SQL-on-Hadoop and NoSQL using HBase.

Part III, "Managing Hadoop," covers scaling, management, and administration of Hadoop and its various related technologies, including advanced configuration, securing, monitoring, and troubleshooting Hadoop.

Data Used in the Exercises

Data for the Try it Yourself exercises can be downloaded from the book's Amazon Web Services (AWS) S3 bucket. If you are not familiar with AWS, don't worry—I cover this topic in the book as well.

Conventions Used in This Book

Each hour begins with "What You'll Learn in This Hour," which provides a list of bullet points highlighting the topics covered in that hour. Each hour concludes with a "Summary" page summarizing the main points covered in the hour, as well as "Q&A" and "Quiz" sections to help you consolidate your learning from that hour.

Key topics being introduced for the first time are typically *italicized* by convention. Most hours also include programming examples in numbered code listings. Where functions, commands, classes, or objects are referred to in text, they appear in `monospace` type.

Other asides in this book include the following:

NOTE

Content not integral to the subject matter but worth noting or being aware of.

TIP

TIP Subtitle

A hint or tip relating to the current topic that could be useful.

CAUTION

Caution Subtitle

Something related to the current topic that could lead to issues if not addressed.

TRY IT YOURSELF ▼

Exercise Title

An exercise related to the current topic including a step-by-step guide and descriptions of expected outputs.

About the Author

Jeffrey Aven is a big data, open source software, and cloud computing consultant and instructor based in Melbourne, Australia. Jeff has several years' experience with Hadoop, NoSQL, Spark, and related technologies, and has been involved in key roles with several major big data implementations in Australia. Jeffrey is the author of *SAMS Teach Yourself Apache Spark* and was awarded Cloudera Hadoop Instructor of the Year for APAC in 2013.

Acknowledgments

I would like to acknowledge the team at Pearson who work hard behind the scenes on all of these projects. I would also like to acknowledge Adam Shook for his help as a technical editor for this project.

We Want to Hear from You

As the reader of this book, *you* are our most important critic and commentator. We value your opinion and want to know what we're doing right, what we could do better, what areas you'd like to see us publish in, and any other words of wisdom you're willing to pass our way.

We welcome your comments. You can email or write to let us know what you did or didn't like about this book—as well as what we can do to make our books better.

Please note that we cannot help you with technical problems related to the topic of this book.

When you write, please be sure to include this book's title and author as well as your name and email address. We will carefully review your comments and share them with the author and editors who worked on the book.

E-mail: feedback@samspublishing.com

Mail: Sams Publishing
ATTN: Reader Feedback
800 East 96th Street
Indianapolis, IN 46240 USA

Reader Services

Visit our website and register this book at informit.com/register for convenient access to any updates, downloads, or errata that might be available for this book.

HOUR 1
Introducing Hadoop

What You'll Learn in This Hour:

▶ Background on Big Data and Hadoop
▶ Typical Hadoop use cases
▶ Introduction to the Hadoop core components
▶ Introduction to the Hadoop ecosystem

Big Data and Hadoop are inexorably linked together. From its early beginnings as a search platform to its vast array of current applications that range from data warehousing to event processing to machine learning, Hadoop has indelibly altered the data landscape.

This hour introduces the background and history behind the Hadoop movement as well as the core concepts of Hadoop and typical use cases.

Hadoop and a Brief History of Big Data

The set of storage and processing methodologies commonly known as "Big Data" emerged from the search engine providers in the early 2000s, principally Google and Yahoo!.

The search engine providers were the first group of users faced with Internet scale problems, mainly how to process and store indexes of all of the documents in the Internet universe. This seemed an insurmountable challenge at the time, even though the entire body of content in the Internet was a fraction of what it is today.

Yahoo! and Google independently set about developing a set of capabilities to meet this challenge. In 2003, Google released a whitepaper called "The Google File System." Subsequently, in 2004, Google released another whitepaper called "MapReduce: Simplified Data Processing on Large Clusters." At the same time, at Yahoo!, Doug Cutting (who is generally acknowledged as the initial creator of Hadoop) was working on a web indexing project called Nutch.

The Google whitepapers inspired Doug Cutting to take the work he had done to date on the Nutch project and incorporate the storage and processing principles outlined in these whitepapers. The resultant product is what is known today as Hadoop.

Hadoop was born in 2006 as an open source project under the Apache Software Foundation licensing scheme.

NOTE

The Apache Software Foundation (ASF) is a non-profit organization founded in 1999 to provide an open source software structure and framework for developers to contribute to projects, encouraging collaboration and community involvement, and protecting volunteers from litigation. ASF is premised upon the concept of meritocracy, meaning projects are governed by merit.

Contributors are developers who contribute code or documentation to projects. They are also typically active on mailing lists and support forums, and provide suggestions, criticism and patches to address defects. Committers are developers whose expertise merits giving them access to a commit code to the main repository for the project. Committers have signed a Contributor License Agreement (CLA) and have an apache.org email address. Committers act as a committee to make decisions about the project.

Around the same time as the birth of the Hadoop project, several other technology innovations were afoot. These included:

- The rapid expansion of ecommerce

- The birth and rapid growth of the mobile Internet

- Blogs and user-driven web content

- Social media

These innovations cumulatively led to what is now known as the data deluge. This accelerated the expansion of the big data movement and led to the emergence of other related projects such as Spark, open source messaging systems, and NoSQL platforms, all of which I will discuss in much more detail later in this book.

But it all started with Hadoop.

Hadoop Explained

Hadoop is a data storage and processing platform, based upon a central concept: data locality. *Data locality* refers to the processing of data where it resides by bringing the computation to the data, rather than the typical pattern of requesting data from its location (for example, a database management system) and sending this data to a remote processing system or host.

With Internet-scale data—"Big Data"—it is no longer efficient, or even possible in some cases, to move the large volumes of data required for processing across the network at compute time. Hadoop enables large datasets to be processed locally on the nodes of a cluster using a *shared nothing* approach, where each node can independently process a much smaller subset of the entire dataset without needing to communicate with one another.

Hadoop is schemaless with respect to its write operations (it is what's known as a *schema-on-read* system). This means that it can store and process a wide range of data, from unstructured text documents, to semi-structured JSON (JavaScript Object Notation) or XML documents, to well-structured extracts from relational database systems.

Schema-on-read systems are a fundamental departure from the relational databases we are accustomed to, which are, in contrast, broadly categorized as schema-on-write systems, where data is typically strongly typed and a schema is predefined and enforced upon INSERT, UPDATE, or UPSERT operations. NoSQL platforms (such as Apache HBase or Cassandra) are typically classified as schema-on-read systems as well. You will learn more about NoSQL platforms later in this book.

Because the schema is not interpreted during write operations to Hadoop, there are no indexes, statistics, or other constructs typically employed by database systems to optimize query operations and filter or reduce the amount of data returned to a client. This further necessitates the requirement for data locality.

Hadoop is designed to find needles in haystacks, doing so by dividing and conquering a large problem into a set of smaller problems applying the concepts of data locality and shared nothing as previously introduced.

Core Components of Hadoop

Hadoop has two core components: Hadoop Distributed File System (HDFS) and YARN (which stands for Yet Another Resource Negotiator). HDFS is Hadoop's storage subsystem, whereas YARN can be thought of as Hadoop's process scheduling subsystem (Figure 1.1).

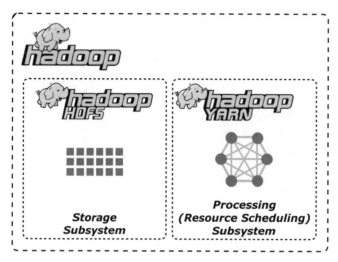

FIGURE 1.1
Hadoop core components.

Each component is independent of one another and can operate in its own cluster; for example, a HDFS cluster and a YARN cluster can operate independently. However, when they are co-located with one another, the combination of both systems is considered to be a Hadoop cluster.

NOTE

A cluster is a collection of systems that work together to perform functions, such as computational or processing functions. Individual servers within a cluster are referred to as nodes.

I will explain each core component including its functionality and internals in much more detail in the next few hours.

Hadoop Ecosystem Components

Any other projects that interact or integrate with Hadoop in some way—for instance, data ingestion projects such as Flume or Sqoop, or data analysis tools such as Pig or Hive—are called Hadoop "ecosystem" projects. In many ways, you could consider Spark an ecosystem project, although this can be disputed because Spark does not require Hadoop to run.

Figure 1.2 depicts the Hadoop ecosystem landscape. By no means is this a comprehensive list—there are many other ecosystem projects. In fact, ecosystem utilities span many additional categories including governance, management, machine learning, search, workflow coordination, and much more. The ecosystem is continually evolving with new projects being incubated or graduating to top level status on a regular basis, so your challenge is to keep current with new and emerging projects.

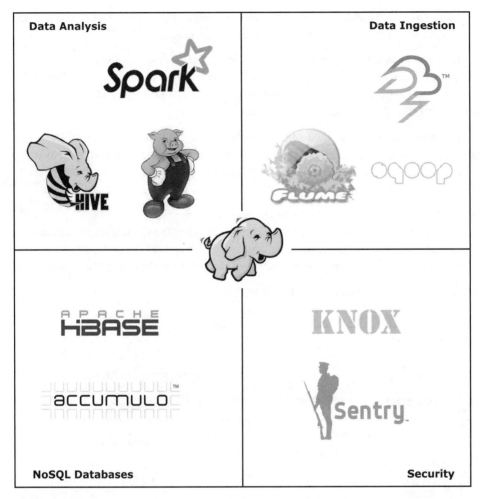

FIGURE 1.2
Example Hadoop ecosystem projects.

Throughout this book I will introduce you to the key ecosystem projects, including Spark, Hive, and many others.

The Commercial Hadoop Landscape

Although Hadoop is an open source project there are many commercial vendors who supply commercial distributions, support, management utilities and more. In 2008, the first commercial vendor, Cloudera, was formed by engineers from Google, Yahoo!, and Facebook, along with Mike Olson, an executive at Oracle formerly the CEO of Sleepycat Software, creator of BerkleyDB (an open source embedded database engine). Cloudera subsequently released the first commercial distribution of Hadoop, called CDH (Cloudera Distribution of Hadoop).

In 2009, MapR was founded as a company delivering a "Hadoop-derived" software solution implementing a custom adaptation of the Hadoop filesystem (called MapRFS) with Hadoop API compatibility. In 2011, Hortonworks was spun off from Yahoo! as a Hadoop vendor providing a distribution called HDP (Hortonworks Data Platform).

Cloudera, Hortonworks, and MapR are referred to as "pure play" Hadoop vendors as their business models are founded upon Hadoop. Many other vendors would follow with their own distribution—such as IBM, Pivotal, and Teradata. However, Hadoop was not necessarily their core business, unlike the pure-play vendors.

In late 2014, the Open Data Platform initiative (ODPi) was announced, founded by Hortonworks. The ODPi was formed to provide a consistent, commercial ready set of Hadoop core and selected ecosystem components. Other vendors, including IBM, Teradata, SAS, and Pivotal, joined this alliance, enabling them to leverage the ODPi code base with their solutions.

Figure 1.3 depicts the commercial Hadoop landscape.

FIGURE 1.3
Commercial Hadoop landscape.

Typical Hadoop Use Cases

Hadoop is essentially a linearly scalable distributed filesystem and a parallel processing SDK (software development kit), and as such its uses are numerous. However, typical large scale Hadoop implementations tend to fall into one of a handful of categories. These include the following:

▶ Data warehouse, extract load transform (ELT), extract transform load (ETL) offload

▶ Event and complex event processing

▶ Data mining and machine learning (advanced analytics)

Lets look at each with some examples.

Data Warehouse Offload

Perhaps the most common use for Hadoop, data warehouse offload, is the process of using Hadoop for long-term storage as well as for performing pre-integration ETL routines. The lower cost storage and distributing processing capabilities of Hadoop result in significant cost savings as compared to higher cost, specialized MPP platforms such as Teradata or Oracle Exadata. Although specialized MPP data warehouse platforms will typically offer better performance and query responsiveness for relational and reporting workloads, Hadoop can be used for aged historical data, freeing up capacity on your MPP platform and deferring high cost hardware upgrades.

Storing unstructured, unprocessed data in Hadoop (or other object-based storage) prior to being staged or integrated into a data warehouse or exposed in a data mart is also considered to be an implementation of a data lake.

Event Processing

Event processing usually involves the ingestion and processing of streaming data sources, such as sensor data, message data, or log data. Event processing is often associated with the IoT concept (Internet of Things), which involves the collection and processing of data from thousands of end points, including temperature sensors, RFID, NFC scanners, CCTV cameras, signalling systems, and more. Hadoop provides low-cost storage to accumulate millions of messages and a computational platform to mine volumes of messages to identify patterns or peculiarities.

Event processing using Hadoop typically involves one or more specialized Hadoop ecosystem platforms or utilities including Storm, Flume, Spark Streaming, Kafka, or others, all of which will be discussed later in this book.

Advanced Analytics

Advanced analytics (also referred to as data science) is the process of identifying patterns in data and building mathematical models to represent these patterns, which can be used to predict outcomes from subsequent data. Advanced analytics expands beyond traditional business intelligence processes, which are largely used for descriptive analytics (describing or analyzing what has happened), to predicting or preempting what may happen or is likely to happen. Some specific applications include customer churn or attrition prediction, propensity modelling (how likely a prospect may be to take up an offer), fraud detection, image or facial recognition, and much more.

Advanced analytics encompasses the specific disciplines of data mining, predictive modelling, and machine learning, which are typically search-based, iterative, trial-and-error–based problem solving approaches. Hadoop enables these recursive approaches at scale.

These usages can (and often are) combined with one another—in fact, it is common for Hadoop implementation to serve all three purposes.

Summary

Hadoop is the most prolific big data platform to date and is now an accepted part of many enterprise environments, both on-premise and in the cloud.

Hadoop is predicated on the concept of data locality, whereby processes are dispatched to where the data to be processed resides. This is the concept of bringing the computation to the data.

Two other concepts integral to Hadoop are shared nothing and schema-on-read. Shared nothing refers to tasks running independently so that nodes do not need to share state or synchronize with other nodes during key processing phases. Schema-on-read refers to the property of accepting data in any format, which is only described when it is processed, making Hadoop a schemaless platform capable of true multi-structured data storage and processing.

Hadoop consists of two core technologies, HDFS and YARN. HDFS is the storage subsystem, and YARN is the process scheduling subsystem. Other projects or utilities that integrate or interact with Hadoop specifically are considered to be Hadoop ecosysyem components. These include projects such as Hive and Spark.

Hadoop is an extensible, programmable platform that has a wide variety of usages. However, the most common usages fall into one or more of the following categories: data warehouse offload, event processing, advanced analytics.

This hour was a gentle,high-level introduction to Hadoop. In the subsequent hours you will deep dive into the Hadoop cluster and runtime internals.

Q&A

Q. To what does the term *data locality* refer?

A. Data locality is the concept of processing data locally wherever possible. This concept is central to Hadoop, a platform that intentionally attempts to minimize the amount of data transferred across the network by bringing the processing to the data instead of the reverse.

Q. What does the term *shared nothing* **refer to?**

A. Shared nothing refers to tasks that can be executed independently on a distributed processing platform such as Hadoop that do not require synchronization or sharing of state with one another.

Q. What are the core components of Hadoop and what are their respective functions?

A. The Hadoop core consists of HDFS (Hadoop Distributed File System), the storage subsystem of Hadoop, and YARN (Yet Another Resource Negotiatior), the process and resource scheduling subsystem of Hadoop. Each core component can operate independently or as a cluster of one or another (e.g., a HDFS cluster or a YARN cluster), but when they are combined it is considered to be a Hadoop cluster.

Workshop

The workshop contains quiz questions to help you solidify your understanding of the material covered. Try to answer all questions before looking at the "Answers" section that follows.

Quiz

1. Which of the following systems or data structures is typically not an example of a schema-on-read source?

  A. Hadoop

  B. A table in an Oracle database

  C. A NoSQL database such as Apache HBase

2. True or False: The Hadoop ecosystem consists of projects or utilities that integrate or are designed to interact with Hadoop.

3. Typical usages of Hadoop include which of the following?

  A. Data warehouse offload

  B. Complex event processing

  C. Machine learning

  D. Any or all of the above

Answers

1. B. Typically, tables in a relational database system such as Oracle have a well-defined schema that is imposed upon write, sometimes referred to as a schema-on-write structure rather than a schema-on-read structure.

2. True.

3. D.

Understanding the Hadoop Cluster Architecture

What You'll Learn in This Hour:

▶ HDFS and YARN cluster processes
▶ The Hadoop cluster architecture
▶ The different Hadoop cluster deployment modes

In this hour you are introduced to the processes involved in the Hadoop platform and how they operate in the Hadoop cluster framework. You learn to distinguish between master and slave node processes in Hadoop's master-slave cluster architecture. You also learn about the different modes of deployment with Hadoop. This hour gives you the high-level understanding you need to deploy Hadoop in the following hour.

HDFS Cluster Processes

HDFS includes a set of Java processes that manage and orchestrate Hadoop's distributed filesystem. As discussed, HDFS can exist as a self-contained cluster that is independent of other processes such as YARN. HDFS has a master-slave cluster architecture, which means different HDFS processes, known as daemons or services, run on cluster nodes and are classified as either master or slave nodes.

NOTE

Daemons are a type of program which run on Linux or Unix operating systems. Daemons run in the background and respond to events such as client requests. Daemons in Linux are the equivalent of services in Windows.

Before I go any further—it is probably worthwhile discussing some key concepts relating to HDFS, which I will do now.

Master-Slave Cluster Architecture

Master-slave is a model of communication whereby one process has control over one or more other processes. In some systems a master is selected from a group of eligible processes at runtime or during processing, while in other cases, such as HDFS, the master and slave processes are predesignated, static roles for the lifetime of the cluster.

Files, Blocks, and Metadata

I cover HDFS in much more detail in **Hour 4, "Understanding the Hadoop Distributed File System (HDFS)"**. However, I need to explain some HDFS concepts at a very high level now. These include files, blocks, and metadata. HDFS is a virtual filesystem where files are comprised of blocks that are distributed across one or more nodes of the cluster. Files are split indiscriminately according to a configured block size upon uploading data into the filesystem, a process known as ingestion. The blocks are then distributed and replicated across cluster nodes to achieve fault tolerance and additional opportunities for processing data locally (recall the design goal of "bringing the computation to the data").

NOTE

Fault tolerance is the capability of a system to continue normal operations even if some of its components fail or develop faults (as defined in Wikipedia).

The information about the filesystem and its virtual directories, and files and the physical blocks that comprise the files is stored in the filesystem metadata. You will learn much more about these concepts as you progress through the book.

The NameNode

The NameNode is the HDFS master node process which manages the filesystem metadata. The NameNode keeps the metadata in resident memory to service client read and write requests efficiently. The NameNode is also responsible for assuring durability and consistency of the filesystem's metadata, which it does through its journaling functions—all of which will be covered in detail in Hour 4. For now you just need to know that the NameNode is a mandatory process necessary for HDFS to operate.

All of the Hadoop server processes (daemons) serve a web user interface (UI). The NameNode serves this UI on port 50070 of the host running the NameNode daemon, as shown in Figure 2.1.

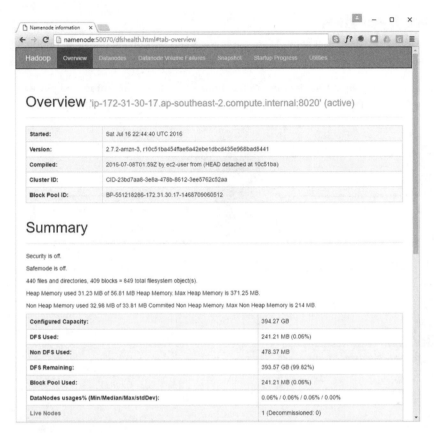

FIGURE 2.1
HDFS NameNode Web UI.

The SecondaryNameNode and Standby Namenode

The SecondaryNameNode and Standby NameNode are optional processes that either expedite filesystem metadata recovery or provide a failover process in the event of a NameNode failure. Again, these are processes I will detail in Hour 4—for now, just realize that they are optional HDFS master node daemon processes.

DataNode Daemons

The DataNode process is a HDFS slave node daemon that runs on one or more nodes of the HDFS cluster. DataNodes are responsible for managing block storage and access for both reading or writing of data as well for block replication, which is part of the data ingestion process.

HDFS Cluster Overview

A typical Hadoop cluster consists of one NameNode, one of either a Standby NameNode or SecondaryNameNode—although these are not required—and many DataNodes.

I will cover some alternate deployment modes later in this hour where the composition and placement of services may vary, but Figure 2.2 represents the daemons involved in a typical HDFS cluster.

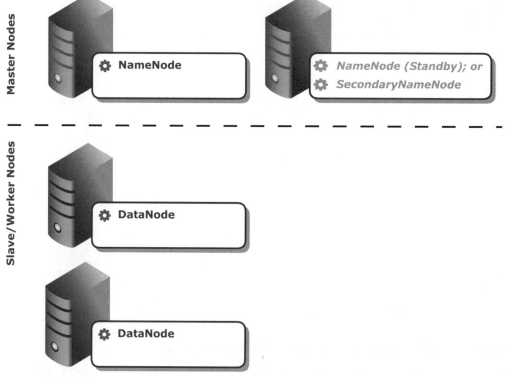

FIGURE 2.2
HDFS cluster processes.

Note that the Standby NameNode and SecondaryNameNode processes are shown in italic to symbolize their optional nature.

YARN Cluster Processes

YARN governs and orchestrates the processing of data in Hadoop, which typically is data sourced from and written to HDFS. I will provide a primer on YARN here for the purpose of introducing the daemons and processes involved in a YARN cluster. However, YARN will be covered in much more detail in **Hour 6, "Understanding Data Processing in Hadoop."**

The YARN cluster architecture is a master-slave cluster framework like HDFS, with a master node daemon called the ResourceManager and one or more slave node daemons called NodeManagers running on worker or slave nodes in the cluster. Let's introduce these now.

The ResourceManager

The ResourceManager is responsible for granting cluster compute resources to applications running on the cluster. Resources are granted in units called *containers*, which are predefined combinations of CPU cores and memory. Container allotments, including minimum and maximum thresholds, are configurable on the cluster. I will cover configuration specifically in **Hour 20, "Understanding Advanced Cluster Configuration."** However, configuration options and configuration in general will be covered throughout the book.

The ResourceManager also tracks available capacity on the cluster as applications finish and release their reserved resources as well as the status of applications running on the cluster. Similar to the NameNode, the ResourceManager serves an embedded web UI on port 8088 of the host running this daemon, which is useful for displaying the status of applications running, completed, or failed on the cluster, as shown in Figure 2.3.

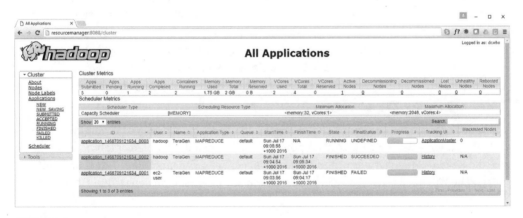

FIGURE 2.3
YARN ResourceManager Web UI.

Clients submit applications to the ResourceManager, the ResourceManager then allocates the first container on an available NodeManager in the cluster as a delegate process for the application called the ApplicationMaster, and the ApplicationMaster then negotiates all of the further containers required to run the application. I discuss this allocation and negotiation process some more later on.

NodeManager Daemons

The NodeManager is the slave node YARN daemon that manages containers on the slave node host. Containers execute the tasks involved in an application. As Hadoop's approach to solving large problems is to "divide and conquer," a large problem is decomposed into a set of tasks, many of which can be run in parallel—recall the concept of shared nothing. These tasks are run in containers on hosts running the NodeManager process.

Most containers simply run tasks. However, one special container that I have already mentioned—the ApplicationMaster—has some additional responsibilities for the applications.

The ApplicationMaster

As discussed, the ApplicationMaster is the first container allocated by the ResourceManager to run on a NodeManager for an application. Its job is to plan the application, including determining what resources are required—often based upon how much data is being processed—and to work out resourcing for application stages (for instance the map and reduce stages of a MapReduce application which you will learn about shortly). The ApplicationMaster requests these resources from the ResourceManager on behalf of the application. The ResourceManager grants resources on the same or other NodeManagers to the ApplicationMaster, to use within the lifetime of the specific application. The ApplicationMaster also monitors progress of tasks, stages (groups of tasks that can be performed in parallel), and dependencies. The summary information is provided to the ResourceManager to display in its user interface as shown previously.

YARN Cluster Overview

Recall that YARN is a self-contained cluster framework, and can be deployed as a fully functional cluster without HDFS. YARN supports a high availability implementation mode, where the ResourceManager has a standby to use in case of a system failure. This is optional, however. The YARN master-slave architecture and cluster processes are depicted in Figure 2.4.

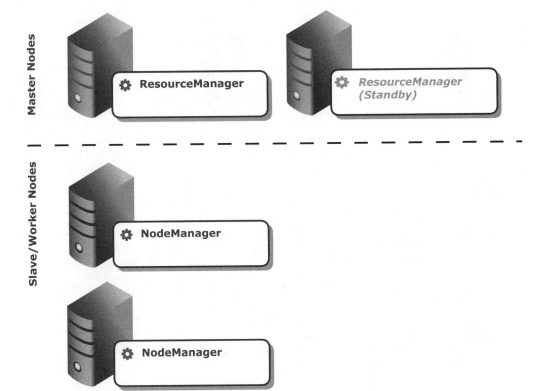

FIGURE 2.4
YARN cluster processes.

Hadoop Cluster Architecture and Deployment Modes

You have seen the components and hierarchies of both a HDFS and a YARN cluster. Now we'll look at them together as part of an entire Hadoop cluster.

Hadoop Cluster Architecture

When you combine both core subsystems you have a Hadoop cluster as shown in Figure 2.5. Typically you would host the NameNode and ResourceManager on separate hosts. You may also choose to host the Standby NameNode or ResourceManager processes—if implemented—on separate hosts as well.

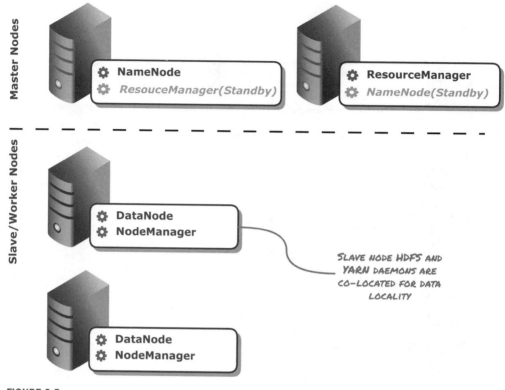

FIGURE 2.5
Hadoop cluster processes.

Notice that the Hadoop slave node processes (the DataNode and NodeManager) are co-located. This provides the maximum opportunity for data locality.

Hadoop Cluster Deployment Modes

Hadoop supports three different deployment modes. Let's discuss these now.

Fully Distributed Mode

Fully distributed mode deploys slave node processes on different hosts than master node processes. Figure 2.5 is an example of a fully distributed Hadoop cluster. There are permutations to this deployment mode; for instance, one host could run both the NameNode and ResourceManager daemons with one or more hosts running both the DataNode and NodeManager daemons. Fully distributed mode is the typical deployment mode for production systems.

Pseudo-Distributed Mode

Pseudo-distributed mode has all Hadoop daemons, which are Java processes, running in separate Java Virtual Machines (JVMs) on a single host to simulate how a fully distributed cluster would function. Pseudo-distributed mode is useful for testing where you need to simulate the interaction that would occur in a typical production cluster while only using a single machine. Many of the sandbox or quick-start environments provided by the various commercial Hadoop distributors are virtual machines with a Hadoop instance running in pseudo-distributed mode. Figure 2.6 shows an example of a Hadoop cluster running in pseudo-distributed mode.

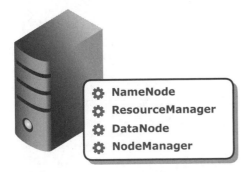

FIGURE 2.6
Pseudo-distributed Hadoop cluster.

NOTE

A Java Virtual Machine (JVM) is a cross-platform runtime engine that can execute instructions compiled from source code into Java bytecode. This is in contrast to programs compiled into machine code for a target platform, such as a C program compiled to run on a Linux x64 platform, for instance. Java bytecode is theoretically cross-platform and portable between different target platforms running the JRE (Java Runtime Environment). All of the major Hadoop processes, tasks and dameons, are written in Java and run in Java virtual machines.

LocalJobRunner Mode

LocalJobRunner mode runs all of the map reduce components in a single JVM. I will be covering map reduce in **Hour 7, "Programming MapReduce Applications,"** but LocalJobRunner allows map reduce developers to integrate with IDEs (Integrated Development Environments) such as Eclipse, and to be able to perform unit tests and debugging, tracing or single stepping within this environment. LocalJobRunner uses the local filesystem as opposed to HDFS as its filesystem. Figure 2.7 shows a screen shot of the Eclipse IDE.

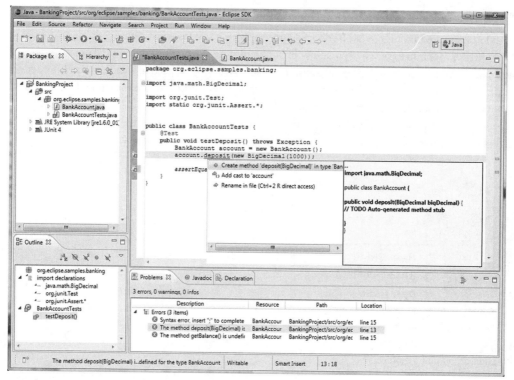

FIGURE 2.7
Eclipse Java Integrated Development Environment (IDE).

Summary

In this hour you learned more about the core processes that comprise a Hadoop cluster, including the daemons (or services) and processes involved in the operation of the HDFS and YARN subsystems. A HDFS cluster manages and orchestrates Hadoop's distributed filesystem and includes the NameNode process—which manages the filesystem metadata—and one or more DataNode processes running on different hosts—which manage block storage, access, and replication. A YARN cluster that manages process scheduling for applications running on the Hadoop platform consists of a ResourceManager process—which governs and allocates processing resources throughout the cluster—and one or more NodeManagers running on different hosts, which execute tasks in an application. The NodeManager process can also host the ApplicationMaster process upon request by the ResourceManager, which is a delegate process created to request resources and govern processing for an application.

You learned the distinction between master and slave node processes, and how the slave node HDFS and YARN processes (DataNode and NodeManager, respectively) are typically co-located to achieve data locality for processing where possible. Finally, you learned about the different deployment modes available with Hadoop, which include the fully distributed deployment mode (which has master and slave node processes on different hosts), the pseudo distributed deployment mode (which has all processes running on a single host) and the LocalJobRunner mode (which runs the map reduce framework in a single JVM using the local filesystem for storage). LocalJobRunner is typically used for map reduce development and unit testing, before graduating to the other modes for integration testing and deployment.

Next hour you will roll up your sleeves and deploy Hadoop!

Q&A

Q. **What daemons are involved in HDFS and what are their respective roles?**

A. Daemons involved in a HDFS cluster include the NameNode, which is responsible for storing and managing the filesystem metadata, and the DataNode, which is responsible for block storage and access.

Q. **What daemons and processes are involved in YARN and what are their respective roles?**

A. Daemons involved in YARN include the ResourceManager, which tracks and manages cluster processing capacity and high level application status, and the NodeManager, which executes tasks for an application. The NodeManager can also host a delegate subprocess for an application called the ApplicationMaster, which negotiates resources with the ResourceManager on behalf of the application and orchestrates task and stage processing for the application.

Q. **What is the advantage of co-locating the slave node processes in a Hadoop cluster?**

A. Co-locating the DataNode and NodeManager daemons on slave nodes increases opportunities for data locality, where tasks can be scheduled to execute where the blocks of input data for the task reside.

Workshop

The workshop contains quiz questions to help you solidify your understanding of the material covered. Try to answer all questions before looking at the "Answers" section that follows.

Quiz

1. **True or False**: A Hadoop cluster deployed in Fully Distributed Mode has all master and slave node HDFS and YARN processes running on the same host.

2. Which two of the following are slave node daemons in a Hadoop cluster?

   A. ApplicationMaster

   B. NodeManager

   C. DataNode

   D. ResourceManager

3. The HDFS master node daemon, the NameNode, manages the filesystem _____.

4. **True or False**: NodeManagers execute tasks at the request of an ApplicationMaster, which is a delegate process for a specific application hosted on one NodeManager in the cluster.

Answers

1. False. A Fully Distributed Mode cluster has master and slave node processes running on different hosts.

2. B and C.

3. metadata.

4. True.

Deploying Hadoop

What You'll Learn in This Hour:

▶ Installation platforms and prerequisites

▶ How to install Hadoop from Apache releases

▶ How to deploy Hadoop using commercial distributions

▶ How to deploy Hadoop in the cloud using AWS

Now that you have been introduced to Hadoop and learned about its core components, HDFS and YARN and their related processes, as well as different deployment modes for Hadoop, let's look at the different options for getting a functioning Hadoop cluster up and running. By the end of this hour you will have set up a working Hadoop cluster that we will use throughout the remainder of the book.

Installation Platforms and Prerequisites

Before you install Hadoop there are a few installation requirements, prerequisites, and recommendations of which you should be aware.

Operating System Requirements

The vast majority of Hadoop implementations are platformed on Linux hosts. This is due to a number of reasons:

▶ The Hadoop project, although cross-platform in principle, was originally targeted at Linux. It was several years after the initial release that a Windows-compatible distribution was introduced.

▶ Many of the commercial vendors only support Linux.

▶ Many other projects in the open source and Hadoop ecosystem have compatibility issues with non-Linux platforms.

That said there are options for installing Hadoop on Windows, should this be your platform of choice. We will use Linux for all of our exercises and examples in this book, but consult the documentation for your preferred Hadoop distribution for Windows installation and support information if required.

If you are using Linux, choose a distribution you are comfortable with. All major distributions are supported (Red Hat, Centos, Ubuntu, SLES, etc.). You can even mix distributions if appropriate; for instance, master nodes running Red Hat and slave nodes running Ubuntu.

CAUTION

Don't Use Logical Volume Manager (LVM) in Linux

If you are using Linux to deploy Hadoop nodes, master or slaves, it is strongly recommended that you not use LVM in Linux. This will restrict performance, especially on slave nodes.

Hardware Requirements

Although there are no hard and fast requirements, there are some general heuristics used in sizing instances, or hosts, appropriately for roles within a Hadoop cluster. First, you need to distinguish between master and slave node instances, and their requirements.

Master Nodes

A Hadoop cluster relies on its master nodes, which host the NameNode and ResourceManager, to operate, although you can implement high availability for each subsystem as I discussed in the last hour. Failure and failover of these components is not desired. Furthermore, the master node processes, particularly the NameNode, require a large amount of memory to operate efficiently, as you will appreciate in the next hour when we dive into the internals of HDFS. Therefore, when specifying hardware requirements the following guidelines can be used for medium to large-scale production Hadoop implementations:

▶ 16 or more CPU cores (preferably 32)

▶ 128GB or more RAM (preferably 256GB)

▶ RAID Hard Drive Configuration (preferably with hot-swappable drives)

▶ Redundant power supplies

▶ Bonded Gigabit Ethernet or 10Gigabit Ethernet

This is only a guide, and as technology moves on quickly, these recommendations will change as well. The bottom line is that you need *carrier class* hardware with as much CPU and memory capacity as you can get!

Slave Nodes

Slave nodes do the actual work in Hadoop, both for processing and storage so they will benefit from more CPU and memory—physical memory, not virtual memory. That said, slave nodes are designed with the expectation of failure, which is one of the reasons blocks are replicated in HDFS. Slave nodes can also be scaled out linearly. For instance, you can simply add more nodes to add more aggregate storage or processing capacity to the cluster, which you cannot do with master nodes. With this in mind, economic scalability is the objective when it comes to slave nodes. The following is a guide for slave nodes for a well-subscribed, computationally intensive Hadoop cluster; for instance, a cluster hosting machine learning and in memory processing using Spark.

▶ 16-32 CPU cores

▶ 64-512 GB of RAM

▶ 12-24 1-4 TB hard disks in a JBOD Configuration

NOTE
___

JBOD

JBOD is an acronym for *just a bunch of disks*, meaning directly attached storage that is not in a RAID configuration, where each disk operates independently of the other disks. RAID is not recommended for block storage on slave nodes as the access speed is limited by the slowest disk in the array, unlike JBOD where the average speed can be greater than that of the slowest disk. JBOD has been proven to outperform RAID 0 for block storage by 30% to 50% in benchmarks conducted at Yahoo!.

___

CAUTION
___

Storing Too Much Data on Any Slave Node May Cause Issues

As slave nodes typically host the blocks in a Hadoop filesystem, and as storage costs, particularly for JBOD configurations, are relatively inexpensive, it may be tempting to allocate excess block storage capacity to each slave node. However, as you will learn in the next hour on HDFS, you need to consider the network impact of a failed node, which will trigger re-replication of all blocks that were stored on the slave node.

___

Slave nodes are designed to be deployed on commodity-class hardware, and yet while they still need ample processing power in the form of CPU cores and memory, as they will be executing computational and data transformation tasks, they don't require the same degree of fault tolerance that master nodes do.

Networking Considerations

Fully distributed Hadoop clusters are very chatty, with control messages, status updates and heartbeats, block reports, data shuffling, and block replication, and there is often heavy network utilization between nodes of the cluster. If you are deploying Hadoop on-premise, you should always deploy Hadoop clusters on private subnets with dedicated switches. If you are using multiple racks for your Hadoop cluster (you will learn more about this in **Hour 21, "Understanding Advanced HDFS"**), you should consider redundant core and "top of rack" switches.

Hostname resolution is essential between nodes of a Hadoop cluster, so both forward and reverse DNS lookups must work correctly between each node (master-slave and slave-slave) for Hadoop to function. Either DNS or a hosts files can be used for resolution. IPv6 should also be disabled on all hosts in the cluster.

Time synchronization between nodes of the cluster is essential as well, as some components, such as Kerberos, which is discussed in **Hour 22, "Securing Hadoop,"** rely on this being the case. It is recommended you use ntp (Network Time Protocol) to keep clocks synchronized between all nodes.

Software Requirements

As discussed, Hadoop is almost entirely written in Java and compiled to run in a Java Runtime Environment (JRE); therefore Java is a prerequisite to installing Hadoop. Current prerequisites include:

▸ Java Runtime Envrionment (JRE) 1.7 or above

▸ Java Development Kit (JDK) 1.7 or above—required if you will be compiling Java classes such as MapReduce applications

Other ecosystem projects will have their specific prerequisites; for instance, Apache Spark requires Scala and Python as well, so you should always refer to the documentation for these specific projects.

Installing Hadoop

You have numerous options for installing Hadoop and setting up Hadoop clusters. As Hadoop is a top-level Apache Software Foundation (ASF) open source project, one method is to install directly from the Apache builds on **http://hadoop.apache.org/**. To do this you first need one or more hosts, depending upon the mode you wish to use, with appropriate hardware specifications, an appropriate operating system, and a Java runtime environment available (all of the prerequisites and considerations discussed in the previous section).

Once you have this, it is simply a matter of downloading and unpacking the desired release. There may be some additional configuration to be done afterwards, but then you simply start the relevant services (master and slave node daemons) on their designated hosts and you are up and running.

Non-Commercial Hadoop

Let's deploy a Hadoop cluster using the latest Apache release now.

Installing Hadoop Using the Apache Release

In this exercise we will install a pseudo-distributed mode Hadoop cluster using the latest Hadoop release downloaded from hadoop.apache.org.

As this is a test cluster the following specifications will be used in our example:

- ▶ Red Hat Enterprise Linux 7.2 (The installation steps would be similar using other Linux distributions such as Ubuntu)
- ▶ 2 CPU cores
- ▶ 8GB RAM
- ▶ 30GB HDD
- ▶ hostname: **hadoopnode0**

1. Disable SELinux (this is known to cause issues with Hadoop):

   ```
   $ sudo sed -i 's/SELINUX=enforcing/SELINUX=disabled/g' \
   /etc/selinux/config
   ```

2. Disable IPv6 (this is also known to cause issues with Hadoop):

   ```
   $ sudo sed -i "\$anet.ipv6.conf.all.disable_ipv6 = 1" \
   /etc/sysctl.conf
   $ sudo sed -i "\$anet.ipv6.conf.default.disable_ipv6 = 1" \
   /etc/sysctl.conf
   $ sudo sysctl -p
   ```

3. Reboot

4. Run the `sestatus` command to ensure SELinux is not enabled:

   ```
   $ sestatus
   ```

5. Install Java. We will install the OpenJDK, which will install both a JDK and JRE:

```
$ sudo yum install java-1.7.0-openjdk-devel
```

a. Test that Java has been successfully installed by running the following command:

```
$ java -version
```

If Java has been installed correctly you should see output similar to the following:

```
java version "1.7.0_101"
OpenJDK Runtime Environment (rhel-2.6.6.1.el7_2-x86_64..)
OpenJDK 64-Bit Server VM (build 24.95-b01, mixed mode)
```

Note that depending upon which operating system you are deploying on, you may have a version of Java and a JDK installed already. In these cases it may not be necessary to install the JDK, or you may need to set up alternatives so you do not have conflicting Java versions.

6. Locate the installation path for Java, and set the JAVA_HOME environment variable:

```
$ export JAVA_HOME=/usr/lib/jvm/REPLACE_WITH_YOUR_PATH/
```

7. Download Hadoop from your nearest Apache download mirror. You can obtain the link by selecting the binary option for the version of your choice at http://hadoop.apache.org/releases.html. We will use Hadoop version 2.7.2 for our example.

```
$ wget http://REPLACE_WITH_YOUR_MIRROR/hadoop-2.7.2.tar.gz
```

8. Unpack the Hadoop release, move it into a system directory, and set an environment variable from the Hadoop home directory:

```
$ tar -xvf hadoop-2.7.2.tar.gz
$ mv hadoop-2.7.2 hadoop
$ sudo mv hadoop/ /usr/share/
$ export HADOOP_HOME=/usr/share/hadoop
```

9. Create a directory which we will use as an alternative to the Hadoop configuration directory:

```
$ sudo mkdir -p /etc/hadoop/conf
```

10. Create a mapred-site.xml file (I will discuss this later) in the Hadoop configuration directory:

```
$ sudo cp $HADOOP_HOME/etc/hadoop/mapred-site.xml.template \
$HADOOP_HOME/etc/hadoop/mapred-site.xml
```

11. Add JAVA_HOME environment variable to `hadoop-env.sh` (file used to source environment variables for Hadoop processes):

```
$ sed -i "\$aexport JAVA_HOME=/REPLACE_WITH_YOUR_JDK_PATH/" \
$HADOOP_HOME/etc/hadoop/hadoop-env.sh
```

Substitute the correct path to your Java home directory as defined in Step 6.

12. Create a symbolic link between the Hadoop configuration directory and the `/etc/hadoop/conf` directory created in Step 10:

```
$ sudo ln -s $HADOOP_HOME/etc/hadoop/* \
/etc/hadoop/conf/
```

13. Create a logs directory for Hadoop:

```
$ mkdir $HADOOP_HOME/logs
```

14. Create users and groups for HDFS and YARN:

```
$ sudo groupadd hadoop
$ sudo useradd -g hadoop hdfs
$ sudo useradd -g hadoop yarn
```

15. Change the group and permissions for the Hadoop release files:

```
$ sudo chgrp -R hadoop /usr/share/hadoop
$ sudo chmod -R 777 /usr/share/hadoop
```

16. Run the built in Pi Estimator example included with the Hadoop release.

```
$ cd $HADOOP_HOME
$ sudo -u hdfs bin/hadoop jar \
share/hadoop/mapreduce/hadoop-mapreduce-examples-2.7.2.jar \
pi 16 1000
```

As we have not started any daemons or initialized HDFS, this program runs in `LocalJobRunner` mode (recall that I discussed this in **Hour 2, "Understanding the Hadoop Cluster Architecture"**). If this runs correctly you should see output similar to the following:

```
. . .
Job Finished in 2.571 seconds
Estimated value of Pi is 3.14250000000000000000
```

Now let's configure a pseudo-distributed mode Hadoop cluster from your installation.

17. Use the `vi` editor to update the `core-site.xml` file, which contains important information about the cluster, specifically the location of the namenode:

```
$ sudo vi /etc/hadoop/conf/core-site.xml
# add the following config between the <configuration>
# and </configuration> tags:
<property>
<name>fs.defaultFS</name>
<value>hdfs://hadoopnode0:8020</value>
</property>
```

Note that the value for the `fs.defaultFS` configuration parameter needs to be set to `hdfs://HOSTNAME:8020`, where the `HOSTNAME` is the name of the NameNode host, which happens to be the localhost in this case.

18. Adapt the instructions in Step 17 to similarly update the `hdfs-site.xml` file, which contains information specific to HDFS, including the replication factor, which is set to 1 in this case as it is a pseudo-distributed mode cluster:

```
sudo vi /etc/hadoop/conf/hdfs-site.xml
# add the following config between the <configuration>
# and </configuration> tags:
<property>
<name>dfs.replication</name>
<value>1</value>
</property>
```

19. Adapt the instructions in Step 17 to similarly update the `yarn-site.xml` file, which contains information specific to YARN. Importantly, this configuration file contains the address of the resourcemanager for the cluster—in this case it happens to be the localhost, as we are using pseudo-distributed mode:

```
$ sudo vi /etc/hadoop/conf/yarn-site.xml
# add the following config between the <configuration>
# and </configuration> tags:
<property>
<name>yarn.resourcemanager.hostname</name>
<value>hadoopnode0</value>
</property>
<property>
<name>yarn.nodemanager.aux-services</name>
<value>mapreduce_shuffle</value>
</property>
```

20. Adapt the instructions in Step 17 to similarly update the `mapred-site.xml` file, which contains information specific to running MapReduce applications using YARN:

```
$ sudo vi /etc/hadoop/conf/mapred-site.xml
# add the following config between the <configuration>
```

```
# and </configuration> tags:
<property>
<name>mapreduce.framework.name</name>
<value>yarn</value>
</property>
```

21. Format HDFS on the NameNode:

```
$ sudo -u hdfs bin/hdfs namenode -format
```

Enter [Y] to re-format if prompted.

22. Start the NameNode and DataNode (HDFS) daemons:

```
$ sudo -u hdfs sbin/hadoop-daemon.sh start namenode
$ sudo -u hdfs sbin/hadoop-daemon.sh start datanode
```

23. Start the ResourceManager and NodeManager (YARN) daemons:

```
$ sudo -u yarn sbin/yarn-daemon.sh start resourcemanager
$ sudo -u yarn sbin/yarn-daemon.sh start nodemanager
```

24. Use the `jps` command included with the Java JDK to see the Java processes that are running:

```
$ sudo jps
```

You should see output similar to the following:

```
2374 DataNode
2835 Jps
2280 NameNode
2485 ResourceManager
2737 NodeManager
```

25. Create user directories and a `tmp` directory in HDFS and set the appropriate permissions and ownership:

```
$ sudo -u hdfs bin/hadoop fs -mkdir -p /user/<your_user>
$ sudo -u hdfs bin/hadoop fs -chown <your_user>:<your_user> /user/<your_user>
$ sudo -u hdfs bin/hadoop fs -mkdir /tmp
$ sudo -u hdfs bin/hadoop fs -chmod 777 /tmp
```

26. Now run the same Pi Estimator example you ran in Step 16. This will now run in pseudo-distributed mode:

```
$ bin/hadoop jar \
share/hadoop/mapreduce/hadoop-mapreduce-examples-2.7.2.jar \
pi 16 1000
```

The output you will see in the console will be similar to that in Step 16. Open a browser and go to localhost:8088. You will see the YARN ResourceManager Web UI (which I discuss in **Hour 6, "Understanding Data Processing in Hadoop") (Figure 3.1):**

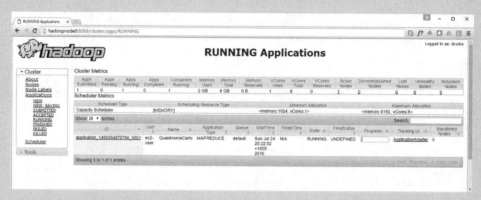

FIGURE 3.1
YARN ResourceManager Web UI.

Congratulations! You have just set up your first pseudo-distributed mode Hadoop cluster. We will use this cluster in other exercises in the book, so keep it available if you can.

Using a Commercial Hadoop Distribution

As I had discussed in **Hour 1, "Introducing Hadoop,"** the commercial Hadoop landscape is well established. With the advent of the ODPi (the Open Data Platform initiative), a once-numerous array of vendors and derivative distributions has been consolidated to a much simpler landscape which includes three primary *pure-play* Hadoop vendors:

▶ Cloudera

▶ Hortonworks

▶ MapR

Importantly, enterprise support agreements and subscriptions can be purchased from the various Hadoop vendors for their distributions. Each vendor also supplies a suite of management utilities to help you deploy and manage Hadoop clusters. Let's look at each of the three major pure play Hadoop vendors and their respective distributions.

Cloudera

Cloudera was the first mover in the commercial Hadoop space, establishing their first commercial release in 2008. Cloudera provides a Hadoop distribution called CDH (Cloudera Distribution of Hadoop), which includes the Hadoop core and many ecosystem projects. CDH is entirely open source.

Cloudera also provides a management utility called Cloudera Manager (which is not open source). Cloudera Manager provides a management console and framework enabling the deployment, management, and monitoring of Hadoop clusters, and which makes many administrative tasks such as setting up high availability or security much easier. The mix of open source and proprietary software is often referred to as **open core**. A screenshot showing Cloudera Manager is pictured in Figure 3.2.

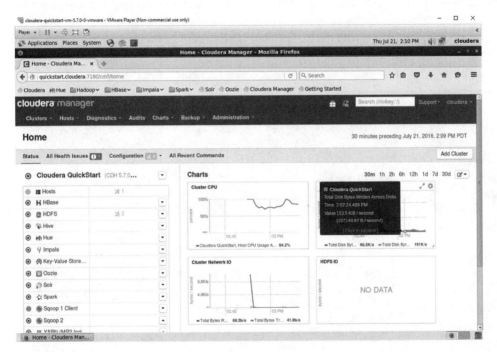

FIGURE 3.2
Cloudera Manager.

As mentioned, Cloudera Manager can be used to deploy Hadoop clusters, including master nodes, slave nodes, and ecosystem technologies. Cloudera Manager distributes installation packages for Hadoop components through a mechanism called *parcels*. As Hadoop installations are typically isolated from public networks, Cloudera Manager, which is technically not part of the cluster and will often have access to the Internet, will download parcels and distribute these to new target hosts nominated to perform roles in a Hadoop cluster or to existing hosts to upgrade components.

Deploying a fully distributed CDH cluster using Cloudera Manager would involve the following steps at a high level:

1. Install Cloudera Manager on a host that has access to other hosts targeted for roles in the cluster.

2. Specify target hosts for the cluster using Cloudera Manager.

3. Use Cloudera Manager to provision Hadoop services, including master and slave nodes.

Cloudera also provides a Quickstart virtual machine, which is a pre-configured pseudo-distributed Hadoop cluster with the entire CDH stack, including core and ecosystem components, as well as a Cloudera Manager installation. This virtual machine is available for VirtualBox, VMware, and KVM, and works with the free editions of each of the virtualization platforms. The Cloudera Quickstart VM is pictured in Figure 3.3.

FIGURE 3.3
Cloudera Quickstart VM.

The Quickstart VM is a great way to get started with the Cloudera Hadoop offering. To find out more, go to **http://www.cloudera.com/downloads.html**.

More information about Cloudera is available at **http://www.cloudera.com/**.

Hortonworks

Hortonworks provides pure open source Hadoop distribution and a founding member of the open data platform initiative (ODPi) discussed in **Hour 1**. Hortonworks delivers a distribution called HDP (Hortonworks Data Platform), which is a complete Hadoop stack including the Hadoop core and selected ecosystem components. Hortonworks uses the Apache Ambari project to provide its deployment configuration management and cluster monitoring facilities. A screenshot of Ambari is shown in Figure 3.4.

FIGURE 3.4
Ambari console.

The simplest method to deploy a Hortonworks Hadoop cluster would involve the following steps:

1. Install Ambari using the Hortonworks installer on a selected host.

2. Add hosts to the cluster using Ambari.

3. Deploy Hadoop services (such as HDFS and YARN) using Ambari.

Hortonworks provides a fully functional, pseudo-distributed HDP cluster with the complete Hortonworks application stack in a virtual machine called the Hortonworks Sandbox. The Hortonworks Sandbox is available for VirtualBox, VMware, and KVM. The Sandbox virtual machine includes several demo applications and learning tools to use to explore Hadoop and its various projects and components. The Hortonworks Sandbox welcome screen is shown in Figure 3.5.

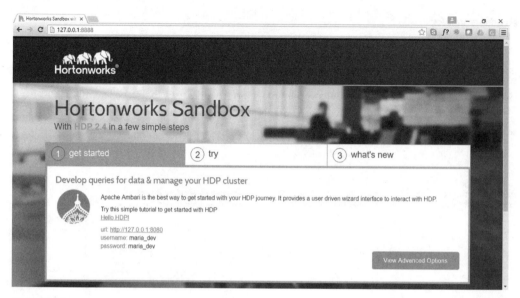

FIGURE 3.5
Hortonworks Sandbox.

You can download the Hortonworks Sandbox from **http://hortonworks.com/products/
sandbox/**. More information about Hortonworks and HDP can be obtained from
http://hortonworks.com/.

MapR

MapR delivers a "Hadoop-derived" software platform that implements an API-compatible
distributed filesystem called MapRFS (the MapR distributed Filesystem). MapRFS has been
designed to maximize performance and provide read-write capabilities not offered by native
HDFS. MapR delivers three versions of their offering called the "Converged Data Platform."
These include:

▶ M3 or "Converged Community Edition" (free version)

▶ M5 or "Converged Enterprise Edition" (supported version)

▶ M7 (M5 version that includes MapR's custom HBase-derived data store)

Like the other distributions, MapR has a demo offering called the "MapR Sandbox," which is
available for VirtualBox or VMware. It is pictured in Figure 3.6.

FIGURE 3.6
MapR Sandbox VM.

The MapR Sandbox can be downloaded from **https://www.mapr.com/products/
mapr-sandbox-hadoop/download**.

MapR's management offering is called the MapR Control System (MCS), which offers a central
console to configure, monitor and manage MapR clusters. It is shown in Figure 3.7.

FIGURE 3.7
MapR Control System (MCS).

Much more information about MapR and the Converged Data Platform is available at https://www.mapr.com/.

Deploying Hadoop in the Cloud

The rise and proliferation of cloud computing and virtualization technologies has definitely been a game changer for the way organizations think about and deploy technology, and Hadoop is no exception. The availability and maturity around IaaS (Infrastructure-as-a-Service), PaaS (Platform-as-a-Service) and SaaS (Software-as-a-Service) solutions makes deploying Hadoop in the cloud not only viable but, in some cases, desirable.

There are many public cloud variants that can be used to deploy Hadoop including Google, IBM, Rackspace, and others. Perhaps the most pervasive cloud platform to date has been AWS (Amazon Web Services), which I will use as the basis for our discussions.

Before you learn about deployment options for Hadoop in AWS, let's go through a quick primer and background on some of the key AWS components. If you are familiar with AWS, feel free to jump straight to the Try it Yourself exercise on deploying Hadoop using AWS EMR.

EC2

Elastic Compute Cloud (EC2) EC2 is Amazon's web service-enabled virtual computing platform. EC2 enables users to create virtual servers and networks in the cloud. The virtual servers are called instances. EC2 instances can be created with a variety of different instance permutations. The Instance Type property determines the number of virtual CPUs and the amount of memory and storage an EC2 instance has available to it. An example instance type is m4.large. A complete list of the different EC2 instance types available can be found at **https:// aws.amazon.com/ec2/instance-types/**.

EC2 instances can be optimized for compute, memory, storage and mixed purposes and can even include GPUs (Graphics Processing Units), a popular option for machine learning and deep analytics.

There are numerous options for operating systems with EC2 instances. All of the popular Linux distributions are supported, including Red Hat, Ubuntu, and SLES, as well various Microsoft Windows options.

EC2 instances are created in security groups. Security groups govern network permissions and Access Control Lists (ACLs). Instances can also be created in a Virtual Private Cloud (VPC). A VPC is a private network, not exposed directly to the Internet. This is a popular option for organizations looking to minimize exposure of EC2 instances to the public Internet.

EC2 instances can be provisioned with various storage options, including instance storage or ephemeral storage, which are terms for volatile storage that is lost when an instance is stopped, and Elastic Block Store (EBS), which is persistent, fault-tolerant storage. There are different options with each, such as SSD (solid state) for instance storage, or provisioned IOPS with EBS.

Additionally, AWS offers Spot instances, which enable you to bid on spare Amazon EC2 computing capacity, often available at a discount compared to normal on-demand EC2 instance pricing.

EC2, as well as all other AWS services, is located in an AWS region. There are currently nine regions, which include the following:

▶ US East (N. Virginia)

▶ US West (Oregon)

▶ US West (N. California)

▶ EU (Ireland)

▶ EU (Frankfurt)

▶ Asia Pacific (Singapore)

▶ Asia Pacific (Sydney)

▶ Asia Pacific (Tokyo)

▶ South America (Sao Paulo)

S3

Simple Storage Service (S3) is Amazon's cloud-based object store. An object store manages data (such as files) as objects. These objects exist in buckets. Buckets are logical, user-created containers with properties and permissions. S3 provides APIs for users to create and manage buckets as well as to create, read, and delete objects from buckets.

The S3 bucket namespace is global, meaning that any buckets created must have a globally unique name. The AWS console or APIs will let you know if you are trying to create a bucket with a name that already exists.

S3 objects, like files in HDFS, are immutable, meaning they are write once, read many. When an S3 object is created and uploaded, an ETag is created, which is effectively a signature for the object. This can be used to ensure integrity when the object is accessed (downloaded) in the future.

There are also public buckets in S3 containing public data sets. These are datasets provided for informational or educational purposes, but they can be used for data operations such as processing with Hadoop. Public datasets, many of which are in the tens or hundreds of terabytes, are available, and topics range from historical weather data to census data, and from astronomical data to genetic data.

More information about S3 is available at **https://aws.amazon.com/s3/**.

Elastic MapReduce (EMR)

Elastic MapReduce (EMR) is Amazon's Hadoop-as-a-Service platform. EMR clusters can be provisioned using the AWS Management Console or via the AWS APIs. Options for creating EMR clusters include number of nodes, node instance types, Hadoop distribution, and additional ecosystem applications to install.

EMR clusters can read data and output results directly to and from S3. They are intended to be provisioned on demand, run a discrete workflow, a job flow, and terminate. They do have local storage, but they are not intended to run in perpetuity. You should only use this local storage for transient data.

EMR is a quick and scalable deployment method for Hadoop. More information about EMR can be found at **https://aws.amazon.com/elasticmapreduce/**.

AWS Pricing and Getting Started

AWS products, including EC2, S3, and EMR, are charged based upon usage. Each EC2 instance type within each region has an instance per hour cost associated with it. The usage costs per hour are usually relatively low and the medium- to long-term costs are quite reasonable, but the more resources you use for a longer period of time, the more you are charged.

If you have not already signed up with AWS, you're in luck! AWS has a free tier available for new accounts that enables you to use certain instance types and services for free for the first year. You can find out more at **https://aws.amazon.com/free/**. This page walks you through setting up an account with no ongoing obligations.

Once you are up and running with AWS, you can create an EMR cluster by navigating to the EMR link in the AWS console as shown in Figure 3.8.

FIGURE 3.8
AWS console—EMR option.

Then click Create Cluster on the EMR welcome page as shown in Figure 3.9, and simply follow the dialog prompts.

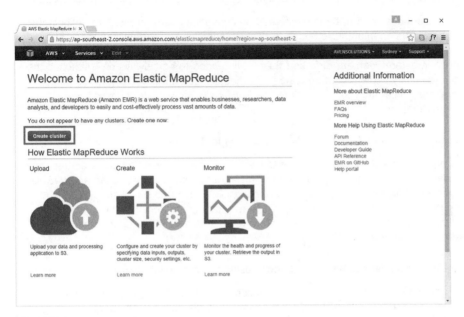

FIGURE 3.9
AWS EMR welcome screen.

You can use an EMR cluster for many of our exercises. However, be aware that leaving the cluster up and running will incur usage charges.

Summary

In this hour you learned about the various approaches to deploying a Hadoop cluster including the Apache releases, commercial distributions and cloud deployment options. Commercial distributions are often the best approach to deploying Hadoop on premise in most organizations as these distributions provide a stable, tested combination of core and ecosystem releases, as well as typically providing a suite of management capabilities useful for deploying and managing Hadoop clusters at scale.

You also learned how to provision Hadoop clusters in the cloud by using the Amazon Web Services Hadoop-as-a-Service offering—Elastic MapReduce (EMR). You are encouraged to explore all the options available to deploy Hadoop. As you progress through the book you will be performing hands-on exercises using Hadoop, so you will need to have a functional cluster. This could be one of the sandbox or quickstart commercial offerings or the Apache Hadoop cluster we set up in the Try it Yourself exercise in this hour.

Q&A

Q. Why do master nodes normally require a higher degree of fault tolerance than slave nodes?

A. Slave nodes are designed to be implemented on commodity hardware with the expectation of failure, and this enables slave nodes to scale economically. The fault tolerance and resiliency built into HDFS and YARN enables the system to recover seamlessly from a failed slave node. Master nodes are different; they are intended to be "always on." Although there are high availability implementation options for master nodes, failover is not desirable. Therefore, more local fault tolerance, such as RAID disks, dual power supplies, etc., is preferred for master nodes.

Q. What does JBOD stand for, and what is its relevance for Hadoop?

A. JBOD is an acronym for "Just a Bunch of Disks," which means spinning disks that operate independently of one another, in contrast to RAID, where disks operate as an array. JBOD is recommended for slave nodes, which are responsible for HDFS block storage. This is because the average speed of all disks on a slave node is greater than the speed of the slowest disk. By comparison, RAID read and write speeds are limited by the speed of the slowest disk in the array.

Q. What are the advantages to deploying Hadoop using a commercial distribution?

A. Commercial distributions contain a "stack" of core and ecosystem components that are tested with one another and certified for the respective distribution. The commercial vendors typically include a management application, which is very useful for managing multi-node Hadoop clusters at scale. The commercial vendors also offer enterprise support as an option as well.

Workshop

The workshop contains quiz questions to help you solidify your understanding of the material covered. Try to answer all questions before looking at the "Answers" section that follows.

Quiz

1. **True or False:** A Java Runtime Environment (JRE) is required on hosts that run Hadoop services.

2. Which AWS PaaS product is used to deploy Hadoop as a service?

    A. EC2

    B. EMR

    C. S3

    D. DynamoDB

3. Slave nodes are typically deployed on what class of hardware?

4. The open source Hadoop cluster management utility used by Hortonworks is called _____.

Answers

1. True. Hadoop services and processes are written in Java, are compiled to Java bytecode, and run in Java Virtual Machines (JVMs), and therefore require a JRE to operate.

2. B. Elastic MapReduce (EMR).

3. Commodity.

4. Ambari.

Understanding the Hadoop Distributed File System (HDFS)

What You'll Learn in This Hour:

- ▶ HDFS blocks, replication, and fault tolerance
- ▶ NameNode metadata operations
- ▶ NameNode on disk structures, durability and recovery
- ▶ The role and operations of the SecondaryNameNode

HDFS is the source and target for nearly all data transformation and analysis operations in Hadoop. Understanding HDFS is essential to understanding and ultimately mastering Hadoop. In this hour I dive deep into the internals of HDFS, including key concepts such as blocks and the NameNode metadata. By the end of this hour you will have a solid understanding of HDFS, which you will build on throughout the remainder of the book.

HDFS Overview

The Hadoop Distributed Filesystem (HDFS) is Hadoop's storage platform. Although Hadoop can interact with many different filesystems, HDFS is Hadoop's primary input data source and target for data processing operations. As discussed previously, Hadoop was originally developed as a platform to support the requirements of search engine providers such as Yahoo!. HDFS was inspired by the GoogleFS whitepaper released in 2003, in which Google outlined how they were storing the large amount of data captured by their web crawlers.

There are several key design principles behind HDFS, which came from the underpinnings of Google's early distributed filesystem implementation (GoogleFS). These principles require that the filesystem

- ▶ is scalable (economically),
- ▶ is fault tolerant,
- ▶ uses commodity hardware,

▶ supports high concurrency,

▶ favors high sustained bandwidth over low latency random access.

HDFS Files, Blocks, and Replication

HDFS is a virtual filesystem, meaning that it appears to a client as if it is one system, but the underlying data is located in multiple different locations. HDFS is deployed on top of native filesystems such as the ext3, ext4, and xfs filesystems available in Linux, or the Windows NTFS filesystem.

One of the most important properties of HDFS is its immutability. Immutability refers to the inability to update data after it is committed to the filesystem. HDFS is often referred to as a WORM (write once, read many) filesystem.

Files in HDFS consist of blocks. HDFS blocks default to 128MB in size, although this is configurable by the client or the server. Files are split into blocks upon ingestion into HDFS as shown in Figure 4.1.

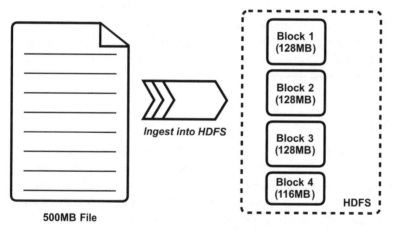

FIGURE 4.1
HDFS blocks.

As seen in Figure 4.1, when a 500MB file is ingested into HDFS, it is split indiscriminately on 128MB boundaries, meaning that at this stage, no assumptions are made about the file's format or definition of a record. As the file in this case is not evenly divisible by 128MB, which is often the case, the last block, Block 4, contains the remaining contents of the file. This is still considered to be a HDFS block, no different than any other block in the filesystem, except this block contains less data than the other three blocks in this example. In the HDFS filesystem, the file is logically presented to users as a 500MB file.

NOTE

If you are familiar with local filesystem programming, you will note that HDFS block sizes are significantly larger than operating system filesystem block sizes (which tend to be in the KB range). This is intentional, as HDFS blocks are actually files themselves that reside on slave node filesystems.

Blocks Are Distributed

If a cluster contains more than one node, blocks are distributed among slave nodes in the cluster upon ingestion. This enables shared nothing—distributed, parallel processing of data. Figure 4.2 shows an example ingested into a three-node cluster.

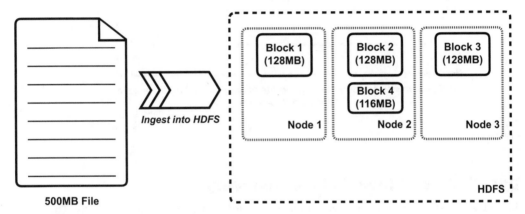

FIGURE 4.2
HDFS block distribution.

Blocks Are Replicated

Blocks are replicated according to a preconfigured replication factor. In a fully distributed cluster environment (with three or more nodes), this configuration value is typically set to 3, whereas in a pseudo-distributed Hadoop cluster this value is set to 1, as there is only one DataNode by definition. Block replication happens upon ingestion, as does the splitting of files into blocks. Block replication serves two key purposes:

▶ Increased opportunities for data locality

▶ Fault tolerance

The replication process happens between DataNodes on the cluster during ingestion as shown in Figure 4.3.

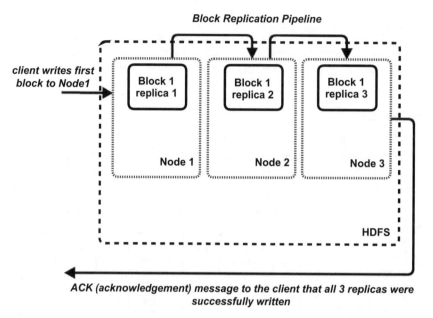

FIGURE 4.3
HDFS block replication.

DataNode or Block Failure Recovery

Each object in HDFS is configured with a replication factor, which we will see shortly. The NameNode gets regular block inventories (block reports) from each DataNode in the cluster. This information is used to determine whether blocks are corrupt or under-replicated, possibly due to the failure of a DataNode which hosted a replica of the block. If the NameNode detects this condition, it will instruct one of the DataNodes containing a valid replica of the same block to replicate that block to another node to restore the configured number of replicas.

Review of the HDFS Roles

Before I detail concepts around the NameNode metadata in the next section, it would be worthwhile to recap the roles and functions provided by the daemons in a HDFS cluster. Let's do this now.

The NameNode

The NameNode is the HDFS master node process, which governs the distributed filesystem. The NameNode's most important function is management of the filesystem's metadata. The HDFS metadata is the filesystem catalog, which contains all of the directory and file objects and their related properties and attributes, such as Access Control Lists (ACLs), which define what users or groups have access to certain objects.

The metadata is stored in resident memory on the NameNode instance to efficiently service client queries related to the filesystem. There are also disk images of the metadata, including a snapshot and a journaling function to ensure durability and crash consistency, similar to a relational database.

Most importantly, the NameNode's in-memory representation of the metadata includes the locations of the blocks which comprise files in HDFS. This is the only stateful representation of the relationship between files and blocks in HDFS.

The NameNode services queries from clients, which could be users querying the filesystem or a MapReduce, Spark, or other application wishing to write output files to a directory in HDFS.

TIP

Data Does Not Go Through the NameNode

It is a common misconception that data goes into HDFS via the NameNode. This is not the case as it would create a bottleneck. Instead, the client interacts with the NameNode to get directives on which cluster node(s) to communicate with to get or put blocks that pertain to the file the client is trying to read or write.

The DataNodes

The DataNodes are the nodes of the cluster on which HDFS blocks are stored and managed. DataNodes are responsible for:

▶ participating in the block replication pipeline (as seen in Figure 4.3 in the previous section)

▶ managing local volumes and storage

▶ providing block reports to the NameNode

Block reports are regular messages sent from the DataNode to the NameNode to provide the NameNode with an inventory of blocks stored on the DataNode. This inventory is then used to populate and maintain the NameNode's metadata discussed previously.

Checksums are calculated upon ingestion into HDFS and are kept with the blocks. The DataNode recalculates and compares these checksums periodically and reports mismatches to the NameNode. Because HDFS is an immutable filesystem (where objects are not updatable after they are written to the filesystem), the checksums should never change for the lifetime of the block. If they do differ from the initial checksums, it's evidence of block corruption, which will be handled by HDFS.

Blocks are stored on local volumes on the hosts running the DataNode daemon (recall from the last hour the recommendation that these volumes be implemented in a JBOD configuration). The storage location is configured on the slave node hosts' local HDFS configuration. You will learn more about this in **Hour 20, "Understanding Cluster Configuration"**.

As the blocks themselves are simply files stored on slave nodes, you can navigate to the directory containing these files and inspect them, although this is typically not required, and it is not recommended that you tamper with these files. Figure 4.4 shows a DataNode's block storage directory.

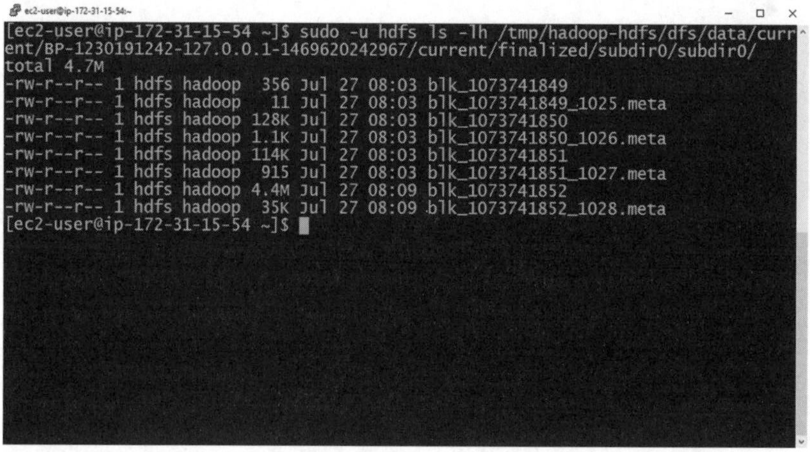

```
ec2-user@ip-172-31-15-54:~                                                    -  □  ×
[ec2-user@ip-172-31-15-54 ~]$ sudo -u hdfs ls -lh /tmp/hadoop-hdfs/dfs/data/curr
ent/BP-1230191242-127.0.0.1-1469620242967/current/finalized/subdir0/subdir0/
total 4.7M
-rw-r--r-- 1 hdfs hadoop  356 Jul 27 08:03 blk_1073741849
-rw-r--r-- 1 hdfs hadoop   11 Jul 27 08:03 blk_1073741849_1025.meta
-rw-r--r-- 1 hdfs hadoop 128K Jul 27 08:03 blk_1073741850
-rw-r--r-- 1 hdfs hadoop 1.1K Jul 27 08:03 blk_1073741850_1026.meta
-rw-r--r-- 1 hdfs hadoop 114K Jul 27 08:03 blk_1073741851
-rw-r--r-- 1 hdfs hadoop  915 Jul 27 08:03 blk_1073741851_1027.meta
-rw-r--r-- 1 hdfs hadoop 4.4M Jul 27 08:09 blk_1073741852
-rw-r--r-- 1 hdfs hadoop  35K Jul 27 08:09 blk_1073741852_1028.meta
[ec2-user@ip-172-31-15-54 ~]$ 
```

FIGURE 4.4
HDFS blocks stored as files.

CAUTION
DataNodes Are Not Aware of HDFS Files and Directories

DataNodes store and manage physical HDFS blocks only, without having any knowledge of how these blocks are related to files and directories in the HDFS filesystem. This relationship is held only in the NameNode's metadata. A common misconception is that because DataNodes store all of the data in a HDFS filesystem, they can be used to reconstruct the filesystem if the NameNode's metadata was lost. This is not the case.

Reading and Writing Files in HDFS

With a good understanding of the NameNode and DataNode roles, let's look at the HDFS file read and write operations. The functions involved with a HDFS file write operation are pictured in Figure 4.5, followed by a legend with more information about each step.

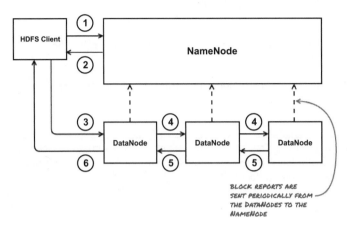

FIGURE 4.5
HDFS write operation.

1. The HDFS Client requests to write a file block.

2. The NameNode responds to the Client with the DataNode to which to write the block.

3. The Client requests to write the block to the specified DataNode.

4. The DataNode opens a block replication pipeline with another DataNode in the cluster, and this process continues until all configured replicas are written.

5. A write acknowledgment is sent back through the replication pipeline.

6. The Client is informed that the write operation was successful.

The functions involved with a HDFS file read operation are pictured in Figure 4.6 followed by a legend.

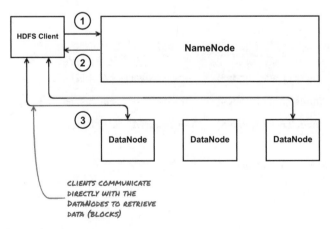

FIGURE 4.6
HDFS read operation.

1. The HDFS Client requests to read a file.

2. The NameNode responds to the request with a list of DataNodes containing the blocks that comprise the file.

3. The Client communicates directly with the DataNodes to retrieve blocks for the file.

NOTE

Block locations are provided to the client in lists. This enables the client to find alternate replicas of a block if a DataNode is not available or if a block is corrupt, meaning that the Client does not have to go back to the NameNode to get these alternate locations.

NameNode Metadata

The NameNode's metadata is perhaps the single most critical component in the HDFS architecture. Without it the filesystem is not accessible, usable, or recoverable. The NameNode's metadata contains the critical link between blocks stored on each of the DataNodes' respective filesystems and their context within files and directories in the Hadoop virtual filesystem.

The metadata persists in resident memory on the NameNode to facilitate fast lookup operations for clients, predominantly read and write operations. It is important to reiterate that data does not flow through the NameNode. The NameNode simply uses its metadata to direct clients where to read and write data—specifically which DataNodes to interact with. The clients then perform data operations directly with the specified DataNodes in the cluster.

Think of the metadata as a giant lookup table, which includes HDFS blocks, the HDFS object (file or directory) they are associated with, and their sequence in the file, as well as ACLs and ownership for the object and block checksums for integrity. This conceptual representation is shown in Figure 4.7.

object	block_id	seq	locations	ACL	Checksum
/data/file.txt	blk_00123	1	[node1,node2,node3]	-rwxrwxrwx	8743b52063 ..
/data/file.txt	blk_00124	2	[node2,node3,node4]	-rwxrwxrwx	cd84097a65 ..
/data/file.txt	blk_00125	3	[node2,node4,node5]	-rwxrwxrwx	d1633f5c74 ..

FIGURE 4.7
Conceptual Representation of In-Memory NameNode Metadata.

HDFS Prefers Fewer, Larger Files

Each object in HDFS consumes approximately 150–200 bytes of memory on the NameNode. As there is a finite amount of memory available on the NameNode, fewer larger files are preferred over many smaller files. Consider the example in the following table, which illustrates ingesting 10GB of data into HDFS with a 128MB block size configured.

Files	Name Entries	Block Metadata	Total Objects
10 × 1GB files	10	80	**90**
10,000 × 1MB files	10,000	10,000	**20,000**

You will learn about methods you can use to concatenate files (or batch files together) upon ingestion in the next hour. Fewer larger files will also make processing more efficient, as you will see later in the book.

The metadata is also represented on disk through a journaling function much like transaction logs in an ACID database. This is to provide durability, recoverability, and crash consistency. I will cover this in more detail shortly.

HDFS Access Control Lists and Permissions

As discussed, objects in HDFS have associated ACLs, which define the owner of the object and permissions that the owner, groups, and others have to the object. These ACLs are part of the metadata structure as previously shown.

The permissions are applied using a Unix-style object permissions mask, including bits representing read(r), write(w), and execute(x) permissions. As there are no executables in HDFS, execute(x) is only used for directories to represent the ability of an assignee to list the contents of a directory. The chown and chmod Hadoop filesystem shell commands are used to assign groups and permissions respectively. Listing 4.1 demonstrates using these commands.

LISTING 4.1 Assigning HDFS Object Permissions and Ownership

```
$ sudo -u hdfs hadoop fs -chown javen /data/books
$ sudo -u hdfs hadoop fs -chmod 777 /data/books
```

The hadoop fs command will be covered in more detail in the "**Interacting with HDFS**" section in this hour. You will also notice that we sudoed as the hdfs user. This is because the hdfs user is typically the owner or root user of Hadoop filesystem.

The process of determining what access a particular user has to an object is referred to as *authorization*.

CAUTION

Don't Rely Solely on HDFS Authorization as HDFS Authentication is Weak

In the absence of using Kerberos (which will be discussed in **Hour 22, "Securing Hadoop"**), authentication in Hadoop is generally weak and can be easily defeated. Users are able to impersonate other users with greater privileges. With this in mind, HDFS permissions are useful for stopping honest people from making honest mistakes, not for stopping nefarious people accessing data they shouldn't be accessing.

On-Disk Structures, Consistency, and Recovery

The on-disk representation of the NameNode metadata consists of two components:

► `fsimage` file—A point-in-time snapshot of the metadata without the specific block locations, this file is typically only written to at the end of recovery or by the SecondaryNameNode process I will discuss shortly.

► `edits` files—Containing updates to the metadata and akin to a transaction log in a traditional database, these files are updated for every filesystem change: new data, deleted data, modified permissions, etc.

During the NameNode's recovery process, which happens during each startup of the NameNode, the following steps are performed:

1. The `fsimage` snapshot is mounted.

2. The `edits` (updates) are applied in sequence.

3. A new `fsimage` is created for the next recovery process.

4. New `edits` files are created to capture new changes post-recovery.

After the NameNode is started and the filesystem is recovered, DataNodes in the cluster start sending their block reports to the NameNode. It is by this process that the NameNode starts associating block locations for block replicas in the in-memory representation of the metadata.

It is important to note that block locations can change due to replication and rebalancing operations, so these are considered dynamic. This is why they only persist in memory and not in the `fsimage` or `edits` files).

Safe Mode

During the NameNode startup process and recovery process, the NameNode is placed into safe mode. Safe mode allows HDFS read operations only. Any operations that require updates to the metadata, including creating new files, modifying directories, or changing object permissions are not allowed, as shown in Figure 4.8.

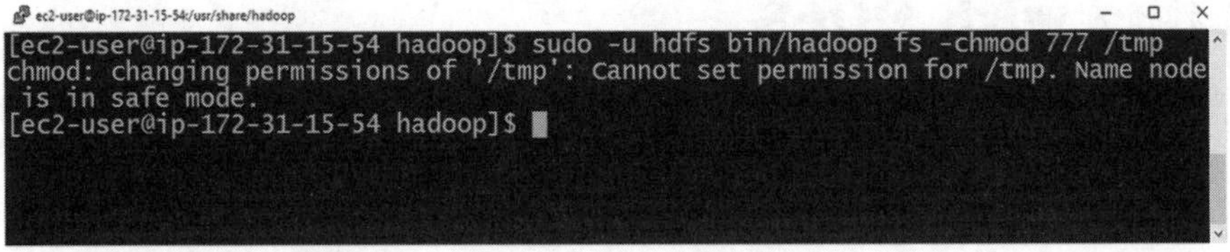

FIGURE 4.8
HDFS safe mode.

You will learn about specific commands to manually place HDFS into safe mode or to leave safe mode in **Hour 23, "Administering and Troubleshooting Hadoop."**

SecondaryNameNode Role

An optional HDFS master node process is the *SecondaryNameNode,* often simplified to 2NN. The SecondaryNameNode is located on a different host from the NameNode, and periodically performs a recovery operation on behalf of the primary NameNode, going through the same sequence of operations that the primary NameNode would do under a normal startup routine). This includes taking the current `fsimage` file from the NameNode, applying all updates from the `edits` files in sequence, and then creating a new `fsimage` file. The resultant point-in-time filesysytem snapshot (`fsimage` file) is then replaced on the primary NameNode, meaning subsequent recovery operations are substantially shortened. This process is called *checkpointing* and is scheduled to occur on the SecondaryNameNode at a configured frequency. The checkpointing process also has the side benefit of reducing the amount of disk space consumed by the journaling function (`edits` files).

The SecondaryNameNode is not a high availability (HA) solution as the SecondaryNameNode is not a hot standby for the NameNode. The SecondaryNameNode, however, does provide an alternate storage location for the on-disk representation of the NameNode's metadata in case of a catastrophic failure on the NameNode.

If you are running HDFS in HA mode, which will be covered in **Hour 21, "Understanding Advanced HDFS,"** then the Standby NameNode assumes the same responsibilities (for checkpointing) that the SecondaryNameNode would normally do.

CAUTION

The NameNode Can Be a Single Point of Failure for Hadoop

HDFS can be deployed in a high availability (or **always on**) configuration as I will discuss in **Hour 21**. Without implementing HA, the NameNode is a single point of failure (SPOF). If the NameNode goes down, the filesystem is completely inaccessible. The SecondaryNameNode does not address this. If the metadata is unrecoverable due to a catastrophic disk failure, for example, then the entire HDFS cluster is unrecoverable. For this reason, a 2NN is recommended along with a `fsimage` and `edits` file backup strategy—which I will discuss in **Hour 23, "Administering and Troubleshooting Hadoop,"**—is recommended, especially if you are not implementing HA.

Interacting with HDFS

HDFS provides multiple interfaces to read, write, interrogate, and manage the filesystem, including the following:

▶ The filesystem shell (`hadoop fs` or `hdfs dfs`)

▶ The Hadoop Filesystem Java API

▶ RESTful proxy interfaces such as HttpFS and WebHDFS

There are many other ways to access HDFS as well. For simplicity, I will demonstrate using the filesystem shell in the examples that follow.

Hadoop's filesystem is based on the POSIX (Portable Operating System Interface) standard, using POSIX conventions found in Unix and Linux for representations of files and directories.

The Hadoop filesystem shell uses verbs similar to the FTP commands, so you will notice some semantic similarities if you are familiar with the FTP syntax.

Examples of some common simple file or directory operations are shown next.

Uploading (or Ingesting) a File

To put a local file named `warandpeace.txt` in the current local directory into an existing directory in HDFS called `/data/books`, you would execute the following:

```
$ hadoop fs -put warandpeace.txt /data/books/
```

Synonymous commands include:

```
$ hadoop fs -copyFromLocal warandpeace.txt /data/books
# or
$ hdfs dfs -put warandpeace.txt /data/books
```

NOTE
_____

Hadoop has no concept of current directory. Every filesystem command starts from a relative path beginning in the user's home directory in HDFS: `/user/<username>`. In the preceding example, I have used an absolute path to specify the destination location for the file in HDFS. If a user `javen` were to specify `hadoop fs -put warandpeace.txt`, the file would be created as `/user/javen/warandpeace.txt`.
_____

Downloading a File

Many applications cannot interact directly with HDFS, so often you will need to retrieve a file from HDFS into a local or network filesystem to use the file with one of these applications.

As an example, suppose you need to retrieve a file called `report.csv` from `/data/reports` in HDFS and place it into the user's current directory on his or her local filesystem. It could be done as follows:

```
$ hadoop fs -get /data/reports/report.csv
```

As with the uploading example, there are similar, synonymous commands to perform other actions such as downloading a file. For the sake of brevity, I won't list these.

Listing a Directory's Contents

To list the contents of /data/reports, you would simply execute:

```
$ hadoop fs -ls /data/reports
```

Deleting Objects in HDFS

To delete `report.csv` from `/data/reports` in HDFS, you would execute:

```
$ hadoop fs -rm /data/reports/report.csv
```

To delete the entire `/data/reports` directory, you would execute:

```
$ hadoop fs -rm -r /data/reports
```

CAUTION

Ensure the Trash Setting Is Enabled

HDFS has the concept of a Trash folder or Recycling Bin. This is configured by a parameter set either on the client or the server called `fs.trash.interval`, which is set in the configuration file `hdfs-site.xml`. This parameter is the amount of time (in minutes) to keep a deleted object in a hidden Trash directory before it is permanently removed from the filesystem. The default is 0, meaning all deletes are immediate and irreversible, so ensure your administrator has set this to a non-zero value before performing a delete.

▼ TRY IT YOURSELF

Interacting with HDFS

In this exercise we will use the `hadoop fs` commands to put data into HDFS and get data out of HDFS. We will also locate and explore the block storage and on-disk NameNode metadata.

We will be using the pseudo-distributed mode cluster set up in the previous hour, though you could also use one of the commercial quickstart pseudo-distributed clusters as well, if you have one available.

1. Set your `HADOOP_HOME` environment variable if it is not still set from the last exercise, and change directories to `$HADOOP_HOME`:

```
$ export HADOOP_HOME=/usr/share/hadoop
$ cd $HADOOP_HOME
```

2. Upload a file to your user's HDFS home directory (as we are not supplying an absolute path) using the `hadoop fs -put` command:

```
$ cd $HADOOP_HOME
$ bin/hadoop fs -put LICENSE.txt
```

3. Now use the `hadoop fs -cat` command to show the contents of the file in HDFS:

```
$ bin/hadoop fs -cat LICENSE.txt
```

4. Use the `hadoop fs -get` command to download the file with a new extension:

```
$ $HADOOP_HOME/bin/hadoop fs -get LICENSE.txt.from_hdfs
```

5. Open the file in the local filesystem to confirm it is the same as the file that was uploaded to HDFS in Step 3:

```
$ cat LICENSE.txt.from_hdfs
```

You can now delete this file using the following:

```
$ rm LICENSE.txt.from_hdfs
```

6. Now explore the block directory on the local filesystem (as the pseudo-distributed cluster has a running DataNode daemon):

```
$ sudo su hdfs
$ cd /tmp/hadoop-hdfs/dfs/data/current
$ ls -lh
```

You will see a directory starting with *BP-...* (this stands for *Block Pool*). In this directory you will find subdirectories containing the actual block files, which are distinguishable because of their *blk_* prefix.

7. Now let's explore the on-disk metadata, as this host is running the NameNode daemon as well:

```
$ cd /tmp/hadoop-hdfs/dfs/name/current
$ ls -lh
```

You should see files beginning with *fsimage..* or *edits..;* these are the `fsimage` and `edits` on-disk metadata files you learned about earlier in this hour.

TIP

Set Up Environment Variables for All Users Using `/etc/profile.d`

It is helpful to set up environment variables such as `HADOOP_HOME` and `JAVA_HOME` for all users of the system. It is also useful to add `$HADOOP_HOME/bin` to the `PATH` for all users as well. This saves having to change directories each time you wish to use the `hadoop` command (which we will use often in this book). These tasks can be accomplished by creating a custom shell script (`hadoop.sh`) in the `/etc/profile.d` directory of your Linux system. Such a script is shown in Listing 4.2.

LISTING 4.2   Adding Hadoop Environment Variables for all Users

```
sudo su
echo "export JAVA_HOME=/PATH_TO_JAVA_HOME/" > /etc/profile.d/hadoop.sh
echo "export HADOOP_HOME=/usr/share/hadoop" >> /etc/profile.d/hadoop.sh
echo "export PATH=/usr/share/hadoop/bin:$PATH" >> /etc/profile.d/hadoop.sh
chmod +x /etc/profile.d/hadoop.sh
```

In later exercises and examples in this book if you see the `hadoop` command used without a directory, you can assume that `$HADOOP_HOME/bin` is in the system `PATH`.

In **Hour 5: "Getting Data into Hadoop,"** you will learn about other methods to ingest data into HDFS, but you will undoubtedly use the `hadoop fs` shell command routinely when using the Hadoop platform.

Summary

In this hour you learned about HDFS, the Hadoop storage subsystem. I discussed how HDFS files are stored as physical blocks that are distributed and replicated across multiple nodes in a typical HDFS cluster, as well as how block failures are handled seamlessly by HDFS. You also learned more about the NameNode's metadata, both its in-memory form and its associated on-disk structures (`fsimage` and `edits` files) and how the filesystem is mounted and recovered.

You learned about the role of the SecondaryNameNode in assisting the NameNode with recovery through its checkpointing function. You learned about object permissions and ownership in HDFS as well. Finally, you learned how to interact with the filesystem using the `hadoop fs` shell commands.

Many other HDFS concepts are covered in the coming hours, including HA, federation, rack awareness, administration, configuration, and more. It has certainly been an intense hour, but one upon which you will be able to build a solid foundation!

Q&A

Q. What is the key difference between the in-memory representation of the NameNode's metadata and the on-disk representation of the metadata, and why?

A. The in-memory representation of the NameNode's metadata includes block locations within the cluster which the on-disk structures do not. This is because the locations could change and are considered dynamic and not part of the core recovery process. Instead, this information is sourced through the DataNode's frequent block report process, whereby the memory-resident metadata structures are updated.

Q. Explain the role of the SecondaryNameNode.

A. The SecondaryNameNode performs a mock recovery process using the NameNode's `fsimage` and `edits` files, creating a new `fsimage` (point-in-time snapshot) file and managing the `edits` file on the NameNode. This new `fsimage` file is then sent back to the NameNode, thereby significantly reducing NameNode recovery time in the event of a restart.

Q. What is the sequence of events that occurs in a HDFS filesystem write operation?

A. In a HDFS write operation, the HDFS client communicates with the NameNode, informing the NameNode of what blocks it needs to write. The NameNode then directs the HDFS client as to which DataNodes to write blocks to. The DataNodes then communicate with one another to form a replication pipeline until all configured replicas of a block have been written. The client is then sent an acknowledgment from the first DataNode, and the write is considered successful. The DataNodes, through their normal operation, will report their storage of the block to the NameNode so the NameNode can update its in-memory metadata.

Workshop

The workshop contains quiz questions to help you solidify your understanding of the material covered. Try to answer all questions before looking at the "Answers" section that follows.

Quiz

1. HDFS is a _____ filesystem. (*write once, read many* or *write many, read many*)

2. **True or False:** The NameNode is not a single point of failure for a Hadoop cluster if you have deployed a SecondaryNameNode.

3. Which `hadoop fs` shell command is used to ingest a new file into HDFS?

    A. `hadoop fs get`

    B. `hadoop fs put`

    C. `hadoop fs ls`

    D. `hadoop fs rm`

4. _____ are regular messages sent from DataNodes to the NameNode and are used to identify the physical location of blocks in the cluster as well as to validate the integrity of HDFS blocks.

Answers

1. write once, read many (or WORM).

2. False.

3. B.

4. Block reports.

HOUR 5
Getting Data into Hadoop

What You'll Learn in This Hour:

▶ Introduction to Apache Flume

▶ Ingesting data from a database using Sqoop

▶ Data ingestion using WebHDFS and HttpFS

▶ Data ingestion best practices

Last hour you learned how to interact with the Hadoop filesystem using the filesystem shell commands. These commands are useful for getting data into and out of Hadoop. However, in many cases you will need to establish interfaces to capture data produced from source systems in real time, such as web logs, or schedule batch snapshots from a relational database, such as a transaction processing system. In such cases you will need some additional approaches, which is exactly what I will cover in this hour!

Data Ingestion Using Apache Flume

Apache Flume is a Hadoop ecosystem project originally developed by Cloudera designed to capture, transform, and ingest data into HDFS using one or more agents. The initial use case was based upon capturing log files, or web logs, from a source system like a web server, and routing these files and their messages into HDFS as they are generated.

NOTE

The project name Flume is actually a reference to logs—the timber variety. For those of you unfamiliar with the logging industry, a flume is the apparatus used to channel timber logs into the sawmill where they are cut into 2 × 4's and sent to your local timber yard. For the non-lumberjacks, the log ride at Disneyland or your local theme park is usually called the flume.

Flume Architecture

Flume is implemented using one or more **agents**. Agents can connect a data source directly to HDFS or to other downstream agents. A few valid flume agent topologies are shown in Figure 5.1.

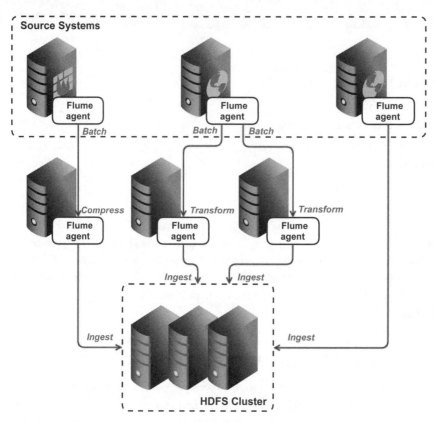

FIGURE 5.1
Flume topologies.

As seen from Figure 5.1, agents can be chained together or can be used in parallel to one another. The latter configuration can be used for horizontal scalability or agent fault tolerance. Also as shown, agents can also perform in-flight data operations, including basic transformations, compression, encryption, batching of events (recall our discussion last hour that fewer larger files are preferred in most cases), and more.

Flume agents contain a **sink**, a **source**, and a **channel** as pictured in Figure 5.2.

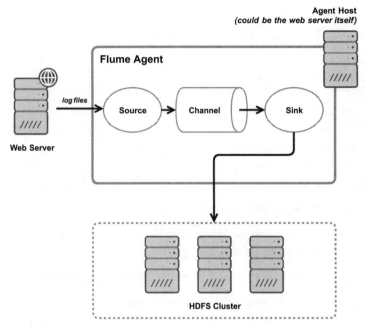

FIGURE 5.2
Flume agent architecture.

Let's look at each component now.

Source

A Flume agent source instructs the agent where the data is to be received from. Example sources include:

- ▶ *HTTP*—Used to consume data from RESTful services using POST and GET methods

- ▶ *Syslog*—Log protocol to capture system events

- ▶ *JMS*—Java Message Service

- ▶ *Kafka*—Popular open source messaging platform

- ▶ *Avro*—Open source, cross platform data serialization framework for Hadoop

- ▶ *Twitter*—Flume source that connects to Twitter's Streaming API to continuously download tweets

- ▶ and more.

An example source configuration to tail a log file is shown in Listing 5.1. You will use this configuration in our next Try it Yourself exercise in this section.

LISTING 5.1   Flume Agent Source Configuration

```
agent1.sources = source1
agent1.sources.source1.type = exec
agent1.sources.source1.command = tail -F /tmp/events
```

Sink

A Flume agent sink tells the agent where to send data. Often the destination is HDFS, which was the original intention for the project. However, the destination could be another agent that will do some further in-flight processing, or another filesystem such as S3. Example sinks include:

▶ *HDFS*—Most common sink used to ingest data into HDFS

▶ *Hive*—Ingests data into HDFS while updating the Hive partitions and the Hive metastore (concepts covered in **Hour 10, "Analyzing Data Using Apache Hive"**)

▶ *HBase*—NoSQL data store built on HDFS (discussed in **Hour 15, "Introducing NoSQL"**)

▶ *Kafka*—Open source, cross-platform data serialization framework for Hadoop

▶ *Solr*—Open source search platform

▶ and more.

An example sink configuration to send data to HDFS is shown in Listing 5.2. You will use this configuration along with the previous sink configuration in the next Try it Yourself exercise.

LISTING 5.2   Flume Agent Sink Configuration

```
agent1.sinks = sink1
agent1.sinks.sink1.type = hdfs
agent1.sinks.sink1.hdfs.path = /flume/events
agent1.sinks.sink1.hdfs.filePrefix = events-
agent1.sinks.sink1.hdfs.round = true
agent1.sinks.sink1.hdfs.roundValue = 10
agent1.sinks.sink1.hdfs.roundUnit = minute
```

Extending Flume with Custom Sources and Sinks

Flume is written in Java and is completely open source and intentionally extensible, so if you cannot find a built-in source or sink to do what you need it to do, you can always write your own!

Channel

The Flume agent channel is a queue between the agent's source and sink. Flume implements a transactional architecture for added reliability. This enables rollback and retry operations if required. The channel or queue used to transfer the data and manage transactions can be implemented in one of the following configurations:

▶ In-memory

▶ Durable

Durable channels use persistent storage (disk) to maintain state (transactional integrity), meaning that these channels are guaranteed not to lose data in the event of a power failure. Examples of durable channel implementations include:

▶ File Channel

▶ JDBC Channel

▶ Kafka Channel

Listing 5.3 shows an example of a memory channel configuration for a Flume agent.

LISTING 5.3   Flume Agent Channel Configuration

```
agent1.channels = channel1
agent1.channels.channel1.type = memory
agent1.channels.channel1.capacity = 100
agent1.channels.channel1.transactionCapacity = 100
agent1.channels.channel1.byteCapacityBufferPercentage = 20
```

Installing Flume

Flume is included in many of the mainstream commercial vendors' Hadoop stacks, and is also available from **https://flume.apache.org/** along with detailed documentation, including more information about available sources, sinks, and more.

Let's install and test Flume on our pseudo-distributed mode Hadoop cluster now.

▼ TRY IT YOURSELF

Deploying Apache Flume

In this exercise we will install and configure a Flume agent to capture data by tailing a log file. The data will then be batched and ingested into HDFS. We will use the pseudo-distributed mode cluster we deployed in **Hour 3, "Deploying Hadoop."** However, feel free to use a commercial distribution or EMR as well. In many cases the agent will already be installed, and you can skip directly to the configuration steps).

1. Find your closest download mirror and download the latest release of Apache Flume from https://flume.apache.org/download.html (we will use release 1.6.0 for this exercise):

   ```
   $ wget http://MIRROR_PATH/apache-flume-1.6.0-bin.tar.gz
   ```

2. Unpack and install Flume:

   ```
   $ tar -xvf apache-flume-1.6.0-bin.tar.gz
   $ mv apache-flume-1.6.0-bin flume
   $ sudo mv flume/ /usr/share/
   ```

3. Create a Flume agent configuration, by creating a `flume-conf.properties` file in `/usr/share/flume/conf` and copying the configuration in sequence from Listings 5.1, 5.2, and 5.3 as well as the additional lines of configuration shown:

   ```
   $ vi /usr/share/flume/conf/flume-conf.properties
   # copy and paste the contents from Listing 5.1
   # copy and paste the contents from Listing 5.2
   # copy and paste the contents from Listing 5.3
   # then add the following lines:
   agent1.sources.source1.channels = channel1
   agent1.sinks.sink1.channel = channel1
   ```

4. We will now set up a test script to generate log messages using random dictionary words. To do this you will first need to install the words package in Linux:

   ```
   $ sudo yum install words
   ```

   This will create a file with approximately 450,000 to 500,000 English words (or words derived from English words) in the `/usr/share/dict` directory.

5. Create a Python script to generate random events using words from `/usr/share/dict/words` by creating a file in your home directory named `gen_events.py` and copying the following code into this file:

   ```
   from random import randint
   from datetime import datetime
   word_file = "/usr/share/dict/words"
   WORDS = open(word_file).read().splitlines()
   ```

```
while True:
  currtime = datetime.now()
  words = ""
  for i in range(0,9):
    words = words + WORDS[randint(0,400000)] + " "
  print currtime.strftime('%Y/%m/%d %H:%M:%S') + "\t" + words
```

6. Make a directory in HDFS to ingest data from Flume (use your particular user in the chown statement):

```
$ sudo -u hdfs $HADOOP_HOME/bin/hdfs dfs -mkdir -p \
/flume/events
$ sudo -u hdfs $HADOOP_HOME/bin/hdfs dfs -chown -R \
ec2-user /flume
```

7. Open three separate terminal windows.

8. In one window, start the Flume agent using the configuration you created in Step 3.

```
$ /usr/share/flume/bin/flume-ng agent \
--conf /etc/hadoop/conf/ \
--conf-file /usr/share/flume/conf/flume-conf.properties \
--name agent1
```

9. In a second window, run the Python script to generate random log messages:

```
$ python gen_events.py >> /tmp/events
```

10. In a third window, inspect the HDFS directory configured to capture the log events (/flume/events):

```
$ hadoop fs -ls /flume/events
```

You should see files created by Flume prefixed by events- (as specified in the configuration) (Figure 5.3).

```
[ec2-user@ip-172-31-15-54 ~]$ hadoop fs -ls /flume/events
Found 9 items
-rw-r--r--   1 ec2-user supergroup       1299 2016-07-31 00:51 /flume/events/events-.1469940660644
-rw-r--r--   1 ec2-user supergroup       1432 2016-07-31 00:51 /flume/events/events-.1469940660645
-rw-r--r--   1 ec2-user supergroup       1407 2016-07-31 00:51 /flume/events/events-.1469940660646
-rw-r--r--   1 ec2-user supergroup       1369 2016-07-31 00:51 /flume/events/events-.1469940660647
-rw-r--r--   1 ec2-user supergroup       1349 2016-07-31 00:51 /flume/events/events-.1469940660648
-rw-r--r--   1 ec2-user supergroup       1313 2016-07-31 00:51 /flume/events/events-.1469940660649
-rw-r--r--   1 ec2-user supergroup       1431 2016-07-31 00:51 /flume/events/events-.1469940660650
-rw-r--r--   1 ec2-user supergroup       1311 2016-07-31 00:51 /flume/events/events-.1469940660651
-rw-r--r--   1 ec2-user supergroup        748 2016-07-31 00:51 /flume/events/events-.1469940660652
[ec2-user@ip-172-31-15-54 ~]$
```

FIGURE 5.3
HDFS files created by Flume.

11. Stop the `gen_events.py` script by entering Ctrl-C in the window where this script is running. You should also stop the Flume agent by entering Ctrl-C in the window where the agent process was started.

12. Inspect one of the files; you should see records generated by the `gen_events.py` script.

```
$ hadoop fs -cat /flume/events/events-.<timestamp>
```

Note that you may see some non-printable characters along with the random words generated. This is because the file generated is a special file using Hadoop serialization, something you will learn about in **Hour 7, "Programming MapReduce Applications".**

Congratulations! You have just set up and tested a Flume agent. I encourage you to test other sources, sinks, and channels available in the project.

Ingesting Data from a Database using Sqoop

Sqoop (which is a portmanteau for "sql-to-hadoop") is a top-level ASF project designed to source data from a relational database and ingest this data into files (typically delimited files) in HDFS. This data can then be used for processing with MapReduce, Hive, Pig, Spark, or any of the other distributed programming platforms or interfaces available in the Hadoop ecosystem.

Sqoop can also be used to send data from Hadoop to a relational database, useful for sending results processed in Hadoop to an operational transaction processing system. Sqoop integrates with Hive, which is a SQL abstraction to MapReduce and other processing technologies on the Hadoop platform. Sqoop can automatically create Hive tables from imported data from a RDBMS (Relational Database Management System) table. I will discuss Hive in more detail in **Hour 10, "Analyzing Data Using Apache Hive."**

Sqoop was originally developed by Cloudera but is now included in most pure-play Hadoop vendors' commercial distributions. Sqoop includes tools for the following operations:

▶ Listing databases and tables on a database system

▶ Importing a single table from a database system, including

    ▶ Specifying which columns to import

    ▶ Specifying which rows to import using a WHERE clause

▶ Importing data from one or more tables using a SELECT statement

▶ Incremental imports from a table on a database system (importing only what has changed since a known previous state)

▶ Exporting of data from HDFS to a table on a remote database system

How Sqoop Works

Sqoop is an abstraction for MapReduce, meaning it takes a command, such as a request to import a table from an RDBMS into HDFS, and implements this using a MapReduce processing routine. Specifically, Sqoop implements a **Map-only** MapReduce process. MapReduce is discussed in much more detail starting in **Hour 7, "Programming MapReduce Applications."**

Sqoop performs the following steps to complete an import operation:

1. Connect to the database system using JDBC or a customer connector, to be discussed shortly.

2. Examine the table to be imported.

3. Create a Java class to represent the structure (schema) for the specified table. This class can then be reused for future import operations.

4. Use YARN to execute a Map-only MapReduce job with a specified number of tasks (mappers) to connect to the database system and import data from the specified table in parallel. The default number of parallel tasks is 4.

NOTE

Java Database Connectivity (JDBC) is a popular Java API for accessing different, mainly relational, database management systems (DBMS). JDBC manages functions such as connecting and disconnecting from the DBMS and running queries. Database vendors typically supply drivers or connectors to provide access to their database platforms via JDBC.

Figure 5.4 demonstrates how four nodes on a Hadoop cluster, each running a map task for a Sqoop application, connect to and ingest data from a database system.

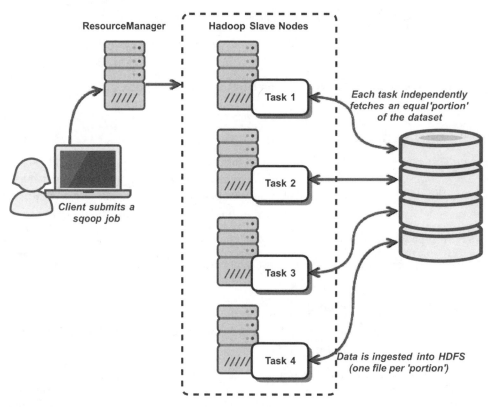

FIGURE 5.4
Sqoop.

Sqoop exposes its functions as **tools**. Available tools are shown in Listing 5.4.

LISTING 5.4   Sqoop Tools

```
$ sqoop help
16/07/31 06:10:26 INFO sqoop.Sqoop: Running Sqoop version: 1.4.6
usage: sqoop COMMAND [ARGS]
Available commands:
codegen             Generate code to interact with database records
create-hive-table   Import a table definition into Hive
eval                Evaluate a SQL statement and display the results
export              Export a HDFS directory to a database table
help                List available commands
import              Import a table from a database to HDFS
import-all-tables   Import tables from a database to HDFS
import-mainframe    Import datasets from a mainframe server to HDFS
job                 Work with saved jobs
```

list-databases	List available databases on a server
list-tables	List available tables in a database
merge	Merge results of incremental imports
metastore	Run a standalone Sqoop metastore
version	Display version information

An example Sqoop operation to import all tables from a MySQL database named "mydb" is shown in Listing 5.5.

LISTING 5.5 Importing All Tables from a Database Using Sqoop

```
$ sqoop import-all-tables \
--username javen \
--password ***** \
--connect jdbc:mysql://mydbserver.local/mydb
```

JDBC and Custom Connectors for Sqoop

Sqoop supports native JDBC as previously discussed. Although JDBC supports connectivity to most database platforms, it may not be as efficient and fast as native connectivity libraries supplied by the respective database platform vendors.

Custom connectors are available from database vendors or third parties for popular database platforms including:

▶ Oracle

▶ Teradata

▶ Microsoft SQL Server

To download these connectors or find more information, check your specific vendor's website.

Sqoop2 (Sqoop-as-a-Service)

Sqoop is available as an application where the Sqoop binaries reside on a client system. It is also available as a service where a server hosts the application and connectors, and a lightweight client, web UI, or API connects to the server to submit a Sqoop request. The server then executes the request on the client's behalf. The advantages to this approach include:

▶ Centralized management of security, as credentials are centrally stored and managed

▶ Capability to restrict or control the number of connections to a database system

▶ Capability to implement network isolation between client systems and subnets and database systems

▶ Eliminates the need to manage software on client systems (e.g., custom connectors, binaries, etc.)

The server-based implementation of Sqoop is called *Sqoop2*.

More information on Sqoop including Sqoop2 (Sqoop-as-a-service) is available from any of the following sources:

▶ Apache Sqoop (http://sqoop.apache.org/)

▶ Cloudera (http://www.cloudera.com/)

▶ Hortonworks (http://hortonworks.com/)

▶ MapR (https://www.mapr.com/)

Data Ingestion Using HDFS RESTful Interfaces

REST (Representational State Transfer) is a pattern used to provide stateless responses to client requests, mostly over HTTP or HTTPS. There are several methods available to provide access to HDFS via REST interfaces. These methods include WebHDFS and HttpFS. Let's discuss them now.

WebHDFS

WebHDFS provides RESTful access to HDFS using HTTP or HTTPS, supporting both read and write operations. This is the simplest implementation of RESTful access to HDFS, only requiring one Hadoop configuration parameter to be modified (which you will do in our next Try it Yourself exercise). Command line utilities such as wget or curl can be used to access HDFS. An example of this is shown in Listing 5.6.

LISTING 5.6   REST Access to HDFS Using WebHDFS

```
$ curl -i -L "http://namenode:50070/webhdfs/v1/data/file.txt?op=OPEN"
```

Let's set up WebHDFS.

Enabling WebHDFS

In the exercise we will enable WebHDFS on our pseudo-distributed Hadoop cluster.

1. Add a new configuration property to `hdfs-site.xml` to enable WebHDFS:

```
$ sudo vi /etc/hadoop/conf/hdfs-site.xml
```

Add the following property between the `<configuration>` and `</configuration>` tags:

```
<configuration>
...
<property>
<name>dfs.webhdfs.enabled</name>
<value>true</value>
</property>
</configuration>
```

2. Restart the NameNode:

```
$ sudo -u hdfs $HADOOP_HOME/sbin/hadoop-daemon.sh stop namenode
$ sudo -u hdfs $HADOOP_HOME/sbin/hadoop-daemon.sh start namenode
```

3. Execute the following `curl` command to list objects created earlier in the hour in the Flume exercise:

```
$ curl -i \
"http://localhost:50070/webhdfs/v1/flume/events?op=GETFILESTATUS"
```

You should see output similar to the following:

```
HTTP/1.1 200 OK
Cache-Control: no-cache
Expires: Sun, 31 Jul 2016 07:37:17 GMT
Date: Sun, 31 Jul 2016 07:37:17 GMT
Pragma: no-cache
Expires: Sun, 31 Jul 2016 07:37:17 GMT
Date: Sun, 31 Jul 2016 07:37:17 GMT
Pragma: no-cache
Content-Type: application/json
Transfer-Encoding: chunked
Server: Jetty(6.1.26)
{
  "FileStatus": {
  "accessTime": 0,
  "blockSize": 0,
  "childrenNum": 20,
```

```
     "fileId": 16650,
     "group": "supergroup",
     "length": 0,
     "modificationTime": 1469941293732,
     "owner": "ec2-user",
     "pathSuffix": "",
     "permission": "755",
     "replication": 0,
     "storagePolicy": 0,
     "type": "DIRECTORY"
     }
   }
```

Although this approach is simple and useful, there are some limitations to be aware of which include the following:

▶ WebHDFS does not support High Availability (HA) HDFS implementations.

▶ Clients must be able to access every DataNode in the cluster.

HttpFS

HttpFS provides RESTful access via a service. The configuration of HttpFS is not as simple as WebHDFS, but the solution is more scalable, supporting HA HDFS implementations and not requiring direct client accessibility to DataNodes in the cluster.

The HttpFS server acts as a proxy accepting REST requests from clients and submitting them to HDFS on the clients' behalf, as depicted in Figure 5.5.

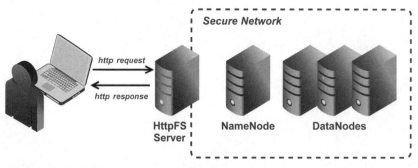

FIGURE 5.5
HDFS access using a HttpFS server.

Steps to configure HttpFS include:

1. Install and configure a HttpFS server.

2. Create a HttpFS user.

3. Enable access to HDFS for the HttpFS user.

4. Restart the NameNode (or NameNodes if HA is implemented).

Clients then submit their requests to the HttpFS server as shown in Listing 5.7:

LISTING 5.7   RESTful HDFS Access Using HttpFS

```
$ curl http://httpfs-host:14000/webhdfs/v1/user/foo/README.txt
```

I will revisit network isolation and discuss how to implement a secure gateway to HDFS using authentication, authorization, and auditing using the Apache Knox project in **Hour 22, "Securing Hadoop."**

Data Ingestion Considerations

There are some considerations and best practices which need to be applied for data ingestion onto production Hadoop clusters. Before I cover these you should first understand how data is made available during the ingestion process.

When a file is being written to HDFS, the file initially appears to clients as a zero byte file in the incoming directory with a `._COPYING_` suffix as shown in Figure 5.6.

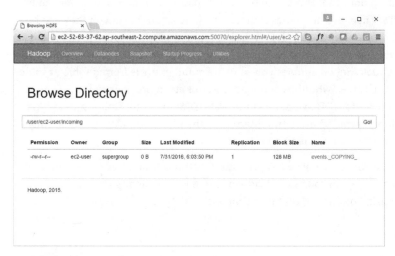

FIGURE 5.6
HDFS files during ingestion.

As data is written to the file, it is committed (or flushed) in block size increments—typically 128MB. So a client watching a directory to which a file is being ingested will see the file grow in 128MB increments from 0MB to its target file size.

The important point here is that the file is visible in the target HDFS directory and can be read (and therefore used as input for processing) while the file is not yet complete. As you will see in the coming hours, the input for processing in Hadoop using MapReduce, Pig, Hive, or Spark, is typically a directory and all files available within it.

For this reason a better practice for data ingestion into HDFS is to do the following:

1. Ingest into a "working" directory in HDFS, e.g., `/../incoming`.

2. Once the write operation is complete, move the file into a directory accessible to users, e.g., `/../ingested`.

The move operation is a metadata operation, so it happens (almost) instantaneously.

This is a fail-safe practice for ingesting data into HDFS, and can easily be orchestrated by a script or batch process. Flume will take care of this automatically, but you should be aware of this behavior for other methods used for ingestion.

Summary

In this hour you learned about several methods used to ingest data from source systems into HDFS. You learned about the Apache Flume project, which implements a series of agents that include sources, channels, and sinks to acquire, transform, and ingest data into HDFS. Flume is useful for capturing data as it is produced—for instance, logs from a web server—and channeling this into HDFS. There are numerous sources and sinks available to you that can be used to capture and ingest data from Syslog, HTTP, Kafka, and even Twitter sources. Sqoop is another useful utility that is used to acquire and ingest data from a relational database such as Teradata, SQL Server, or Oracle. Sqoop enables you to perform full extracts from a table or tables as well as incremental extracts (i.e., what has changed since a known previous state). Lastly we looked at RESTful interfaces to HDFS, which include WebHDFS and HttpFS, that provide API gateways used to upload to, download from and interrogate the filesystem. HttpFS is especially useful where perimeter security is implemented for Hadoop clusters.

Spark Streaming, Apache Storm and Apache NiFi are other methods which can be used to transform and ingest streaming data sources in Hadoop. These will be discussed in **Hour 13, "Introducing Apache Spark,"** and **Hour 17, "Working with the Hadoop Ecosystem,"** respectively.

Q&A

Q. What are the components of a Flume agent and what are their respective functions?

A. Flume agents consist of a source, a sink and a channel. The source defines where to get the data from, the sink defines where to send the data to, and the channel is the queue between the source and sink.

Q. What are the advantages of HttpFS over WebHDFS?

A. HttpFS is implemented as a HDFS proxy, which allows Hadoop cluster nodes to be isolated from client networks, whereas WebHDFS is a process running on the NameNode itself. Furthermore, HttpFS is able to access HDFS clusters implementing High Availability (HA), which WebHDFS is not.

Q. What issues could arise if a client is ingesting a file into the `/data` directory in HDFS and another client is reading the `/data` directory for processing at the same time?

A. As a file is being ingested into the `/data` directory, the file will be seen by other processes to have a `._COPYING_` extension. Although this file is clearly seen to be uploading, the file is still accessible by processes reading the directory at the time. This could lead to integrity issues for the client reading files in the directory because Hadoop processing operations typically read all files in a directory regardless of their extension.

Workshop

The workshop contains quiz questions to help you solidify your understanding of the material covered. Try to answer all questions before looking at the "Answers" section that follows.

Quiz

1. **True or False:** HttpFS does not support HDFS deployed in High Availability mode.

2. **True or False:** Native connectors provided by the database vendor typically provide better performance for Sqoop operations than using built-in JDBC connectivity.

3. Flume can be used to capture, transform, and ingest data from which type of source?

    A. HTTP

    B. Syslog

    C. Twitter

    D. All of the above

4. A client ingests a 1GB file into HDFS, and the configured HDFS block size is the Hadoop default (128MB). The client has uploaded 450MB thus far. If another client browses the HDFS directory where the file is being uploaded to what will they see?

Answers

1. False. WebHDFS does not support HDFS deployed in High Availability mode. HttpFS does support HDFS HA mode.

2. True.

3. D.

4. 384MB, as 3 blocks have been completely written to HDFS.

Understanding Data Processing in Hadoop

What You'll Learn in This Hour:

▶ The history of MapReduce

▶ The basic concepts of the MapReduce programming model

▶ Understanding WordCount, the "Hello World" of Hadoop programming

▶ The implementation of MapReduce in Hadoop

▶ Application scheduling on Hadoop using YARN

To understand data processing in Hadoop, it is imperative that you understand the MapReduce programming model and its implementation on Hadoop. MapReduce is a platform- and language-independent programming model at the heart of most big data and NoSQL platforms. Many common processing platforms are abstractions of MapReduce (such as Pig and Hive) or are heavily influenced by MapReduce concepts (the very popular Spark project, for example). Understanding and mastering the concepts behind MapReduce is fundamental to truly understanding distributed programming and data processing in Hadoop. This hour is packed with concepts which you will use throughout the course of this book and throughout your career in Big Data!

Introduction to MapReduce

Following Google's release of the "The Google File System" whitepaper in 2003, which influenced the Hadoop Distributed File System, Google released another whitepaper called "MapReduce: Simplified Data Processing on Large Clusters" in December 2004.

The MapReduce whitepaper gave a high-level description of Google's approach to processing, specifically indexing and ranking, large volumes of text data for search-engine processing. This whitepaper had a major influence on the Nutch project that was underway at the time at Yahoo!. The creators of the Nutch project, including Doug Cutting, incorporated the principles outlined in the Google MapReduce and Google File System papers into the project now known as Hadoop.

The Motivation for MapReduce

When the original scale-up approach to increasing processing capacity started to reach its limits, a new paradigm emerged: the distributed system. Distributed programming frameworks had existed for decades before the Google MapReduce paper was released in 2004, including Message Passing Interface (MPI), Parallel Virtual Machine (PVM), HTCondor, and others.

The early distributed computing and grid computing frameworks had several limitations, including the following:

▶ *Complexity in programming*—Developers would often need to concern themselves with state and synchronization between distributed processes, including temporal dependencies.

▶ *Partial failures, which are difficult to recover from*—Synchronization and data exchange between processes in a distributed system made dealing with partial failures much more challenging.

▶ *Bottlenecks in getting data to the processor*—Many distributed systems sourced data from shared or remote storage. Movement of this data, along with the data exchanged between remote processes, would ultimately result in a processing bottleneck.

▶ *Limited scalability*—Finite bandwidth between processes would ultimately limit the extent to which early distributed systems could scale.

Because synchronization and data movement overheads increase with every node added, at a certain point adding additional nodes results in diminishing performance returns. This concept is pictured in Figure 6.1.

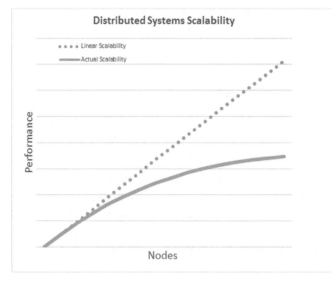

FIGURE 6.1
Diminishing returns with early distributed systems.

The Design Goals for MapReduce

Distributed systems that existed before the seminal Google whitepapers were adequate for handling the scale of data at that time. At that stage, the Internet was in its formative years—or not in existence at all—and data volumes were modest. This was all about to change.

The search-engine providers, including Google and Yahoo!, had a requirement to collect, store, and index an exponentially expanding number of unstructured text documents. This was the beginning of the "data deluge." The expansion of mobile data networks and social media would further exacerbate the issues.

Google set out to address the scalability limitations and develop a storage and processing platform that could scale linearly to hundreds or thousands of nodes running on commodity hardware, and leverage thousands of CPUs running thousands of concurrent tasks. The design goals outlined in the 2004 Google MapReduce white paper included the following:

▶ *Automatic parallelization and distribution*—The programming model should make it easy to parallelize and distribute computations.

▶ *Fault tolerance*—The system must be able to handle partial failure. If a node or process fails, its workload should be assumed by other functioning components in the system.

▶ *Input/output (I/O) scheduling*—Task scheduling and allocation aim to limit the amount of network bandwidth used. Tasks are dynamically scheduled on available workers so that faster workers process more tasks.

▶ *Status and monitoring*—Status of each component and its running tasks, including progress and counters, are reported to a master process. This makes it easy to diagnose issues, optimize jobs, or perform system capacity planning.

In the subsequent sections, I will describe the MapReduce programming model in detail, but the Google whitepaper established some key distributed processing framework concepts that are still present today in Hadoop and many other ecosystem projects such as Spark. The Google MapReduce whitepaper is available at http://research.google.com/archive/mapreduce.html.

MapReduce Explained

Before diving into the MapReduce model, you first need to understand some basic data elements that I will frequently refer to, particularly key value pairs.

Key Value Pairs and Records

Input, output, and intermediate records in MapReduce are represented in the form of key value pairs (KV or KVP), also known as name-value pairs or attribute-value pairs. Key value pairs are commonly used in programming to define a unit of data. The key is an identifier; for instance, the name of the attribute. In some systems, the key needs to be unique with respect to other keys in the same system—such is the case with most distributed NoSQL key value stores. However, in the case of MapReduce programming in Hadoop, the key is not required to be unique, as you will see later in the next hour.

The value is the data that corresponds to the key. This value can be a simple, scalar value such as an integer, or a complex object such as a list of other objects. Some example key value pairs are shown in Table 6.1.

TABLE 6.1   Example Key Value Pairs

Key	Value
City	Chicago
Temperatures	[35,38,27,16]

Key value pairs are implemented in many programming languages and often are used to express configuration parameters and metadata. In Python, dictionaries, or dicts, are sets of key-value pairs. Similarly, Ruby hashes are collections of key value pairs.

Often, the implementation of key value pairs is abstracted from the programmer; however, in low-level programming in Hadoop (MapReduce implemented in Java, for example), key value pairs are the atomic data unit against which all processing is done.

You will need to be comfortable with key value pairs because this concept is central to MapReduce, and frequently is referred to in schema-on-read platforms, including Hadoop. You will often decompose complex problems in Hadoop into a series of operations against key value pairs.

The MapReduce Programming Model

There is some ambiguity between MapReduce the programming model, and MapReduce the processing framework in Hadoop. Unfortunately, the two concepts are unavoidably conflated. I will mainly discuss MapReduce in the context of a programming model while making reference to how it's implemented as a framework in Hadoop. The latter will be discussed in **Hour 7, "Programming MapReduce Applications."**

MapReduce, the programming model (or programming abstraction), was inspired by the map and reduce primitives in Lisp and other functional programming languages.

NOTE

Lisp

Lisp is a programming language inspired by lambda calculus that was originally specified in 1958. The name is believed to be an abbreviation for list processor. Lisp was created by John McCarthy, an artificial intelligence (AI) researcher at the Massachusetts Institute of Technology (MIT).

MapReduce includes two developer-implemented processing phases, the Map phase and the Reduce phase, along with a Shuffle-and-Sort phase, which is implemented by the processing framework. Figure 6.2 describes the overall MapReduce process. This is an adaptation of the diagram provided in the original Google MapReduce whitepaper.

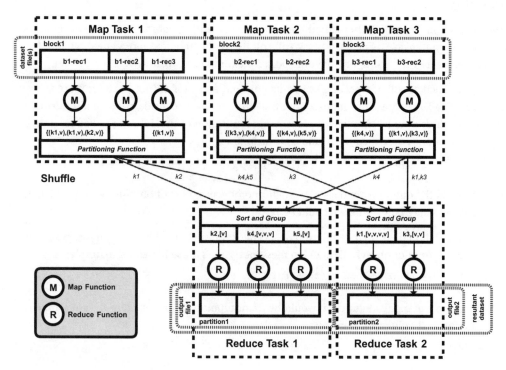

FIGURE 6.2
MapReduce Overview.

Map Phase

The Map phase is the initial phase of processing in which you'll use an input dataset as a datasource for processing. The Map phase uses input format and record reader functions in its specific implementation to derive records in the form of key value pairs for the input data.

The Map phase then applies a function or functions to each key value pair over a portion of the dataset. In the case of a dataset hosted in files in HDFS, this portion would be a block in the filesystem. If there were *n* blocks of data in the input dataset, there would be *n* Map tasks (also referred to as Mappers). In reality, there may be more Map task attempts, as a task may fail due to node failure. Another way of looking at this is that the input data dictates the number of Map tasks implemented, whereas the number of Reduce tasks in the Reduce phase, as I will explain later, is explicitly specified by the developer.

The Map phase is purposely designed not to share state between processes; in other words, it is a true shared nothing processing stage. Each Map task iterates through its portion of the dataset in parallel with the other Map tasks in such a way that every record (key value pair) is processed once and only once (with exceptions only for task failure or speculative execution, which I will discuss later).

In the diagram in Figure 6.2, there are three Map tasks operating against three filesystem blocks (*block1*, *block2*, and *block3*). Each Map task will call its map() function, represented by *M* in the diagram, once for each record, or key value pair; for example, *b1-rec1*, *b1-rec2*, and so on.

Each map() function call accepts one key value pair and emits (or outputs) zero or more key-value pairs. The key value pairs emitted from the Map phase are considered to be intermediate data because there may be subsequent processing or mutation of the data in the Reduce phase. The map() function is described in pseudo-code as follows:

```
map (in_key, in_value) → list (intermediate_key, intermediate_value)
```

The list refers to the output from a map() function producing a list of outputs, with a list length of *n* output key value pairs (where *n* could be zero).

Common map() functions include filtering of specific keys, such as filtering log messages if you only wanted to count or analyze ERROR log messages. Here's a pseudo-coded example:

```
let map (k, v) = if (ERROR in v) then emit (k, v)
```

Another example of a map() function would be to manipulate values, such as a map() function that converts a text value to lowercase:

```
let map (k, v) = emit (k, v. toLower ( ))
```

There are many other examples of map() functions that can be chained into a pipeline or sequence of individual functions, including conditional logic. Any map() function is valid as long as the function can be executed against a record contained in a portion of the dataset, in isolation from other Map tasks in the application that are processing other portions of the dataset.

The Map task then collects all of the individual lists of intermediate data key value pairs emitted from each map function (or each input record of the Map task's unique portion of the input dataset) into a single list grouped by the intermediate key. The combined list of intermediate values grouped by their intermediate keys is then passed to a partitioning function.

Partitioning Function

The role of the partitioning function, or Partitioner, is to ensure each key and its list of values is passed to one and only one Reduce task or Reducer. The most common implementation is a hash partitioner, which creates a hash (or unique signature) for the key and then arbitrarily divides the hashed key space into *n* partitions. The number of partitions is directly related to the number of Reducers specified by the developer.

A developer could implement a custom Partitioner for various reasons. For example, if you were processing a year's worth of data and you wanted each month to be processed by its own Reducer, you would implement a Partitioner to partition by the month.

The partitioning function is called for each key with an output representing the target Reducer for the key, typically a number between 0 and $n - 1$, where n is the number of Reducers requested by the developer).

Shuffle and Sort

So far, all of the processing you've done has been fully parallelized and individual nodes or processes did not need to communicate or exchange data or state with one another. Now you need to know how to combine intermediate keys and their associated intermediate values from multiple Map tasks, in many cases running on different nodes of the cluster, to perform further processing in the Reduce phase.

During the Shuffle-and-Sort phase, the output from each separate Map task is sent to a target Reduce task as specified by the application's partitioning function. This is typically the most expensive phase of the overall MapReduce process because it requires data to be physically transferred between nodes, requiring network I/O and consuming bandwidth, which is finite at best and scarce at worst.

NOTE

Shuffle and Sort

The Shuffle-and-Sort operation groups keys and their values together and presents the data to the target Reducer in key-sorted order. For instance, if the key is a Text value then the keys would be presented to the Reducer in ascending alphabetical order. This is the "Sort" in the "Shuffle-and-Sort" operation.

Reduce Phase

After all of the Map tasks have completed and the Shuffle phase has transferred all of the intermediate keys and their lists of intermediate values to their target Reducer (or Reduce task), the Reduce phase can begin.

Each Reduce task (or Reducer) executes a `reduce()` function for each intermediate key and its list of associated intermediate values. The output from each `reduce()` function is zero or more key value pairs considered to be part of the final output. In reality, this output may be the input to another Map phase in a complex multistage computational workflow, but in the context of the individual MapReduce application, the output from the Reduce task is final. Here is a pseudo-code representation of the reduce() function:

```
reduce (key, list (intermediate_value)) → key, out_value
```

reduce() functions are often aggregate functions such as sums, counts, and averages. The simplest and most common reduce() function is the Sum Reducer, which simply sums a list of values for each key. Here's a pseudo-coded sum reduce function:

```
let reduce (k, list <v>) =
        sum = 0
        for int  i  in  list <v> :
          sum + = i
        emit (k, sum)
```

A count operation is as simple as summing a set of ones representing instances of the values you which to count. I will present examples of this in the next section on word count.

NOTE

All Map tasks and the Shuffle phase must complete before the first reduce() function of any Reducer can be executed. This is because any portion (block) of the input data could contain keys and values that could affect the final output from the application. For instance, if our Reduce phase is implementing an aggregate function such as an average() or sum() of values by key, the output of this function would be erroneous if intermediate values from unfinished Map tasks are not included.

Fault Tolerance

The MapReduce model enables fault tolerance. In fact, it was purposely designed with the expectation of node failure because it was originally intended to run at scale on commodity hardware, or even cheap, unreliable hardware.

In Hadoop, for instance, if a Map task fails, it will automatically be rescheduled by the master process on another node, preferably a node that has a copy of the same block(s), maintaining data locality. By default, a task can fail and be rescheduled four times before the job is deemed to have failed. Similarly, because intermediate data is retained for the life of the job, if a Reduce task fails, it also can be rescheduled and its input data resupplied.

Combiner Functions

In the case of commutative and associative Reduce operations such as sums or counts, these operations can often be performed after the Map task is complete on the node executing it; that is, before the Shuffle-and-Sort phase. This is done by the use of a Combiner function, or Combiner.

Because the Map phase is naturally more distributed, using a Combiner where possible can be advantageous. It will reduce the amount of data transferred in the Shuffle phase and reduce the computational load in the Reduce phase. The Combiner function is often the same function as the `reduce()` function; it's simply executed on the Map task node against the output from the Map task.

A Combiner function can be implemented as long as running the function on the Mapper, as well as running the function more than once, will have no effect on the final result. For example, a sum function could be implemented in a Combiner, because summing a list of sums would still provide the same result. However, an average function could not be used as a Combiner function because averaging a list of averages would give an erroneous result. Figure 6.3 depicts a Combiner function.

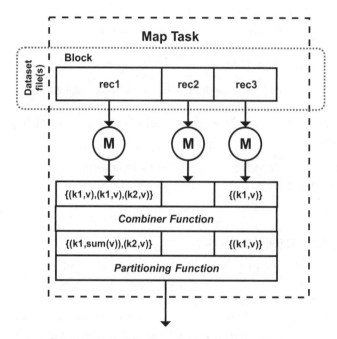

Pre-aggregated, Partitioned Data Sent to a Reducer

FIGURE 6.3
The Combiner function.

Asymmetry and Speculative Execution

The Map and Reduce phases are, respectively, asymmetrical in nature. For instance, one instance of a Map task may do more processing than other Map tasks mapping over the same dataset. This may be a result of more relevant keys existing in one portion or block of the input dataset.

An example would be a MapReduce application looking at weblogs and filtering for a particular IP address and then doing some subsequent processing. Records with the desired IP address may be clustered in multiple contiguous records in one of the blocks in the dataset and not present in others. Therefore, one of the Map tasks would naturally have more processing to do than the others. Similarly, a Reducer may work harder than others because there are more keys (and therefore more values) in its partition.

This asymmetry can lead to some Map and/or Reduce tasks running much slower than others. Because completion of the entire Map phase is a prerequisite for beginning the Reduce phase, this asymmetry could be a bottleneck.

You can configure a behavior called speculative execution that looks for a configurable, tolerated difference in progress between tasks. This will be governed by the ResourceManager and ApplicationsMaster in Hadoop. If a task falls outside of the configured tolerance, the governing process would create a duplicate task to run simultaneously against the same data (the same block, that is) as the initial slow-running task. The results of the first task to complete would be used, and the other task would be killed and its output discarded.

For instance, if you had five Map tasks, four of which were approximately 80% complete and the fifth task was 20% complete, speculative execution would start a duplicate task for the fifth task, looking at the same portion of the dataset. The results of whichever task finished first would be used, and the other task would be killed.

This behavior is designed to prevent a slow, overloaded, or unstable node from becoming a bottleneck. If the issue was solely related to asymmetry in the data, this behavior would have little or no effect.

Map-only MapReduce Applications

A MapReduce application can have zero Reduce tasks: This is considered to be a Map-only MapReduce application. Common applications for Map-only MapReduce jobs are ETL routines where the data is not intended to be summarized, aggregated, or reduced; file format conversion jobs; image processing jobs; and more. With Map-only applications, there is no partitioning function, and the output from the Map task in this case is considered to be the final output. Map-only jobs have the advantage of massive parallelization and avoiding the expensive Shuffle-and-Sort operation. Figure 6.4 depicts a Map-only MapReduce application.

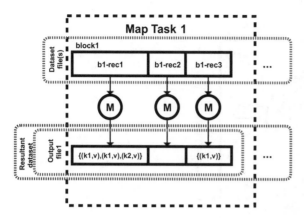

FIGURE 6.4
A Map-only MapReduce application.

You have seen a practical example of a Map-only MapReduce application in Sqoop, which was discussed in the previous hour.

An Election Analogy for MapReduce

Think about the analogy of an election and a simulation of manually tallying votes to incorporate all of the MapReduce concepts together. In an election, there are multiple polling booths located in different areas that produce completed ballot papers containing votes for candidates (representing the input data in our analogy). Each polling booth will have a teller, who groups and tallies the votes generated in their polling booth, including the filtering out of incomplete ballot papers (representing the Map and Combiner functions in our analogy). The votes grouped and counted for each candidate at each booth are then sent to a counting station for a particular candidate or candidates (representing the partitioning function and Shuffle phase). Vote counters from the central counting station now collect all of the votes for their particular candidate or candidates from all of the polling booths and tally these up (representing the Reduce phase in our analogy). The respective candidates' tallies can then be easily compared against one another to determine the winner of the election. This example is shown in Figure 6.5.

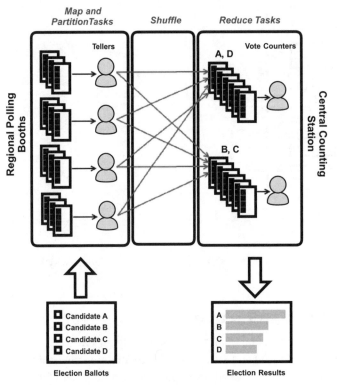

FIGURE 6.5
A MapReduce election analogy.

Word Count: The "Hello, World" of MapReduce

Word count is a simple algorithm that is often used to represent and demonstrate the MapReduce programming model. In this section, I break it down and then look at its implementation in Hadoop.

Why Count Words?

If you have previously read any Hadoop training material or tutorials, you are probably sick and tired of seeing word count examples, or you may be scratching your head trying to work out what the fixation with counting words is—a seemingly uninteresting task.

Word count is the most prevalent example used when describing the MapReduce programming model because it is easy to understand and demonstrates all of the components of the MapReduce model.

Having said that, many real-life problems solved with MapReduce are simply derivations of word count: for instance, counting occurrences of events in a large corpus of log files, or text mining functions such as TF-IDF (Term Frequency-Inverse Document Frequency). After you understand word count, you understand MapReduce too, and the problem-solving possibilities are endless.

How It Works

Counting words requires us to read a text file and count occurrences of each word and then rank these counts to determine the most frequently occurring words in the body of text being analyzed. Consider a text document containing the works of Shakespeare.

> O Romeo, Romeo! wherefore art thou Romeo?
> Deny thy father, and refuse thy name
>
> William Shakespeare

The first question you need to answer is how to derive a key and value from this unstructured collection of text to form an input record. Fortunately, Hadoop has a mechanism for this; it's called the **TextInputFormat**.

The TextInputFormat considers each newline-terminated line of text to be a record. Each record (line) is assigned an arbitrary key, usually a byte offset representing the start of the line, and the value is the complete line of text. So in the Shakespeare excerpt from Romeo and Juliet, the input records would be as shown in Listing 6.1.

LISTING 6.1   Input to the Map Task

```
(0, 'O Romeo , Romeo ! wherefore art thou Romeo ?')
(45, 'Deny thy father, and refuse thy name')
```

You will soon see that the input key is not used in further processing; therefore, anything could have been used. Now you have your input records, which will be processed in the Map phase. Recalling that this is a distributed phase, each Mapper will have a unique set of lines of text, represented as records. Each Mapper or Map task running on a worker or slave node calls a map() function for each record in its set of records, which is called an *InputSplit*. For each record, you split the line of text into a collection of words based upon whitespace or punctuation, a process known as *tokenization*. You then output each individual word or token as the intermediate key and the number 1 as the value. The resulting output of the map() functions for each record in the input split from Listing 6.1 would be as shown in Listing 6.2.

NOTE

Accessing the TextInputFormat Key

You can access the TextInputFormat key (the byte offset) when programming low-level Java
MapReduce in Hadoop, although this is rarely required.

LISTING 6.2   Output from the Map Task

```
('O', 1)
('Romeo', 1)
('Romeo', 1)
('wherefore', 1)
('art', 1)
('thou', 1)
('Romeo', 1)
('Deny', 1)
('thy', 1)
('father', 1)
('and', 1)
('refuse', 1)
('thy', 1)
('name', 1)
```

As an aside, if you were doing this seriously, you would filter out stopwords (such as "and,"
"a," "the," and so on) in the Map phase. You would generally also normalize the case—
either all uppercase or all lowercase—and perform a process called stemming, which removes
pluralization and possessives to make related terms uniform. You will note that the output from
our map() functions has changed the keyspace from the arbitrary byte offset to the individual
word. This demonstrates that the key can change during phases of the application. The output
from each Map task is then grouped and sorted into a key (word) and list of values (1's). The
resultant output—which is the input to the Reduce task—is shown in Listing 6.3.

LISTING 6.3   Intermediate Data Sent to the Reducer

```
('and', [1])
('art', [1])
('Deny', [1])
('father', [1])
('name', [1])
('O', [1])
('refuse', [1])
('Romeo', [1,1,1])
('thou', [1])
('thy', [1,1])
('wherefore', [1])
```

The output from a Map task, along with similar output from every other Map task running in parallel, is the intermediate data for the job. If you have more than one Reducer specified by the developer, this is the stage when you would apply the partitioning function. For simplicity, assume there is a single Reduce task in this example, so all intermediate keys and their values go to this one Reducer. Now the intermediate data output from the Map tasks gets sent to the Reducer and merged into one set of keys and their associated list of values. The Reducer runs its `reduce()` function for each intermediate record and simply sums the list of ones for each key and outputs a key (word) and the sum of the 1's for that word (the count). Our final output from the Reduce task, which is the final output for the job, is shown in Listing 6.4.

LISTING 6.4 **Final Output**

```
('and', 1)
('art', 1)
('Deny', 1)
('father', 1)
('name', 1)
('O', 1)
('refuse', 1)
('Romeo', 3)
('thou', 1)
('thy', 2)
('wherefore', 1)
```

And that's Word Count! You will do this for real in **Hour 7, "Programming MapReduce Applications."**

MapReduce in Hadoop

MapReduce is implemented in Hadoop either by using the original MapReduce cluster framework (commonly referred to as MR1 or MapReduce version 1), or by using YARN and the second-generation MapReduce framework known as MR2.

Clusters implementing MR1 are distinguished by the presence of the following daemons:

▶ *JobTracker* instead of the ResourceManager master node daemon in YARN

▶ *TaskTracker* instead of the NodeManager slave node daemon in YARN

Although the MR1 cluster framework was very adept at scheduling MapReduce programs written in Java or programming abstractions such as Apache Pig or Apache Hive, it had three major shortcomings:

- ▶ It was not intended to schedule and manage non-MapReduce programs such as Spark
- ▶ It had a practical upper limit to its scalability
- ▶ It was inflexible for leveraging underutilized processing assets

The solution to these limitations was the YARN cluster framework, and in the case of MapReduce applications, the solution was MR2 on YARN. MR1 is not as prevalent now, so for this reason I will focus primarily on YARN for this book.

Before discussing MapReduce on YARN, let's first look further at how applications in general are scheduled, executed and managed on YARN.

Running an Application on YARN

YARN schedules and orchestrates applications and tasks in Hadoop. When tasks to be run require data from HDFS, YARN will attempt to schedule these tasks on the node where the data resides, applying the concept of data locality discussed previously.

YARN is designed to distribute an application's workload across multiple worker daemons or processes called NodeManagers. NodeManagers are the workers or agents responsible for carrying out tasks, the complete set of which comprise an application. A YARN daemon called the ResourceManager is responsible for assigning an ApplicationMaster, a delegate process for managing the execution and status of an application. In addition, the ResourceManager, the YARN master node process, keeps track of available resources on the NodeManagers, such as CPU cores and memory. Compute and memory resources are presented to applications in processing units called *containers*.

NOTE

Terminology

In Hadoop or YARN terminology, an application or job is a complete set of tasks, which are individual units of work, such as Map tasks. Each task will have at least one task attempt. A task may be attempted more than once due to task failure or the phenomena I discussed previously known as speculative execution. Remember that speculative execution occurs when a parallel processing task is running slowly relative to other concurrent tasks. In this case, a separate task is started on another NodeManager and the results of the first successfully completed task are used.

The ApplicationMaster determines container requirements for the application and negotiates these resources with the ResourceManager, hence the name Yet Another Resource Negotiator, or YARN. The process is detailed in Figure 6.6.

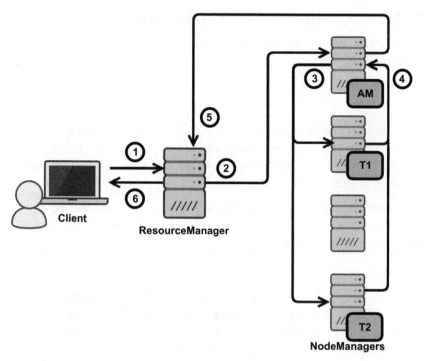

FIGURE 6.6
YARN application submission, scheduling, and execution.

The process pictured in Figure 6.6 is described here:

1. A client submits an application to the ResourceManager.

2. The ResourceManager allocates an ApplicationMaster process on a NodeManager with sufficient capacity to be assigned this role.

3. The ApplicationMaster negotiates task containers with the ResourceManager to be run on NodeManagers—this can include the NodeManager on which the ApplicationMaster is running as well—and dispatches processing to the NodeManagers hosting the task containers for the application.

4. The NodeManagers report their task attempt status and progress to the ApplicationMaster.

5. The ApplicationMaster in turn reports progress and the status of the application to the ResourceManager.

6. The ResourceManager reports application progress, status, and results to the client.

Mappers, Reducers, and the Shuffle Service

As discussed previously in this hour, a MapReduce application consists of three discrete phases: the Map, Reduce, and Shuffle-and-Sort phases. Let's discuss these in the context of a MapReduce application running on YARN.

Map Phase

Map and Reduce tasks (Mappers and Reducers) are scheduled to run in containers running on NodeManagers in the cluster. Map tasks are scheduled according to InputSplits. InputSplits are upper bounded by the HDFS block size for the input data, but for the sake of simplicity can be thought of as equivalent to HDFS blocks.

The ApplicationMaster (AM) will attempt to schedule the Map tasks on the same nodes that contain the blocks that comprise the input data set for the application. The ApplicationMaster will then monitor the progress of the Map tasks.

Shuffle-and-Sort Phase

A configuration setting, `mapreduce.job.reduce.slowstart.completed.maps` in the `mapred-site.xml` file on the system sets a threshold for the percentage of Map tasks to complete before the AM can schedule the Reduce phase. The key word here is schedule—not start. Scheduling the Reduce phase involves identifying the NodeManagers with resource availability to instantiate containers to run the Reduce tasks. It is important to note that there is no requirement or attempt to achieve data locality in the Reduce phase. The number of Reduce tasks is explicitly specified by the developer or configured at the time of application submission.

Once the Reducers are identified and their containers are spawned, intermediate data from completed Map tasks (keys and lists of values) is sent to the appropriate Reducer, depending upon the partitioning function specified. This intermediate data transfer is from the local disk on the Map task node to the local disk on the Reduce task node.

The keys and their lists of values are then merged into one list of keys and their associated values per Reducer, with the keys stored in key-sorted order according the key datatype.

The entire process of transferring intermediate data from Mappers to Reducers and merging the lists of key value pairs into lists in key-sorted order on each Reducer is called the Shuffle-and-Sort phase, as introduced previously.

Reduce Phase

Once all Map tasks have completed and all keys and values have been transferred to their respective target Reducers and the data has been merged and sorted, the first Reduce phase can begin, where each Reducer executes a `reduce()` method for each intermediate key until all keys have been processed. Typically, a MapReduce job will write out data to a target directory in HDFS; in such cases each Reduce task will write out its own output file, seen in the target HDFS directory as part-r-nnnnn, where *nnnnn* is the identifier for the Reducer. For instance, the first nominated Reducer would be 00000; therefore, the file written from this Reduce task would be named part-r-00000).

Once all Reduce tasks are complete and their output has been written to HDFS, the application is complete. The ApplicationMaster informs the ResourceManager, and the containers and resources used for the application are released and made available to future applications and tasks to be run on the cluster.

The inputs and outputs to a MapReduce application are generally directories in HDFS, whereas the intermediate data is stored on local disk of the Map and Reduce task nodes. This is illustrated in Figure 6.7.

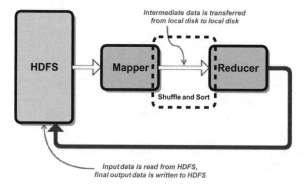

FIGURE 6.7
MapReduce input, output, and intermediate data.

Storing the final output data from reduce tasks in HDFS enables this data to be used as input for subsequent processing; for instance, a subsequent MapReduce application.

Summary

In this hour, I covered MapReduce, a fundamental programming model and framework at the heart of most big data processing systems including Hadoop. The MapReduce model is a programming abstraction that maximizes parallelization and takes full advantage of distributed data and data locality during execution.

You learned how MapReduce uses key value pairs to represent input, intermediate, and output data, and how the different phases of processing (the Map and Reduce phases) interact with one another. I discussed the Shuffle-and-Sort phase used to transfer data from Mappers to Reducers. I also discussed speculative execution and how fault tolerance is implemented in MapReduce. I then used the Word Count example to demonstrate the MapReduce model.

A solid understanding of MapReduce and the concepts behind MapReduce enables you to solve complex, non-relational problems in schema-on-read environments with solutions that are not possible using other conventional approaches. You will put these concepts into action in the next hour!

Q&A

Q. What purpose does *speculative execution* serve?

A. Speculative execution "speculates" about the cause of a Map or Reduce task node running comparatively slowly in contrast to other Map or Reduce task nodes running tasks for the same application. It assumes that these nodes are running slower due to being overloaded or under-resourced, and dispatches the same task(s) on different nodes to prevent these slow nodes from becoming a bottleneck in the overall process.

Q. Where does a Reduce task normally write its output data to? Why?

A. Reduce tasks typically write their final output data to HDFS. Doing this enables the output data to be used as input data for subsequent operations, in a workflow, for instance.

Q. What were the primary reasons behind the development of YARN as a process management framework for Hadoop?

A. Major factors that led to the development of YARN included the requirement to schedule and manage non-MapReduce applications, as well as increasing scalability and achieving more effective resource utilization across the cluster.

Workshop

The workshop contains quiz questions to help you solidify your understanding of the material covered. Try to answer all questions before looking at the "Answers" section that follows.

Quiz

1. **True or False:** A Partitioner ensures each key will be passed to one and only one Reducer.

2. **True or False:** A Combiner function usually implements a different function than a Reducer in the same application.

3. The YARN process that monitors the status of an application is called the...

    A. The ResourceManager

    B. The NodeManager

    C. The ApplicationMaster

4. Intermediate data is presented to a Reducer in ___ sorted order.

Answers

1. True.

2. False. If a Combiner is implemented, it will usually run the same function as the Reducer, but this function will be run on the node executing the Map task.

3. C. The ApplicationMaster is the delegate process that is responsible for negotiating containers to run task attempts for the application as well as monitoring the progress and status of these tasks, the complete set of which define a YARN application.

4. key.

Programming MapReduce Applications

What You'll Learn in This Hour:

- ▶ An introduction to serialization and Hadoop datatypes
- ▶ Hadoop input and output formats
- ▶ Writing a Java MapReduce application
- ▶ Advanced MapReduce API Concepts

MapReduce is the foundational processing framework on which Hadoop was built. The MapReduce API implemented in Java still forms the basic building blocks for many other programming interfaces such as Hive or Pig. This hour builds upon the previous hour's discussion of MapReduce concepts, putting these concepts into action using the Java MapReduce API.

Introducing the Java MapReduce API

Some familiarity with object-oriented programming (OOP) and specifically Java would be very helpful for this hour. However, Java is a very intuitive and readable language, so you should be able to follow along even if you are not a seasoned Java programmer. Before we start programming MapReduce using Java, we need to establish some introductory concepts first, which I will do in this hour.

Serialization in Hadoop

Serialization is the process of converting data structures to a byte stream prior to storing the object or transferring the object between two processes, whether over the network or on the same host. Deserialization is the inverse process: taking a serialized object, a byte stream, and reconstructing the original data structure.

Serialization in one form or another is common in many platforms and systems, from messaging systems to database management systems to serialization constructs built into the Java framework. Serialization is omnipresent in Hadoop, especially when you deal with the lower-level APIs such as MapReduce in Java.

Hadoop Datatypes

Keys and values are serializable objects in Hadoop. This is a subtle but very important distinction. When we define most data elements we use simple, or primitive, datatypes such as int, long, or char. The difference in Hadoop is that a key or value is an object that is an instantiation of a class, with attributes and defined methods, that contains (or encapsulates) the data with methods defined for reading and writing data from and to the object.

As you will see in the next section, this means you cannot operate directly on a Hadoop data object without using the defined accessor or mutator methods, which are the terms for the methods used to read data from or write data to the object.

Hadoop defines a special interface—the Writable interface—to define the accessor and mutator methods. Specifically, methods named readFields and write are defined through the Writable interface. The Writable interface is used for all serializable data objects in Hadoop.

Recall that keys are presented to Reducers in key sorted order. This is facilitated by a superclass to the Writable interface called the WritableComparable interface. The WritableComparable interface adds additional methods used to determine sort order between key objects; these methods are the compareTo, equals and hashCode methods.

Hadoop defines its own built-in data object types to represent the common primitive types we as programmers are accustomed to working with; for instance int, long, etc. These built-in object types are referred to as *box classes* as they encapsulate data. These box classes and the primitive datatypes they contain are summarized in Table 7.1.

TABLE 7.1 Hadoop Box Classes

Hadoop Box Class	Java Primitive
BooleanWritable	boolean
ByteWritable	byte
IntWritable	int
FloatWritable	float
LongWritable	long
DoubleWritable	double
NullWritable	null
Text	String

Although the suffix to many of these is Writable, these classes are in fact WritableComparable and therefore can be used to represent keys or values alike.

InputFormats and OutputFormats

As discussed, InputFormats and OutputFormats determine how files are read from and written to and how keys and values are extracted from the data. Lets take a closer look at each now.

InputFormats

InputFormats specify how data (keys and values) are extracted from a file. InputFormats provide a factory for RecordReader objects. The RecordReader objects are then used to actually extract the data from an input split, which is typically a HDFS block. You will not normally need to concern yourself with RecordReaders unless you are writing your own custom InputFormat, but you should know that they exist. Some common InputFormats are summarized in Table 7.2.

TABLE 7.2   Hadoop InputFormats

InputFormat	Description
TextInputFormat	InputFormat for plain text files. Files are broken into lines. Either linefeed or carriage-return are used to signal end of line. Keys are the position in the file, and values are the line of text.
KeyValueTextInputFormat	Same as TextInputFormat except each line is divided into a key and value by a separator.
SequenceFileInputFormat	InputFormat for SequenceFiles (discussed next).
NLineInputFormat	Similar to TextInputFormat and specifies how many lines should go to each map task.
DBInputFormat	InputFormat to read data from a JDBC data source.
FixedLengthInputFormat	InputFormat to read input files which contain fixed length records

SequenceFiles

SequenceFiles are binary encoded, serialized data files designed for use in Hadoop. SequenceFiles contain metadata which define the datatypes for key and value objects within the file. SequenceFiles can be uncompressed or compressed on an HDFS block or record (key value pair) boundary. SequenceFiles are especially efficient when the output of one MapReduce process becomes the direct input to another MapReduce process; for instance, in a multi-stage workflow.

SequenceFiles can be explicitly read within your MapReduce Java code using the SequenceFile.Reader object, although this is not typically necessary. One of the disadvantages of SequenceFiles is that they are not accessible from languages other than Java. The Apache Avro project, created by Doug Cutting, attempts to address this shortcoming by defining a cross-language serialization format specification and access libraries as an alternative to SequenceFiles in Java. The Avro format, as well as the SequenceFile formats, are natively supported in Hadoop and, more specifically, in the MapReduce API.

OutputFormats

OutputFormats are similar to InputFormats except that OutputFormats determine how data is written out to files as opposed to how data is read. Some common OutputFormats are shown in Table 7.3.

TABLE 7.3 Hadoop OutputFormats

OutputFormat	Description
FileOutputFormat	OutputFormat to write output data to a file.
DBOutputFormat	OutputFormat to write output data to a JDBC data source.

Anatomy of a MapReduce Program

A MapReduce program written in Java contains the following components:

- ▶ Driver

- ▶ Mapper

- ▶ Reducer (except in the case of a Map-only application)

Let's discuss each of these now, and then I will show an example of each in the subsequent section where we will build and run a MapReduce application.

NOTE

Java Class Names Capitalization

You may have noted the capitalization used when referring to Mappers, Reducers, and Drivers. This is not accidental. For those unfamiliar, or less familiar, it is common convention to capitalize the first letter of a Java class name.

Driver

The Driver is the program which sets up and starts the MapReduce application. Driver code is executed on the client; this code submits the application to the ResourceManager along with the application's configuration. The Driver can submit the job asynchronously (in a non-blocking fashion) or synchronously (waiting for the application to complete before performing another action). Drivers can also configure and submit more than one application; for instance, running a workflow consisting of multiple MapReduce applications, although this is not usually done (there are better workflow solutions available to accomplish this which I will discuss later in this book).

The Driver can accept parameters such as where the input data is to be read from, where to write the output data to, which HDFS cluster to use for the application, or which YARN cluster to submit the application to.

In Java MapReduce the Driver is implemented as a Java class containing the entry point (`main()` method) for the program.

Configuration and the Job Object

The Driver class instantiates a Job object. The Job object creates and stores the configuration options for the Job, including the classes to be used as the Mapper and Reducer, input and output directories, and other options, such as the Job name that will display in the YARN ResourceManager UI.

I will discuss configuration and the various configuration options available in much more detail in **Hour 20, "Understanding Advanced Cluster Configuration."** However, you should be aware of how options are set and configuration precedence. The following list determines how options are applied, which also determines which settings get higher precedence if the same configuration option is supplied with different values:

1. Apache defaults (`*-default.xml`, e.g. `core-default.xml`). These can be found through the Apache Hadoop project documentation.

2. `*-site.xml` file(s) on a slave node or nodes the client communications with, e.g., where a Mapper is executed on

3. `*-site.xml` file(s) on the client node, e.g., where the Driver code is executed

4. Configuration properties set at the command line as arguments to the MapReduce application

5. Configuration properties set explicitly in code and compiled through the Job object

Option 5 is generally only recommended for static options, such as the Mapper and Reducer classes associated with the application.

The Job object can also be used by the Driver to control the application's submission and execution and to query the state of the application.

Mapper

The Mapper is the Java class that contains the `map()` method. Each object instance of the Mapper iterates through its assigned input split executing its `map()` method against each record read from the InputSplit, using the InputFormat and its associated RecordReader as discussed previously.

The number of InputSplits (most commonly the number of HDFS blocks) in the input data set will dictate the number of Mapper objects (or Map tasks) which run for any given MapReduce application.

Mappers can also include setup and cleanup code to run in any given object lifespan. Mappers do most of the heavy lifting when it comes to data processing in MapReduce, as by definition they read ALL of the data in scope for the application. Programmed to find a needle in a haystack, the Mappers search through their portions of the haystack—the dataset—grain by grain, looking for the needle.

The Map phase, which can be defined as running the code defined in the Mapper class, is a true shared nothing and potentially massively parallel processing phase. With this in mind, there are some key considerations when developing Mapper code:

▶ **No saving or sharing of state**—You should not attempt to persist or share data between Map tasks. However, you can keep state within a Map task; for example, between `map()` method calls within the same Mapper class. As the Map phase is an unordered set of map tasks, you cannot guarantee when and where these tasks will run—or if they will be run more than once as is the case with speculative execution mentioned in the previous hour. Therefore, attempting to save or share state during the Map phase is bad practice.

▶ **No side effects**—As Map tasks may be executed in any sequence and may be executed more than once, any given Map task must not create any side effects, such as creating external events or triggering external processes.

▶ **No attempt to communicate with other map tasks**—For the same reasons as the first point regarding sharing state, Map tasks are not intended to communicate with one another, and in many cases this is not possible.

You should also be careful of external IO operations inside of Map tasks, such as writing to a network filesystem or updating a table in a remote database. Although these operations are possible, they can result in unintended consequences such as being perceived as a DDoS (Distributed Denial-of-Service) attack or an event swarm or storm, as numerous activities would occur from different hosts (different nodes running map tasks for the same application) at the same or similar time.

Reducer

The Reducer runs against a partition and each key and its associated values are passed to a `reduce()` method inside the Reducer class. As with the Map task, the Reduce task may run more than once if speculative execution is enabled for the reduce phase, although it is less common for this to occur, except in the case of node failure. With this said, the same caveats that applied to Mappers (no side effects, no sharing of state, etc.) generally apply to Reducers as well.

Writing a MapReduce Program in Java

Having looked at the anatomy of a MapReduce application in Java, let's have a crack at writing one. We can use WordCount as an example for this. The example code in each listing will be used in our next Try it Yourself exercise.

Driver Code

Listing 7.1 is an example Driver class for our WordCount application.

LISTING 7.1   WordCount Driver Class

```java
import org.apache.hadoop.fs.Path;
import org.apache.hadoop.io.IntWritable;
import org.apache.hadoop.io.Text;
import org.apache.hadoop.mapreduce.lib.input.FileInputFormat;
import org.apache.hadoop.mapreduce.lib.output.FileOutputFormat;
import org.apache.hadoop.mapreduce.Job;
import org.apache.hadoop.conf.Configured;
import org.apache.hadoop.conf.Configuration;
import org.apache.hadoop.util.Tool;
import org.apache.hadoop.util.ToolRunner;

public class WordCountDriver extends Configured implements Tool {
  public int run(String[] args) throws Exception {
    if (args.length != 2) {
      System.out.printf("Usage: %s [generic options] <inputdir> <outputdir>\n",
getClass().getSimpleName());
      return -1;
    }
    Job job = new Job(getConf());
    job.setJarByClass(WordCountDriver.class);
    job.setJobName("Word Count");
    FileInputFormat.setInputPaths(job, new Path(args[0]));
    FileOutputFormat.setOutputPath(job, new Path(args[1]));
    job.setMapperClass(WordCountMapper.class);
    job.setReducerClass(WordCountReducer.class);
    job.setMapOutputKeyClass(Text.class);
    job.setMapOutputValueClass(IntWritable.class);
    job.setOutputKeyClass(Text.class);
    job.setOutputValueClass(IntWritable.class);
    boolean success = job.waitForCompletion(true);
    return success ? 0 : 1;
  }

  public static void main(String[] args) throws Exception {
    int exitCode = ToolRunner.run(new Configuration(), new WordCountDriver(), args);
    System.exit(exitCode);
  }
}
```

The Driver leverages a class called ToolRunner, which is used to parse command-line options. Although ToolRunner is not mandatory, it should be used in most cases as it enables flexibility in supplying configuration parameters at the command line when submitting a MapReduce job. Another advantage to using the ToolRunner class with your Driver is that you can specify items for the DistributedCache which I discuss later in the hour.

An example of submitting a command-line option to direct your application to a specific HDFS cluster is shown in Listing 7.2. This is only possible if you implement the ToolRunner interfaces in your Driver class.

LISTING 7.2   ToolRunner Command-Line Generic Options

```
$ hadoop jar mr.jar MyDriver -D fs.defaultFS=hdfs://mycluster:8020 \
  myinputdir myoutputdir
```

Note the -D switch used to supply a named Hadoop configuration parameter. Another common example of this is to supply the number of Reduce tasks requested to be run for any given MapReduce application as shown in Listing 7.3.

LISTING 7.3   Specifying the Number of Reduce Tasks from the Command Line

```
$ hadoop jar mr.jar MyDriver -D mapreduce.job.reduces=10 \
  myinputdir myoutputdir
```

To summarize the Driver class code in Listing 7.1, the main() method in your Driver calls the ToolRunner.run() method. The run() method then performs the following actions:

1. Parses the command line for positional arguments – inputdir and outputdir

2. Creates a new Job object instance, using the getConf() method to obtain configuration from the various sources (*-default.xml and *-site.xml files and properties submitted using the -D argument)

3. Gives the Job a friendly name (the name you will see in the ResourceManager UI)

4. Sets the InputFormat and OutputFormat for the Job and determines the InputSplits for the Job

5. Defines the Mapper and Reducer classes to be used for the Job (These must be available in the Java classpath where the Driver is run—typically these classes are packaged alongside the Driver.)

6. Sets the Intermediate Key and Value Classes (Box classes in this case). Recall that these are the key value pairs emitted by the Mapper and serve as input to the Reducer

7. Sets the final output key and value classes, which will be written out files in the outputdir

8. Submits the Job (in this case synchronously)

NOTE

InputPaths and File Globs

`FileInputFormat.setInputPaths()` reads all files the in the specified directory by default with the exception of objects that begin with an underscore or a period (_ or .), which are the conventions for hiding or escaping files in a Posix filesystem. File globs can also be used as input paths to filter input; for example, `'/2016/*'`.

After submitting the Job, the Mapper and Reducer classes, along with the configuration, are passed to the ResourceManager, which will in turn pass this information to the nominated ApplicationMaster for the Job. The ApplicationMaster will request resources (containers) to run tasks (Map and/or Reduce tasks). These tasks will be provided with the respective code and configuration to use against their allocated part of the data set: an InputSplit in the case of a Mapper or an intermediate data partition in the case of a Reducer.

Let's break down the Mapper and Reducer code next.

Mapper Code

Listing 7.4 shows the Mapper code for our WordCount example application.

LISTING 7.4   WordCount Mapper Class

```
import java.io.IOException;
import org.apache.hadoop.io.IntWritable;
import org.apache.hadoop.io.LongWritable;
import org.apache.hadoop.io.Text;
import org.apache.hadoop.mapreduce.Mapper;

public class WordCountMapper extends Mapper<LongWritable, Text, Text, IntWritable>
{
  private final static IntWritable one = new IntWritable(1);
  private Text wordObject = new Text();

  @Override
  public void map(LongWritable key, Text value, Context context)
      throws IOException, InterruptedException {

    String line = value.toString();
    for (String word : line.split("\\W+")) {
      if (word.length() > 0) {
        wordObject.set(word);
        context.write(wordObject, one);
      }
    }
  }
}
```

The Mapper class extends the base Mapper class included with the Hadoop libraries and implements four generics, located in the angle brackets `<>` on the class signature. The generics are Hadoop datatypes (Writeables and/or WriteableComparables) which correspond to the input and output of the map function. An easy way to think about this is:

```
<map_input_key, map_input_value, map_output_key, map_output_value>
```

These generics must correspond to:

▶ Key value pair types as defined by the InputFormat in the Driver

▶ `job.setMapOutputKeyClass` and `job.setMapOutputValueClass` defined in the Driver

▶ Input and output to the `map()` method

The Mapper must implement a `map()` method. The `map()` method is where the map function is implemented. As mentioned, its input, the first two arguments of the `map()` method signature, must match the Driver definition and the Mapper class signature generics; otherwise you will get compile time and/or runtime exceptions.

Looking at our example code in the `map()` method, note that before we can perform any functions against a key or a value (Java functions in this case such as `split()`), we need to get the value that is contained in the serialized Writable or WritableComparable object. In this case we do this using the `value.get()` method.

Once we have performed the necessary operations against the input data (key/value pair) to the `map()` method, the output data (intermediate data) in the form of a key value pair—consisting of WritableComparable and Writable objects, respectively—is emitted using the Context object, which I will detail shortly.

In the case of a Map-only job, the output from the Map phase, and consequently the complete set of key value pairs emitted from all `map()` methods in all map tasks for the job, is the final output, and there is no intermediate data or Shuffle-and-Sort phase. As such the output from a Map-only job is not sorted or ordered by key and is not deliberately partitioned.

The Mapper can also include `setup()` and `cleanup()` methods used to perform operations before the first `map()` method is run and after the last `map()` method is run for the InputSplit.

Context Object

The Context object is used to pass information between processes in Hadoop. It performs some important functions in both the Mapper and Reducer. Some of these key functions are listed here:

▶ Contains configuration and state needed for processes within the MapReduce application, including enabling parameters to be passed to distributed processes

▸ Writes intermediate and final data from Map and Reduce tasks respectively using the `Context.write()` method

▸ Used in the optional `setup()` and `cleanup()` methods within a Mapper or Reducer, which define work to be done before and after processing of an individual task

▸ Can also be used to get other information during processing, such as retrieving the name of a file being processed

Reducer Code

Listing 7.5 shows the Mapper code for our WordCount example application.

LISTING 7.5   WordCount Reducer Class

```
import java.io.IOException;
import org.apache.hadoop.io.IntWritable;
import org.apache.hadoop.io.Text;
import org.apache.hadoop.mapreduce.Reducer;

public class WordCountReducer extends Reducer<Text, IntWritable, Text, IntWritable>
{
  private IntWritable wordCountWritable = new IntWritable();
  @Override
    public void reduce(Text key, Iterable<IntWritable> values, Context context)
                    throws IOException, InterruptedException {
            int wordCount = 0;
            for (IntWritable value : values) {
                    wordCount += value.get();
            }
            wordCountWritable.set(wordCount);
            context.write(key, wordCountWritable);
    }
}
```

The Reducer extends the base Reducer class in a fashion similar to the Mapper's extension of the base Mapper class and implements generics similarly as well:

```
<reduce_input_key, reduce_input_value, reduce_output_key, reduce_output_value>
```

As with the generics in the Mapper class, the keys and values are Hadoop WritableComparable and/or Writable types (serialized data objects).

The Reducer must implement a `reduce()` method. Once the Map phase is complete, meaning all Map tasks have completed, and the Shuffle-and-Sort phase is complete, meaning all keys and their intermediate values have been passed to their target Reducers and the data is presented to the Reducer in key sorted order, the first `reduce()` method can be run.

The reduce() method accepts a key and an Iterable list of values as input, denoted by the angle brackets <>. As with the map() method, to operate or perform Java string or numeric operations against keys or values from the input list of values, you must first extract the value the Hadoop object contains, in this case the number contained in the value.

Finally the reduce() method emits a key value pair in the form of Hadoop WritableComparable objects for keys and Writable (or WriteableComparable) objects for values. This is done using the Context object, similarly to the way keys and values were emitted from the map() method.

TIP
Keys and Values Are Critical
I'm sure you have seen by now that the concept and implementation of key/value pairs is integral and critical to Java MapReduce programming and that these keys and values are Hadoop serialized objects. The diagram in Figure 7.1 depicts this for review and consolidation.

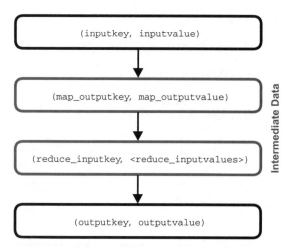

FIGURE 7.1
Keys and Values in Java MapReduce Programming

Compiling and Packaging a MapReduce Application
After writing the code for the Driver, Mapper, and Reducer Java classes, you then need to compile the code into byte code and package the libraries into a jar file (Java Archive). You can use build tools such as Maven to do this, or simply use the javac and jar executables provided in the Java Development Kit (JDK).

Once you have a Java package containing your compiled classes, the package, now a jar file, can be submitted to YARN using the hadoop jar command. Lets do this now in our Try it Yourself exercise.

Writing a WordCount Application using Java MapReduce

In this exercise we will put all of the concepts covered in the last two hours into action to perform a WordCount operation. We will use the complete works of Shakespeare as our input data for the exercise.

To run this exercise you can use the pseudo-distributed cluster we deployed in Hour 3, or you can choose to use your own distribution. You will also need to download the shakespeare.txt file from the book's download page (code is provided in the exercise to do this).

1. Create an input directory called shakespeare in HDFS:

```
$ hadoop fs -mkdir shakespeare
```

2. Download the shakespeare.txt data file from the book's download page:

```
$ wget https://s3.amazonaws.com/sty-hadoop/shakespeare/shakespeare.txt
```

3. Put the shakespeare.txt file into the shakespeare directory in HDFS you created in Step 1.

```
$ hadoop fs -put shakespeare.txt shakespeare
```

4. Create a directory in your local filesystem home directory called word_count.

5. Change directories to the word_count directory, create three empty text files in this directory (WordCountMapper.java, WordCountReducer.java and WordCountDriver.java).

6. Copy the code from Listing 7.1 in the WordCountDriver.java file (using a text editor such as vi or nano), save, and exit.

7. Copy the code from Listing 7.4 in the WordCountMapper.java file, save, and exit.

8. Copy the code from Listing 7.5 in the WordCountReducer.java file, save, and exit.

9. Compile the source code into Java byte code using the javac compiler:

```
$ javac -classpath `$HADOOP_HOME/bin/hadoop classpath` *.java
```

The `hadoop classpath` statement will enable all of the imports you used in your code to be resolved.

10. Package the compiled class files into a Java archive file using the jar command in the JDK:

```
$ jar cvf wc.jar *.class
```

11. Submit the application using the Hadoop `jar` command:

```
$ $HADOOP_HOME/bin/hadoop jar wc.jar WordCountDriver \
  -D mapreduce.job.reduces=2 shakespeare wordcount
```

Disregard any warning messages you may get at this stage.

You should now see progress in the terminal. Note that once submitted, the program is running in the cluster as an asynchronous distributed process. Although you can use Ctrl-C to kill the terminal window you used to launch the application, the job will continue to run on the cluster. I will discuss how to properly kill running jobs later in the book.

12. Once the job is complete, check the output HDFS directory:

```
$ hadoop fs -ls wordcount
```

You should see two files: `wordcount/part-r-00000` and `wordcount/part-r-00001`.

13. Inspect the contents of one of the files:

```
$ hadoop fs -tail wordcount/part-r-00000
```

You should see output similar to the following:

```
...
your         6132
yourself     271
yourselves   74
youth        253
yslaked      1
zealous      5
zeals        1
zed          1
zephyrs      1
zo           1
zodiacs      1
zounds       1
zur          2
```

14. Now run Step 11 again. You should see a failure.

Because HDFS is an immutable filesystem, the output directory for a MapReduce job must not exist when the job is launched, as it cannot be overwritten. You can run the job again specifying a different output directory or move or remove the directory prior to re-submitting.

Congratulations, you have just written, compiled and run your first MapReduce application!

Advanced MapReduce API Concepts

Having learned the basics of MapReduce, there are some common advanced concepts you should be familiar with. Let's discuss some of them now.

Using Combiners

Combiner functions, as discussed in **Hour 6, "Understanding Data Processing in Hadoop,"** are used to decrease the amount of intermediate data sent between Mappers and Reducers as part of the Shuffle-and-Sort process. Combiners can be thought of as "mini reducers" or "map-side reducers." Their implementation in Java MapReduce is quite straightforward, assuming the following caveats are satisfied:

▶ The `combiner()` function is identical to the `reduce()` function defined in your Reducer class.

▶ The output key and value object types from the `map()` function implemented in the Mapper match the input to the function used in the Combiner.

▶ The output key and value object types from the function used in the Combiner match the input key and value object types used in the Reducer's `reduce()` method.

▶ The operation to be performed is commutative and associative.

The Combiner class in most cases simply reuses your existing Reducer class as the combiner. This is specified in the Driver as shown in Listing 7.6 (using our WordCount application example).

LISTING 7.6   Declaring a Combiner in your Driver Class

```
job.setCombinerClass(WordCountReducer.class);
```

Understanding Partitioners

The role of the Partitioner is to divide the output keyspace for a MapReduce application, controlling which Reducers get which intermediate data. This can be useful for process distribution or load balancing (e.g., getting more Reduce tasks running in parallel) or to segregate the output; for instance, creating 12 partitions, one for each month of the year.

Even though we did not explicitly define a Partitioner in our previous example, a default Partitioner was used; the HashPartitioner. The HashPartitioner arbitrarily hashes the key space so the same keys go to the same Reducers, and the keyspace is distributed roughly equally among the number of Reducers requested by the developer. For instance, if 100MB of intermediate data consisting of different keys was generated for an application with two Reduce tasks, each Reduce task would get roughly 50MB worth of data.

If you have one Reduce task, which is the default, the Partitioner is academic as all of the intermediate data goes to the same Reducer.

If a Partitioner other than the default HashPartitioner is required, it is specified in the Driver as shown in Listing 7.7.

LISTING 7.7   Declaring a Partitioner in your Driver Class

```
job.setPartitionerClass(MyCustomPartitioner.class);
```

The Partitioner class extends the base Partitioner class and must implement a `getPartition()` method. This method accepts the key value pair and the number of reduce tasks as input and returns a number between `0` and the `numReduceTasks` argument to the method. A custom Partitioner, in this case to separate words by their first letter, is shown in Listing 7.8.

LISTING 7.8   Custom Partitioner

```
public static class LetterPartitioner extends Partitioner <Text, IntWritable>
{
  @Override
  public int getPartition(Text key, Text value, int numReduceTasks)
  {
    String word = value.toString();
        if (word.toLowerCase().matches("^[a-m].*$")) {
                // if word starts with a to m, go to the first Reducer or partition
            return 0
        } else {
                // else go to the second Reducer or partition
                return 1
        }
  }
}
```

Using the DistributedCache

When programming in a distributed environment, it is often necessary to access additional data to supplement your input data set. The need to supply reference data to a process is an example of this. Another example would be the need to supply lookup data such as geo-IP lookup data that might be required for a Map process.

Additionally, you may need to supply Mappers or Reducers with custom-developed supplementary functions. For instance, you could supply them with functions in custom classes to perform specialized operations.

Fortunately, the MapReduce API provides a facility to disseminate either side data or additional class libraries at runtime to Mappers or Reducers in a fully distributed Hadoop cluster environment. This facility is called the DistributedCache.

The DistributedCache pushes the data or libraries to all slave nodes as a prerequisite background task before any task for the application is executed. The distributed data is then available in read-only format on any node running a task for the application. After the application terminates, the files are removed automatically.

Using the previously mentioned ToolRunner class in your Driver, you can easily add items to the DistributedCache using command-line arguments when you submit your application. There is no need to upload these files to HDFS beforehand. Table 7.4 describes the command-line arguments used with the ToolRunner class to submit items to the DistributedCache.

TABLE 7.4   DistributedCache Command-Line Switches

Switch	Description
-files	Used to distribute files; for instance, lookup data, reference data, etc.
-archives	Used to distribute archived files; for instance, tar files or tar.gz files. These files are then unpacked on the slave nodes.
-libjars	Used to distribute jar files (Java packages) to slave nodes, these files are automatically added to the runtime classpath for the application's tasks running on the slave node.

Listing 7.9 shows an example of using these arguments from the command line when submitting a MapReduce job.

LISTING 7.9   Adding Files to the DistributedCache from the Command Line

```
$ hadoop jar wc.jar WordCountDriver \
  -files stopwords.txt shakespeare wordcount
```

Files added to the DistributedCache are available in the task's local working directory and can be accessed using the File object from within your Mapper or Reducer class as shown in Listing 7.10.

LISTING 7.10   Accessing Files in the DistributedCache

```
File f = new File("stopwords.txt");
```

Extending MapReduce

As MapReduce is implemented in Java and Java is extensible, MapReduce is extensible. You have just seen an example of writing your own custom Partitioner. You could also perform other extensions including:

▶ Writing your own Writable or WritableComparable classes to store custom key or value objects (such as tuples or data structures)

▶ Writing SortComparators to influence the sort order of objects during the Shuffle-and-Sort phase

▶ and more

You can find many examples of extending the MapReduce API on the web. The possibilities are practically infinite!

Using the MapReduce Streaming API

It is possible to implement Map and Reduce functions in languages other than Java, for instance Perl, Python, or Ruby. This can be accomplished using the MapReduce Streaming API (`hadoop-streaming.jar`). This method requires that key value pairs are presented to your Map or Reduce script using standard input (STDIN), and key value pairs are emitted from your script using standard output (STDOUT).

There are pros and cons to doing this, which are shown in Table 7.5.

TABLE 7.5 Pros and Cons of the MapReduce Streaming API

Advantages	Disadvantages
Allows Mappers and Reducers to be developed in languages other than Java	Poor performance as this method adds significant overhead
Increased Agility as the development, build, test cycle may be shortened	Could possibly fork excessive operating system processes or use excessive RAM on slave nodes
	Any additional API constructs must be implemented in Java; for instance, InputFormats, Writables, Partitioners
	Reducers receive intermediate values individually, rather than a complete list per key, adding additional overhead on the Reduce function to keep track of when the key changes
	Only suitable for data which can be represented as text

As you can see, there are some considerations to take into account before using the Streaming API. If you simply want to avoid using Java there are better ways, which you will learn about in the next few hours covering Pig and Hive.

Listing 7.11 shows a word count map function implemented in Python.

LISTING 7.11   Word Count Mapper in Python

```python
#!/usr/bin/env python
import sys
for line in sys.stdin:
  line = line.strip()
  words = line.split()
  for word in words:
    print '%s\t%s' % (word, 1)
```

Listing 7.12 shows a word count Reduce function implemented in Python.

LISTING 7.12   Word Count Reducer in Python

```python
#!/usr/bin/env python
import sys
from operator import itemgetter
this_word = None
wordcount = 0
word = None
for line in sys.stdin:
  line = line.strip()
  word, count = line.split('\t', 1)
  count = int(count)
  if thisword == word:
    wordcount += count
  else:
  if thisword:
    print '%s\t%s' % (thisword, wordcount)
  wordcount = count
  thisword = word
if thisword == word:
  print '%s\t%s' % (thisword, wordcount)
```

Listing 7.13 demonstrates how to submit a streaming MapReduce word count application using the Python Map and Reduce functions from Listing 7.11 and 7.12, respectively.

LISTING 7.13   Submitting a Streaming MapReduce Job

```
$ hadoop jar \
  $HADOOP_HOME/share/hadoop/tools/lib/hadoop-streaming-*.jar \
  -input shakespeare \
  -output wordcount \
  -mapper wordmapper.py \
  -reducer wordreducer.py \
  -file wordmapper.py \
  -file wordreducer.py
```

Once submitted, the Python scripts will be distributed to the Mapper and Reducer nodes designated for the application and will be used to perform the Map and Reduce functions. The Hadoop MapReduce framework will still orchestrate the Shuffle-and-Sort phase.

It is important, as discussed, to consider performance; however, as it is more efficient and performant to use Java MapReduce if possible.

Summary

In this hour I deep-dived into programming MapReduce applications in Java. You learned about serialization and the Hadoop datatypes, or box classes, as well as learning about the various Input and Output Formats available in the MapReduce API. InputFormats use RecordReaders to extract records (key value pairs) from data sources—files in HDFS—and these records then form the input to a Map operation in a MapReduce application.

You also learned about the components of a Java MapReduce application, including the Driver, the Mapper, and the Reducer, and the map() and reduce() methods implemented in each respective class. I discussed Combiners, Partitioners, and the DistributedCache as additional MapReduce API constructs that can be used for functional or non-functional purposes. Finally, I discussed the MapReduce streaming API, which can be used to implement Map and Reduce functions in languages other than Java.

The next four hours devoted to Pig and Hive will build upon the MapReduce implementation concepts covered in this hour.

Q&A

Q. **Explain the role of the Driver in a MapReduce application.**

A. The Driver includes the `main()` method, which is the entry point for a MapReduce application. The role of the Driver is to set up, configure, and submit the MapReduce Job. This includes calculating InputSplits for input data, defining the Mapper and Reducer classes to be used by the application, and defining the InputFormat and OutputFormat and key value pair definitions for the application.

Q. **What is the DistributedCache? What are some examples of uses for the DistributedCache?**

A. The DistributedCache is used to supply side data or code libraries (Java classes) to tasks running on slave nodes in a Hadoop cluster. Examples of side data could include reference data or lookup values. Examples of code libraries could be custom functions used in your `map()` or `reduce()` methods.

Q. **Why is it not recommended to implement a call to a remote database or a network file system in your Mapper code's `map()` method?**

A. The `map()` method will get called at least once (and possibly more than once) for every record in an input data set, which could be potentially millions of times or more. Furthermore, this method will be executed on many machines in parallel, which could appear to the remote system as a distributed denial-of-service (DDoS) attack.

Workshop

The workshop contains quiz questions and exercises to help you solidify your understanding of the material covered. Try to answer all questions before looking at the "Answers" section that follows.

Quiz

1. **True or False:** ToolRunner provides a method to supply configuration parameters to a MapReduce application at the command line.

2. The object that is responsible for creating, configuring, and managing a MapReduce application is which of the following?

    A. Context Object

    B. Job Object

    C. Application Object

3. The object that is responsible for writing intermediate and final data in a MapReduce application is which of the following?

   A. Context Object

   B. Job Object

   C. Writer Object

4. What class would be used to perform the summary operations against intermediate data on the Mapper node?

Answers

1. True.

2. A.

3. B.

4. Combiner.

Analyzing Data in HDFS Using Apache Pig

What You'll Learn in This Hour:

▶ An introduction to Apache Pig
▶ Basics of Pig programming
▶ How to load data into Pig
▶ How to use the built-in functions in Pig

As the Hadoop platform gained traction, alternatives to MapReduce programming in Java started to emerge. One such alternative was the Pig project; in this hour I introduce Apache Pig as a high-level dataflow language used to analyze data in HDFS. Using Pig leverages the Hadoop distributed programming environment while enabling rapid application development and speed to value.

Introducing Pig

In 2006, a new research project was initiated at Yahoo! called Pig. The premise behind Pig was to provide an alternative language interface to programming MapReduce using Java. Pig is considered a MapReduce abstraction as it abstracts the developer or analyst from the underlying MapReduce code, enabling the developer to code in an interpreted data flow language, which is then converted to a series of map and reduce operations.

The dataflow scripting language used by Pig is called Pig Latin. An interpreter running on a client machine takes the Pig Latin instructions and turns these into a series of MapReduce jobs, submitting these jobs to the cluster, monitoring their progress and then returning results to the console or saving results to files in HDFS. This process is pictured in Figure 8.1.

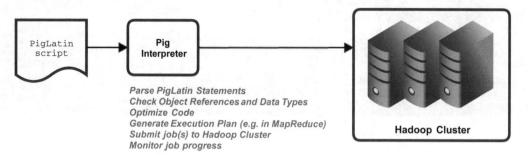

FIGURE 8.1
Pig Flow.

An example Pig application is shown in Listing 8.1. As you can see the code is very intuitive (we will discuss the statements in detail soon).

LISTING 8.1   Pig Program

```
A = LOAD 'customer' USING PigStorage() AS (name:chararray, age:int);
B = FOREACH A GENERATE name;
```

Pig offers productivity and agility for analysts and developers, specifically because

▶ Developers do not need to know how to program in Java

▶ Pig code does not need to be compiled and packaged, unlike Java MapReduce applications

▶ Pig does not force developers to describe objects, allowing for easier data discovery

In 2008, Pig became an Apache Software Foundation project with adoption and contribution from the likes of LinkedIn, Twitter, and many others. Pig remains an active top-level Apache project with extensions into Spark as an execution engine, and projects such as Spork—Pig on Spark.

Pig Latin Basics

To install Pig you simply need a system with a Hadoop client and configuration, which of course would require a Java Runtime Engine to be present.

Pig is easily installed on a client system by downloading and unpacking a Pig release. There are no additional steps required. However, there may be some additional customization or configuration desired for your cluster. This is typically done using the `pig.properties` file in the `conf` directory of the Pig release.

You will install (and test) Pig in the Try it Yourself exercise at the end of this hour.

Pig Modes

Pig, like MapReduce, has different modes it can be run in, and they include the following:

▶ MapReduce (the default)

▶ Local (similar to the LocalJobRunner Hadoop mode discussed previously)

▶ Tez (on Hortonworks clusters or where Tez is available. We will discuss Tez in **Hour 12, "Using SQL on Hadoop Solutions"**)

▶ Spark (on some systems)

These modes determine how the Pig instructions will be executed on the client or cluster. Typically, you would use `local` mode for development and testing and one of `mapreduce`, `tez` or `spark` modes for production applications.

Grunt—The Pig Shell

The interactive Pig programming shell is called *grunt* (as you may have already noticed, the Pig project is full of porcine references!). Using the grunt shell, you can enter Pig Latin statements interactively. Each statement is parsed and interpreted as it is entered, with execution beginning when output is requested, either to the console or to an output directory. This process is called lazy evaluation.

Grunt is useful for development as it allows you to sample and inspect data as you develop a routine. Figure 8.2 shows an example grunt shell.

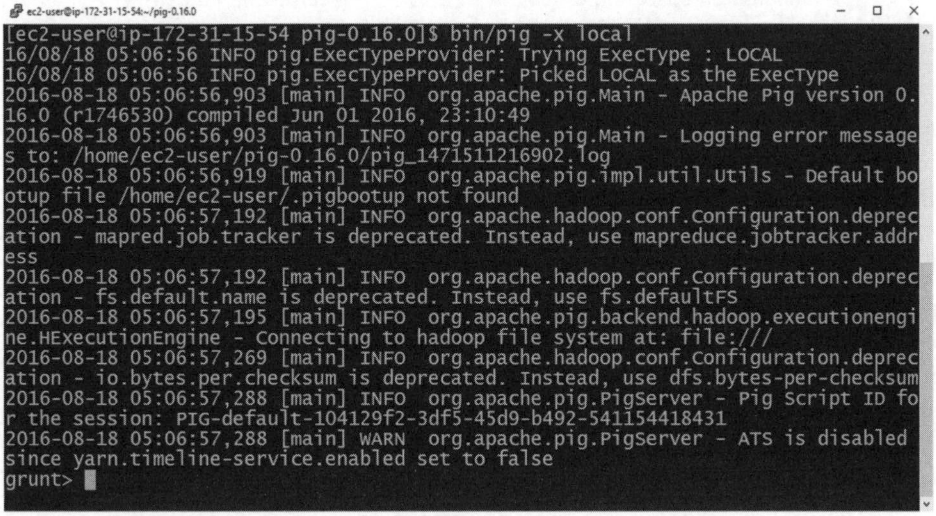

```
ec2-user@ip-172-31-15-54:~/pig-0.16.0                                    —  □  ×
[ec2-user@ip-172-31-15-54 pig-0.16.0]$ bin/pig -x local
16/08/18 05:06:56 INFO pig.ExecTypeProvider: Trying ExecType : LOCAL
16/08/18 05:06:56 INFO pig.ExecTypeProvider: Picked LOCAL as the ExecType
2016-08-18 05:06:56,903 [main] INFO  org.apache.pig.Main - Apache Pig version 0.
16.0 (r1746530) compiled Jun 01 2016, 23:10:49
2016-08-18 05:06:56,903 [main] INFO  org.apache.pig.Main - Logging error message
s to: /home/ec2-user/pig-0.16.0/pig_1471511216902.log
2016-08-18 05:06:56,919 [main] INFO  org.apache.pig.impl.util.Utils - Default bo
otup file /home/ec2-user/.pigbootup not found
2016-08-18 05:06:57,192 [main] INFO  org.apache.hadoop.conf.Configuration.deprec
ation - mapred.job.tracker is deprecated. Instead, use mapreduce.jobtracker.addr
ess
2016-08-18 05:06:57,192 [main] INFO  org.apache.hadoop.conf.Configuration.deprec
ation - fs.default.name is deprecated. Instead, use fs.defaultFS
2016-08-18 05:06:57,195 [main] INFO  org.apache.pig.backend.hadoop.executionengi
ne.HExecutionEngine - Connecting to hadoop file system at: file:///
2016-08-18 05:06:57,269 [main] INFO  org.apache.hadoop.conf.Configuration.deprec
ation - io.bytes.per.checksum is deprecated. Instead, use dfs.bytes-per-checksum
2016-08-18 05:06:57,288 [main] INFO  org.apache.pig.PigServer - Pig Script ID fo
r the session: PIG-default-104129f2-3df5-45d9-b492-541154418431
2016-08-18 05:06:57,288 [main] WARN  org.apache.pig.PigServer - ATS is disabled
since yarn.timeline-service.enabled set to false
grunt> █
```

FIGURE 8.2
Grunt shell.

Pig can be run in a non-interactive or batch mode as well. We will use both interactive and non-interactive modes in our Try it Yourself exercise later this hour.

Pig Latin Basics

As discussed, Pig Latin is a data flow language; it is not a SQL language or an object-oriented language. Pig Latin programs are a sequence of statements that follow the pattern described here:

1. Load data into a named dataset.

2. Create a new dataset by manipulating the input dataset.

3. Repeat step 2 *n* times, creating a dataset each time (these intermediate datasets are not necessarily materialized).

4. Output the final dataset to the screen or to an output directory.

Pig Data Structures

The datasets used by Pig are called **relations** or **bags**. Bags contain records called **tuples**. Tuples contain **fields**, and fields can contain data structures such as other bags or tuples, or atomic data called **atoms**. Pig's data structures are described in Table 8.1.

TABLE 8.1 Pig Data Structures

Type	Description	Example
tuple	ordered set of fields	('Jeff',47)
bag	unordered collection of tuples	{('Jeff',47),('Paul',44)}
map	set of key value pairs	[name#Jeff]

Bags, tuples, and maps have distinctive notation as seen in the example. This notation will be displayed in the console when returning data as well as shown in the schema for objects when describing them, which we will do later.

Object Identifiers

Bags, maps, tuples, and fields within tuples typically have named identifiers. An example of this is shown in Listing 8.2, where a bag is created from an input data set, the bag is assigned an identifier (students) and a schema is applied to the tuples in the bag with each field assigned an identifier (name, age, gpa).

LISTING 8.2   Pig Identifiers

```
students = LOAD 'student' AS (name: chararray, age: int, gpa: float);
```

Identifier names are case sensitive and cannot be the same as any of the keywords in the Pig Latin language. Listing 8.3 lists some of the common Pig Latin keywords.

LISTING 8.3   Pig Reserved Keywords

```
assert, and, any, all, arrange, as, asc, AVG, bag, BinStorage, by,
bytearray, BIGINTEGER, BIGDECIMAL, cache, CASE, cat, cd, chararray,
cogroup, CONCAT, copyFromLocal, copyToLocal, COUNT, cp, cross,
datetime, %declare, %default, define, dense, desc, describe, DIFF,
distinct, double, du, dump, e, E, eval, exec, explain, f, F, filter,
flatten, float, foreach, full, generate, group, help, if, illustrate,
import, inner, input, int, into, is, join, kill, l, L, left, limit,
load, long, ls, map, matches, MAX, MIN, mkdir, mv, not, null, onschema,
or, order, outer, output, parallel, pig, PigDump, PigStorage, pwd,
quit, register, returns, right, rm, rmf, rollup, run, sample, set,
ship, SIZE, split, stderr, stdin, stdout, store, stream, SUM, TextLoader,
TOKENIZE, through, tuple, union, using, void
```

Aside from not using keywords to name objects, the other rules for identifiers are:

▶ Must begin with a letter

▶ Can only include letters, numbers, and underscores

An example of some valid and invalid identifiers are shown in Listing 8.4.

LISTING 8.4   Valid and Invalid Pig Identifiers

```
/* invalid identifiers! */
$names = LOAD 'names';
1names = LOAD 'names';

/* valid identifiers */
student_names = LOAD 'names';
names_1 = LOAD 'names';
```

Pig Simple Datatypes

Atoms (atomic units of data) can be of different datatypes. The simple datatypes used in the Pig programming model are listed in Table 8.2.

TABLE 8.2 Pig Simple Datatypes

Type	Description	Example
int	32-bit signed integer	20
long	64-bit signed integer	20L
float	32-bit floating point	20.5F
double	64-bit floating point	20.5
chararray	UTF-8 string	'Jeff'
bytearray	uninterpreted byte array	<BLOB>
boolean	True or False	true
datetime	datetime	1970-01-01T00:00:00.000+00:00
biginteger	Java BigInteger	200000000000
bigdecimal	Java BigDecimal	33.456783321323441233442

Pig supports equality and relational operators, similar to many common programming languages, which are primarily used in filtering operations. These operators are described in Table 8.3.

TABLE 8.3 Pig Relational Operators

Operator	Notation
equal	==
not equal	!=
less than	<
greater than	>
less than or equal to	<=
greater than or equal to	>=
pattern matching	matches

Furthermore, as you would expect, Pig supports the standard set of mathematical operators as described in Table 8.4.

TABLE 8.4 Pig Mathematical Operators

Operator	Notation
Addition	+
Subtraction	-
Multiplication	*
Division	/
Modulo	%

Statements, Comments, and Conventions in Pig

As you will have noticed by now, there are some different requirements and common conventions when it comes to Pig programming. First, statements must be terminated by a semicolon, although they may span multiple lines and can include indentation. Second, statements always begin by assigning a dataset to a bag, either through the process of loading data or manipulating a previously defined bag. The only exception is when output is required, which is typically the last line in a Pig program, using a DUMP or STORE statement.

Keywords (such as LOAD, STORE, FOREACH, etc.) are capitalized by convention but are otherwise case insensitive (recall that they cannot be used as identifiers, however, regardless of case). Also note that many of the built-in functions in Pig (such as COUNT or SUM) are case sensitive.

Pig supports inline comments using the double hyphen (--) as well as block comments using the /* */ notation. An example of this is shown in Listing 8.5.

LISTING 8.5 Comments in Pig

```
-- This is an inline comment
/*
This is a block comment
*/
```

Loading Data into Pig

Loading data into a bag is the first step for any Pig program. Pig uses load functions similar to the InputFormats discussed in the previous hour, which determine how a schema is extracted from the data. Some of the key load functions in Pig are summarized in Table 8.5.

TABLE 8.5 Common Pig Load Functions

Function	Syntax	Description
PigStorage (default)	`PigStorage([delim])`	Loads and stores data as structured text files
TextLoader	`TextLoader()`	Loads unstructured data in UTF-8 format
JsonLoader	`JsonLoader([schema])`	Loads JSON data

The load function is supplied using the USING clause. If the USING clause is omitted, the data is assumed to be tab delimited text data.

An example of a LOAD statement for a new line terminated, comma delimited dataset in Pig using the PigStorage function is shown in Listing 8.6.

LISTING 8.6 `PigStorage LOAD` **Function**

```
stations = LOAD 'stations' USING PigStorage(',') AS
            station_id,
            name,
            lat,
            long,
            dockcount,
            landmark,
            installation;
```

There are many other additional load functions in Pig including HBaseStorage, AvroStorage, AccumuloStorage, OrcStorage, and more, used for columnar storage files or NoSQL data storage. We will mainly use PigStorage, the default, for all of our examples.

There are many permutations to loading data initially such as the following:

▶ Loading data with no defined schema

▶ Loading data with a schema (named fields) but no assigned data types

▶ Loading data with a schema and assigned data types

This is demonstrated in Listing 8.7.

LISTING 8.7 Supplying Schemas for Bags in Pig

```
--load data with no schema defined
stations = LOAD 'stations' USING PigStorage(',');
/*
elements are accessed using their relative position, e.g. $0
all fields are typed as bytearray
*/
```

```
--load data with an untyped schema
stations = LOAD 'stations' USING PigStorage(',') AS
          (station_id,name,lat,long,dockcount,landmark,installation);
/*
elements are accessed using their named identifier, e.g. name
all fields with an unassigned datatype are typed as bytearray
*/

--load data with a typed schema
stations = LOAD 'stations' USING PigStorage(',') AS
          (station_id:int, name:chararray, lat:float,
           long:float, dockcount:int, landmark:chararray,
           installation:chararray);
/*
elements are accessed using their named identifier, e.g. name
*/
```

Loading data without having to provide a schema or datatypes can be useful when you are exploring a dataset for the first time. However, it is generally recommended that you supply this information if known, as it will make for better program optimization.

Filtering, Projecting, and Sorting Data using Pig

Once you have a bag "loaded" with data (virtually, not physically, of course), you would generally start manipulating this bag. Let's discuss some simple operations with Pig.

FILTER Statement

The most basic operation is simply to filter data. In this case, the schema is not changed—tuples that match a given criterion are retained in the target bag while tuples that don't satisfy the filter condition are not retained. Filtering tuples from a bag in Pig is accomplished by using the FILTER statement. A simple example of this is shown in Listing 8.8.

LISTING 8.8   FILTER **Statement**

```
sj_stations = FILTER stations BY landmark == 'San Jose';
```

TIP

Naming Bags in Pig

There is no right or wrong approach to naming bags in Pig. Some texts and examples you will find will use nondescript bag names such as A, B, C, etc. I personally prefer to give these meaningful names that describe them at a high level, but this is a personal choice.

Projecting and Transforming Fields Using FOREACH

Projecting or transforming fields within tuples in bags in Pig is accomplished using the FOREACH statement. FOREACH can be thought of as the Pig equivalent of a map operation in a MapReduce job; in fact, these operations would inevitably be executed using map functions. Each tuple in a given bag is iterated through performing the requested operation, which could include the following:

- ▸ Removing a field or fields; for instance, projecting 3 selected fields from an input bag with 4 fields

- ▸ Adding a field or fields; for instance, adding a computed field based upon data in the input bag

- ▸ Transforming a field or fields; for instance, performing an in-place manipulation of a field—such as converting a chararray field to lowercase

- ▸ Performing an aggregate function on a complex field; for instance, a COUNT operation against a field which is itself a bag—we will look at this in the next hour)

FOREACH is the most commonly used operation in Pig behind LOAD, DUMP and STORE. Listing 8.9 shows an example of a FOREACH operation to project specific fields in a target bag in Pig.

LISTING 8.9   FOREACH **Statement**

```
station_ids_names = FOREACH stations GENERATE station_id, name;
```

We will look at using FOREACH to execute built-in functions shortly.

ORDER **Statement**

Ordering tuples by a given field is another common Pig data processing and analysis requirement. Knowing what you know about MapReduce, you can deduce that this will leverage the Shuffle and Sort feature of the MapReduce framework at a physical level.

Ordering in Pig is accomplished using the ORDER BY statement. An example of ordering a bag by a given field using this operator is shown in Listing 8.10.

LISTING 8.10   ORDER **Statement**

```
ordered = ORDER station_ids_names BY name;
```

DESCRIBE and ILLUSTRATE Statements

Having created and manipulated bags in a Pig program, it is often useful to inspect the schema of a bag. A simple inspection of a bag at any stage of a Pig program can be done using the DESCRIBE statement. DESCRIBE will show the fields and their types from a given relation (bag). This does not require or invoke execution. An example of the DESCRIBE statement is shown in Listing 8.11.

LISTING 8.11   DESCRIBE Statement

```
DESCRIBE stations;
stations: {station_id: int,name: chararray,lat: float,long: float,
dockcount: int,landmark: chararray,installation: chararray}
```

Another useful command for inspection is ILLUSTRATE. The ILLUSTRATE command shows not only the bag's schema but the lineage for the bag as well—its predecessors in the program—along with showing some sample data (tuples) taken all the way through the program, showing the state at each step.

To do this, ILLUSTRATE must do some actual processing, unlike DESCRIBE, so it will take longer than the DESCRIBE command. However, it is a handy command when doing advanced programming in Pig. An example ILLUSTRATE command is shown in Listing 8.12.

LISTING 8.12   ILLUSTRATE Statement

```
ILLUSTRATE ordered;
---------------------------------------------------------------------
| stations        | station_id:int  | name:chararray           ...  |
---------------------------------------------------------------------
|                 | 23              | San Mateo County Center        |
|                 | 70              | San Francisco Caltrain (Townsend at
---------------------------------------------------------------------
---------------------------------------------------------------------
| station_ids_names  | station_id:int  | name:chararray        ...  |
---------------------------------------------------------------------
|                    | 23              | San Mateo County Center     |
|                    | 70              | San Francisco Caltrain      |
---------------------------------------------------------------------
---------------------------------------------------------------------
| ordered         | station_id:int  | name:chararray           ...  |
---------------------------------------------------------------------
|                 | 70              | San Francisco Caltrain (Townsend at
|                 | 23              | San Mateo County Center        |
---------------------------------------------------------------------
```

Built-in Functions in Pig

Pig includes several common built-in functions; these typically operate against a field and are used with the FOREACH operator. An example using a built-in function is provided in Listing 8.13.

LISTING 8.13   Built-in Functions in Pig

```
lcase_stations = FOREACH stations GENERATE station_id, LOWER(name),
                 lat, long, landmark;
```

There are built-in functions for common string or text operations, date functions, and numeric functions. Listing 8.14 lists some of the key built-in functions included with the Pig release. Many of these are analogous to functions included in most SQL dialects. Additional functions are available in community libraries, or you can write your own functions. We will discuss that more in the next hour.

LISTING 8.14   Some Common Built-in Functions Included with Pig

```
--Eval Functions
AVG, COUNT, MAX, MIN, SIZE, SUM, TOKENIZE

--Math Functions
ABS, CEIL, EXP, FLOOR, LOG, RANDOM, ROUND

--String Functions
STARTSWITH, ENDSWITH, LOWER, UPPER, LTRIM, RTRIM, TRIM, REGEX_EXTRACT

--Datetime Functions
CurrentTime, DaysBetween, GetDay, GetHour, GetMinute, ToDate
```

▼ TRY IT YOURSELF

Installing and Using Apache Pig

In this exercise you will download and install Pig on your pseudo-distributed cluster, and then you will run some interactive and batch Pig queries.

For this example we will be using data from the Bay Area Bike Share Data Challenge. The Bay Area Bike Share program enables members to pick up bikes from designated stations, which they can then drop off at the same or a different station. Bay Area Bike Share has made their trip data available for public use through their Open Data program. More information can be found at:

http://www.bayareabikeshare.com/open-data

The data for this exercise has also been made available in the book's download site.

1. Download the latest Pig release from the Apache Pig website (http://pig.apache.org/)—in our case this is release 0.16.0.

2. On your test cluster, unpack the Pig release:

```
$ tar -xvf pig-0.16.0.tar.gz
```

3. Change directories into your Pig release:

```
$ cd pig-0.16.0
```

4. Run the `pig` command with the `--version` switch to verify your release:

```
$ bin/pig --version
Apache Pig version 0.16.0 (r1746530)
compiled Jun 01 2016, 23:10:49
```

5. Download the stations data from the bike-share dataset:

```
$ wget https://s3.amazonaws.com/sty-hadoop/bike-share/stations/stations.csv
```

6. Create a directory called `stations` in HDFS and upload the `stations.csv` file to this directory:

```
$ hadoop fs -mkdir stations
$ hadoop fs -put stations.csv stations
```

7. Pig requires a MapReduce JobHistory server to be running to collect statistics and messages. We can start one using the command shown here:

```
$HADOOP_HOME/sbin/mr-jobhistory-daemon.sh \
start historyserver
```

8. Open a grunt session in the default mapreduce mode:

```
$ bin/pig
```

9. Enter the following commands in the terminal one by one:

```
stations = LOAD 'stations' USING PigStorage(',') AS
(station_id:int, name:chararray, lat:float,
long:float, dockcount:int, landmark:chararray,
installation:chararray);
station_ids_names = FOREACH stations GENERATE
                  station_id, name;
ordered = ORDER station_ids_names BY name;
```

10. Try the `DESCRIBE` and `ILLUSTRATE` commands:

```
DESCRIBE stations;
ILLUSTRATE ordered;
```

11. Request output to the terminal:

```
DUMP ordered;
```

12. Now exit the session by pressing Ctrl-D.

13. Save the commands in **Step 9** and **Step 11** to a file named `list_stations.pig`.

14. Run the program in batch mode:

```
$ bin/pig list_stations.pig
```

15. Change the DUMP command to a STORE command (you can comment out the DUMP command as shown):

```
--DUMP ordered;
STORE ordered INTO 'ordered';
```

16. Run the program again in batch mode:

```
$ bin/pig list_stations.pig
```

17. Inspect the output directory in HDFS. This should look similar to the output directory you saw when we executed our Java MapReduce program in the previous hour:

```
$ hadoop fs -ls ordered
```

18. Inspect the file produced to see the data returned:

```
$ hadoop fs -tail ordered/part-r-00000
```

Note that the data is in tab-delimited format by default, and that the bag and tuple notation is not written to the file(s).

Congratulations! You have written and executed your first Pig program.

You will use this Pig installation again in the next hour where we will look at some advanced Pig concepts.

CAUTION

Use Caution with the DUMP Statement

Using the DUMP statement to return data to the terminal should be used with caution and generally only when you know the volume of data which will be returned. For unknown or large datasets in Pig, you are usually advised to use the STORE command to output the resultant data to a directory in HDFS, from which you can subsequently inspect the data. Alternatively you can, and in many cases should, use the LIMIT operator to restrict the number of tuples returned from a DUMP operation.

Summary

In this hour, you had a gentle introduction to Apache Pig, a simple yet powerful data processing language and platform used to transform and analyze data in Hadoop. Pig was created at Yahoo! to enable developers and analysts to be more productive and agile when using the Hadoop platform. Pig enables users to effectively implement routines using the MapReduce or other execution frameworks without having to develop in Java or other low-level programming languages.

Pig's data model consists primarily of bags, tuples, fields, and atoms. Operations in Pig consist of either loading data into a bag, creating a bag from manipulating another bag or requesting a bag's data as output using the DUMP or STORE commands. You learned about Pig's datatypes as well as Pig's load functions, used to interpret input data files (similar to the InputFormats you learned about in the previous hour about Java MapReduce). You learned that Pig can be used to inspect data with or without declaring a schema or datatypes, making it useful for data inspection and discovery operations.

Finally, you looked at some simple operations in Pig to perform filtering, projection, and transformation of fields, and ordering of tuples by a given field. In the next hour we build on this knowledge to do some more advanced Pig programming.

Q&A

Q. What data structures exist in Pig? Briefly explain each of these.

A. The data structures in Pig are *bags*, *tuples*, and *maps*. Tuples are structures containing fields. Tuples can be thought of as equivalent to records in a relational table. Fields in tuples can hold atoms, or atomic units of data—for instance, an integer or a string value, or fields can hold complex data structures such as bags, tuples, or maps containing nested data. Bags are unordered collections of tuples, and maps contain collections of key value pairs.

Q. What are some example uses for the FOREACH statement in Pig?

A. FOREACH is typically used to project certain fields from a bag (for instance, returning specific fields from a bag), to perform transformations on a field through a function or functions, or to add fields to a bag (for instance, a computed field).

Q. Explain the concept of lazy evaluation with Pig.

A. Pig parses each statement presented to the interpreter either interactively through the grunt shell or in batch mode for syntax and object references. Planning, optimizing, and executing the jobs required to perform the required function is delayed until output is requested through the issuing of a DUMP or STORE command. This delayed execution is referred to as lazy evaluation.

Workshop

The workshop contains quiz questions and exercises to help you solidify your understanding of the material covered. Try to answer all questions before looking at the "Answers" section that follows.

Quiz

1. Which of the following are legal names for Pig identifiers (choose one or more)?

    A. `name`

    B. `name_1`

    C. `1name`

    D. `$name`

2. **True or False:** Built-in functions in Pig can be invoked using the `FOREACH` statement.

3. What statement is used to sort a bag by a specific field?

4. If you create a bag from an input data set using a `LOAD` statement and do not supply a schema, how would you refer to the first field in the bag?

Answers

1. A and B.

2. True.

3. `ORDER`.

4. `$0`.

HOUR 9
Using Advanced Pig

What You'll Learn in This Hour:

▶ Grouping and aggregating data in Pig
▶ Co-grouping and joining data in Pig
▶ User-defined functions in Pig
▶ Automating Pig using macros and variables

In this hour we will build on our introduction to Pig, looking deeper into the Pig programming language and execution framework. You will learn about processing multiple datasets using Pig, including joining and co-grouping operations, as well as how to process data in nested data structures. You will also learn about user-defined functions and how to automate Pig routines.

Grouping Data in Pig

Grouping data is a common and frequently used technique in relational database programming, usually for the purposes of aggregating data by a key, such as performing a COUNT, AVG, MIN, MAX, or SUM operation. Conceptually, the approach is the same in Pig. However, the underlying implementation takes some getting used to for those of you coming from a SQL background. Nevertheless, once you understand this, you will find the construct exceptionally powerful in Pig. Let's look at the GROUP statement now.

GROUP Statement

The GROUP statement enables you to group records by a specified field. The result of a GROUP operation in Pig is a structure with one record per unique value in the field by which you are grouping. Tuples in the resultant relation have two fields:

▶ A field named *group* of the same type as the field by which you are grouping from the input bag

▶ A field named after the relation you are grouping by, which is a bag of tuples from this relation that contain the element by which you are grouping

Consider the data sets in Listing 9.1, which I will use to illustrate grouping, co-grouping, and joining operations in Pig during this hour.

LISTING 9.1 Sample Datasets

```
--salespeople
--schema: salespersonid, name, storeid
1,Henry,100
2,Karen,100
3,Paul,101
4,Jimmy,102
5,Janice,

--stores
--schema: storeid, name
100,Hayward
101,Baumholder
102,Alexandria
103,Melbourne

--sales
--schema: salespersonid, storeid, salesamt
1,100,38
1,100,84
2,100,26
2,100,75
3,101,55
3,101,46
4,102,12
4,102,67
```

Listing 9.2 performs a group operation and describes and demonstrates the output data structure.

LISTING 9.2 GROUP Statement

```
grouped = GROUP sales BY salespersonid;
DESCRIBE grouped;
grouped: {group: int,
          sales: {(salespersonid: int,storeid: int,salesamt: int)}}
DUMP grouped;
(1,{(1,100,84),(1,100,38)})
(2,{(2,100,75),(2,100,26)})
(3,{(3,101,46),(3,101,55)})
(4,{(4,102,67),(4,102,12)})
```

Aggregate Functions in Pig

As discussed, you typically group data as a precursor to performing an aggregate function (COUNT, SUM, AVG, etc.). Pig includes most of these functions as part of the built-in functions included with Pig. Listing 9.3 demonstrates a SUM function performed against the grouped dataset created in Listing 9.2.

LISTING 9.3   SUM **Function**

```
salesbyid = FOREACH grouped GENERATE group AS salespersonid,
            SUM(sales.salesamt) AS total_sales;
DUMP salesbyid;
(1,122)
(2,101)
(3,101)
(4,79)
```

Note that the *<bag>.<field>* notation is used to refer to a specific field in a grouped bag. This is referred to as a **dereferencing** operator.

To perform an aggregate operation against all tuples in a bag, such as counting all tuples in a bag or summing fields from all tuples in a bag, you would use the GROUP ALL statement. It groups all tuples into one structure that can then be counted using the COUNT or COUNT_STAR method (which includes NULL values), or summed using the SUM method. An example demonstrating GROUP ALL with a subsequent SUM and COUNT operation is provided in Listing 9.4.

LISTING 9.4   GROUP ALL **Statement**

```
allsales = GROUP sales ALL;
DUMP allsales;
(all,{(4,102,67),(4,102,12),(3,101,46),(3,101,55),(2,100,75),...})

--COUNT all tuples in the sales bag
sales_trans = FOREACH allsales GENERATE COUNT(sales);
DUMP sales_trans;
(8)

--SUM all salesamts in the sales bag
sales_total = FOREACH allsales GENERATE SUM(sales.salesamt);
DUMP sales_total;
(403)
```

Nested FOREACH Statements

As well as performing aggregate functions against grouped data, you can operate directly against the nested structure that is returned as a result of a GROUP operation using a nested

FOREACH statement. The nested FOREACH statement iterates through every item in the nested structure (bag). There are some rules that apply to nested FOREACH operations that require the following:

▶ Only relational operations are allowed within the nested operation (e.g., LIMIT, FILTER, ORDER).

▶ GENERATE must be the last line in the nested code block.

Listing 9.5 shows an example of a nested FOREACH statement to show the top two sales for each salesperson using the grouped dataset created in Listing 9.2.

LISTING 9.5   Nested FOREACH **Statement**

```
top_sales = FOREACH grouped {
            sorted = ORDER sales BY salesamt DESC;
            limited = LIMIT sorted 2;
            GENERATE group, limited.salesamt;
            };
DUMP top_sales;
(1, { (84) , (38) })
(2, { (75) , (26) })
(3, { (55) , (46) })
(4, { (67) , (12) })
```

Notice that the top sales are in a nested structure as well (a bag). Typically you would follow this operation by another FOREACH to flatten the resultant structure, depending upon the desired output.

Multiple Dataset Processing in Pig

So far, all of the processing we have done has been against one dataset (one bag in a Pig routine). Often the true magic of Pig programming, as with most SQL programming, involves analyzing multiple datasets in one program. Let's look at some of the methods available to analyze multiple datasets in Pig.

Cogrouping Datasets

Previously you looked at grouping items from a single bag, co-grouping items allows you to group items from multiple bags. Co-grouping is accomplished by using a COGROUP operation which collects values from the all bags into a new bag. This new bag is quite similar to the structure returned by the GROUP statement; however, unlike GROUP, which contained one field literally named group and one bag named after the relation that was grouped, the resultant co-grouped structure contains one bag for each input bag to the COGROUP statement.

Consider the dataset we introduced in Listing 9.1. Listing 9.6 demonstrates the use and output from a COGROUP operation using this dataset.

LISTING 9.6   COGROUP **Statement**

```
cogrouped = COGROUP stores BY storeid, salespeople BY storeid;
cogrouped: {group: int,stores: {(storeid: int,name: chararray)},
      salespeople: {(salespersonid: int,name: chararray,storeid: int)}}
DUMP cogrouped;
(100,{(100,Hayward)},{(2,Karen,100),(1,Henry,100)})
(101,{(101,Baumholder)},{(3,Paul,101)})
(102,{(102,Alexandria)},{(4,Jimmy,102)})
(103,{(103,Melbourne)},{})
(,{},{(5,Janice,)})
```

Joining Multiple Datasets

Join operations in Pig are analogous to the join operations we routinely see is SQL programming. Join functions combine records from two bags based on a common field.

Join Types

A quick refresher on joins—you can skip this if you have a relational database background. Joins operate on two different datasets where one field in each dataset is nominated as a key (or a join key). The datasets are referred to in the order in which they are specified. For instance, the first dataset specified is considered as the left entity or dataset, the second dataset specified is considered as the right entity or dataset.

An *inner join*, often simply called a join (where the "inner" is inferred), returns all elements or records from both datasets where the nominated key is present in both datasets.

An *outer join* does not require keys to match in both datasets. Outer joins are implemented as either a left outer join, right outer join, or a full outer join.

A *left outer join* returns all records from the left, or first, dataset along with matched records only (by the specified key) from the right, or second, dataset.

A *right outer join* returns all records from the right, or second, dataset along with matched records only (by the specified key) from the left, or first, dataset.

A *full outer join* returns all records from both datasets whether there is a key match or not.

Joins in Pig

The bag returned from a JOIN operation in Pig is a structure containing the entire matched records from both input bags. This is where it may sound a bit foreign to you if you are used to performing join operations in SQL—which returns a flattened list of columns from both entities. Let's work through an example.

Considering from our fictitious retailer from Listing 9.1, with a list of stores and a list of salespeople with the stores they are assigned to. Figure 9.1 is a logical depiction of how a JOIN operation works in Pig.

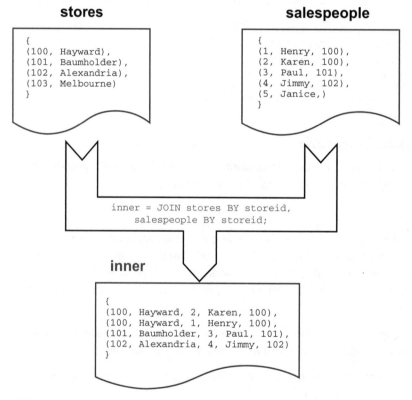

FIGURE 9.1
Inner Join in Pig.

An inner join operation shows all stores and salespeople with a matching *storeid*. Salespeople without stores and stores without salespeople are not included.

TIP

Optimizing Joins in Pig

Unlike most databases, there are no indexes or statistics used by Pig to optimize the JOIN, so the optimizations you can provide are essential to maximizing performance. One such optimization is the order in which you reference bags in a JOIN statement. A simple axiom to remember is "join large by small." This means referencing the larger of the two input bags (the one containing the most tuples if this is known) first, followed by the smaller of the two bags. This will seem strange for users coming from relational database programming backgrounds, but unlike relational database systems, joins are relatively inefficient in Hadoop.

Figures 9.2, 9.3, and 9.4 logically depict a LEFT OUTER JOIN, RIGHT OUTER JOIN, and FULL OUTER JOIN in Pig.

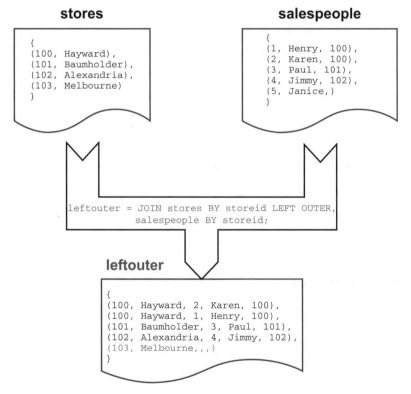

FIGURE 9.2
Left Outer Join in Pig.

A left outer join operation shows all stores with or without salespeople.

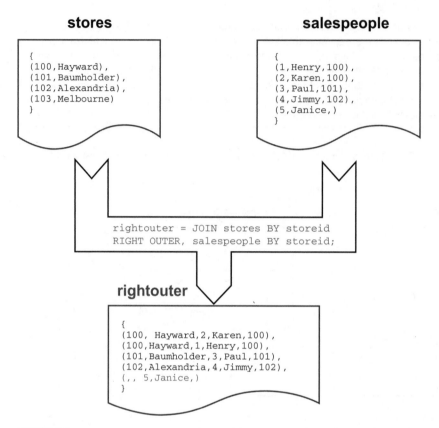

FIGURE 9.3
Right Outer Join in Pig.

A right outer join operation shows all salespeople with or without stores.

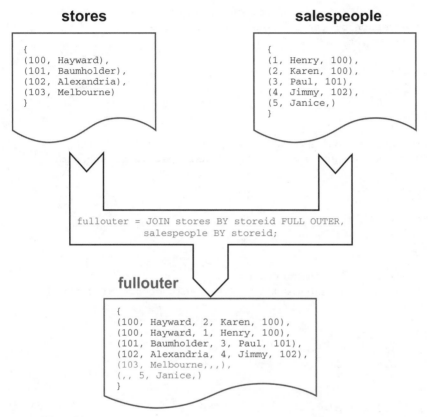

FIGURE 9.4
Full Outer Join in Pig.

A full outer join operation shows all salespeople with all stores whether there is an association or not.

JOIN Statement

Having an understanding of the types of joins available and how data is returned from join operations in Pig, lets look at some examples. Listing 9.8 shows examples using our sample dataset, showing the data and schema for bags returned by a JOIN statement. Notice the distinctive object identifier assigned to the fields in the bag returned. The "::" syntax is referred to as a disambiguation operator as you may have namespace clashes if fields have the same name in both bags. Listing 9.7 demonstrates the various JOIN operations in Pig.

LISTING 9.7   JOIN Statement

```
--Stores and their salespeople
inner = JOIN stores BY storeid, salespeople BY storeid;
DESCRIBE inner;
```

```
inner: {stores::storeid: int,stores::name: chararray,
salespeople::salespersonid: int,salespeople::name: chararray,
salespeople::storeid: int}
```
DUMP inner;
```
(100,Hayward,2,Karen,100)
(100,Hayward,1,Henry,100)
(101,Baumholder,3,Paul,101)
(102,Alexandria,4,Jimmy,102)
```

```
--All stores with and without salespeople
```
leftouter = JOIN stores BY storeid LEFT OUTER, salespeople BY storeid;
DUMP leftouter;
```
(100,Hayward,2,Karen,100)
(100,Hayward,1,Henry,100)
(101,Baumholder,3,Paul,101)
(102,Alexandria,4,Jimmy,102)
(103,Melbourne,,,)
```

```
--All salespeople with and without stores
```
rightouter = JOIN stores BY storeid RIGHT OUTER, salespeople BY storeid;
DUMP rightouter;
```
(100,Hayward,2,Karen,100)
(100,Hayward,1,Henry,100)
(101,Baumholder,3,Paul,101)
(102,Alexandria,4,Jimmy,102)
(,,5,Janice,)
```

```
--All stores, all salespeople
```
fullouter = JOIN stores BY storeid FULL OUTER, salespeople BY storeid;
DUMP fullouter;
```
(100,Hayward,2,Karen,100)
(100,Hayward,1,Henry,100)
(101,Baumholder,3,Paul,101)
(102,Alexandria,4,Jimmy,102)
(103,Melbourne,,,)
(,,5,Janice,)
```

TIP

Filter Early, Filter Often

As you will have noticed, the bags returned by GROUP, COGROUP, and JOIN operations will contain duplicate fields; for instance, the field you are grouping, co-grouping, or joining on will be duplicated in the nested or flattened data structures returned. A common convention is to follow a COGROUP operation with a FOREACH operation to remove duplicate fields. This will assist the Pig optimizer in making the execution of your programs more efficient as well.

The golden rule of big data processing is *"Filter early, filter often."*

WordCount in Pig

In this exercise, we will use Pig to perform a word count operation against our *shakespeare.txt* file, which will use the `GROUP` relational operator and the `COUNT` function. We will also introduce a new dataset, *stop-words-list.csv*, containing known English stopwords, to remove words like "the," "and," "a," etc., using a `RIGHT OUTER JOIN`.

1. Download the `stopwords.txt` file from the books download site:

   ```
   $ wget https://s3.amazonaws.com/sty-hadoop/stopwords/stop-word-list.csv
   ```

2. Create a directory in HDFS and put the `stopwords.txt` file in this directory:

   ```
   $ hadoop fs -mkdir stopwords
   $ hadoop fs -put stop-word-list.csv stopwords
   ```

3. From the Pig installation directory, start a grunt session:

   ```
   $ bin/pig
   ```

4. Use the `SET` command in the grunt session to give the program a friendly name, which can be seen in the YARN ResourceManager UI:

   ```
   SET job.name 'Word Count in Pig';
   ```

5. Load the `shakespeare` dataset:

   ```
   shakespeare = LOAD 'shakespeare' AS (lineoftext:chararray);
   ```

6. Load the `stopwords` dataset:

   ```
   stopwords = LOAD 'stopwords' USING PigStorage()
           AS (stopword:chararray);
   ```

7. `TOKENIZE` and `FLATTEN` and normalize text (making all lowercase) in the `shakespeare` dataset, creating a bag of words:

   ```
   words = FOREACH shakespeare GENERATE
           FLATTEN(TOKENIZE(REPLACE(LOWER(TRIM(lineoftext)),
           '[\\p{Punct},\\p{Cntrl}]','''))) AS word;
   ```

8. `FILTER` the `words` bag to remove empty words:

   ```
   realwords = FILTER words BY SIZE(word) > 0;
   ```

9. `TOKENIZE` and `FLATTEN` the `stopwords` dataset:

   ```
   flattened_stopwords = FOREACH stopwords GENERATE
           FLATTEN(TOKENIZE(stopword)) AS stopword;
   ```

10. Perform a `RIGHT OUTER JOIN` between the `stopwords` dataset and the `realwords` bag:

```
right_joined = JOIN flattened_stopwords
                    BY stopword RIGHT OUTER,
                    realwords BY word;
```

11. Perform a `FILTER` operation to remove stopwords:

```
meaningful_words = FILTER right_joined BY
                    (flattened_stopwords::stopword IS NULL);
```

12. Perform a `FOREACH` to remove duplicate fields:

```
shakespeare_real_words = FOREACH meaningful_words
                    GENERATE realwords::word AS word;
```

13. Perform a `GROUP` operations on the remaining words:

```
grouped = GROUP shakespeare_real_words BY word;
```

14. Count the remaining meaningful words using the `COUNT` function:

```
counted = FOREACH grouped GENERATE group AS word,
            COUNT(shakespeare_real_words) AS wordcount;
```

15. Order the count using the `ORDER` operator:

```
ordered = ORDER counted BY wordcount;
```

16. Check the output using the `DUMP` command:

```
DUMP ordered;
```

17. Now combine all of the Pig commands into a single file `wordcount.pig`, replace the `DUMP` statement with a `STORE` operation at the end of the script, and run the Pig program in non-interactive mode as we did in the Try it Yourself exercise in the previous hour.

Set Operations in Pig

Pig supports several common set operations which operate on the entire tuple as opposed to fields in a tuple. Let's look at a few of these now, using the two sets *odds* and *fibonacci* pictured in Figure 9.5.

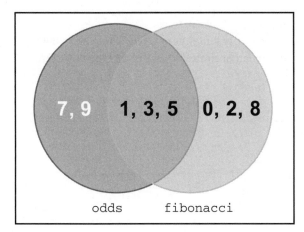

FIGURE 9.5
Example Sets.

UNION Statement

Sometimes it in necessary to concatenate two datasets with one another; that is, combine the tuples in one bag with the tuples in another. This is accomplished using the UNION operator. Listing 9.8 demonstrates the UNION operator.

LISTING 9.8   UNION **Statement**

```
unioned = UNION odds, fibonacci;
DUMP unioned;
(0)
(1)
(2)
(3)
(5)
(8)
(1)
(3)
(5)
(7)
(9)
```

NOTE

UNION Does Not Preserve Order or Filter Duplicates

Be aware that UNION does not eliminate duplicates. You should follow a UNION with a DISTINCT operation, which I will cover next, to accomplish this. Furthermore, UNION does not preserve the order of either of the input bags. For this you should use the ORDER statement after the UNION operation.

DISTINCT Statement

A common requirement is to remove duplicate records or tuples from a bag where every field is identical to one or more other tuples. Listing 9.9 demonstrates the use of the DISTINCT statement.

LISTING 9.9   DISTINCT Statement

```
no_duplicates = DISTINCT unioned;
DUMP no_duplicates;
(0)
(1)
(2)
(3)
(5)
(7)
(8)
(9)
```

SUBTRACT Statement

The SUBTRACT operator is another common set operation which returns tuples from one bag that are not present in another bag. Listing 9.10 demonstrates the use of the SUBTRACT operator. Notice that tuples that negate one another, in this case odd numbers, are represented as empty sets.

LISTING 9.10   SUBTRACT Statement

```
cogrouped = COGROUP odds by $0, fibonacci by $0;
subtracted = FOREACH cogrouped GENERATE SUBTRACT(fibonacci, odds);
DUMP subtracted;
({(0)})
({(2)})
({(8)})
({})
({})
({})
({})
({})
```

CROSS Statement

Pig also includes a CROSS operator which produces a cross product of all tuples from one bag with all tuples from another bag. This can be useful for data science applications where you want to test all possible combinations of records from two disparate datasets.

Listing 9.11 shows an example of a CROSS operation with abridged output for brevity.

LISTING 9.11   CROSS **Statement**

```
crossed = CROSS odds, fibonacci;
DUMP crossed;
(9,8)
(9,5)
(9,3)
(9,2)
(9,1)
(9,0)
(7,8)
(7,5)
(7,3)
...
```

CAUTION

Cross Joins can Create Massive Datasets

Cross joins or Cartesian products of two or more datasets can result in extremely large volumes of data and should be used sparingly. Although Hadoop is a Big Data platform by definition, you should not inadvertently create a big data problem where one did not need to exist!

Splitting Datasets in Pig

Not only can you combine datasets using the UNION operator but you can also split one bag into multiple bags using the SPLIT operator. SPLIT can be used to create independent datasets which do not have to be mutually exclusive. These datasets can then be processed in parallel or can be used to segregate output.

Listing 9.12 provides an example of the SPLIT operator.

LISTING 9.12   SPLIT **Statement**

```
SPLIT unioned INTO evens IF ($0 % 2 == 0), odds IF ($0 % 2 != 0);
DUMP evens;
(0)
(2)
(8)
DUMP odds;
(1)
(3)
```

(5)
(1)
(3)
(5)
(7)
(9)

User-Defined Functions in Pig

Although Pig provides some built-in functions, which I discussed in the previous hour, there are often requirements to perform more advanced functions for which there are no built-in options. Fortunately, Pig supports and encourages the use of built-in functions that can be written or sourced from the Pig community. Let's look at these now.

Writing UDFs for Pig

Like most projects in the Hadoop ecosystem, Pig is extensible by design. The most obvious example of this is its support for user-defined functions (UDFs). UDFs in Pig are generally classified into one of the following categories:

- ▶ Eval functions
- ▶ Load/Store Functions

User-defined load/store functions are the Pig equivalent of custom InputFormats, OutputFormats, and RecordReaders in MapReduce, and can be used to define custom input and output data sources and structures. Eval functions in Pig are functions which can be used in Pig expressions and statements to return any simple or complex Pig datatype.

Unlike user-defined extensions to MapReduce which can only be implemented in Java, Pig allows you to write UDFs in multiple languages. The languages include the following:

- ▶ Java
- ▶ Python and Jython (Python code compiled to run in a JVM)
- ▶ JavaScript
- ▶ Groovy
- ▶ JRuby

For performance reasons, JVM-based platforms such as Java, Jython, JRuby and Groovy are recommended. There is much more information available on writing and implementing UDFs in the various languages at **https://pig.apache.org**. Listing 9.13 shows an example Pig Eval UDF written in Jython to return a bag of **n-grams** (*n*-sized fragments of a word, a construct used frequently in text comparison) from a given bag of words.

LISTING 9.13   Pig UDF Written in Jython

```
@outputSchema("n:bag{t:tuple(ngram:chararray)}")
def return_ngrams(s,n):
  outBag = []
  if s is None: return None
  input_list = list(s)
  for i in range(len(input_list)-(n-1)):
    ngram_arr = input_list[i:i+n]
    if (all(isinstance(item, int) for item in ngram_arr)):
      ngram_str = "".join(chr(l).lower() for l in ngram_arr)
    else:
      return None
    outBag.append(ngram_str)
  return outBag
```

Once your UDF is written, you use the REGISTER command to include the function in your program, then use the function as you would any built-in function in Pig. Note that you can include multiple functions in one registered UDF library in a Pig program. Listing 9.14 demonstrates how to register and reference the Jython Pig UDF defined in Listing 9.13.

LISTING 9.14   Registering and Using a Pig UDF

```
REGISTER 'fuzzymatchingudf.py' USING jython as fuzzymatchingudf;
raw_data = LOAD 'test.data' USING PigStorage();
names_with_ngrams = FOREACH raw_data GENERATE $0,
                    fuzzymatchingudf.return_ngrams($0,3);
DUMP names_with_ngrams;
```

Community Function Libraries in Pig

Pig includes a library of community-contributed user-defined functions called PiggyBank. Generally, functions get contributed and committed to PiggyBank, a separate project, before they graduate to become built-in functions. However, some more obscure or less commonly required functions will stay in the PiggyBank.

PiggyBank is a very useful source of functions that you should be familiar with. A code example of how to register and access PiggyBank in a Pig program is provided in Listing 9.15.

LISTING 9.15   PiggyBank Function Library

```
REGISTER 'lib/piggybank.jar';
DEFINE ISOToUnix
     org.apache.pig.piggybank.evaluation.datetime.convert.ISOToUnix();
...
toEpoch = FOREACH toISO GENERATE id,
          (long)ISOToUnix(ISOTime) as epoch:long;
...
```

Another library you should be familiar with is DataFu. Apache DataFu is a library of Pig UDFs contributed by LinkedIn. DataFu includes several useful statistical and set processing functions that aren't available as built-in functions or in PiggyBank. A sample DataFu function used to create quantiles from web response time is shown in Listing 9.16. This is one of many useful statistical functions in the DataFu library.

LISTING 9.16   Apache DataFu Function Library

```
REGISTER 'datafu-1.2.0.jar';
DEFINE Quantile datafu.pig.stats.StreamingQuantile('5');
quantiles = FOREACH resp_time_only {
      sorted = ORDER resp_time_bag BY resp_time;
      GENERATE url_date, Quantile(sorted.resp_time) as quantile_bins;
      }
...
```

Before writing your own function, you should check the documentation for both PiggyBank and DataFu (as well as a general search in GitHub at **https://github.com**). The links for the PiggyBank and DataFu projects are given here:

▶ **https://cwiki.apache.org/confluence/display/PIG/PiggyBank** (PiggyBank)

▶ **https://datafu.incubator.apache.org/** (DataFu)

Stream Operator in Pig

In **Hour 7, "Programming MapReduce Applications,"** I discussed how Map and Reduce functions could be written in languages other than Java using the MapReduce Streaming API. Pig exposes the same functionality using the STREAM operator.

The STREAM operator enables you to write functions in languages such as Perl, BASH, and other languages not supported for UDF development. Like the MapReduce Streaming API, records are read in as tab-delimited text on STDIN, and records are emitted from your custom function as tab-delimited text using STDOUT.

Given a function in a Perl script called myfunction.pl, Listing 9.17 demonstrates how to use the STREAM operator.

LISTING 9.17   STREAM **Statement**

```
DEFINE MYFUNCTION `myfunction.pl` SHIP('myfunction.pl');
output = STREAM recs THROUGH MYFUNCTION AS (col1:chararray, col2:long);
...
```

NOTE

Performance Considerations When Using the STREAM **Operator**

As with MapReduce streaming, a performance tax is applicable. You should try to implement a JVM-based UDF using the Pig UDF API discussed earlier, if at all possible, before resorting to using the STREAM operator.

Automating Pig Using Macros and Variables

You have seen how powerful Pig can be as a language and framework for data transformation and analysis, but Pig also provides some key automation features and capabilities to productionize and scale Pig applications. These features include the capability to parameterize Pig programs and define Pig macros. Parameters and macros enable code reuse, sharing, and agility. Lets discuss these useful features now.

Parameterizing Pig Programs

Parameters enable flexibility in your code. Parameters passed to an application can enable programs to be reused for different purposes; for instance, the same program can be used with different input search or filter criteria. Pig enables you to parameterize just about anything, from input and output paths to filter criteria and more. This is because Pig parameterization is simple string substitution, replacing designated values with parameter values at runtime. An example of a parameterized Pig script is shown in Listing 9.18.

LISTING 9.18   Pig Program Variables Sourced from Parameters

```
...
longwords = FILTER words BY SIZE(word) > $WORDLENGTH;
...
```

Listing 9.19 demonstrates how to invoke your script, passing in the designated parameters.

LISTING 9.19   Passing Parameters to your Pig Script

```
$ bin/pig -p WORDLENGTH=10 wordcount.pig
```

You can also utilize shell commands when passing in parameters. An example of this is shown in Listing 9.20.

LISTING 9.20   Passing Shell Command Return Values to a Pig Script

```
$ bin/pig -p NOW=`date +%s` wordcount.pig
```

If you have a large number of parameters to pass in you can supply these in a text file instead of passing each parameter at the command line. An example parameters file is shown in Listing 9.21.

LISTING 9.21   Multiple Pig Parameters in a Text File

```
INPUTDIR=shakespeare
STOPWORDS=stopwords
WORDLENGTH=10
NOW=`date +%s`
```

To supply your parameters file you simply use the -m option at the command line as shown in Listing 9.22.

LISTING 9.22   Passing Pig Parameters using a Text File

```
$ bin/pig -m myparameters.txt wordcount.pig
```

Reusing Code with Pig Macros

Often processing in Pig is repetitive and sometimes recursive. Macros in Pig are designed to improve the reusability of code (or more specifically, functional groupings of code). Using macros, you can designate a block of code, which can then be easily reused multiple times in your program.

Macros are created using the DEFINE statement and can then be called by the alias assigned to them, as shown in Listing 9.23.

LISTING 9.23   Defining and Calling a Pig Macro

```
define remove_stopwords (BAG_OF_IDS_AND_TERMS, STOPWORDS_TERMS_ONLY)
returns result {
/**** GET RID OF STOPWORDS HERE... ****/
```

```
stopwords = FOREACH $STOPWORDS_TERMS_ONLY GENERATE
                FLATTEN(TOKENIZE(stopword)) as stopword;
tokenized_stopwords_join = JOIN stopwords BY stopword RIGHT OUTER,
                           $BAG_OF_IDS_AND_TERMS by term PARALLEL 5;
meaningful_terms = FILTER tokenized_stopwords_join BY
                   (stopwords::stopword IS NULL);
$result = FOREACH meaningful_terms GENERATE
          $BAG_OF_IDS_AND_TERMS::id AS id,
          $BAG_OF_IDS_AND_TERMS::term AS term;
};
...
terms_final = remove_stopwords(tokens, known_stop_words);
...
```

As with parameters, macros use simple string substitution at runtime. Pig enables you to see the substituted code without running the code using the -dryrun argument. This can be quite useful when using parameters and macros to automate Pig. Listing 9.24 demonstrates a dryrun operation.

LISTING 9.24 Pig dryrun **Option**

```
$ bin/pig -p WORDLENGTH=10 -dryrun wordcount.pig
```

In the case of the last code listing, the dryrun option will create a file called wordcount.pig. substituted, which will have all of the parameter and macro variables substituted with their respective input values and code.

You can create a file with multiple macros in it and then import this file for use anywhere in your program. This is a clean way to import commonly used macros. If you had multiple macros defined in a file called functions.pig you would import this file using the IMPORT statement as shown in Listing 9.25.

LISTING 9.25 **IMPORT Statement**

```
IMPORT 'functions.pig';
```

Summary

In this hour you learned some more advanced Pig concepts related to grouping and joining data. Conceptually, this is very similar to the join operations we are familiar with from relational database programming. However, their implementation in Pig is quite different in terms of the resultant structures these functions return. You learned that many functions, including GROUP and COGROUP, return complex or nested data structures (fields containing bags that contain tuples). You learned how to process these structures using a nested FOREACH operation.

I also discussed extending Pig with user-defined functions (UDFs), which could be written or sourced from a variety of publicly available libraries such as PiggyBank or DataFu.

Finally, you learned how to automate Pig using macros, variables, and parameter substitution. This concludes our discussion of Pig (sadly...), but hopefully this is just the beginning of your journey!

Q&A

Q. What is a nested FOREACH operation used for? What are some of the restrictions on and caveats for a nested FOREACH operation?

A. A nested FOREACH statement iterates through every item in the nested structure (bag), usually created by another operation such as a GROUP statement. This can be used for operations such as *TOP n* items based upon a filter criteria. Restrictions that apply to nested FOREACH operations include the requirement that only relational operations are allowed within the nested operation (e.g. LIMIT, FILTER, ORDER), and GENERATE must be the last line in the nested code block.

Q. Describe a COGROUP operation in Pig.

A. A COGROUP operation groups two bags by a field with a matching value in each input bag. The return bag contains one field literally called group and two bags each named after the respective input bag. The contents of each bag are the entire set of tuples from each respective bag with a given field matching the grouped value.

Q. How does a JOIN operation work in Pig? Describe the output schema from a JOIN.

A. A JOIN operation in Pig matches a given value in one or both input bags. Joins can be inner joins (finding only values that match in both bags) or outer joins where values can be present in only one of the given bags. The return structure from a JOIN is a flattened bag of tuples containing all fields from both bags, using the input bag name and field name separated by a disambiguation operator "::".

Workshop

The workshop contains quiz questions and exercises to help you solidify your understanding of the material covered. Try to answer all questions before looking at the "Answers" section that follows.

Quiz

1. **True or False:** A GROUP statement in Pig is often a precursor to an aggregate function such as SUM or COUNT.

2. When performing a COGROUP operation in Pig, what is the first field of the resultant output structure named?

3. Given a Pig script that includes the following statement

   ```
   ...
   highvalue = FILTER customers BY ltv > $LTV;
   ...
   ```

   which invocation of the Pig program from the command line would be used to pass the $LTV parameter?

   A. `$ pig -p $LTV=1000000`

   B. `$ pig -p LTV=1000000`

   C. `$ pig LTV=1000000`

   D. `$ pig $LTV=1000000`

7. What is the name of the community-contributed user-defined function library included with Pig?

Answers

1. True.

2. group.

3. B.

4. PiggyBank.

Analyzing Data Using Apache Hive

What You'll Learn in This Hour:

▸ Introduction to Apache Hive

▸ Hive deployment and configuration

▸ Hive objects and the Hive metastore

▸ Basic programming in HiveQL

Hive is perhaps the most commonly used tool in the Hadoop ecosystem (followed closely by Spark, which will be discussed later in the book, and which itself leverages some of the Hive constructs). Hive has proliferated due to its ease of use and familiar programming interface, and can often be the best way to quickly achieve adoption and productivity on the Hadoop platform. In this hour I will introduce Hive and get you up and running, analyzing data in HDFS using HiveQL.

Introducing Hive

Similar to the Apache Pig project I have discussed over the previous two hours that started at Yahoo!, the Apache Hive project started at Facebook in 2010 to provide a high-level interface to Hadoop MapReduce. Instead of creating a new language, as was done with PigLatin, the Hive project set out to put a SQL-like abstraction on top of MapReduce.

The Hive project introduced a new language called HiveQL (or Hive Query Language), which implements a subset of SQL-92, an internationally agreed-upon standard specification for the SQL language, with some extensions.

Similar to Pig, the motivation for Hive was that few analysts were available with Java MapReduce programming skills. Facebook recognized, however, that many analysts were proficient in SQL. Furthermore, SQL is the common language for BI, visualization tools, and reporting tools, which commonly use ODBC/JDBC as a standard interface.

In Hive's original implementation, HiveQL would get parsed by the Hive client and mapped to a sequence of Java MapReduce operations, which would then be submitted as jobs on the Hadoop cluster. The progress would be monitored and the results returned to the client (or written back to the desired location in HDFS). Figure 10.1 provides a high-level depiction of how Hive processes data on HDFS. I will discuss the Hive metastore next.

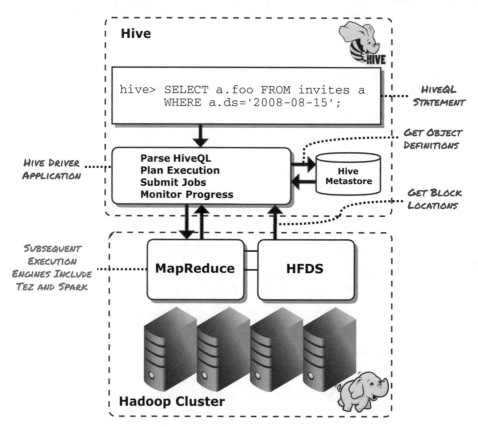

FIGURE 10.1
Hive High-Level Overview.

Hive Objects and the Hive Metastore

Hive implements a tabular abstraction to objects in HDFS, presenting directories and all files they contain as a table in its programming model. Just as in a conventional relational database, tables have predefined columns with designated datatypes created using SQL Data Definition Language (DDL) commands. The data in HDFS can then be accessed via SQL Data Manipulation Language (DML) statements, just as with a normal database management system.

This is where the similarity ends, however, as Hadoop is a schema-on-read platform, backed by an immutable filesystem, HDFS. The following key differences exist between Hive and a conventional database platform:

▶ UPDATE is not (really) supported

Although UPDATE has been introduced into the HiveQL dialect, HDFS is still an immutable filesystem, so this abstraction involves applying **coarse-grained** transformations, whereas a true UPDATE in a RDBMS is a **fine-grained** operation.

▶ No transactions, no journaling, no rollbacks, no (real) transaction isolation level

▶ No declarative referential integrity (DRI), no primary keys, no foreign keys

▶ Incorrectly formatted data (for example, mistyped data or malformed records) are simply represented to the client as NULL

The mapping of tables to their directory locations in HDFS and the columns and their definitions are maintained in the Hive metastore. The metastore is a relational database (somewhat ironic) that is written to and read by the Hive client. The object definitions also include the input and output formats for the files represented by the table objects (for example, CSVInputFormat, and so on) and SerDes (short for Serialization/Deserialization functions), which instruct Hive how to extract records and fields from the files.

Figure 10.2 shows a high-level example of the interactions between Hive and the metastore.

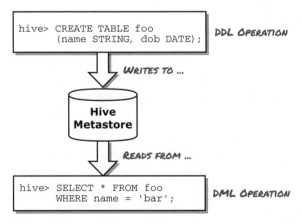

FIGURE 10.2
Hive Metastore Interaction

The metastore can be an embedded Derby database (the default) or a local or remote database (such as MySQL or PostgreSQL). In most cases, a shared database is implemented, which enables developers and analysts to share object definitions.

There is also a Hive subproject called HCatalog, which was an initiative to extend objects created in Hive to other projects, such as Apache Pig, with a common interface.

I will refer to the Hive metastore again in the book as it is leveraged by several other projects in the Hadoop ecosystem.

Hive CLI, HiveServer2, Beeswax, and Beeline

Hive provides a client command-line interface (CLI) that accepts and parses HiveQL input commands. This is a common method for performing ad hoc queries. Figure 10.3 shows the Hive CLI.

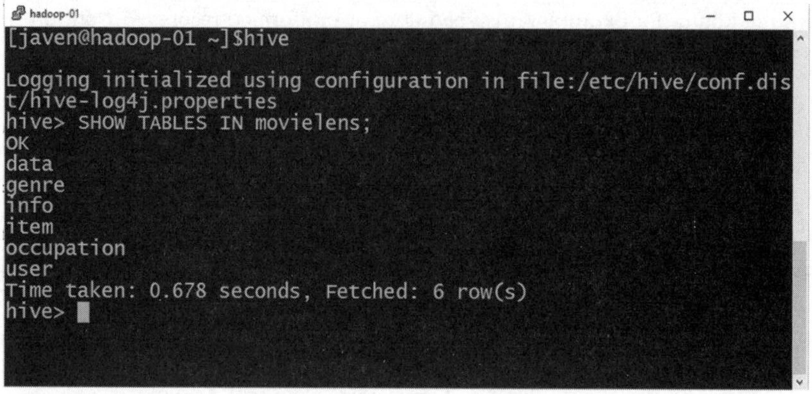

FIGURE 10.3
The Hive Command-Line Interface.

The Hive CLI is used when the Hive client or driver application is deployed to the local machine, including the connection to the metastore. For large-scale implementations, a client/server approach is often more appropriate because the connection details to the metastore are kept in one place (on the server), and access can be controlled to the cluster. This approach is called HiveServer2.

HiveServer2 can now act as a multi-session driver application for multiple clients. HiveServer2 provides a JDBC interface that can be used by external clients, such as visualization tools, as well as a lightweight CLI called Beeline. There is also a web-based interface called Beeswax, which is used within the HUE (or Hadoop User Environment) project, which will be covered in **Hour 14, "Using the Hadoop User Environment (HUE)."**

You can also run Hive statements and scripts in non-interactive, or batch mode, using the -f or -e option as shown in Listing 10.1.

LISTING 10.1 Running Hive Queries in Batch Mode

```
# run all statements in a file
$ hive -f MyHiveQuery.hql
# run an individual statement
$ hive -e "SELECT * FROM mytable"
```

Deploying and Configuring Hive

Hive is typically made available for you on all of the commercial Hadoop distributions, with management capabilities to deploy Hive client and server components and make changes to Hive-specific configuration parameters. If you have to install Hive from the Apache release, it is quite straightforward. You simply download and unpack the release and link to the Hadoop configuration. We will do this in the Try it Yourself exercise later this hour.

This basic deployment will get you up and running with an embedded metastore using a Derby database. To change to a shared metastore, you would need to modify your configuration to supply the connection details for the shared metastore—for example, on a shared MySQL server instance. The remote database server will need a Hive metastore schema deployed which contains tables that support the metastore data model. You can get this from the Hive release.

Hive Databases and Tables

Hive objects consist of databases and tables. Hive databases are used for organization, authorization, and namespace management. Hive tables exist in a Hive database. The default database in Hive is (aptly) named default. Database context can be changed using the USE statement as shown in Listing 10.2.

LISTING 10.2 Changing Hive Database Contexts

```
hive> USE bikeshare;
```

You can also reference objects using their fully qualified object identifier (which includes the database and table name) as shown in Listing 10.3.

LISTING 10.3 Referencing Hive Objects

```
hive> SELECT * FROM bikeshare.trips;
```

Hive Authorization

Hive supports basic authorization, which determines access levels to objects within a Hive instance. Hive authorization is not enabled by default; to enable Hive authorization you need to add the configuration values to Hive's main configuration file (`hive-site.xml`) as shown in Listing 10.4.

LISTING 10.4 Configuring Hive Authorization

```
...
<property>
  <name>hive.security.authorization.enabled</name>
  <value>true</value>
</property>
<property>
  <name>hive.security.authorization.createtable.owner.grants</name>
  <value>ALL</value>
</property>
...
```

Once enabled, object-level privileges can be assigned using the GRANT statement. This is generally synonymous with the GRANT semantics available in most relational database management platforms. An example privilege assignment to a table in Hive is shown in Listing 10.5.

LISTING 10.5 The GRANT Statement

```
hive> GRANT SELECT ON TABLE trips TO USER javen;
```

The specific privileges available in Hive include SELECT, CREATE, ALTER, DROP, and more. There is also an ALL privilege that grants all actions to a particular user.

Hive also supports privilege assignments to a GROUP or ROLE as well as a USER. Roles make it easy to grant access rights depending upon what role a user is performing at the time, such as defining roles called developer or analyst and assigning appropriate privileges to these roles. Listing 10.6 demonstrates the creation and privilege assignment to a role named analyst.

LISTING 10.6 Creating Roles in Hive

```
hive> CREATE ROLE analyst;
```

Privileges can be revoked as well, as shown in Listing 10.7.

LISTING 10.7 REVOKE Statement

```
hive> REVOKE SELECT ON TABLE trips FROM USER javen;
```

There is also a SHOW GRANT command, which can be used to show all privileges assigned to a specific user, group, or role on a particular object or all objects.

CAUTION

Hive Authorization on Its Own Is Not Secure

Hive authorization is built on top of HDFS authorization, which is weak in the absence of strong cluster authentication. If security is a paramount design consideration, you should use Kerberos authentication, along with Hive authorization and HDFS authorization. I will discuss this further in **Hour 22, "Securing Hadoop."**

Creating Hive Objects

Through its datatypes and Data Definition Language (DDL), Hive supports most common primitive datatypes, similar to those found in most database systems, as well as several complex datatypes. The simple datatypes used in Hive are listed in Table 10.1.

TABLE 10.1   Hive Simple Datatypes

Datatype	Category	Description
TINYINT	Numeric	1-byte signed integer (−128 to 127)
SMALLINT	Numeric	2-byte signed integer (−32,768 to 32,767)
INT	Numeric	4-byte signed integer
BIGINT	Numeric	8-byte signed integer
FLOAT	Numeric	4-byte single precision floating point
DOUBLE	Numeric	8-byte double precision floating point
DECIMAL(p,s)	Numeric	User definable precision and scale
TIMESTAMP	Date/Time	Unix timestamp
DATE	Date/Time	Date (formatted as YYYY-MM-DD)
STRING	String	Character sequence (variable length)
VARCHAR	String	Character sequence (variable length)
CHAR(n)	String	Character sequence (fixed length)
BOOLEAN	Misc	True or False
BINARY	Misc	Raw binary data

There are complex (or nested) datatypes in Hive as well, which I will discuss in the next hour.

A typical Hive DDL statement used to create a table in Hive is shown in Listing 10.8.

LISTING 10.8   CREATE TABLE **Statement**

```
hive> CREATE TABLE stations
> (
> station_id INT,
> name STRING,
> lat DOUBLE,
> long DOUBLE,
> dockcount INT,
> landmark STRING,
> installation STRING
> )
> ROW FORMAT DELIMITED
> FIELDS TERMINATED BY ','
> STORED AS TEXTFILE;
```

The CREATE TABLE statement in Listing 10.8 did not include an EXTERNAL directive, which you will use in the Try it Yourself exercise later in this hour, or a LOCATION directive. As such, the table is simply a reference to an empty directory created in Hive's internal warehouse directory (/user/hive/warehouse).

Hive supplies a useful DESCRIBE statement that can be used for showing the schema of Hive tables. An example DESCRIBE statement and its output are provided in Listing 10.9.

LISTING 10.9   DESCRIBE **Statement**

```
hive> DESCRIBE stations;
OK
station_id              int
name                    string
lat                     double
long                    double
dockcount               int
landmark                string
installation            string
Time taken: 0.035 seconds, Fetched: 7 row(s)
```

There is also an alternative DESCRIBE FORMATTED command that provides additional information, such as the physical location of the data in HDFS and other metadata about the object.

Internal Tables versus External Tables in Hive

When you create tables in Hive, the default option is to create a Hive "internal" table. Directories for internal tables are managed by Hive, and a DROP TABLE statement for an internal table will delete the corresponding files from HDFS. It is typically recommended to use external tables by specifying the keyword EXTERNAL in the CREATE TABLE statement. This provides the schema and location for the object in HDFS, but a DROP TABLE operation does not delete the directory and files.

Input/Output Formats and SerDes in Hive

Hive uses an InputFormat and a **SerDe** (short for Serializer/Deserializer) to determine how to read input files and extract records for processing.

The InputFormat is specified using the STORED AS directive in the CREATE TABLE statement. In Listing 10.8, STORED AS TEXTFILE was specified, which in turn corresponds to the TextInputFormat. The TextInputFormat is the same InputFormat used in our MapReduce examples and is used for all text files in Hive.

Similarly, other supported STORED AS directives included in the Hive CREATE TABLE DDL syntax are as follows:

▶ SEQUENCEFILE

▶ ORC

▶ PARQUET

▶ AVRO

Avro and SequenceFile are pre-serialized, self-describing file formats, while ORC and Parquet are optimized columnar formats, which I will discuss further in **Hour 12, "Using SQL-on-Hadoop Solutions."**

These directives map to their associated InputFormat classes in Hive to support the associated filetype.

The default SerDe used by Hive is the LazySimpleSerDe. This SerDe expects the file to be delimited by a character (printable or non-printable). The FIELDS TERMINATED BY clause is used to specify a delimiter. If this is not present, the delimiter defaults to Ctrl-A, which is a non-printable control character.

Other SerDes are available, such as the RegexSerDe, which is useful for describing the schema for fixed-width data, a common extract format from many legacy systems. Alternative SerDes to the LazySimpleSerDe are specified using the ROW FORMAT SERDE directive in the Hive CREATE TABLE statement.

Similarly to MapReduce and Pig, Hive uses an OutputFormat to specify how to write data out as a result of a Hive query. The default OutputFormat for Hive is the `HiveIgnoreKeyTextOutputFormat`. This OutputFormat class is used to write data out to text files in Hadoop. Alternative OutputFormats are available for ORC, Parquet, Avro, SequenceFiles, and more.

Loading Data into Hive

Data can be loaded into tables in one of the following ways:

▶ Simply put, move, or copy the file(s) into the HDFS directory for the table object

▶ Use the Hive `LOAD DATA INPATH` command for data that exists in HDFS, which uses an underlying HDFS move function

▶ Use the Hive `LOAD DATA LOCAL INPATH` command for data that does not exist in HDFS, which uses an underlying HDFS put function

An example of the `LOAD DATA INPATH` command is provided in Listing 10.10.

LISTING 10.10   LOAD **Statement**

```
hive> LOAD DATA INPATH '/bikeshare/stations' INTO TABLE stations;
```

With any load operation you can add the `OVERWRITE` directive to replace the existing directory contents with new data as desired. This is shown in Listing 10.11.

LISTING 10.11   OVERWRITE **Option**

```
hive> LOAD DATA INPATH '/bikeshare/stations'
> OVERWRITE INTO TABLE stations;
```

Hive also supports the loading (or materializing) of data during the table creation process using a `CREATE TABLE AS SELECT` (or CTAS) operation. An example of this is provided in Listing 10.12.

LISTING 10.12   CREATE TABLE AS SELECT

```
hive> CREATE TABLE stations_copy AS
> SELECT * FROM stations;
```

Sqoop, the project discussed in **Hour 5, "Getting Data into Hadoop,"** also has built-in support for loading data into a Hive table using the `--hive-import` option. This option will create the table in Hive if it does not already exist and load the data from the source database into the corresponding directory in HDFS.

Analyzing Data with Hive

The Hive Query Language (HiveQL) is based on the SQL-92 specification, with some additional Hive-specific functions and some limitations due to the inherent immutable properties of HDFS.

Hive keywords such as SELECT and CREATE are not case sensitive, but are usually capitalized by convention (as was the case with Pig). HiveQL statements can span multiple lines and are terminated by a semicolon. Single line comments are supported using the double hyphen (--). Typical SQL semantics such as column lists and WHERE clauses are fully supported in Hive.

An example SELECT statement in Hive is shown in Listing 10.13.

LISTING 10.13   SELECT **Statement**

```
-- this is a comment
hive> SELECT name, lat, long
> FROM stations
> WHERE landmark = 'San Jose';
```

Using Hive's Built-in Functions

Hive includes numerous built-in functions to perform common mathematical operations such as ROUND, CEIL, FLOOR, RAND, and so on, as well as string and date manipulation such as SUBSTRING, LOWER, UPPER, RTRIM, LTRIM, CONCAT, TO_DATE, DAY, MONTH, YEAR, and so on. Many of these functions are identical to their counterparts available in the SQL dialects in most popular RDBMS.

TIP

Writing Hive UDFs

If you can't find a function that performs the operation you require, you can always write your own. Hive UDFs can be written in Java. More information on writing Hive UDFs is available at https://hive.apache.org.

An example of invoking a Hive built-in function is shown in Listing 10.14.

LISTING 10.14   Hive Built-in Functions

```
hive> SELECT LOWER(name) FROM stations;
```

You can also use the DESCRIBE command to show help and usage for the function as shown in Listing 10.15.

LISTING 10.15   DESCRIBE FUNCTION **Statement**

```
hive> DESCRIBE FUNCTION RAND;
OK
RAND([seed]) - Returns a pseudorandom number between 0 and 1
Time taken: 0.013 seconds, Fetched: 1 row(s)
```

Grouping and Aggregating Data with Hive

HiveQL provides semantics for grouping and aggregating data that would be familiar to most SQL analysts or developers. An example of this is provided in Listing 10.16.

LISTING 10.16   Grouping and Aggregating Data in Hive

```
hive> SELECT landmark, COUNT(*) FROM stations
> GROUP BY landmark;
OK
Mountain View    7
Palo Alto        5
Redwood City     7
San Francisco    35
San Jose         16
Time taken: 19.443 seconds, Fetched: 5 row(s)
```

Joining Data using Hive

Joins in Hive work synonymously with their counterparts in standard SQL dialects, including the assignment of table aliases to de-reference columns in a joined dataset. An example JOIN operation is shown in Listing 10.17.

LISTING 10.17   JOIN **Statement**

```
hive> SELECT t.trip_id
> ,t.duration
> ,t.start_date
> ,s.name
> FROM
> stations s
> JOIN trips t ON s.station_id = t.start_terminal;
```

Hive supports all of the common join types, INNER JOIN (default), LEFT OUTER JOIN, RIGHT OUTER JOIN and FULL OUTER JOIN. Only equality join conditions are supported with Hive; for instance, an ON condition such as s.station_id <> t.start_terminal is not supported in a Hive JOIN statement.

Hive also supports the CROSS JOIN operation, but as with the CROSS operator in Pig that I discussed in the last hour, use this operation with caution, as it could generate massive amounts of data.

In addition to the typical join types, Hive also supports the LEFT SEMI JOIN. The LEFT SEMI JOIN operation is useful where you would typically use an IN clause with a subquery in some SQL dialects. The use of IN or EXISTS clauses with subqueries is not supported in Hive, so the LEFT SEMI JOIN serves as a practical workaround. An example of this is provided in Listing 10.18.

LISTING 10.18　LEFT SEMI JOIN **Statement**

```
hive> SELECT t.trip_id
> ,t.duration
> ,t.start_date
> FROM trips t LEFT SEMI JOIN stations s
> ON (s.station_id = t.start_terminal AND s.landmark = 'San Jose');
```

TRY IT YOURSELF ▼

Getting Started with Apache Hive

In this exercise, we will install and configure Hive on your pseudo-distributed Hadoop cluster using the default embedded Derby database. You will then use this local instance of Hive to create some Hive tables, load the tables with data, and then run some simple HiveQL queries.

1. Download the Bike Share *stations* and *trips* datasets from the book's download site if you have not done so already in a previous exercise:

   ```
   $ wget https://s3.amazonaws.com/sty-hadoop/bike-share/stations/stations.csv
   $ wget https://s3.amazonaws.com/sty-hadoop/bike-share/trips/trips.csv
   ```

2. Make directories in HDFS and upload both datasets:

   ```
   $ sudo -u hdfs hadoop fs -mkdir -p /bikeshare/stations
   $ sudo -u hdfs hadoop fs -chmod 777 /bikeshare/stations
   $ hadoop fs -put stations.csv /bikeshare/stations
   $ hadoop fs -mkdir -p /bikeshare/trips
   $ hadoop fs -put trips.csv /bikeshare/trips
   ```

3. Download the latest release of Hive from the Hive Apache downloads page (https://hive.apache.org/downloads.html). Download the *bin* package. In this case we will download release 2.1.0.

4. Unpack the release:

   ```
   $ tar -xzvf apache-hive-2.1.0-bin.tar.gz
   ```

5. Create a HIVE_HOME environment variable:

```
$ cd apache-hive-2.1.0-bin
$ export HIVE_HOME=`pwd`
```

You may wish to set this permanently using the `/etc/profile.d/hadoop.sh` script we created in a previous exercise. You may also wish to add the Hive bin directory to your system path as well (although this is not mandatory):

```
$ export PATH=$HIVE_HOME/bin:$PATH
```

6. Make directories in HDFS for use by Hive, including the Hive warehouse directory:

```
$ sudo -u hdfs hadoop fs -mkdir /tmp
$ sudo -u hdfs hadoop fs -mkdir -p /user/hive/warehouse
$ sudo -u hdfs hadoop fs -chmod g+w /tmp
$ sudo -u hdfs hadoop fs -chmod g+w /user/hive/warehouse
```

7. Initialize a new Hive metastore using a local Derby embedded database:

```
$HIVE_HOME/bin/schematool -dbType derby -initSchema
```

For Hive production installations, you should use a shared metastore such as MySQL or PostgreSQL. In either case you would use the same `schematool` connecting to your target database to create the Hive metastore objects.

8. Open a Hive CLI session:

```
$HIVE_HOME/bin/hive
```

9. Create a new database called *bikeshare*:

```
CREATE DATABASE bikeshare;
```

10. List the Hive databases available on your system:

```
SHOW DATABASES;
```

You should see the *bikeshare* database you just created along with the *default* database.

11. Change your database context to the *bikeshare* database:

```
USE bikeshare;
```

12. Create a table for the *stations* dataset:

```
CREATE EXTERNAL TABLE stations
 (
station_id INT,
name STRING,
lat DOUBLE,
```

```
long DOUBLE,
dockcount INT,
landmark STRING,
installation STRING
)
ROW FORMAT DELIMITED
FIELDS TERMINATED BY ',' 
STORED AS TEXTFILE
LOCATION 'hdfs:///bikeshare/stations';
```

13. Create a table for the *trips* dataset:

```
CREATE EXTERNAL TABLE trips
 (
trip_id INT,
duration INT,
start_date STRING,
start_station STRING,
start_terminal INT,
end_date STRING,
end_station STRING,
end_terminal INT,
bike_num INT,
subscription_type STRING,
zip_code STRING
)
ROW FORMAT DELIMITED
FIELDS TERMINATED BY ',' 
STORED AS TEXTFILE
LOCATION 'hdfs:///bikeshare/trips';
```

14. List the tables in the *bikeshare* database:

```
SHOW TABLES;
```

You should see the *stations* and *trips* tables you just created. Try the DESCRIBE and DESCRIBE FORMATTED commands for each of the tables as well.

15. Run a query to count the number of trips by each start terminal:

```
SELECT start_terminal
,start_station
,COUNT(1) AS count
FROM trips
GROUP BY
start_terminal, start_station
ORDER BY count
DESC LIMIT 10;
```

16. Run a query to join the *stations* and *trips* datasets:

```
SELECT t.trip_id
,t.duration
,t.start_date
,s.name
,s.lat
,s.long
,s.landmark
FROM
stations s
JOIN trips t ON s.station_id = t.start_terminal
LIMIT 10;
```

You now have a basic Hive installation up and running with a local metastore and the default configuration. To make configuration changes to your installation you would need to copy the `hive-default.xml.template` located in the `$HIVE_HOME/conf` directory to a new file named `hive-site.xml` in the same directory. You would then make any necessary configuration changes to the `hive-site.xml` file.

Data Output with Hive

Thus far we have seen the use of the `SELECT` statement to execute HiveQL queries. The `SELECT` statement in Hive sends the query results back to the Hive client, in much the same way a query tool such as SQLPlus or SQL Server Query Analyzer would. Oftentimes, as part of an ETL workflow, for example, you need to persist the output of a query to a local or distributed filesystem—specifically HDFS.

Hive supports several methods to accomplish this, including the following:

▶ `INSERT OVERWRITE`, which will send the query results to another Hive table (a directory in HDFS), overwriting the existing contents

▶ `INSERT INTO TABLE`, which will send the query results to another Hive table, appending the output to the existing table (directory) contents

▶ `INSERT OVERWRITE DIRECTORY`, which will save the results to a directory in HDFS which may or may not be assigned to a Hive table

▶ `INSERT OVERWRITE LOCAL DIRECTORY`, which will save the results to a local directory, not to HDFS

Examples of using the various `INSERT` commands to output query results are provided in Listing 10.19.

LISTING 10.19   INSERT **Statement**

```
hive> INSERT INTO TABLE trips_counts
> SELECT start_terminal
> , start_station
> , COUNT(*) AS count
> FROM trips
> GROUP BY
> start_terminal, start_station
> ORDER BY count
> DESC LIMIT 10;
```

As discussed, Hive's default output format uses non-printable control characters for field delimiters. This is often not desirable for output to be used outside of Hive. You can control this behavior by creating an output Hive table with your preferred delimiter, for instance, comma or tab delimited, and then use INSERT OVERWRITE or INSERT INTO TABLE to store your query output into the desired format.

Summary

In this hour I introduced Apache Hive, a Hadoop ecosystem project designed to enable fast and simple access to data in HDFS using a familiar SQL-like programming interface. You learned how Hive works internally, including how the metastore stores object definitions for Hive tables—which are metaphors for directories in HDFS. You also learned how to create and access Hive tables using both Hive DDL and DML statements. Detailed documentation on the HiveQL is available at https://hive.apache.org.

In the next hour we look at more advanced programming and text analysis using Hive. However, many of the concepts covered in this hour will be leveraged throughout the book, especially when I discuss the "SQL on Hadoop" landscape and provide an introduction to Apache Spark, and specifically SparkSQL.

Q&A

Q. **What is the role of the Hive metastore? What are the implementation options for the Hive metastore?**

A. The Hive metastore is the repository used to store and manage the metadata in Hive which defines objects (tables) and associates these objects with directories in HDFS. The metastore is written to by clients creating objects (for instance, using DDL commands such as CREATE TABLE) and is read from by clients running Hive queries using DML commands such as SELECT statements. The Hive metastore can be deployed using the default embedded Derby database, which is only available to the local user, or using a shared metastore on a multi-user database system such as PostgreSQL or MySQL. The shared metastore is generally preferred for most implementations as object definitions can be shared among teams or groups of developers or analysts.

Q. What are the various ways Hive can be accessed by clients?

A. Hive can be accessed using the command-line interface (CLI) as a client application. Hive can also be deployed in server mode using the HiveServer2 project, which can then be accessed using a lightweight CLI called Beeline, or through a web interface such as HUE using the Beeswax interface. Deploying in server mode also enables access via JDBC, which is useful for using Hive with other tools, such as visualization tools.

Q. Explain Hive authorization. What are the shortcomings of using Hive authorization in isolation for securing data in Hive/HDFS?

A. Hive authorization involves applying privileges such as SELECT, DROP, etc. to objects within Hive to users, groups or roles. These privileges are assessed along with the underlying object ACLs (HDFS permissions) to allow or disallow access to Hive objects. Hive authorization is weak in the absence of strong authentication. If you require a secure Hive/HDFS environment you need to implement authentication using Kerberos, along with authorization in Hive and HDFS.

Workshop

The workshop contains quiz questions and exercises to help you solidify your understanding of the material covered. Try to answer all questions before looking at the "Answers" section that follows.

Quiz

1. **True or False.** If you use a DROP TABLE statement against an internal Hive managed table, the underlying data in HDFS will not be deleted.

2. What is not a purpose for Hive databases?

   A. Authorization

   B. Authentication

   C. Organization

   D. Namespace Management

3. Which Hive command would be used to load data from files in an existing directory in HDFS?

   A. LOAD DATA LOCAL INPATH

   B. LOAD DATA INPATH

    C. `hadoop fs -put data.txt /data/mytable`

    D. `INSERT OVERWRITE DIRECTORY`

4. **True or False.** Hive only supports equality conditions in JOIN operations.

Answers

1. False. The data in HDFS will be deleted with a `DROP TABLE` statement unless you define the table as an `EXTERNAL TABLE`.

2. B.

3. B.

4. True.

HOUR 11
Using Advanced Hive

What You'll Learn in This Hour:

▶ Automating Hive

▶ Complex data types in Hive

▶ Text processing and analysis using Hive

▶ Partitioning and bucketing using Hive

In the last hour you were introduced to Hive, a project which enables SQL-like access to data stored in Hadoop. In this hour we take a deeper look at some of the advanced capabilities of Hive, including nested data storage and processing, partitioning, bucketing, and text analysis using Hive. You'll also learn about automating and optimizing Hive queries.

Automating Hive

Hive provides a well-known programming interface to help users quickly produce outputs, which can be transformation or analysis routines. Hive also supports query parameterization and runtime substitution, as well as support for custom external scripts—features which provide automation capabilities. Let's explore these capabilities now.

Parameterizing Hive Queries

Hive supports parameterization through variable substitution within HiveQL scripts. Hive variables, which are denoted by unescaped curly braces ({ }), are substituted with a variable's given value at runtime. An example of a Hive query containing a variable is shown in Listing 11.1.

LISTING 11.1 Parameterized HiveQL Query

```
hive> SELECT SUM(amt) FROM sales
> WHERE state = '{hiveconf:state}'
> GROUP BY state;
```

The value from the variable can be set in one of two ways:

▶ It could be set in the query or session using the SET command.

▶ It could be passed in on the command line when the script it executed.

An example of setting a variable in a Hive session (interactive or non-interactive) is shown in Listing 11.2.

LISTING 11.2 SET **Statement**

```
hive> SET state=NV;
```

An example of passing a variable's value in from the command line is shown in Listing 11.3.

LISTING 11.3 **Setting Hive Variable via the Command Line**

```
$ hive -hiveconf state=NV -f salesbystate.hql > nv_total.txt
```

Using Custom Scripts in Hive Queries

Similar to the STREAM operator in Pig or the MapReduce Streaming API, Hive allows you to use external scripts (that is, programs external to Hive) to perform transformation, manipulation, or calculations upon data processed within a Hive query. This is accomplished using the TRANSFORM operator in Hive.

Like the STREAM operator in Pig, the TRANSFORM operator in Hive is an abstraction for the MapReduce Streaming API. Data is passed to this API from Hive and results are returned back to the parent Hive process for output or for incorporation in further processing.

Scripts used to process data with the TRANSFORM operator can be written in any language. The external program receives each record as a line of text on standard input (STDIN). The program performs its transformations or functions and returns a tab-delimited, new line-terminated output record on standard output (STDOUT). The output fields can be named and assigned datatypes to be used in further processing.

An example custom transformation script written in Python is shown in Listing 11.4.

LISTING 11.4 **Custom Transform Script Written in Python**

```
#!/usr/bin/env python

import sys

while True:
    line = sys.stdin.readline()
```

```
if not line:
   break
sales = int(line)
commission = sales * .1
print(str(commission))
```

To use your custom script, you first need to add the file to your program using the `ADD FILE` statement. This will add the file to the DistributedCache discussed in **Hour 7, "Programming MapReduce Applications."** Once the file is added you can reference the script using the `TRANSFORM` operator as show in Listing 11.5.

LISTING 11.5   `ADD FILE` and `TRANSFORM` **Statements**

```
hive> ADD FILE commissions.py;
hive> SELECT salesrepid, amt, TRANSFORM(amt)
> USING 'commissions.py' AS commission
> FROM sales;
```

NOTE

Using External Scripts May Degrade Performance

Just as with the Streaming API in MapReduce and the `STREAM` operator in Pig, the `TRANSFORM` operator should be used with careful consideration, as it can fork excessive processes and degrade performance. You should always weigh the impacts of using this approach against the effort required to write a UDF in Java, to determine which would be more efficient.

Complex Datatypes in Hive

In the previous hour you learned about the simple datatypes in Hive that represent primitive datatypes such as `INT` and `FLOAT`. Hive also provides support for complex or nested datatypes, which are useful for multi-stage or iterative processing. Many complex data objects occur synthetically, as a result of a function; for instance, a text processing function that returns a list of words. However, we also find complex structures occurring naturally more often because of the proliferation of web services, APIs, XML, JSON, and other semi-structured data sources.

ARRAY **Datatype**

An `ARRAY` datatype is used to store an ordered list of elements, all of the same datatype; for instance, an ordered list of strings or an ordered list of integers. Arrays are a common programming construct, often referred to as lists or sequences in different programming languages. They are especially useful for capturing sequences of events or for decomposing text as we will do in the next section.

ARRAY columns are defined in a Hive CREATE TABLE statement using angle brackets (<>) to define the datatype of elements in the list. Creating a table with an ARRAY column is demonstrated in Listing 11.6.

LISTING 11.6 ARRAY **Datatype**

```
hive> CREATE TABLE customers (
    > id INT,
    > fname STRING,
    > lname STRING,
    > email STRING,
    > orderids ARRAY<INT>)
    > ROW FORMAT DELIMITED
    > FIELDS TERMINATED BY '|'
    > COLLECTION ITEMS TERMINATED BY ','
    > ;
```

The COLLECTION ITEMS TERMINATED BY clause determines the delimiter used for reading or deriving elements in the collection. The default delimiter for collection items is Ctrl-B, a non-printable control character. If this is specified, the terminator should be different than the terminator used for fields in the table.

There are several functions which can be used to create ARRAY objects in Hive. One such function is the array() function, which converts input arguments into ARRAY elements. The array() function is demonstrated in Listing 11.7.

LISTING 11.7 array() **Function**

```
hive> SELECT array(1,2,3,4,5);
[1,2,3,4,5]
```

Given an ARRAY column in a Hive table, the column can be returned as a complete list, or individual elements can be returned by referencing the element's position (as a zero-based index). Some examples showing how to access ARRAY column data are provided in Listing 11.8.

LISTING 11.8 Selecting ARRAY **Elements**

```
hive> SELECT orderids[0] FROM customers;
1
```

STRUCT **Datatype**

The STRUCT datatype in Hive consists of named fields that could be of the same or different datatypes. Each STRUCT attribute is defined with its associated datatype denoted by angle brackets , similarly to the ARRAY datatype. An example CREATE TABLE statement, including a column with the STRUCT datatype, is provided in Listing 11.9.

LISTING 11.9   STRUCT **Datatype**

```
hive> CREATE TABLE customers (
    > id INT,
    > fname STRING,
    > lname STRING,
    > email STRING,
    > orderids ARRAY<INT>,
    > email_preferences STRUCT<opcomms:boolean, promos:boolean>)
    > ROW FORMAT DELIMITED
    > FIELDS TERMINATED BY '|'
    > COLLECTION ITEMS TERMINATED BY ','
    > ;
```

As with the ARRAY type, the COLLECTION ITEMS TERMINATED BY clause is used to derive different elements in the STRUCT. As with the ARRAY, this terminator should not appear naturally in the data itself, and should be different from the terminator used for fields in the table.

The STRUCT type is conceptually very similar to the tuple type you learned about in our coverage of Pig. Similar constructs exist in many other languages as well, such as Python. To access elements in the STRUCT in a Hive SELECT statement, you need to supply the column name and field name separated by a period. An example of this is provided in Listing 11.10.

LISTING 11.10   **Selecting** STRUCT **Elements**

```
hive> SELECT email_preferences.opcomms FROM customers;
TRUE
```

MAP **Datatype**

The MAP datatype is used to represent key value pairs or name value pairs with datatypes for the key and value. Maps commonly occur in semi-structured data sources such as JSON and have programmatic equivalents in most languages; for example, dictionaries in Python or hashes in Ruby.

Listing 11.11 demonstrates how to create a table with a column of the MAP datatype.

LISTING 11.11 MAP **Datatype**

```
hive> CREATE TABLE customers (
    > id INT,
    > fname STRING,
    > lname STRING,
    > email STRING,
    > orderids ARRAY<INT>,
    > email_preferences STRUCT<opcomms:boolean, promos:boolean>,
    > address_map MAP<STRING, STRING>)
    > ROW FORMAT DELIMITED
    > FIELDS TERMINATED BY '|'
    > COLLECTION ITEMS TERMINATED BY ','
    > MAP KEYS TERMINATED BY ':';
```

Note that as well as the aforementioned COLLECTION ITEMS TERMINATED BY clause, MAP fields also include the MAP KEYS TERMINATED BY clause used to discern between the key and the value within each element of the MAP object. The default character used if this is not supplied is the Ctrl-C non-printable control character.

Elements in the MAP are accessed by their key using the syntax shown in Listing 11.12.

LISTING 11.12 Selecting MAP **Values**

```
hive> SELECT address_map['city'] FROM customers;
Hayward
```

Text Processing Using Hive

One of the lesser known features of Hive is its powerful built-in text mining, text processing, and text analysis functions. Let's look at some of these now.

Regular Expressions in Hive

Regular expressions (or Regex) are a common programming approach used to extract patterns in text. The purpose of this section is not to cover regular expressions themselves, as there are many other books, cheat sheets, and other resources dedicated to this topic. Instead we will focus on some of the specific functions that support regular expressions in Hive.

Extracting Data Using the Regex SerDe

You learned about the SerDe in the previous hour as a means to extract fields from records in a Hive table, or files in a HDFS directory. The RegEx SerDe can extract fields based on a regular expression.

This is particularly useful with some data sources such as log data or fixed-width data extracts, which are common in many legacy systems such as mid-range and mainframe systems. Consider a file containing the following records:

```
NAB"NATIONAL AUSTRALIA BANK LIMITED""Banks"
BHP"BHP BILLITON LIMITED""Materials"
WOW"WOOLWORTHS LIMITED""Food & Staples Retailing"
```

Listing 11.13 shows a Regex SerDe used to derive fields from the fixed width record.

LISTING 11.13   RegEx SerDe

```
hive> CREATE TABLE securities (
    > code STRING,
    > name STRING,
    > sector STRING)
    > ROW FORMAT SERDE 'org.apache.hadoop.hive.serde2.RegexSerDe'
    > WITH SERDEPROPERTIES ("input.regex" =
    > "(.{3})\"([^\"]*)\"\"([^\"]*)\"");
```

A `SELECT` statement from the table created in Listing 11.13 would return the data shown in Table 11.1.

TABLE 11.1   Table Contents

Code	Name	Sector
NAB	NATIONAL AUSTRALIA BANK LIMITED	Banks
BHP	BHP BILLITON LIMITED	Materials
WOW	WOOLWORTHS LIMITED	Food & Staples Retailing

`REGEXP_EXTRACT` Function

The `REGEXP_EXTRACT` function returns text from a string that matches the regular expression pattern provided. This function is useful for finding and returning a defined string within a larger body of text. An example of the `REGEXP_EXTRACT` function is shown in Listing 11.14.

LISTING 11.14   `REGEXP_EXTRACT` Function

```
hive> SELECT REGEXP_EXTRACT('foothebar', 'foo(.*?)(bar)', 2);
bar
```

REGEXP_REPLACE Function

The `REGEXP_REPLACE` function is used to replace a matched pattern in a body of text with another string. The `REGEXP_REPLACE` function is especially useful for text manipulation. An example of this function is provided in Listing 11.15.

LISTING 11.15   `REGEXP_REPLACE` Function

```
hive> SELECT REGEXP_REPLACE("foobar", "oo|ar", "");
fb
```

Text Processing Functions

Many of Hive's built-in text processing functions are considered table functions as they often return one of the nested or complex object types covered in the previous section. Let's discuss some of the key text functions now.

SPLIT Function

The SPLIT function takes a string and splits it by a delimiter or expression. The resultant output is an array of string elements. An example of the `SPLIT` function is shown in Listing 11.16.

LISTING 11.16   `SPLIT` Function

```
hive> SELECT SPLIT('1,2,3,4,5',',');
["1","2","3","4","5"]
```

EXPLODE Function

The `EXPLODE` function takes an input array and creates a record for each element. This is conceptually similar to the `FLATTEN` operator in Pig. Consider the array created from the `SPLIT` operation in Listing 11.16. Listing 11.17 shows an example using the `EXPLODE` function to flatten this array into individual records.

LISTING 11.17   `EXPLODE` Function

```
hive> SELECT EXPLODE(SPLIT('1,2,3,4,5',','));
1
2
3
4
5
```

LATERAL VIEW **Clause**

The LATERAL VIEW clause is used on the output of a table-generating function such as EXPLODE to join the results of the table function to a given base table. An example of the LATERAL VIEW clause operating on an EXPLODE function is shown in Listing 11.18.

LISTING 11.18   LATERAL VIEW **Clause**

```
hive> SELECT word FROM shakespeare
    > LATERAL VIEW EXPLODE(SPLIT(text, ' ')) exploded AS word;
A
MIDSUMMER-NIGHT'S
DREAM
. . .
```

POSEXPLODE **Function**

The POSEXPLODE function works similarly to the EXPLODE function but returns the element along with its position (or index) in the input array. An example of the POSEXPLODE function is given in Listing 11.19.

LISTING 11.19   POSEXPLODE **Function**

```
hive> SELECT POSEXPLODE(SPLIT('1,2,3,4,5',','));
0       1
1       2
2       3
3       4
4       5
```

Let's try some text processing in Hive.

TRY IT YOURSELF ▼

Text Processing in Hive

In this exercise, we will use some of the text processing functions discussed to perform word count in Hive using the *shakespeare* text used in the MapReduce and Pig exercises. You can use the pseudo-distributed cluster we deployed in Hour 3, or you can use a commercial or cloud instance for this exercise. You will need the *shakespeare* dataset in HDFS, however.

1. Create a table in Hive for the *shakespeare* dataset loaded into HDFS from previous exercises.

```
CREATE EXTERNAL TABLE shakespeare (
text STRING)
```

```
ROW FORMAT DELIMITED
FIELDS TERMINATED BY '\n'
STORED AS TEXTFILE
LOCATION '/user/<youruser>/shakespeare';
```

2. Run the following Hive query using the EXPLODE, SPLIT, and LATERAL VIEW functions to perform word count on the *shakespeare* data.

```
SELECT word, COUNT(*)
FROM shakespeare
LATERAL VIEW explode(split(text, ' ')) exploded as word
GROUP BY word;
```

3. CHALLENGE: Modify the query from **Step 2** to list the three most frequently occurring words.

Sentiment Analysis Using Hive

Much of the text analysis capability that is built in to Hive stems from its use at Facebook for sentiment analytics; that is, the measurement of emotions and opinions embodied in text or conversation. This is often a feature of social media analytics. There are several functions that were purpose-built to gauge sentiment in text. These include the SENTENCES, NGRAMS, and CONTEXT_NGRAMS functions, which we will cover now.

SENTENCES Function

The SENTENCES function takes an input string containing one or more sentences separated by periods or punctuation. The string is parsed into an output nested ARRAY type, where the outer array contains one inner array per sentence, and the inner array contains one element per word in the sentence. The SENTENCES function is often a precursor to further processing for sentiment analysis. Listing 11.20 demonstrates the use of the SENTENCES function.

LISTING 11.20 SENTENCES Function

```
hive> SELECT SENTENCES('Hello there! How are you?');
[["Hello","there"],["How","are","you"]]
```

NGRAMS Function

An *n-gram* is a combination of words or letters where *n* is the number of words in the sequence. *n*-grams can be used to identify combinations of words or letters that frequently appear together in a body of text. *n*-grams are a popular text processing approach to finding relevant words, concepts, trends, or sentiment in text as well as to assess item similarity, including document or text.

The NGRAMS function in Hive calculates *n*-grams from an input array of sentences (typically produced by the SENTENCES function) along with the value of *n*. The output of the NGRAMS function is a STRUCT type consisting of each *n*-gram, along with the estimated frequency at which the *n*-gram occurs in the text. Listing 11.21 demonstrates the use of the NGRAMS function.

LISTING 11.21 NGRAMS **Function**

```
-- review:
-- 'This Hadoop book is really helpful!
--   This Hadoop book helped me greatly!'
hive> SELECT EXPLODE(NGRAMS(SENTENCES(review), 2, 5));
{"ngram":["hadoop","book"],"estfrequency":2.0}
{"ngram":["this","hadoop"],"estfrequency":2.0}
{"ngram":["book","helped"],"estfrequency":1.0}
{"ngram":["helped","me"],"estfrequency":1.0}
{"ngram":["really","helpful"],"estfrequency":1.0}
```

TIP

Normalize Case When Analyzing Text

It is often recommended to normalize case in text before performing any text processing or analytics; for instance, converting strings to lowercase using the LOWER function. This will prevent the same word or token from being analyzed differently—for instance, the word "Hadoop" being treated differently than the word "hadoop."

CONTEXT_NGRAMS **Function**

Placing text in the context in which it is used is necessary in natural language processing and text analytics. Not considering context can lead to erroneous assertions or conclusions.

The CONTEXT_NGRAMS function is similar to the NGRAMS function, but filters for specific combinations of words. This is used to consider *n*-grams in the context in which they are used and, commonly, for sentiment analysis. It consists of an additional input parameter that supplies an array of words to find in the text, with NULL values used as placeholders for other words (for instance, stop words).

An example of the CONTEXT_NGRAMS function is provided in Listing 11.22.

LISTING 11.22 CONTEXT_NGRAMS **Function**

```
hive> SELECT EXPLODE(CONTEXT_NGRAMS(SENTENCES(review),
    > ARRAY("hadoop", "book", NULL, NULL, NULL), 4, 3));
{"ngram":["is","really","helpful"],"estfrequency":1.0}
{"ngram":["helped","me","greatly"],"estfrequency":1.0}
```

LEVENSHTEIN **Function**

The *Levenshtein distance* is named after Vladimir Levenshtein, a Russian scientist specializing in information theory. It is the distance between two strings in terms of the number of edits of single characters required to convert one word into another. The lower the Levenshtein distance, the more similar two words or strings are to one another. This technique is commonly used to find close matches or identify misspellings in text.

Hive includes the built-in function LEVENSHTEIN, which returns the Levenshtein distance between two strings. An example of the LEVENSHTEIN function is provided in Listing 11.23.

LISTING 11.23   LEVENSHTEIN **Function**

```
hive> SELECT LEVENSHTEIN('Jeffery', 'Jeffrey');
2
```

SOUNDEX **Function**

Soundex is an algorithm for classifying words by their pronunciation in the English language. This is especially useful for name matching as some names have different spelling permutations but phonetically sound the same (a homophone). The Soundex algorithm has been included in many popular relational database management platforms for several years, including SQL Server and Oracle. An example of the SOUNDEX function in Hive is shown in Listing 11.24.

LISTING 11.24   SOUNDEX **Function**

```
hive> SELECT SOUNDEX('Jeffrey');
J160
hive> SELECT SOUNDEX('Jeffery');
J160
```

Data Masking and Hashing Functions in Hive

Sensitive data includes personally identifiable information (PII) such as names, or Payment Card Industry Data Security Standard data (PCI DSS) such as credit card numbers. Working with this data often requires obfuscation methods to be used during processing. Hive provides several approaches to desensitizing or de-identifying data, which include the following:

▶ masking

▶ hashing

▶ encrypting

Of course you could always remove the fields using a column projection as well.

MASK **Function**

Masking is available from release 2.1.0 of Hive. Masking capabilities in Hive are implemented using the MASK function. The MASK function simply replaces uppercase letters with X, lowercase letters with x, and numbers with n. You can supply alternative characters to be used as well. Listing 11.25 demonstrates the use of the MASK function.

LISTING 11.25   MASK Function

```
hive> SELECT MASK('abcd-EFGH-8765-4321');
xxxx-XXXX-nnnn-nnnn
```

Hashing Functions

Hive provides several methods to calculate hashes or digests for a given string or binary field. Hashes are unique, deterministic values for a given input and are not easily reversible. Hashing functions in Hive include the MD5, SHA, SHA1, SHA2, and CRC32 functions. Listing 11.26 demonstrates hashing a column in Hive using the MD5 method.

LISTING 11.26   MD5 Function

```
hive> SELECT MD5('ABC');
902fbdd2b1df0c4f70b4a5d23525e932
```

More information about hashing techniques and the algorithms behind them is available at https://en.wikipedia.org/wiki/List_of_hash_functions.

Column Encryption Using Hive

Unlike hashing, encryption provides a reversible value for an encrypted column which can be retrieved using the secret key used to encrypt the value. Hive supports the AES_ENCRYPT and AES_DECRYPT built-in methods to encrypt and decrypt an input field using the AES (Advanced Encryption Standard) cryptographic standard.

An example of encrypting and decrypting a field in Hive using a secret key is shown in Listing 11.27.

LISTING 11.27   Encryption and Decryption in Hive

```
hive> SELECT BASE64(AES_ENCRYPT('ABC', '1234567890123456'));
y6Ss+zCYObpCbgfWfyNWTw==
hive> SELECT AES_DECRYPT(UNBASE64('y6Ss+zCYObpCbgfWfyNWTw==')
    > ,'1234567890123456');
ABC
```

URL and Web Log Parsing in Hive

Web log parsing is another foundational use case for Hadoop and Hive. As discussed previously, the RegEx SerDe is a popular method for providing a schema and analyzing web logs in Hive. An example of a RegEx SerDe used to analyse an Apache web log is shown in Listing 11.28.

LISTING 11.28 Web Log Schema using a RegEx SerDe

```
hive> CREATE TABLE access_log (
    > ip STRING,
    > time_local STRING,
    > method STRING,
    > uri STRING,
    > protocol STRING,
    > status STRING,
    > bytes_sent STRING,
    > referer STRING,
    > useragent STRING)
    > ROW FORMAT SERDE 'org.apache.hadoop.hive.contrib.serde2.RegexSerDe'
    > WITH SERDEPROPERTIES (
    > 'input.regex'=
    > '^(\\S+) \\S+ \\S+ \\[([^\\[]+)\\] "(\\w+) (\\S+) (\\S+)" (\\d+) (\\d+)
"([^"]+)" "([^"]+)".*'
    > );
```

URLs (or URIs) are a common component of web logs and often need to be decomposed into their discrete elements. Hive offers built-in functions for parsing URLs in web logs using the `PARSE_URL` and `PARSE_URL_TUPLE` functions.

Input arguments to the `PARSE_URL` function are the URL column and specific element required. The `PARSE_URL` function then parses the input URL and returns the requested element.

Listing 11.29 demonstrates the `PARSE_URL` function in Hive.

LISTING 11.29 `PARSE_URL` Function

```
hive> SELECT PARSE_URL('http://facebook.com/path1/p.php', 'HOST');
facebook.com
```

The `PARSE_URL_TUPLE` function is similar to the `PARSE_URL` function except that it can extract multiple elements from a given URL in one operation, returning the results as a tuple. Listing 11.30 demonstrates the `PARSE_URL_TUPLE` function.

LISTING 11.30 `PARSE_URL_TUPLE` **Function**

```
hive> SELECT PARSE_URL_TUPLE('http://facebook.com/p.php?k1=v1&k2=v2'
    > ,'QUERY:k1', 'QUERY:k2');
v1      v2
```

Optimizing and Managing Queries in Hive

Recall that unlike a traditional relational database platform, Hive does not have some of the built-in capabilities that optimize queries and data access such as indexes and statistics. Therefore, design optimizations you make up front can be invaluable in optimizing performance. One factor you can influence is how much data is read by a particular query. Hive offers two key approaches used to limit or restrict the amount of data that a query needs to read, each doing so in a different way for a different purpose. Let's discuss both approaches now.

Partitioning in Hive

Partitioning is used to divide data into subdirectories based upon one or more conditions that typically would be used in WHERE clauses for the table. This approach is typically used for coarse-grained date grouping (e.g., a date without the time component, month, or year). You can still run queries that span multiple partitions, however; for example, queries that do not include a WHERE clause on the partitioned column. Listing 11.31 shows a CREATE TABLE statement with a partitioned column.

LISTING 11.31 CREATE TABLE **with Partitioning**

```
hive> CREATE TABLE weblogs (
    > ip STRING,
    > time_local STRING,
    > method STRING,
    > uri STRING,
    > protocol STRING,
    > status STRING,
    > bytes_sent STRING,
    > referer STRING,
    > useragent STRING)
    > PARTITIONED BY (date STRING);
```

Figure 11.1 demonstrates how partitioning would work against the weblogs partitioned table created in Listing 11.31.

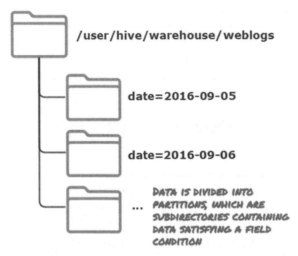

/user/hive/warehouse/weblogs

date=2016-09-05

date=2016-09-06

... DATA IS DIVIDED INTO PARTITIONS, WHICH ARE SUBDIRECTORIES CONTAINING DATA SATISFYING A FIELD CONDITION

FIGURE 11.1
Partitioning in Hive.

Note that the subdirectory created has the column name and value included. You can also create nested partitions.

Partitions can be added manually using the ALTER TABLE ADD PARTITION statement shown in Listing 11.32.

LISTING 11.32 ADD PARTITION **Statement**

```
hive> ALTER TABLE weblogs
    > ADD PARTITION (date='2016-09-05');
```

Conversely, partitions can be removed using the DROP PARTITION clause of an ALTER TABLE statement as shown in Listing 11.33.

LISTING 11.33 DROP PARTITION **Statement**

```
hive> ALTER TABLE weblogs
    > DROP PARTITION (date='2016-09-05');
```

You can use the SHOW PARTITIONS command to view the known partitions for any partitioned table in Hive as shown in Listing 11.34.

LISTING 11.34 SHOW PARTITIONS **Statement**

```
hive> SHOW PARTITIONS weblogs;
date=2016-09-05
date=2016-09-06
```

If you create subdirectories in HDFS without performing an ADD PARTITION operation, the data in these subdirectories will not be returned for any given SELECT statement on the table, including a SELECT statement with a WHERE clause referencing the manually created partition. An alternative solution when manually creating or removing partitions by adding or removing subdirectories of the table object in HDFS is to use the MSCK REPAIR TABLE command, which will find the newly created partitions in HDFS and update the metastore accordingly. An example of the MSCK REPAIR TABLE command is shown in Listing 11.35.

LISTING 11.35 MSCK REPAIR TABLE **Command**

```
hive> MSCK REPAIR TABLE weblogs;
```

CAUTION

Select Appropriate Columns for Partitioning

You should carefully consider the columns used for partitioning based upon the distribution and uniqueness of values in the table. Fields that are generally unique (such as ID columns or timestamps including milliseconds) should not be used as partition columns as they will create excess partitions. Instead, use columns that will typically appear in a WHERE clause and which have a known range of values, such as a month or year.

Bucketing in Hive

Bucketing is used to group items based upon a key hash and is an alternative method for subdividing data in a Hive table. Bucketing involves calculating a hash code for values inserted into bucketed (or clustered) columns. The hash code ranges are then assigned to one or a predefined number of buckets. An example CREATE TABLE statement with a bucketed column is provided in Listing 11.36.

LISTING 11.36 CREATE TABLE **with Bucketing**

```
hive> CREATE TABLE customers
    > (cust_id INT,
    > fname STRING,
    > lname STRING,
    > email STRING
    > )
    > CLUSTERED BY (cust_id) INTO 3 BUCKETS;
```

Partitioning creates subdirectories for each partition, whereas bucketing creates separate data files for each bucket as shown in Figure 11.2.

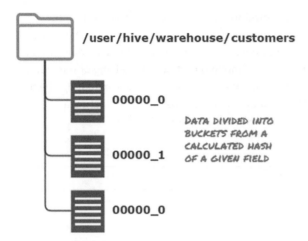

FIGURE 11.2
Bucketing in Hive.

Unlike partitioning, bucketing is desirable where you have largely unique values such as ID fields. Joins against two bucketed tables that are bucketed on the same column will be more efficient: the buckets can be joined to one another, as opposed to each record from each table having to be mapped against each other.

Furthermore, this approach is useful for random sampling, as each bucket will contain a known random percentage of the overall dataset. Sampling is accomplished using the using the TABLESAMPLE operator as shown in Listing 11.37.

LISTING 11.37   TABLESAMPLE **Operator**

```
hive> SELECT * FROM customers
    > TABLESAMPLE (BUCKET 1 OUT OF 3 ON cust_id);
```

NOTE

Enforcing Bucketing During INSERT **Operations**

Bucketing is not enforced by default when inserting data. To enable automatic bucketing, you need to set the hive.enforce.bucketing property to true in your hive-site.xml configuration file, or through the SET command in a Hive session. You should also consider changing the number of Reducers used in processing operations against the table to match the number of buckets in the table using the mapred.reduce.tasks property.

Understanding Query Execution in Hive

Hive queries are planned by the Hive query optimizer. To understand the query execution plan for any given query you can use the EXPLAIN command as shown in Listing 11.38.

LISTING 11.38 EXPLAIN **Statement**

```
hive> EXPLAIN SELECT method, COUNT(*) FROM weblogs GROUP BY method;
STAGE DEPENDENCIES:
Stage-1 is a root stage
Stage-0 depends on stages: Stage-1
STAGE PLANS:
Stage: Stage-1
Map Reduce
Map Operator Tree:
TableScan
alias: weblogs
...
```

Parallel Execution in Hive

Query execution, especially for more complex operations, is generally divided into stages. Stages may or may not have dependencies. If stages lack dependencies then they can be executed in parallel. However, this feature is not enabled by default. To enable parallel execution, set the hive.exec.parallel property to true in your hive-site.xml file.

Managing and Killing Hive Queries Control

Once you submit a query in Hive, the query will be executed asynchronously on the cluster. You cannot kill the query by simply pressing Ctrl-C, for example, as you may be able to on many conventional database platforms. Hive queries can be killed using the yarn command. Listing 11.39 demonstrates using the yarn command to list applications and then to kill a specific Hive query using its *application_id*.

LISTING 11.39 **Killing a Hive Query**

```
$ yarn application --list
Application-Id                 Application-Name      ...
application_1474361632170_0005  SELECT word, COUNT(*) ...
$ yarn application --kill application_1474361632170_0005
```

Running Hive in Local Mode

Hive can be run in local mode, similarly to the local execution mode in Pig or the LocalJobRunner execution mode in MapReduce. Local execution may be particularly useful for small jobs, where the overhead of cluster execution may be excessive. Local execution can be enforced using the SET command as shown in Listing 11.40.

LISTING 11.40 Local Execution in Hive

```
hive> SET mapreduce.framework.name=local;
...
Job running in-process (local Hadoop)
```

Hive can select local execution mode automatically using its own criteria. This is enabled by setting the hive.exec.mode.local.auto property to true, either by using a SET command in a Hive session or in your hive-site.xml file.

Summary

This hour completes our introductory tour of the Apache Hive project. In this hour you were introduced to profiling Hive queries using the EXPLAIN statement. You also learned how to parameterize queries and pass values to queries at runtime, and how to leverage custom scripts in your Hive queries using the TRANSFORM operator, enabling automation and reuse.

You learned about Hive's powerful text processing and analysis capabilities, which originate from its beginnings as a sentiment analysis tool at Facebook. These capabilities include the EXPLODE, SENTENCES, and NGRAMS functions among others. Hive's text (or unstructured data) processing functions often return complex datatypes or nested data structures such as the MAP, ARRAY, or STRUCT, each of which you learned about in this hour.

In this hour you also learned about the advanced capabilities of Hive, including its storage and processing optimization constructs, partitioning and bucketing. Partitioning is useful for reducing the scope of data which would otherwise need to be processed, whereas bucketing is useful for optimizing joins within Hive objects as well as randomly sampling data in Hive.

Hive and the Hive metastore ecosystem, which includes Spark and the SQL-on-Hadoop ecosystem projects we will cover next, are foundational components of the Hadoop landscape. The last two hours were only an introduction; I would strongly recommend that you familiarize yourself further with Hive beyond this book. The Hive project website and its associated Wiki are great resources to start with. These can be accessed from **https://hive.apache.org**.

Q&A

Q. **Explain the difference between partitioning and bucketing in Hive. When would you use each approach?**

A. Both partitioning and bucketing are used to subdivide the data in a Hive table, reducing the input scope of a Hive query and assisting in parallelization and query optimization. Partitioning is used to divide data into subdirectories based upon one or more conditions that would typically be used in `WHERE` clauses for the table. This approach is typically used for coarse-grained date grouping (e.g., a date without the time component, month, or year). Bucketing is used to group items based upon a key hash. This approach is useful for random sampling using the `TABLESAMPLE` operator, as well as optimizing joins bucketed on the same key.

Q. **What complex datatypes are available in Hive? Briefly explain each.**

A. Complex types in Hive include the `ARRAY`, which is an ordered list of values all of the same type; the `MAP`, which is a set of one or more key value pairs with defined key and value types; and the `STRUCT`, which is a set of named fields with defined datatypes.

Q. **Explain the `SENTENCES`, `NGRAMS`, and `CONTEXT_NGRAMS` functions in Hive. What are some typical usages for these functions?**

A. The `SENTENCES` function takes an input string containing one or more sentences separated by periods or punctuation. The string is parsed into an output nested `ARRAY` type, where the outer array contains one inner array per sentence, and the inner array contains one element per word in the sentence. An *n*-gram is a combination of words or letters where *n* is the number of words in the sequence. *n*-grams are a popular text processing approach to finding relevant words, concepts, or sentiment in text as well as to assessing item similarity, including document or text. The `NGRAMS` function in Hive calculates *n*-grams from an input array of sentences typically produced by the `SENTENCES` function, along with the value of *n*. The output of the `NGRAMS` function is a `STRUCT` type consisting of each *n*-gram along with the estimated frequency at which the *n*-gram occurs in the text.

Workshop

The workshop contains quiz questions and exercises to help you solidify your understanding of the material covered. Try to answer all questions before looking at the "Answers" section that follows.

Quiz

1. Given a Hive query with a parameter *state*, what is the correct way to reference this parameter as a variable in your HiveQL query?

2. Given the same Hive query and its parameter *state*, what is the correct way to pass this parameter to the query from the command line?

3. Suppose you have a partitioned table in Hive. You manually create a directory alongside the other directories containing partition data, but when you query the table, the new data is not present. Which of the following options can be used to rectify this issue? (choose two)

   A. `ALTER TABLE ... ADD PARTITION ...`

   B. `ADD PARTITION ...`

   C. `ALTER TABLE ... DROP PARTITION ...`

   D. `MSCK REPAIR TABLE ...`

4. The Hive complex datatype consisting of an ordered list of values, all of the same datatype, is called what?

Answers

1. `{hiveconf:state}`.

2. `-hiveconf state=<value>`

3. A and D.

4. An `ARRAY`

Using SQL-on-Hadoop Solutions

What You'll Learn in This Hour:

▶ Introduction to SQL-on-Hadoop

▶ Parquet and columnar storage in Hadoop

▶ Introduction to Impala, HAWQ, and Drill

▶ Introduction to Apache Tez and Apache Drill

In the last two hours you were introduced to Hive. As the Hadoop solution matured and experienced greater market uptake, the desire for and expectations of more MPP-like (Massively Parallel Processing) performance grew in the market. This demand paved the way for what is known as SQL-on-Hadoop solutions, which are a set of alternative processing frameworks to MapReduce that provide SQL or SQL-like access to data in HDFS.

What Is SQL on Hadoop?

Although the Hive project was instrumental in providing the pattern of SQL-like access to unstructured data in HDFS, performance and user experience fell well short of existing Relational Database Management Systems (RDBMS) and Massively Parallel Processing (MPP) database technology performance. The batch nature of MapReduce, which was the foundational processing engine behind Hive, was not suited to interactive queries or real-time applications.

In 2010, Google released a seminal whitepaper (yes, another one!) called "Dremel: Interactive Analysis of Web-Scale Datasets" outlining Google's approach to interactive SQL access to schema-on-read systems. This was a major catalyst for the SQL-on-Hadoop movement.

Pure-play Hadoop vendors including Cloudera, Hortonworks, MapR, and Pivotal all set off in different directions to develop the best mousetrap for delivering true interactive, RDBMS-like performance against data stored in HDFS. A performant, enterprise-grade SQL-on-Hadoop solution was seen as a key differentiator by each of the established vendors, and each made a significant investment in their chosen solution.

A brief summary of the SQL on Hadoop landscape immediately after the Dremel whitepaper is provided here:

▶ **Cloudera Impala**—Developed by Cloudera, Impala is written in C++ and is built to short-circuit many of the operations that normally interact with blocks in HDFS. Furthermore, Impala is a memory-intensive solution performing extensive caching of metadata and block locations. Impala was designed to share the metastore with Hive and be (mostly) compatible with HiveQL, but was a completely separate project from Apache Hive.

▶ **Apache Tez**—As Hortonworks' preferred solution for lower-latency SQL on Hadoop operations, Tez created and implemented a smarter DAG (Directed Acyclic Graph) scheduling framework to execute coarse-grained operations against data in HDFS. Tez, as an extension to the Apache Hive project, became an integrated execution engine for Hive, hot-swappable with MapReduce as an execution engine.

▶ **Pivotal HAWQ (now Apache HAWQ)**—HAWQ was built by Pivotal to enable federation of queries across HDFS and Greenplum, Pivotal's MPP database software solution built on top of PostgreSQL. HAWQ then developed into a full-fledged SQL-on-Hadoop solution, with a predominantly memory-centric architecture.

▶ **Apache Drill**—Adopted by MapR as their preferred approach to SQL on Hadoop, Apache Drill is an open source, low-latency query engine for Hadoop with the capability to use objects created with Hive.

Other SQL engines for Hadoop would follow later, including *Apache Presto*, Facebook's next-generation data warehousing solution, and *Apache Flink*, a generalized data–processing framework with a table API supporting relational-like access.

The common performance detractor addressed by all of the implementations was reducing or eliminating the need to write out intermediate data to disk, which was seen as a major shortcoming of the MapReduce architecture.

However, as the battle lines were being drawn and the Hadoop vendors were dueling each other with their respective solutions, another solution was quietly being developed that would alter the landscape of SQL-on-Hadoop as it was commonly understood. This solution was Shark and, ultimately, *Spark SQL* which I discuss in the next hour.

Columnar Storage in Hadoop

Columnar storage is defined by the process of organizing and storing objects by columns instead of organizing data by rows or records. This has a significant performance impact on many analytic access patterns, particularly the distributed access patterns implemented by many of the SQL-on-Hadoop solutions as well as Spark. Figure 12.1 shows the difference between columnar- and row-oriented data storage.

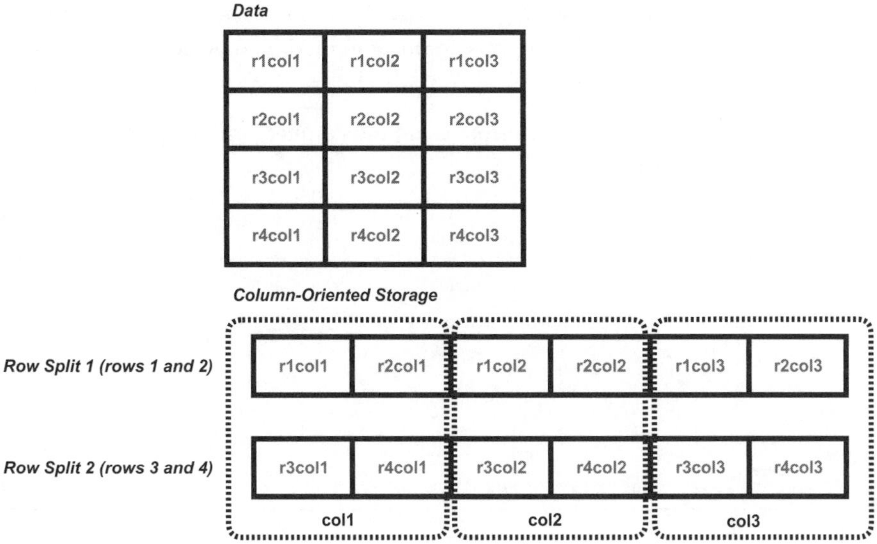

Data

FIGURE 12.1
Column-Oriented Storage.

Columnar or column-oriented storage is implemented in special file–based data storage formats including Parquet, ORC, Trevni, and others. Many of these format specifications were inspired by the encoding principles outlined in the Google Dremel whitepaper. Next, let's look at the most prolific columnar storage formats in use today.

Parquet Format

Apache Parquet was created as a joint project between Cloudera and Twitter to improve performance and make enhancements to the Trevni specification, a subproject of the Avro project which was founded by Doug Cutting, the forefather of Hadoop.

Parquet implements efficient compression and encoding schemes to provide efficient columnar data representation and deserialization savings, all of which contribute to a compact, performant data format suitable for interactive workloads and access patterns.

Compression in Parquet is available on a per-column level using the following lossless compression codecs (a portmanteau of coder-decoder):

► **Snappy**—Splittable compression library developed by Google

► **GZip**—Unsplittable common compression library

► **LZO**—Lempel–Ziv–Oberhumer specification for splittable compression

Platforms such as SQL-on-Hadoop platforms that access data in compressed Parquet format can operate on the compressed data without decompressing the data on disk, a potentially expensive operation.

An example of creating a table in the Hive metastore using the Parquet format with Snappy compression is shown in Listing 12.1.

LISTING 12.1   **Parquet Storage**

```
CREATE TABLE customers (
id INT,
fname STRING,
lname STRING,
email STRING,
phoneno STRING)
STORED AS PARQUET
TBLPROPERTIES ("parquet.compression"="SNAPPY");
```

The columnar storage in Parquet also keeps statistics about columns, such as aggregate calculations. This property, along with Parquet's use of compression and encoding, can greatly reduce the amount of data which needs to be read to execute a given query.

The Parquet format is supported (and included) on most major commercial distributions of Hadoop, as well as natively through the Spark project, which we will discuss in the next hour. More information on Parquet is available at **https://parquet.apache.org/**.

ORC Format

The Optimized Row Columnar file format (ORC) is the successor to the Record Columnar File format (RCFile) specification. The ORC format provides a highly efficient way to store data for access through SQL-on-Hadoop solutions such as Hive using Tez, a technology we will discuss later in this hour.

The ORC file format is a pre-serialized, compact file format, where the structure is self-contained with the data. Column-level aggregates such as count, min, max, and sum are stored with the data as statistics for further optimization.

Data stored in the ORC format is organized into stripes, which are optimized for HDFS read operations. ORC supports compression codecs including Snappy and Zlib. Figure 12.2 describes the ORC format.

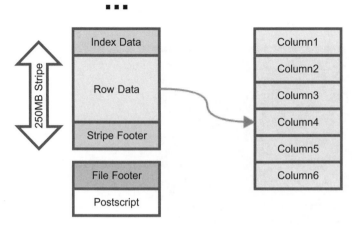

FIGURE 12.2
ORC File Format.

More information about the ORC File specification is available through the Hive project documentation, which can be found a **http://hive.apache.org/**.

Introduction to Impala

Cloudera Impala is an open source project licensed by Apache that implements a massively parallel SQL engine on a Hadoop cluster. The data queried can be stored in HDFS or HBase, a NoSQL platform which I discuss in **Hour 15, "Introducing NoSQL."**

Impala was inspired by the Google Dremel whitepaper and was designed to provide interactive, performant query access to data in Hadoop. Query times can be reduced by 5 to 20 times or more as compared to equivalent queries using Hive/MapReduce.

Impala uses the Hive metastore for its object definitions, and can share the metastore with an existing Hive deployment. Impala supports a subset of the HiveQL language specification, so most Hive queries can be executed verbatim using Impala. Impala can read and write from many of the common file formats used in Hadoop including text files, sequence files, and the columnar Parquet format discussed in the previous section. In fact, many performance benchmarks establish Parquet as the best performing file format to use with Impala.

Impala supports many common interfaces for running queries including the following:

▶ The Impala Shell (similar to the Hive CLI)

▶ The HUE Web-based UI, which I discuss in **Hour 14, "Using the Hadoop User Environment (HUE)"**

▶ ODBC/JDBC, which could be used to connect a visualization tool such as Tableau to an Impala cluster

Running a query using the Impala shell is demonstrated in Figure 12.3.

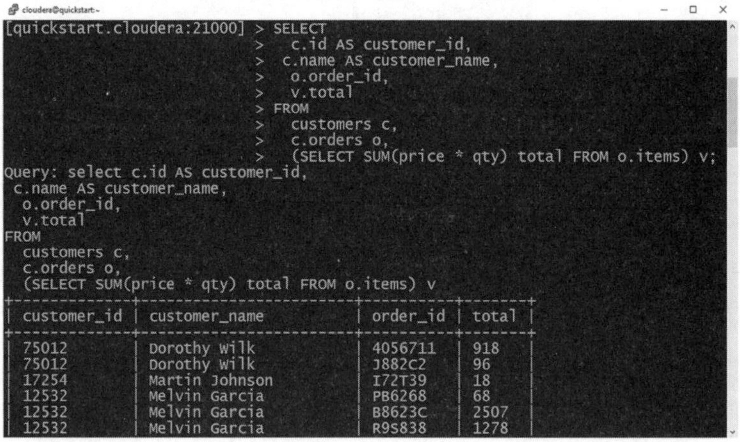

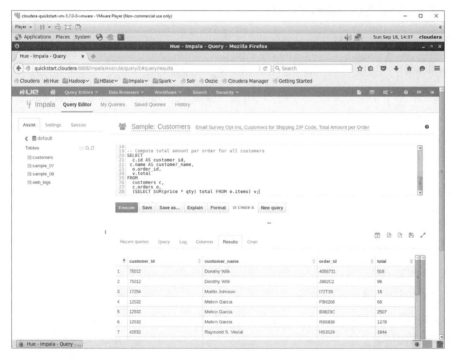

FIGURE 12.3
Impala Shell.

Running a query using the Impala query editor included in HUE is shown in Figure 12.4.

FIGURE 12.4
Querying Impala Using HUE.

One of the major enablers of Impala's performance gains is the fact that Impala does not use MapReduce as its processing engine. Instead, Impala implements its own cluster framework, distributing an Impala query across numerous Impala Server Daemons that are co-located with DataNodes in a Hadoop cluster. An additional daemon called the Impala StateStore daemon provides a lookup service for the Impala Server Daemons in the cluster. The topology of an Impala cluster running on Hadoop is shown in Figure 12.5.

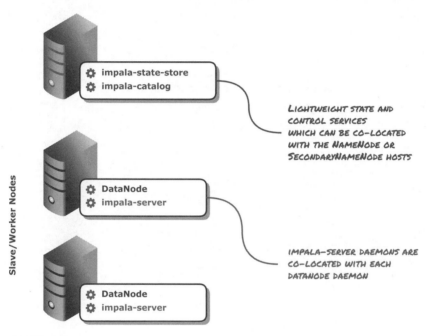

FIGURE 12.5
Impala Cluster.

Unlike many of the other Hadoop ecosystem projects that you will learn about which are written in Java and implemented in libraries compiled to Java bytecode, Impala is written almost entirely in C++ and is implemented in machine code. This method of implementation, along with many other optimizations, enables Impala to have more direct access to block data stored on slave node filesystems, and to have more efficient access to memory on these nodes as well.

Impala is well suited for ad hoc query access to data in Hadoop and can be especially useful for BI/visualization activities.

▼ TRY IT YOURSELF

Using Impala

For this exercise we will use an existing installation of Impala. You can get this by downloading the Cloudera Quickstart VM from http://www.cloudera.com/downloads.html.

1. Import the *shakespeare* dataset and create the *shakespeare* table as you did in the **Hour 11 Try it Yourself exercise.**

2. Launch an Impala shell:

   ```
   impala-shell
   ```

3. At the impala-shell prompt, issue a query to count the records in a table:

   ```
   > SELECT COUNT(*) FROM shakespeare;
   ```

   You should see the following results returned:

   ```
   +----------+
   | count(*) |
   +----------+
   | 129107   |
   +----------+
   ```

4. Try loading some additional datasets (such as comma-delimited datasets) into Hive and compare queries in Impala against their equivalent queries in Hive.

Introduction to Tez

The Apache Tez project is an application processing framework built on YARN to create complex Directed Acyclic Graphs (DAGs) to model, plan, and execute application workflows, such as the workflow required to execute a HiveQL query against data in HDFS. The Tez framework can be used with both Hive and Pig.

A generic DAG is pictured in Figure 12.6.

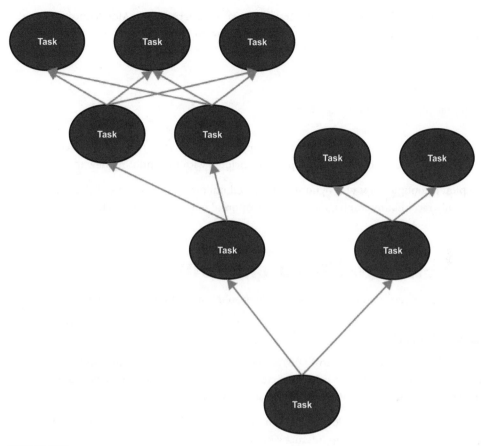

FIGURE 12.6
Apache Tez DAGs.

NOTE

About DAGs

A DAG is a mathematical construct that is commonly used in computer science to represent dataflows and their dependencies. DAGs contain vertices or nodes and edges. Vertices or nodes, in a dataflow context, are steps in the process flow. Edges in a DAG connect vertices to one another in a directed orientation in such a way that it is impossible to have circular references. I will revisit DAGs in the next hour when I discuss Spark.

While Tez itself is not a pure SQL-on-Hadoop solution, technically speaking, its premise of providing an alternative to MapReduce and the design goal to make SQL queries on Hadoop more interactive and performant are shared and closely aligned with the other SQL-on-Hadoop solutions outlined in this hour.

In addition to Tez's DAG-based processing framework as an alternative to MapReduce, Apache Tez's performance increases are also enabled by the following:

- ▶ Optimal resource management

- ▶ Plan reconfiguration at runtime

- ▶ Dynamic physical dataflow decisioning

One of the resource management optimizations employed by Tez is its reuse of YARN containers for task processing. This reduces the startup cost associated with instantiating new tasks.

Runtime plan reconfiguration and dynamic physical dataflow decisioning are Tez's ability to dynamically reconfigure graphs and determine optimal data movement methods during processing.

Introduction to HAWQ and Drill

HAWQ and Drill are two additional SQL-on-Hadoop solutions. Let's discuss these now.

Apache HAWQ

Apache HAWQ (originally Pivotal HAWQ) was Pivotal's solution for interactive MPP SQL processing on Hadoop. HAWQ was originally created as an extension to the Pivotal Greenplum solution, which is an enterprise MPP solution based on PostgreSQL.

HAWQ is able to read-and-write data in HDFS and supports both the Parquet and Avro data formats. HAWQ can also be used to interact with data in HBase.

HAWQ takes complex queries and decomposes them into smaller tasks that can be distributed across multiple segment instances located on slave nodes in the cluster. HAWQ can use YARN for its resource management framework and supports connectivity for external applications, such as visualization tools, through JDBC and ODBC interfaces.

At the time of writing, HAWQ is in Apache Software Foundation (ASF) incubation status. More information on HAWQ is available at **http://hawq.incubator.apache.org/**.

Apache Drill

Many of the other solutions discussed drew inspiration from the Google Dremel project, whereas Apache Drill is the direct open source implementation of Dremel. Google Dremel is available as a platform-as-a-service (PaaS) offering called Google BigQuery.

Like the other solutions discussed, Drill can also leverage the Hive metastore to query objects created in Hive using the Hive Storage Plugin. Drill leverages data locality and runtime, data-aware query optimization to deliver low-latency, interactive SQL access to data at scale.

Drill is a top-level ASF project that is available as a standalone solution and is also included in some Hadoop distributions, including the MapR offering. Drill supports multiple data sources, including distributed filesystems such as HDFS, object stores, and block stores, and NoSQL stores such as HBase and MongoDB. It also enables queries across disparate data sources. Figure 12.7 shows the Drill Web Console, which can be used to submit and monitor queries using Drill.

FIGURE 12.7
Drill Web Console.

More information about Apache Drill can be found at **https://drill.apache.org/**, and information about Google BigQuery is available at **https://cloud.google.com/bigquery/**.

Summary

In this hour you learned about the various SQL-on-Hadoop solutions available. SQL-on-Hadoop solutions and the traditional Hive interface both provide SQL-like access to data stored in HDFS. The difference, however, is that the SQL-on-Hadoop solutions do not use MapReduce. Instead, SQL-on-Hadoop solutions implement a custom processing framework designed to maximize the distributed storage and processing capabilities of Hadoop, while providing vastly greater performance than the Hive/MapReduce equivalent operation.

The SQL-on-Hadoop landscape includes many solutions, from Cloudera's Impala to Apache Tez and Apache Drill to more recent solutions such as Apache Presto.

SQL-on-Hadoop solutions typically make greater use of memory on slave nodes and perform caching, buffering, and statistics collection in a fashion similar to that of many of the traditional MPP or RDBMS platforms. Most of these solutions can still leverage the Hive metastore for object definitions, and in many cases will cache metastore definitions as well as HDFS block locations to minimize the number of recurring lookup operations.

Another common feature of SQL-on-Hadoop solutions is their support for (and bias towards) columnar-based storage formats such as Parquet. These formats are optimized for federated SQL access and can provide performance increases often measured in orders of magnitudes.

In the next hour, I will introduce Apache Spark, which includes its own SQL API, *Spark SQL,* which is widely predicted to further redefine the SQL-on-Hadoop landscape.

Q&A

Q. **What is the principal design goal of a SQL-on-Hadoop solution? What is the main commonality behind all of the SQL-on-Hadoop solutions?**

A. The principal design goal of any SQL-on-Hadoop solution modeled after the Google Dremel whitepaper and project is to deliver a high-performance, interactive, distributed SQL engine used to process data stored in HDFS. None of the SQL-on-Hadoop solutions use MapReduce, instead implementing their own custom cluster or processing framework.

Q. **What are some of the available SQL-on-Hadoop solutions and what commercial distributions or vendors are they associated with?**

A. The main SQL-on-Hadoop solutions include Impala, which was created by Cloudera and is included in the Cloudera application stack; Apache Tez, which is included in the Hortonworks Data Platform; Apache HAWQ (formerly Pivotal HAWQ), which is supported by Pivotal; and Apache Drill, which is included in MapR's Hadoop offering. Other SQL-on-Hadoop solutions such as Apache Presto and Apache Flink are emerging as well.

Q. **What are the performance advantages of using the Parquet columnar data storage format?**

A. The columnar storage in Parquet also keeps statistics about columns, such as aggregate calculations. This property, along with Parquet's use of compression and encoding, can greatly reduce the amount of data that needs to be read to execute a given query.

Workshop

The workshop contains quiz questions to help you solidify your understanding of the material covered. Try to answer all questions before looking at the "Answers" section that follows.

Quiz

1. Which Impala daemon responsible for query planning, distribution, and execution is co-located with the DataNodes on a Hadoop cluster?

2. Apache Tez is an application framework that creates a series of complex _____ for processing data.

3. **True or False**. Apache Drill can be used to join data from disparate data platforms such as joining data from MongoDB to data in Amazon S3.

4. **True or False**. The Apache Tez framework is designed to re-use YARN containers to reduce startup costs for new tasks.

Answers

1. impala-server.

2. DAGs.

3. True.

4. True

HOUR 13
Introducing Apache Spark

What You'll Learn in This Hour:

▶ Introduction to Spark

▶ Understanding the Spark application runtime and cluster architecture

▶ Introduction to RDDs

▶ Using transformations and actions in Spark

▶ Extensions to Spark (including Spark SQL and Spark Streaming)

In the previous hours I have discussed numerous programming interfaces and frameworks for processing data in Hadoop, but I have saved what is widely believed to be the best for last: Apache Spark. Spark was created as an alternative to MapReduce, to gain efficiencies measured in orders of magnitude. Spark also delivers unrivaled extensibility and is effectively a Swiss Army Knife for data processing in Hadoop, delivering SQL access, streaming data processing, graph and NoSQL processing, machine learning, and much more right out of the box.

This hour is only an introduction to Spark as there are entire books devoted to this topic alone, including Sams *Teach Yourself Apache Spark* (http://www.informit.com/store/apache-spark-in-24-hours-sams-teach-yourself-9780672338519).

Introducing Spark

Apache Spark is an open source distributed data processing project that was started in 2009 by Matei Zaharia at the University of California, Berkeley RAD Lab. As a top-level Apache Software Foundation project, Spark has more than 400 individual contributors and committers from companies such as Facebook, Yahoo!, Intel, Netflix, Databricks, and others.

Spark is written in Scala, which is built on top of the Java Virtual Machine (JVM) and Java runtime. This makes Spark a cross-platform application capable of running on Windows as well as Linux and is seen by many to be the future of data processing in Hadoop.

Spark enables developers to create complex, multi-stage data processing routines, providing a high-level API and fault-tolerant framework that lets programmers focus on logic rather than infrastructure or environmental issues, such as hardware failure.

Spark was founded as an alternative to using traditional MapReduce on Hadoop, which was deemed to be unsuited for interactive queries or real-time, low-latency applications. A major disadvantage of Hadoop's MapReduce implementation was its persistence of intermediate data to disk between the Map and Reduce processing phases.

As an alternative to MapReduce, Spark implements a distributed, fault tolerant, in-memory structure called a Resilient Distributed Dataset (RDD). Spark maximizes the use of memory across multiple machines, improving overall performance by orders of magnitude. Spark's reuse of these in-memory structures makes it well-suited to iterative, machine learning operations, as well as interactive queries.

What Sort of Applications Use Spark?

Spark supports a wide range of applications, including the following:

- ▶ Extract-transform-load (ETL) operations
- ▶ Predictive analytics and machine learning
- ▶ Data access operations (such as SQL queries and visualizations)
- ▶ Text mining and text processing
- ▶ Real-time event processing
- ▶ Graph applications
- ▶ Pattern recognition
- ▶ Recommendation engines

As of the time of this writing, more than 500 organizations are known to be using Spark in production, with some organizations running Spark on hundreds to thousands of cluster nodes against petabytes of data.

Spark's speed and versatility have been further complemented by the numerous extensions now included with Spark (including Spark SQL, Spark Streaming, and SparkR, to name a few).

Programming Interfaces to Spark

As mentioned previously, Spark itself is written in Scala. It runs in Java virtual machines (JVMs). Spark provides native support for programming interfaces including the following:

- ▶ Scala

- ▶ Python (using Python's functional programming operators)

- ▶ Java

- ▶ SQL

- ▶ R

Additionally, Spark includes extended support for Clojure and other languages.

Ways to Use Spark

Spark programs can be run interactively or submitted as batch jobs, including mini-batch and micro-batch jobs.

Interactive Use

Interactive programming shells are available in Python and Scala. The PySpark and Scala shells are shown in Figures 13.1 and 13.2, respectively.

FIGURE 13.1
PySpark Shell.

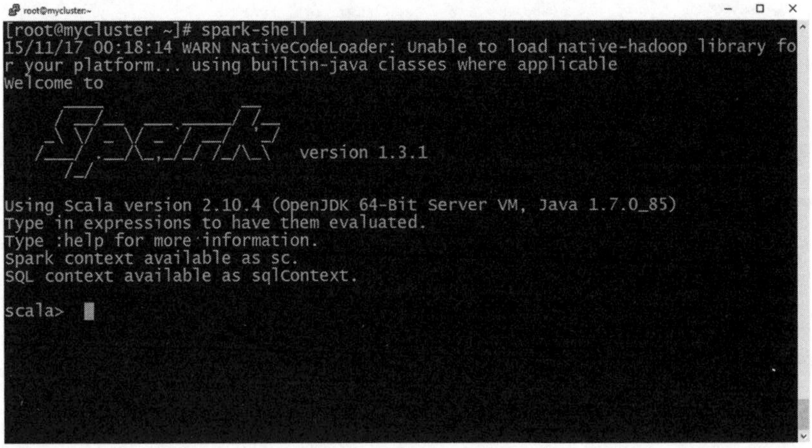

FIGURE 13.2
Scala Shell.

Interactive R and SQL shells are included with Spark as well.

Non-interactive Use

Non-interactive applications can be submitted using the `spark-submit` command, as shown in Listing 13.1.

LISTING 13.1   Submitting a Spark Application

```
$SPARK_HOME/bin/spark-submit \
--class org.apache.spark.examples.SparkPi \
--master yarn-cluster \
--num-executors 4 \
--driver-memory 10g \
--executor-memory 10g \
--executor-cores 1 \
lib/spark-examples*.jar 10
```

Input/Output Types

Although, in the majority of cases, Spark is used to process data in Hadoop, Spark can be used with a multitude of other source and target systems, including the following:

▶ Local or network filesystems

▶ Object storage such as Amazon S3 or Ceph

▶ Relational database systems

► NoSQL stores, including Apache Cassandra, HBase, and others

► Messaging systems such as Kafka

Spark Architecture

A Spark application contains several components, all of which exist whether you are running Spark on a single machine or across a cluster of hundreds or thousands of nodes.

Each component has a specific role in executing a Spark program. Some of these roles are passive during execution, such as the client components, and other roles are active in the execution of the program, such as components executing computation functions.

The components of a Spark application running on the YARN framework are the driver, the master (ApplicationMaster), the cluster manager (ResourceManager), and the executor(s), which run on slave nodes or workers. Figure 13.3 shows all of the Spark components for a running application.

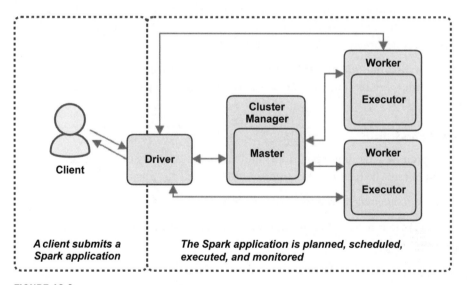

FIGURE 13.3
Spark Runtime Application Components.

All of the Spark components, including the driver, master, and executor processes, run in JVMs. The role of the YARN ResourceManager and ApplicationMaster were discussed in **Hour 6, "Understanding Data Processing in Hadoop,"** but let's discuss the Spark-specific components in more detail now.

Spark Driver

The life of a Spark application starts and finishes with the Spark driver. The Spark driver is the process clients use to submit applications in Spark. The driver is also responsible for planning and coordinating the execution of the Spark program and returning status and/or results (data) to the client.

The Spark Context

The Spark driver is responsible for creating the SparkContext. The SparkContext, which is referred to as `sc` in our Spark examples, is the application instance representing the connection to the Spark master and the Spark executors. The Spark Context is instantiated at the beginning of a Spark application (including the interactive shells) and is used for the entirety of the program.

Application Planning

One of the main functions of the driver is to plan the application. The driver takes the application processing input and plans the execution of the program. The driver takes all of the requested transformations (data manipulation operations) and actions (requests for output or a prompt to execute the program) and creates a DAG similar to the graphs discussed in the previous hour when you learned about Tez and Drill.

The DAG consists of tasks and stages. Tasks are the smallest unit of schedulable work in a Spark program. Stages are sets of tasks that can be run together. Stages are dependent upon one another.

Application Scheduling

The driver also coordinates the running of stages and tasks defined in the DAG. Key driver activities involved in the scheduling and running of tasks include the following:

- ▶ Keeping track of available resources to execute tasks

- ▶ Scheduling tasks to run "close" to the data where possible, which is the data locality concept central to Hadoop

- ▶ Coordinating the location and movement of data between processing stages

Other Driver Functions

In addition to planning and orchestrating the execution of a Spark program, the driver also is responsible for returning the results from an application. These could be return codes or data when an action requests data to be returned to the client; for example, an interactive query.

The driver also serves the Application UI on port 4040, as shown in Figure 13.4. This UI is created automatically, independent of the code submitted or how it was submitted (that is, interactive versus `spark-submit`).

FIGURE 13.4
The Spark Application UI.

Spark Executors

Spark executors are the host processes on which tasks from a Spark DAG are run. Executors reserve CPU and memory resources on slave nodes or workers in a Spark cluster. Executors are dedicated to a specific Spark application and terminated when the application completes. A Spark executor can run hundreds or thousands of tasks within a Spark program.

Typically, a worker node or slave node, which hosts the executor process, has a finite or fixed number of executors that can be allocated at any point in time. Therefore a cluster, being a known number of nodes, has a finite number of executors that can be allocated to run Spark executors.

As I mentioned, Spark executors are hosted in JVMs. The JVMs for executors are allocated a heap, which is a dedicated memory space in which to store and manage objects. This value is configurable.

Executors store output data from tasks in memory or on disk. It is important to note that workers and executors are only aware of the tasks allocated to them, whereas the driver is responsible for understanding the complete set of tasks and their respective dependencies that comprise an application.

Resilient Distributed Datasets in Spark

The Resilient Distributed Dataset (RDD) is the most fundamental data object used in Spark programming. RDDs are datasets within a Spark application, including the initial dataset(s) loaded, any intermediate datasets, and the final resultant dataset(s). Most Spark programming consists of creating new RDDs by performing operations on existing RDDs.

RDDs use various types of elements, from primitive datatypes such as integers, floating point numbers, and strings, to complex types such as lists or hashes, including nested objects, as well as serialized Scala and Java objects.

Although there are options for persisting RDDs to disk, RDDs are predominantly stored in memory (or are intended to be stored in memory, at least). As one of the initial intended uses for Spark was to support machine learning, Spark's RDDs provided a restricted form of shared memory that could make efficient reuse of data for successive/iterative operations.

The term Resilient Distributed Dataset is an accurate and succinct descriptor for the concept. Here's how it breaks down:

▶ **Resilient**—RDDs are resilient, meaning that if a node performing an operation in Spark is lost, the dataset can be reconstructed. This is because Spark knows the lineage of each RDD, which is the sequence of steps to create the RDD.

▶ **Distributed**—RDDs are distributed, meaning the data in RDDs is divided into one or many partitions and distributed as in-memory collections of objects across worker nodes in the cluster. As mentioned, RDDs provide an effective form of shared memory with which to exchange data between processes (executors) on different nodes (workers).

▶ **Dataset**—RDDs are datasets that consist of records. Records are uniquely identifiable data collections within a dataset. Records could be a collection of fields similar to a row in a table in a relational database, a line of text in a file, or multiple other formats. RDDs are partitioned such that each partition contains a unique set of records and can be operated on independently: this is another example of the *shared nothing* approach.

Another key property of RDDs is their *immutability*, which means that after they are instantiated and populated with data, they cannot be updated. Instead, new RDDs are created by performing coarse-grained transformations on existing RDDs in much the same way as bags in Pig are created by performing transformation on other bags.

Listing 13.2 shows a simple Spark program written in Python (PySpark) to search a log file for errors.

LISTING 13.2   **RDDs in Spark**

```
# load log files from local filesystem
logfilesrdd = sc.textFile("file:///var/log/hadoop/hdfs/hadoop-hdfs-*")
# filter log records for errors only
onlyerrorsrdd = logfilesrdd.filter(lambda line: "ERROR" in line)
# save onlyerrorsrdd as a file
onlyerrorsrdd.saveAsTextFile("file:///tmp/onlyerrorsrdd")
```

As shown in Listing 13.2, RDDs are initially created by loading data, typically from a text file or other file in HDFS using the `sc.textFile()` method.

Data Locality with RDDs

By default, Spark tries to read data into an RDD from the nodes that are close to it. Because Spark usually accesses distributed partitioned data, such as data from HDFS, to optimize transformation operations, it creates partitions to hold the underlying blocks from the distributed filesystem. Figure 13.5 depicts how blocks from a file in a distributed filesystem (like HDFS) are used to create RDD partitions on workers, which are co-located with the data.

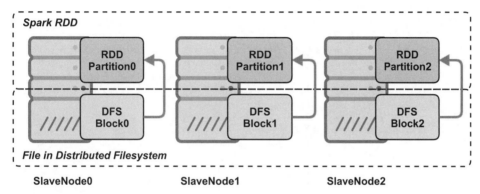

FIGURE 13.5
Loading an RDD From a Text File in a Distributed Filesystem.

RDDs can also be loaded from other data sources such as relational databases using a JDBC interface, as well as by simply parallelizing collections of objects such as data structures in Python or Scala.

RDD Persistence and Re-use

RDDs are created and exist predominantly in memory on executors. By default, RDDs are transient objects that exist only while they are required. Once they are transformed into new RDDs and no longer needed for any other operations, they are removed permanently. This may be problematic if an RDD is required for more than one action because it must be re-evaluated in its entirety each time. To address this issue, Spark provides API methods to persist, cache and checkpoint RDDs.

RDD Lineage

Spark keeps track of each RDD's lineage: that is, the sequence of operations that resulted in the RDD. Every RDD operation recomputes the entire lineage by default unless RDD persistence is requested.

In an RDD's lineage, each RDD will have a parent RDD and/or a child RDD. Spark creates a DAG consisting of dependencies between RDDs. RDDs are processed in stages, which are sets of transformations. RDDs and stages have dependencies that can be considered to be narrow if all operations can be performed in a single stage with no dependencies, or wide if multiple stages are required with a shuffle between stages.

The Spark Application UI enables you to visualize DAGs in a Spark application as shown in Figure 13.6.

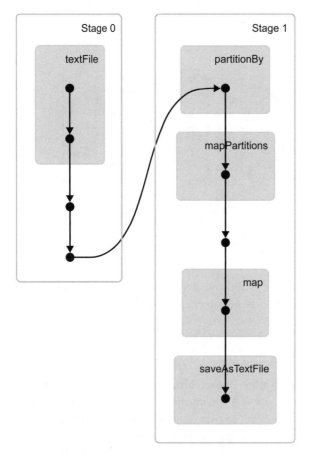

FIGURE 13.6
DAG Visualization through the Spark UI.

Fault Tolerance with RDDs

Since Spark records the lineage of each RDD, including the lineage of all parent RDDs (and parent's parents and so on), any RDD with all of its partitions can be reconstructed to the state it was at the time of failure, which could have resulted from a node failure, for example. Because RDDs are distributed, they can tolerate and recover from the failure of any single node.

Transformations and Actions in Spark

There are two types of operations that can be performed on RDDs: *transformations* and *actions*. Lets discuss each now.

Transformations

Transformations are operations performed against RDDs that result in the creation of new RDDs. Common transformations include map and filter functions. Listing 13.3 shows a new RDD being created from a transformation of an existing RDD.

LISTING 13.3   Transformations in Spark

```
originalrdd = sc.parallelize([0, 1, 2, 3, 4, 5, 6, 7, 8])
newrdd = originalrdd.filter(lambda x: x % 2)
```

In Listing 13.3 we simply parallelized a collection of numbers into an RDD called `originalrdd`. The `filter()` transformation was then applied to each element in the `originalrdd` to bypass even numbers in the collection. The results of this transformation are created in the new RDD called `newrdd`.

Actions

Actions are the other operation that can be performed on RDDs. In contrast to transformations, which return new RDD objects, actions produce output such as data from an RDD returned to a driver program, or save the content of an RDD to a filesystem (local, HDFS, S3, or other). There are many other actions as well, including returning a count of the number of records in a RDD.

Listing 13.4 uses the `collect()` action to return and display the contents of the `newrdd`.

LISTING 13.4   Actions in Spark

```
newrdd.collect() # will return [1, 3, 5, 7]
```

Actions are typically the final statement in a Spark program.

Lazy Evaluation

Spark uses *lazy evaluation* (also called *lazy execution*) in processing Spark programs. Lazy evaluation defers processing until an action is called (therefore when output is required). This is easily demonstrated using one of the interactive shells, where you can enter one of the transformation methods to RDDs one after the other without any processing starting. Instead, each statement is parsed for syntax and object references only. After an action such as `count()` or `saveAsTextFile()` is requested, a DAG is created along with logical and physical execution plans. These are then orchestrated and managed across executors by the driver.

This lazy evaluation allows Spark to combine operations where possible, thereby reducing processing stages and minimizing the amount of data transferred between Spark executors, a process called the *shuffle*.

▼ TRY IT YOURSELF

Installing and Using Spark

In this exercise, you will install and test Spark. You can use your Apache Hadoop cluster for this exercise or any other Hadoop environment you have available.

1. Obtain a download link for the latest Spark release from the Spark project website at http://spark.apache.org/downloads.html (I am using the 2.0 release in this example):

   ```
   $ wget http://<downloadhost>/spark-2.0.0-bin-hadoop2.7.tgz
   ```

2. Unpack the release and move the contents into a new Spark home directory (`/opt/spark`):

   ```
   $ tar -xzf spark-2.0.0-bin-hadoop2.7.tgz
   $ sudo mv spark-2.0.0-bin-hadoop2.7 /opt/spark
   ```

3. Create environment variables required for Spark:

   ```
   $ export SPARK_HOME=/opt/spark
   $ export PATH=$SPARK_HOME/bin:$PATH
   $ export HADOOP_CONF_DIR=/etc/hadoop/conf
   ```

   These environment variable could also be set using the `.bashrc` file or similar user or system profile scripts. You need to do this if you wish to persist these variables beyond the current session.

4. Open the PySpark shell by running the `pyspark` command from any directory, as you've added the Spark bin directory to the `PATH`.

   ```
   $ pyspark
   ```

   If Spark has been successfully installed, you should see the following output (with informational logging messages omitted for brevity):

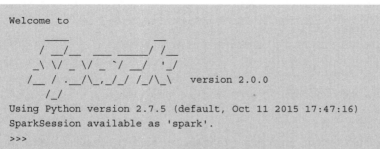

```
Welcome to
      ____              __
     / __/__  ___ _____/ /__
    _\ \/ _ \/ _ `/ __/  '_/
   /__ / .__/\_,_/_/ /_/\_\   version 2.0.0
      /_/

Using Python version 2.7.5 (default, Oct 11 2015 17:47:16)
SparkSession available as 'spark'.
>>>
```

5. Keeping the pyspark shell open, in a browser (on the same machine or another machine with access to your machine) navigate to `http://<your_server>:4040`.

You should see the Spark Application Web UI connected to your pyspark session, similar to the UI shown in Figure 13.7.

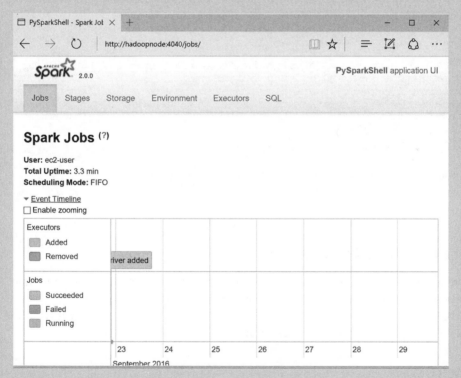

FIGURE 13.7
Spark Application Web UI Screenshot.

6. Press Ctrl-D in the console session to exit the pyspark shell.

7. Open a Scala shell by entering the following at the terminal prompt:

```
$ spark-shell
```

You should see a shell similar to that seen in Step 4, except with a `scala>` prompt.

8. Exit the Scala shell by pressing Ctrl-D.

9. Run the included Pi estimator example in local execution mode by executing the following command:

```
$ spark-submit --class org.apache.spark.examples.SparkPi \
--master local \
$SPARK_HOME/examples/jars/spark-examples*.jar 1
```

You should see output similar to the following (the INFO messages are suppressed for brevity):

```
Pi is roughly 3.138671386713867
```

10. Run the Pi estimator program using YARN execution mode by executing the following command:

```
$ spark-submit --class org.apache.spark.examples.SparkPi \
--master yarn \
--deploy-mode client \
$SPARK_HOME/examples/jars/spark-examples*.jar 1
```

You should see output similar to the output shown in Step 9.

Extensions to Spark

The programming interfaces to Spark discussed thus far have used the Spark core API, which is implemented in Python, Scala, or Java through functional programming interfaces. There are many other extensions or abstractions to the core API designed to make Spark accessible and useful for users with backgrounds in SQL or data science disciplines.

SparkSQL

The first extension to Spark started as a subproject called Shark. Much like the Hive project, Shark was designed to implement a SQL-like abstraction to the Spark core API. Shark would later be re-launched as the SparkSQL project.

SparkSQL implements a new construct called the *DataFrame*. The DataFrame, originally called the SchemaRDD, is a special purpose extension to the Spark RDD that implements an in-memory columnar storage scheme optimized for SQL access. The DataFrame API, as part of the overall Spark architecture, is pictured in Figure 13.8.

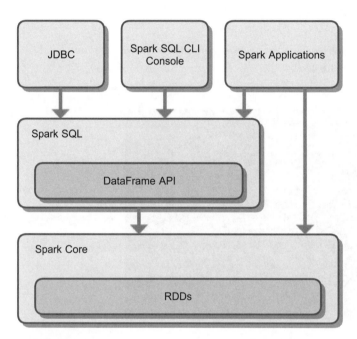

FIGURE 13.8
Spark High-Level Architecture.

An example SparkSQL DataFrame operation is shown in Listing 13.5.

LISTING 13.5   Accessing SparkSQL DataFrames

```
sql_cmd = """SELECT name, lat, long
    FROM stations
    WHERE landmark = 'San Jose'"""
    df = sqlContext.sql(sql_cmd)
    df.show()

+-------------------+---------+-----------+
|               name|      lat|       long|
+-------------------+---------+-----------+
|    Adobe on Almaden|37.331415|  -121.8932|
|    San Pedro Square|37.336721|-121.894074|
|Paseo de San Antonio|37.333798|-121.886943|
| San Salvador at 1st|37.330165|-121.885831|
|           Japantown|37.348742|-121.894715|
```

```
|    San Jose City Hall|37.337391|-121.886995|
|          MLK Library|37.335885| -121.88566|
|        St James Park|37.339301|-121.889937|
|          Ryland Park|37.342725|-121.895617|
|            ...       |   ...   |    ...    |
+--------------------+---------+-----------+
```

SparkSQL can be accessed via JDBC as well as the spark-sql and Beeline shell programs. The spark-sql shell is pictured in Figure 13.9.

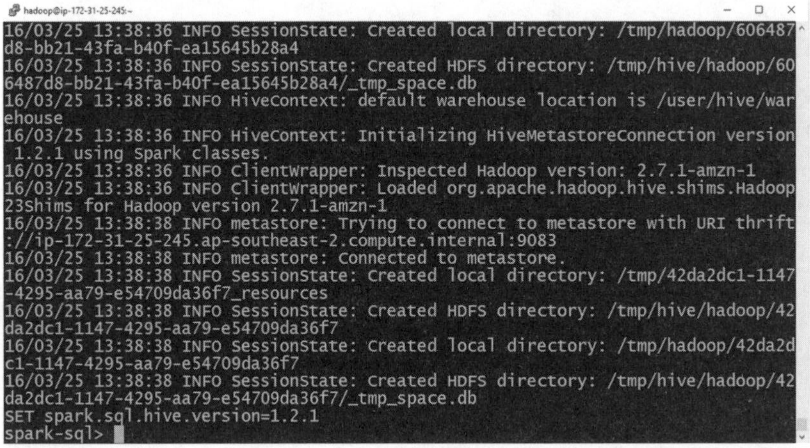

FIGURE 13.9
The spark-sql Shell.

Spark Streaming

Spark Streaming is a key extension to the Spark core API introducing objects and functions designed to process streams of data. The foundational object in Spark Streaming is the discretized stream (or *DStream*), which is an RDD abstraction comprised of streams of data batched into RDDs based on time intervals.

Spark transformations can be applied to DStreams applying functions to each underlying RDD in the DStream. Figure 13.10 demonstrates the implementation of DStreams in Spark Streaming.

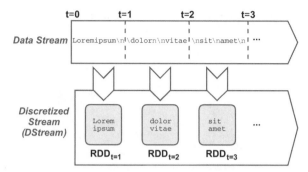

FIGURE 13.10
Spark Discretized Streams (DStreams).

Stream processing operations, including state and sliding window operations, can be applied to DStreams. Examples include operations on data "windows" (such as the last hour, last day, and so on).

Spark Streaming can also be used with messaging systems such as Kafka.

SparkR

R is a powerful programming language and software environment for statistical computing, visual analytics, and predictive modeling. For data analysts, statisticians, mathematicians, and data scientists already using R, Spark provides a scalable runtime engine for R: *SparkR*.

SparkR is an R package that provides access to Spark and distributed data frame operations from an R environment using the R programming language. R data frames can then be used for distributed operations with Spark, such as statistical analysis and building, testing, and deploying simple linear regression models.

SparkR is available through the SparkR shell as shown in Figure 13.11.

FIGURE 13.11
The SparkR shell.

SparkR can also be implemented as the processing engine for the RStudio web interface as shown in Figure 13.12.

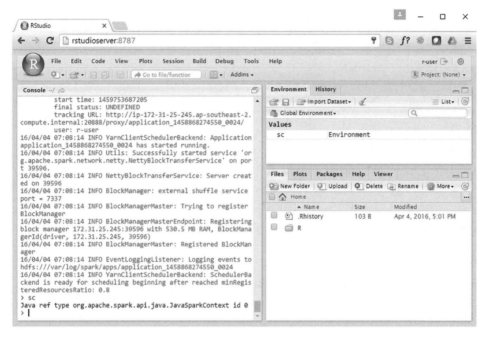

FIGURE 13.12
RStudio Web Interface.

Machine Learning with Spark

Machine learning is the science of creating algorithms that are capable of learning based on the data provided to them. Common applications of machine learning are seen every day, from recommendation engines to spam filters to fraud detection and much more. Spark has included a purpose-built library, MLlib, to make practical machine learning scalable, easy, and seamlessly integrated into Spark.

The MLlib subproject and API are built upon the RDD model. MLlib includes many common machine learning algorithms and utilities to perform data preparation, feature extraction, model training, and testing. MLlib is designed to be a succinct, user-friendly yet functionally rich, powerful, and scalable machine learning abstraction on top of Spark.

Listing 13.6 demonstrates using the Spark MLlib to train a decision tree model.

LISTING 13.6   Training a Decision Tree Model with Spark MLlib

```
from pyspark.mllib.tree import DecisionTree
model = DecisionTree.trainClassifier(data=data,
        numClasses=2,
        categoricalFeaturesInfo={0: 3})
...
print(model.toDebugString())
  If (feature 2 <= 80.0)
      If (feature 1 <= 65.0)
        If (feature 1 <= 64.0)
        Predict: 1.0
        Else (feature 1 > 64.0)
        Predict: 0.0
      Else (feature 1 > 65.0)
      Predict: 1.0
    Else (feature 2 > 80.0)
    If (feature 0 in {0.0})
    Predict: 0.0
    Else (feature 0 not in {0.0})
    If (feature 1 <= 71.0)
      If (feature 1 <= 70.0)
        Predict: 1.0
      Else (feature 1 > 70.0)
        Predict: 0.0
    Else (feature 1 > 71.0)
      Predict: 1.0
```

Graph Processing with Spark

The world is increasingly more interconnected. Many of today's problems and challenges require the modeling of the relationships between different entities or discrete data items. Graph processing provides a framework-based approach to evaluating these relationships. Spark provides a full set of graph data abstractions, transformations, and algorithms to meet these challenges at scale. Spark provides the GraphX and GraphFrames extensions as an approach to graph processing and analysis.

Graphs consist of *vertices* (or *nodes*) and *edges* as shown in Figure 13.13.

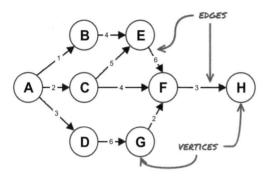

FIGURE 13.13
A Directed Acyclic Graph.

Listing 13.7 demonstrates the use of GraphFrames in Spark (a DataFrame abstraction) to apply the PageRank algorithm to a graph.

LISTING 13.7   PageRank Algorithm in Spark

```
graph = GraphRDD(vertices, edges)
ranks = graph.pageRank(0.0001).vertices
```

PageRank, which was actually named after one of Google's founders, Larry Page, traverses a graph where web pages are the vertices and inbound and outbound links are edges. PageRank is used to determine search engine weightings, web page relevance, and query results based upon the quality and quantity of inbound links to a particular web page.

PageRank is just one of the available graph analysis functions accessible through the Spark GraphX or GraphFrames API.

Summary

Spark is a high-performance data processing framework that can be used with or without YARN to process data in HDFS or other filesystems. Spark implements a distributed shared memory data abstraction called the Resilient Distributed Dataset (RDD). A Spark program consists of a set of DAGs, which manipulate RDDs to achieve a desired output: either transformations such as **map** and **filter**, or actions such as **count** or **saveAsTextFile**.

Spark can leverage the YARN resource scheduling framework included with Hadoop but also supplies its own scheduler, the standalone scheduler. Spark programs consist of a Driver, a Master, a Cluster Manager, and one or more Executors. The Driver plans and monitors the Spark program, the Cluster Manager and Master negotiate and coordinate available resources for the application, and the Executors do the actual data processing. Spark's runtime architecture is highly scalable and efficient.

Spark programs can be written in Python (PySpark), Scala, or Java with extensions for R (SparkR) and SQL (SparkSQL). In addition, there are machine learning, graph analysis, and other libraries and modules available to extend Spark.

Spark is widely expected to ultimately supplant MapReduce and the other SQL-on-Hadoop engines as the predominant processing framework for the Hadoop platform.

For more information on Apache Spark visit **https://spark.apache.org** or **http:// www.informit.com/store/apache-spark-in-24-hours-sams-teach-yourself-9780672338519.**

Q&A

Q. What is the difference between *transformations* and *actions* in Spark? What does *lazy evaluation* refer to?

A. *Transformations* are operations which perform functions against each element in an RDD and result in a new RDD being created. Examples include `map()` and `filter()` operations. *Actions* return a value to the Spark driver or store results to a filesystem or another data store. RDD transformation operations are lazily evaluated, meaning they are only evaluated when an action is requested to return a result.

Q. What is an RDD in Spark?

A. An RDD is a *Resilient Distributed Dataset*. The RDD is the fundamental processing unit in Spark, which is partitioned and distributed across one or more Executors in a Spark cluster. RDD operations are *transformations*, which apply functions to each element of an RDD, producing a new RDD, or *actions*, which request output from an RDD and trigger evaluation of an RDD and its lineage.

Q. What is the role of the Driver in a Spark application?

A. The Driver is responsible for planning and coordinating the execution of the Spark program and returning status and/or results (data) to the client.

Workshop

The workshop contains quiz questions to help you solidify your understanding of the material covered. Try to answer all questions before looking at the "Answers" section that follows.

Quiz

1. What are the two basic classifications of operations in the Spark core API?

2. What is the name of the Spark RDD API abstraction implemented by SparkSQL?

3. What is the fundamental data object in the Spark Streaming API?

4. Which process in the Spark distributed execution framework is responsible for accessing data and executing tasks?

   A. Driver

   D. Worker

   C. Executor

   D. Master

Answers

1. Transformations and Actions.

2. the DataFrame.

3. the DStream.

4. C.

HOUR 14

Using the Hadoop User Environment (HUE)

What You'll Learn in This Hour:

▶ Introducing the Hadoop User Environment (HUE)
▶ Projects that interface with HUE
▶ Installing and configuring HUE
▶ Using HUE

HUE is one of the more significant projects in the evolution of Hadoop. HUE was the first project of its kind to provide graphical user access to data stored in Hadoop for analysts to use. In this hour you learn about the HUE project and its many interfaces and usages.

Introducing HUE

Cloudera, notably the first mover in the commercial Hadoop movement, started a project called Cloudera Desktop soon after releasing their Hadoop distribution around 2008-2009. Cloudera Desktop was designed to provide users easy access to data processing in Hadoop. In June of 2010, Cloudera Desktop version 0.9 was rebranded as the open source HUE (Hadoop User Environment) project, which it is known as today.

HUE provides a web-based interface to Hadoop and its data analysis ecosystem projects such as Hive, Pig, Impala, Oozie, and more. HUE makes the Hadoop platform more accessible to SQL and other data analysts by providing a friendly user environment by which to navigate data in HDFS and Hive and perform data processing and analysis tasks. HUE empowers analysts by providing drag-and-drop and point-and-click development environments.

HUE is included with many commercial vendors' Hadoop distributions such as the Cloudera Hadoop offering. The Cloudera Quickstart VM is a quick and easy way to explore HUE. HUE is also available as a deployment option with Amazon's Elastic MapReduce (EMR). However, HUE can be deployed on any installation of Hadoop, including a pure Apache deployment.

HUE has many file and object browsers, query editors, and integrated development environments for many different ecosystem projects. The list of supported projects is continually expanding as more and more Hadoop ecosystem projects reach maturity. In this hour, we will look at some of the capabilities and notable supported projects that exist now with HUE.

Advantages of Using HUE

Implementing HUE for user access to Hadoop and other on-platform technologies has the benefit of isolating Hadoop cluster resources from direct access by users. HUE could be deployed on an *edge node*, that is, a node or server that has an interface to a public network such as an enterprise LAN, and an interface to a private network such as a private subnet, AWS VPC, or VLAN dedicated to Hadoop cluster nodes. An example of this configuration is shown in Figure 14.1.

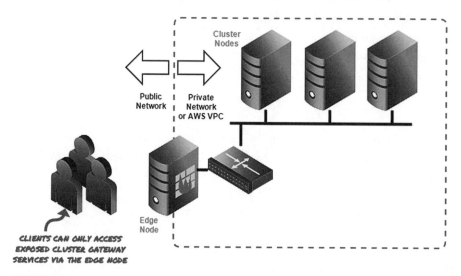

FIGURE 14.1
Using an Edge Node to Control Access to a Hadoop Cluster.

As shown in Figure 14.1, access to Hadoop is concentrated through the HUE server, which enables a control point and the capability to restrict access to the cluster.

Furthermore, with all of the client software located on one instance, there is no need to manage software libraries, compatibility, upgrades, and patches on client systems throughout the network.

Interacting with HDFS

As analysts interacting with Hadoop will often need to upload or download data to or from HDFS, HUE includes a HDFS file browser console where developers or analysts can browse the filesystem and upload or download files in HDFS, make or remove directories, rename objects, and alter permissions to objects they own. The HUE HDFS file browser interface is shown in Figure 14.2.

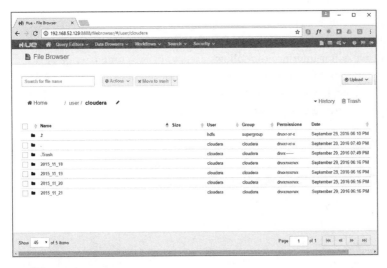

FIGURE 14.2
HDFS File Browser in HUE.

Managing YARN Jobs

HUE also includes a facility for developers or analysts to monitor and control their applications running on YARN. Using the job browser interface in HUE, developers can monitor progress, view logs, and terminate their jobs in YARN rather than having to do so from a terminal. The HUE job browser is shown in Figure 14.3.

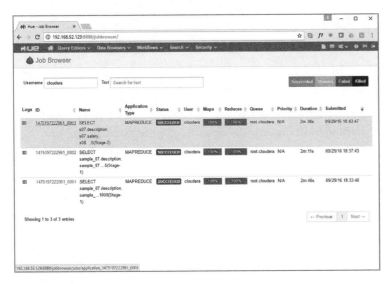

FIGURE 14.3
YARN Job Browser in HUE.

Hive

As discussed previously, Hive is one of the most common programming interfaces in the Hadoop ecosystem. HUE includes a Hive editor interface that allows users to browse and describe objects in Hive, as well as submit queries and return results in a grid format as shown in Figure 14.4. Hive query results can also be downloaded using the Hive editor interface in either CSV or XLS format. Query results can also be saved to HDFS or another table object in Hive.

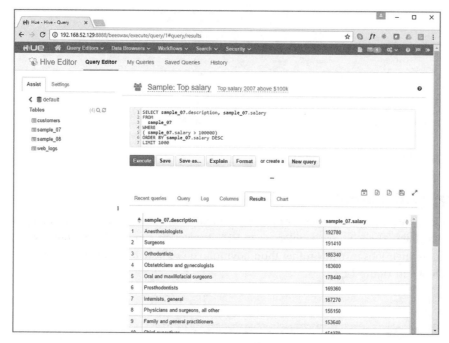

FIGURE 14.4
Hive Editor in HUE.

In addition to returning tabular results from Hive queries, the HUE Hive editor also enables data visualization using the charting function. Available charting options include bar, line, pie, and map charts. An example visualization using results from a query in Hive is shown in Figure 14.5.

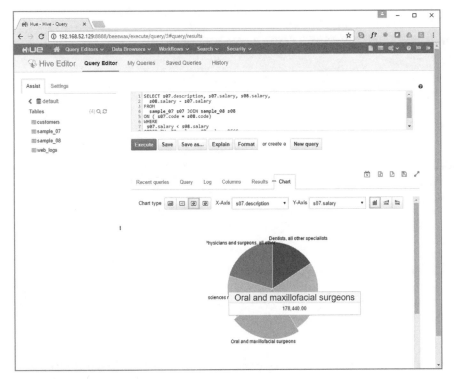

FIGURE 14.5
Visualizing Data Using HUE.

Pig

HUE includes a Pig editor that enables users to create, save, and execute PigLatin programs on a Hadoop cluster. Using the Pig editor, developers can pass parameters to Pig scripts as discussed in **Hour 9, "Using Advanced Pig,"** and store output results to directories in HDFS. An assistant is also available in the editor to show the usage of built-in functions in PigLatin. The HUE Pig editor interface is shown in Figure 14.6.

FIGURE 14.6
Pig Editor in HUE.

Impala

Impala is a popular SQL-on-Hadoop solution discussed in **Hour 12, "Using SQL-on-Hadoop Solutions,"** especially as part of the Cloudera Hadoop application stack. HUE includes an Impala query editor that can be used to execute Impala queries and return grid and visual results as shown in Figure 14.7.

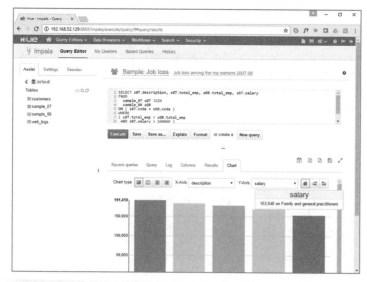

FIGURE 14.7
Impala Queries Using HUE.

HBase

HBase is the NoSQL platform built on Hadoop which I will cover in **Hour 15, "Introducing NoSQL."** HUE provides user and administrative access to tables and objects in HBase using its intuitive interface. The HBase browser interface in HUE can be used to browse tables or to put or get data into or out of a HBase table. The HBase browser is shown in Figure 14.8.

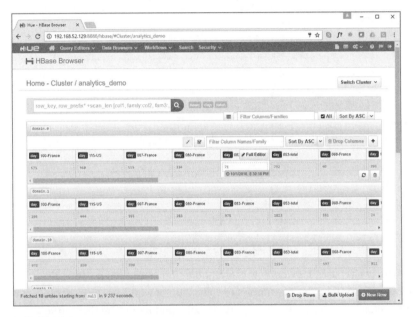

FIGURE 14.8
HBase Browser in HUE.

Solr

Solr is an Apache top-level project that provides full-text indexing and search capabilities. Search (and in particular, web search) was one of the initial use cases and drivers for the Hadoop and GoogleFS/Google MapReduce projects. Solr is a search engine which is built on the foundational Lucene Java library and is an equivalent technology to ElasticSearch, another popular search platform. The Solr interface in HUE enables users to visualize indexes as shown in Figure 14.9.

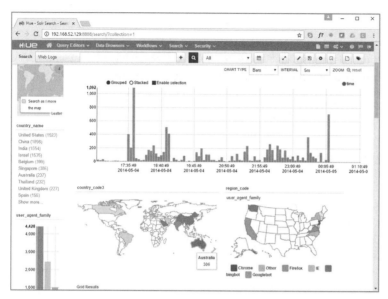

FIGURE 14.9
Accessing Solr Indexes Using HUE.

Oozie

Oozie is a Hadoop ecosystem project used for workflow coordination that is covered in **Hour 17, "Working with the Hadoop Ecosystem."** Oozie enables orchestration of workflows in Hadoop using various Hadoop ecosystem projects such as Hive, Pig, Spark, Impala, and more. The HUE Oozie editor enables users to create workflows using a drag-and-drop interface as shown in Figure 14.10.

FIGURE 14.10
Oozie Editor in HUE.

Sqoop

HUE also includes an interface that enables users to configure and execute Sqoop commands to import or export data to or from a relational database system as discussed in **Hour 5, "Getting Data into Hadoop."**

Installing, Configuring, and Using HUE

HUE can be deployed on any distribution of Hadoop. Let's explore how to install, configure, and use HUE.

Installing HUE

HUE can be obtained from http://gethue.com/. From the HUE home page you can find links with specific installation instructions for the various popular Hadoop distributions, including:

▶ Cloudera, using Cloudera Manager or using CDH packages

▶ Hortonworks HDP

▶ MapR

▶ Pivotal HD

▶ IBM Big Insights

You can also find instructions for deploying HUE on various popular cloud Hadoop Platform-as-a-Service (PaaS) offerings including:

▶ Amazon Elastic MapReduce (EMR)

▶ Microsoft Azure HDInsight

▶ IBM Bluemix

HUE can also be deployed using Docker with ready-made images, instructions for this can be found on the http://gethue.com/ website.

In this hour we will use the release of HUE provided with the Cloudera Hadoop platform for our Try it Yourself exercise.

Configuring HUE

HUE is built upon the *Django* project, a web framework written in Python used by many content management systems. The Django project keeps its configuration in a database engine, typically PostgreSQL or MySQL.

The HUE service acts as a broker between the Django presentation layer and the various Hadoop cluster services. The main configuration file for the HUE service is the hue.ini file. This configuration file is used to supply configuration parameters to allow HUE to connect to and interact with the many supported Hadoop and Hadoop ecosystem components and projects.

The hue.ini file is usually located in the /etc/hue/conf/ directory and can be edited manually using vi or a similar text editor, or if you are using the Cloudera Distribution of Hadoop (CDH), this file can be modified through the Cloudera Manager browser-based interface.

An example excerpt from a hue.ini file is shown in Listing 14.1.

LISTING 14.1   hue.ini **File**

```
# Hue configuration file
# ===================================
#


###########################################################################
# General configuration for core Desktop features (authentication, etc)
###########################################################################

[desktop]
# Webserver listens on this address and port
http_host=0.0.0.0
http_port=8888
# Time zone name
time_zone=America/Los_Angeles
# Configuration options for connecting to LDAP and Active Directory
# ------------------------------------------------------------------

[[ldap]]
# The search base for finding users and groups
base_dn="DC=mycompany,DC=com"
# The NT domain to connect to (only for use with Active Directory)
nt_domain=mycompany.com
# URL of the LDAP server
ldap_url=ldap://auth.mycompany.com
# Configuration options for specifying the Desktop Database.  For more info,
# see http://docs.djangoproject.com/en/1.1/ref/settings/#database-engine
# -------------------------------------------------------------------

[[database]]
engine=mysql
host=quickstart.cloudera
port=3306
user=hue
password=cloudera
name=hue
```

```
#######################################################################
# Settings to configure your Hadoop cluster.
#######################################################################

[hadoop]
# Configuration for HDFS NameNode
# ---------------------------------------------------------------------

[[hdfs_clusters]]
# HA support by using HttpFs

[[[default]]]
# Enter the filesystem uri
fs_defaultfs=hdfs://quickstart.cloudera:8020
# Configuration for YARN (MR2)
# ---------------------------------------------------------------------

[[yarn_clusters]]

[[[default]]]
# Enter the host on which you are running the ResourceManager
resourcemanager_host=localhost
# The port where the ResourceManager IPC listens on
resourcemanager_port=8032

#######################################################################
# Settings to configure liboozie
#######################################################################

[liboozie]
# The URL where the Oozie service runs on. This is required in order for
# users to submit jobs.
oozie_url=http://localhost:11000/oozie

#######################################################################
# Settings to configure Beeswax with Hive
#######################################################################

[beeswax]
# Host where Hive server Thrift daemon is running.
# If Kerberos security is enabled, use fully-qualified domain name (FQDN).
hive_server_host=quickstart.cloudera
# Port where HiveServer2 Thrift server runs on.
hive_server_port=10000
# Hive configuration directory, where hive-site.xml is located
hive_conf_dir=/etc/hive/conf
```

```
##########################################################################
# Settings to configure Pig
##########################################################################

[pig]
# Location of piggybank.jar on local filesystem.
local_sample_dir=/usr/lib/hue/apps/pig/examples
# Location piggybank.jar will be copied to in HDFS.
remote_data_dir=/user/hue/pig/examples

##########################################################################
# Settings to configure Sqoop
##########################################################################

[sqoop]
# For autocompletion, fill out the librdbms section.
# Sqoop server URL
server_url=http://quickstart.cloudera:12000/sqoop

##########################################################################
# Settings to configure Impala
##########################################################################

[impala]
# Host of the Impala Server (one of the Impalad)
server_host=quickstart.cloudera
# Port of the Impala Server
server_port=21050

##########################################################################
# Settings to configure Hbase
##########################################################################

[hbase]
# Comma-separated list of HBase Thrift servers for
# clusters in the format of '(name|host:port)'.
hbase_clusters=(Cluster|quickstart.cloudera:9090)

##########################################################################
# Settings to configure Solr Search
##########################################################################

[search]
# URL of the Solr Server
solr_url=http://quickstart.cloudera:8983/solr/
```

HUE configuration can also be accessed and updated using the Cloudera Manager management console interface.

Controlling Access to HUE

One of the main advantages of HUE, as discussed previously, is the ability to control access to cluster resources. Let's cover some of the basics of authentication and authorization in HUE.

HUE Authentication

Authentication in HUE can be achieved using local users from the system HUE is installed on, or Kerberos principals (users) if Kerberos is deployed. I will discuss Kerberos in **Hour 22, "Securing Hadoop."**

Using the HUE user admin console, HUE administrators can add new users and groups and manage users, as shown in Figure 14.11.

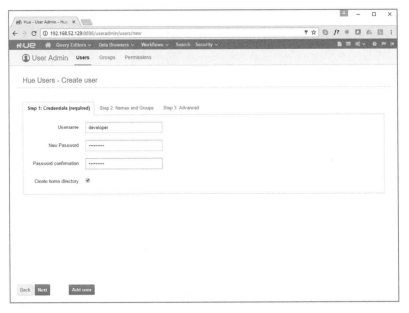

FIGURE 14.11
Adding Users in HUE.

HUE can also integrate with LDAP (Lightweight Directory Access Protocol), which allows user principals to be provided from directory services such as Microsoft Active Directory.

HUE Authorization

Once authenticated, access to resources and associated system and project privileges can be assigned to users in HUE using the HUE console. This access and privileges can only be granted by a HUE administrator. An example of applying granular access to configured projects using the HUE user admin console is shown in Figure 14.12.

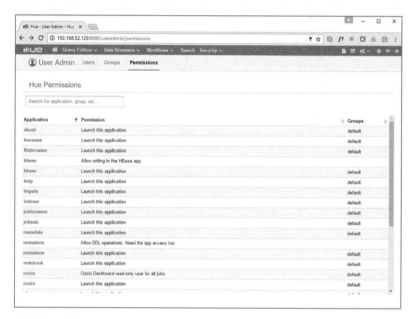

FIGURE 14.12
Granting Access to HUE Users.

NOTE

The First User to Log In to HUE Assumes the HUE Superuser Role

By default, the first user to log in to HUE becomes the administrator, or superuser, and then can assign access, roles, and permissions to additional users.

Using HUE

By default, HUE is available on port 8888 of the server it was deployed on and is accessible via HTTP. You can optionally require secure access via HTTPS. To do this, you will need a certificate installed on your server. Instructions for enabling HTTPS are available at http://gethue.com.

Once you access the HUE server, you will need to log in using the login page shown in Figure 14.13. Recalling that the very first user to log in to HUE becomes the superuser, this is typically the administrator who provisions and configures HUE.

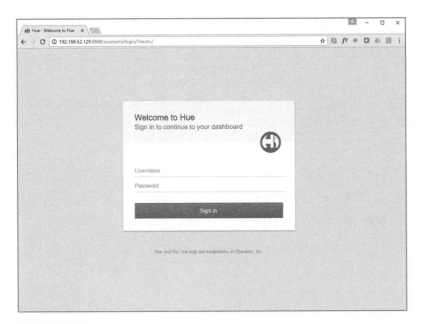

FIGURE 14.13
HUE Login Screen.

If you are logging on for the first time, a wizard interface is displayed that enables you to deploy examples for the various projects supported by HUE. These examples include data and code which are integrated into the HUE environment. This is a great way to road-test HUE, and we do so in our Try it Yourself exercise.

HUE's main console includes the logged-in user's environment, showing the user's workspace and saved documents. From any screen you can access any of the integrated products configured, such as the HDFS browser, Pig editor, or Beeswax Hive interface. The main console is shown in Figure 14.14.

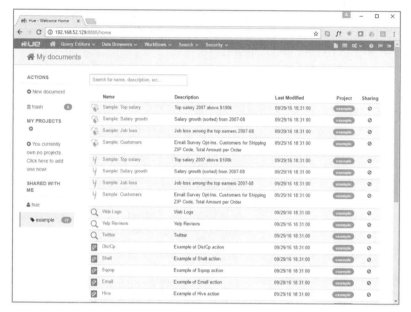

FIGURE 14.14
HUE Main Console.

Let's take HUE for a spin now in our Try it Yourself exercise.

▼ TRY IT YOURSELF

Using HUE

For this exercise, you can use the Cloudera Quickstart VM, which can be downloaded from http://www.cloudera.com/downloads.html. Download the latest version of the Quickstart VM, which will include the latest release of CDH (Cloudera Distribution of Hadoop), along with a release of HUE ready to go. You will need either VMware Player or Oracle Virtual Box running on your host with the recommended specifications (CPU, memory, disk space) to run the VM. Assuming your VM is being started for the first time, follow the steps below to explore HUE.

1. Download and launch the Quickstart VM on your chosen virtualization platform.

2. From the host, open a browser to the VM's IP address port 8888.

3. Log in to HUE using the default Cloudera Quickstart VM user credentials (at the time of writing the credentials are *cloudera/cloudera* but check the latest Quickstart documentation). Recall that the first user to log in is the superuser for HUE.

4. From the Welcome screen, click on the Examples link as shown in Figure 14.15.

FIGURE 14.15
HUE First Time Welcome Screen.

5. Install any or all of the examples (Hive, HBase, etc.) by clicking on its link in the Examples pane as shown in Figure 14.16.

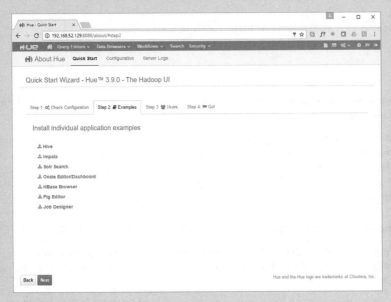

FIGURE 14.16
Installing the HUE Examples.

6. Click **Next** and accept all of the defaults on the remaining wizard screens. Click **Done** on the final wizard screen.

7. You should see a list of examples using the various projects supported by HUE. Select any of the examples by clicking the link.

You can also try HUE using the AWS Elastic MapReduce (EMR) platform.

Summary

HUE is an open source web-based user interface for Hadoop and many of its ecosystem components and technologies. HUE was created by Cloudera but is Hadoop-distribution agnostic, and in fact is included as an option in many other vendors' offerings including the AWS EMR platform.

HUE provides a rich, intuitive, user-friendly experience for analysts who need to work with data on the Hadoop platform. Users can upload data to HDFS, access and manipulate data, visualize data, and manage their own jobs on Hadoop, all within a browser-based client environment.

HUE supports many Hadoop core and ecosystem projects—including most of the projects I have discussed or will discuss in this book. These projects include HDFS, YARN, Hive, Pig, Impala, HBase, and more. The list of supported projects continues to grow as the ecosystem develops and matures.

More information about HUE is available at **http://gethue.com/**.

Q&A

Q. What are the advantages to having users use HUE for accessing Hadoop or Hadoop-related projects such as Hive?

A. HUE can be implemented as a user gateway to the Hadoop platform, enabling isolation of the Hadoop platform resources from direct user access by concentrating access to Hadoop through the HUE server. This also has the benefit of a single point of control and software lifecycle management, as you only need to manage the software libraries to access Hadoop and ecosystem resources on one node instead of having to manage multiple clients.

Q. What are some of the interfaces to projects or capabilities that are exposed through HUE?

A. HUE can be used to browse HDFS or to upload or download files as well as view and manage YARN jobs. Additionally, HUE exposes user interfaces to Hive, Impala, Pig, Oozie, HBase, and Solr.

Workshop

The workshop contains quiz questions to help you solidify your understanding of the material covered. Try to answer all questions before looking at the "Answers" section that follows.

Quiz

1. **True or False.** HUE supports authentication into corporate directory services using LDAP.

2. **True or False.** You do not need a HiveServer2 instance available to use the Beeswax interface provided through HUE.

3. **True or False.** The first user to log in to HUE once installed becomes the superuser.

4. **True or False.** HUE can be used to browse tables or to put or get data into or out of a HBase table.

Answers

1. True.

2. False.

3. True.

4. True.

HOUR 15
Introducing NoSQL

What You'll Learn in This Hour:

▶ Introduction to NoSQL concepts and systems
▶ Types of NoSQL systems and uses for NoSQL
▶ Introduction to HBase and Cassandra
▶ Integrating NoSQL with Hadoop

Moore's law and the birth and explosion of mobile ubiquitous computing have permanently altered the data, computing, and database landscape. That is not to say that the relational database is dead—far from it—but there are now new sets of problems and increasingly aggressive nonfunctional, non-relational requirements that necessitate alternative approaches to data storage, management, and processing. This new data paradigm requires us to look at data in terms of cells rather than just the relational paradigm of tables, rows, and columns. Enter NoSQL, offering a completely new set of tools and capabilities designed to meet the demands of today's and tomorrow's data requirements. In this hour, I introduce you to NoSQL systems and methodologies, and look at their integration into Hadoop and the Hadoop ecosystem.

Introduction to NoSQL

Hadoop's ascension closely follows the ascension and proliferation of NoSQL systems. Before I discuss specific implementations of NoSQL, let's take a step back and review the background of NoSQL.

Bigtable: The Beginnings of the NoSQL Movement

In 2006, Google released a whitepaper that would outline a new paradigm for databases and data storage. The paper was titled "Bigtable: A Distributed Storage System for Structured Data."

Bigtable was the distributed storage system for managing structured data at Google. However, unlike existing RDBMS platforms, Bigtable was designed to reliably scale to petabytes of data and thousands of machines to meet Google's application workload demand. At the time, Bigtable was used by several Google products, including Google Analytics, Google Finance, and Google Earth.

Bigtable introduced some new concepts such as column families, uninterpreted column types, and runtime column definitions and sparsity, while extending some core Massively Parallel Processing (MPP) database concepts such as shared nothing and distributed primary indexes.

Bigtable paved the way for several Apache projects, including HBase, Cassandra, and Accumulo. I will discuss HBase and Cassandra, two direct descendants of Bigtable, in the coming sections, but Google's work and the Bigtable paper inspired a new generation of thinking in data structure and storage. It ultimately paved the way for other popular data stores today, including MongoDB and others.

NoSQL is an integral product of the big data movement, and the Google Bigtable paper was a major catalyst for the movement.

NoSQL System Characteristics

There is some friendly disagreement about what NoSQL means, from not SQL to not only SQL to other interpretations or definitions. Regardless of the ambiguity around the nomenclature, NoSQL systems come in different variants, which I will describe in further detail shortly. All of the variants share some common properties, specifically:

▶ *They are schemaless at design time and "schema-on-read" at runtime*—This means they do not have predefined columns, but columns are created with each PUT (INSERT) operation, and each record, document, or data instance can have a different schema from the previous instance.

▶ *Data has no predefined relationship to any other object*—This means there is no concept of foreign keys or referential integrity, declarative or otherwise. Relationships may exist between data objects or instances, but they are discovered or leveraged at runtime rather than prescribed at design time.

▶ *Joins are typically avoided*—In most NoSQL implementations, joins are kept to an absolute minimum, if not avoided altogether. This is typically accomplished by denormalizing data, often with a trade-off of storing duplicate data. However, with most NoSQL implementations leveraging cost-efficient commodity or cloud infrastructure, the material cost is offset by the computation cost reduction of not having to perform excessive joins when the data is accessed.

In all cases, there is no logical or physical model that dictates how data is structured, unlike a third normal form data warehouse or online transaction processing system.

Moreover, NoSQL systems are typically distributed (like Apache Cassandra or HBase) and are designed for fast lookups. Write operations are typically faster as well, as many of the overheads of traditional relational database systems are not used, like datatype or domain checks, atomic/blocking transactions, or management of transaction isolation levels.

NoSQL systems, in the majority of cases, are built for scale and scalability from petabytes of storage to queries bounded in terabytes, performance, and low friction (having the ability to adapt to changes). NoSQL systems are often more analytically friendly as they are capable of providing a denormalized structure, which is conducive to feature extraction, machine learning, and scoring.

Types of NoSQL Systems

As mentioned, NoSQL systems come in several variants or categories, which are key value stores, document stores, and graph stores, each of which is described here in further detail with examples.

Key Value Stores

Key value stores contain a set or sets of indexed keys and associated values. Values are typically uninterpreted byte arrays, but can represent complex objects such as nested maps, structs, or lists. The schema is not defined at design time; however, some storage properties such as column families, which are effectively storage containers for values, and compression attributes can be defined at table design time. Examples of key value stores include HBase, Cassandra, and Amazon DynamoDB.

Document Stores

Document stores or document databases store documents, complex objects, such as JSON or BSON objects, or other complex, nested objects. The documents are assigned a key or document ID, and the contents would be the semi-structured document data. Examples of document stores include MongoDB and CouchDB.

Graph Stores

Graph stores are based upon graph theory and processing concepts. Examples of graph stores include Neo4J and GraphBase.

With that introduction, in the remaining sections I will look at some examples of popular NoSQL systems and their integrations with Hadoop.

Introducing HBase

HBase is perhaps the closest descendant and purest implementation of Bigtable. HBase was a Hadoop ecosystem project designed to deliver a distributed, massively scalable key value store on top of HDFS.

HBase Data Model

HBase stores data as a sparse, multidimensional, sorted map. The map is indexed by its key (the *row key*), and values are stored in *cells* (consisting of a *column key* and *column value*). The row key and column keys are strings and the column value is an uninterpreted byte array (which could represent any primitive or complex datatype).

HBase is multidimensional, as each cell is versioned with a time stamp.

At table design time, one or more *column families* is defined. Column families will be used as physical storage groups for columns. Different column families may have different physical storage characteristics such as block size, compression settings, or the number of cell versions to retain.

HBase API and Shell

Although there are projects such as Hive and Phoenix to provide SQL access for reading and writing data in HBase, the natural methods to access and update data in HBase are essentially get, put, scan, and delete. HBase includes a shell program as well as programmatic interfaces for multiple languages.

The HBase shell is an interactive Ruby Read-Evaluate-Print-Loop (REPL) shell with access to HBase API functions to create and modify tables and read-and-write data. The shell application can be accessed by entering hbase shell on the terminal of a system with the HBase client binaries available (see Figure 15.1).

FIGURE 15.1
HBase Shell.

Listing 15.1 demonstrates the use of the hbase shell to create a table and to insert data into the table.

LISTING 15.1   Creating a Table and Inserting Data in HBase

```
hbase> create 'my-hbase-table', \
hbase* {NAME => 'cf1', COMPRESSION => 'SNAPPY'}, \
hbase* {NAME => 'cf2'}
=> Hbase::Table - my-hbase-table
hbase> put 'my-hbase-table', 'rowkey1', 'cf1:fname', 'John'
hbase> put 'my-hbase-table', 'rowkey1', 'cf1:lname', 'Doe'
hbase> put 'my-hbase-table', 'rowkey2', 'cf1:fname', 'Jeffrey'
hbase> put 'my-hbase-table', 'rowkey2', 'cf1:lname', 'Aven'
hbase> put 'my-hbase-table', 'rowkey2', 'cf1:city', 'Hayward'
hbase> put 'my-hbase-table', 'rowkey2', 'cf2:photo', '<image>'
```

The create statement creates a new HBase table with two column families (*cf1* and *cf2*). One column family is configured to use compression and the other is not. The subsequent put statements insert data into a cell as defined by the row key (*rowkey1* or *rowkey2*, in this case) and a column specified in the format *<column_family>:<column_name>*.

Unlike a traditional database, the columns are not defined at table design time and are not typed—recall all data is an uninterpreted array of bytes. A scan command of the new table is shown in Listing 15.2.

LISTING 15.2   Scanning Our HBase Table

```
hbase> scan 'my-hbase-table'
ROW            COLUMN+CELL
 rowkey1       column=cf1:fname, timestamp=1461234568799, value=John
 rowkey1       column=cf1:lname, timestamp=1461234568877, value=Doe
 rowkey2       column=cf1:city, timestamp=1461234569032, value=Hayward
 rowkey2       column=cf1:fname, timestamp=1461234568923, value=Jeffrey
 rowkey2       column=cf1:lname, timestamp=1461234568960, value=Aven
 rowkey2       column=cf2:photo, timestamp=1461234570769, value=<image>
```

Figure 15.2 depicts the conceptual view of the data inserted.

Row Key	Column Family "cf1"	Column Family "cf2"
rowkey1	fname: John, lname: Doe	
rowkey2	fname: Jeffrey, lname: Aven, city: Hayward	photo: *<image>*

FIGURE 15.2
HBase Data.

As you can see from Figure 15.2, HBase supports sparsity. Not every column needs to exist in each row in a table and nulls are not stored.

Although HBase data is stored on HDFS, an immutable file system, HBase allows in-place updates to cells within HBase tables. It does this by creating a new version of the cell with a new time stamp if the column key already exists, and then a background compaction process collapses multiple files into a smaller number of larger files.

Listing 15.3 demonstrates an update to an existing cell and the resultant new version.

LISTING 15.3   Updating a Cell in a HBase Table

```
hbase> # update a cell
hbase* put 'my-hbase-table', 'rowkey2', 'cf1:city', 'Melbourne'
hbase> # get the latest version of a cell
hbase* get 'my-hbase-table', 'rowkey2', {COLUMNS => ['cf1:city']}
COLUMN        CELL
cf1:city      timestamp=1461276401653, value=Melbourne
hbase> # get multiple versions of a cell
hbase* get 'my-hbase-table', 'rowkey2', {COLUMNS => ['cf1:city'], VERSIONS
=> 2}
COLUMN        CELL
cf1:city       timestamp=1461276401653, value=Melbourne
cf1:city       timestamp=1461276230733, value=Hayward
```

HBase Data Distribution and Cluster Architecture

HBase data is stored in HFile objects in HDFS. HFile objects are the intersection of a column family (storage group) and a sorted range of row keys. Ranges of sorted row keys are referred to as *regions* (also known as *tablets* in Bigtable). Regions are assigned to a *region server* by HBase (see Figure 15.3). Regions are used to provide fast row key lookups, as the regions and row keys they contain are known by HBase. HBase splits and compacts regions as necessary as part of its normal operation. Non-row key-based lookups, such as looking for a column key and value satisfying some criteria, are slower. However, HBase implements *bloom filters*, a special purpose probabilistic index used to test whether an element is a member of a set, to help expedite the search.

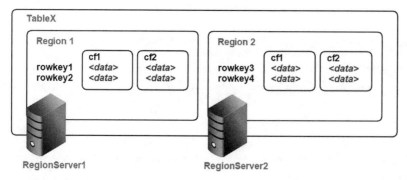

FIGURE 15.3
HBase Regions.

HBase clusters are governed by a master process called the *HMaster*. The HMaster works with a distributed transaction coordination service called ZooKeeper to maintain state across all of the Region Servers in the HBase cluster. The HMaster also orchestrates region splitting and combining. Like many other Hadoop projects, the HMaster serves a web UI on port 60010 of the HMaster node; this is pictured in Figure 15.4. The HBase UI shows the status of all of the Region Servers in the cluster and shows information about HBase tables available on the system.

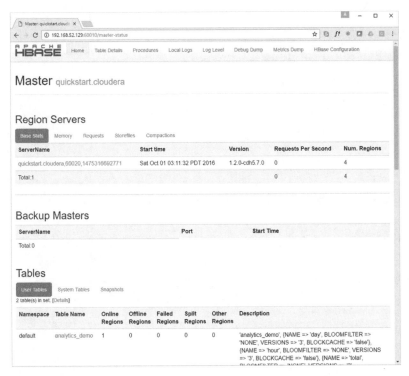

FIGURE 15.4
HBase UI.

Installing HBase

HBase can be installed in either standalone mode, which runs an entire HBase cluster in a single JVM and uses the local filesystem as its store, or distributed mode (either pseudo-distributed or fully distributed mode). In distributed mode, HBase cluster processes run in separate, isolated host processes (daemons), and HDFS is used as the store for HBase data. Fully distributed mode is recommended for production implementations.

HBase is written in Java, so a Java runtime and JAVA_HOME environment variable are required for either standalone or distributed deployment modes for HBase.

Furthermore, in distributed mode, HBase relies on another ecosystem project called ZooKeeper to maintain state across different processes in the HBase cluster.

More information about ZooKeeper can be found at **http://zookeeper.apache.org/**.

HBase's main configuration file is named `hbase-site.xml` and normally lives in `/etc` `/hbase/conf/`. The `hbase-site.xml` file contains configuration for all processes running on an HBase cluster.

Let's try installing HBase in standalone mode in our next Try it Yourself exercise.

▼ TRY IT YOURSELF

Installing HBase in Standalone Mode

You can use any system with Java installed for this exercise. As we are installing HBase in standalone mode, technically Hadoop and HDFS are not required. However, you can install HBase in standalone mode on the same system on which you installed Hadoop.

1. Make local directories for HBase and Zookeeper data:

   ```
   $ mkdir /tmp/hbase_data
   $ mkdir /tmp/zk_data
   ```

2. Download the latest release of HBase from the Apache HBase project site (`http://hbase.apache.org/`):

   ```
   $ wget http://apache.mirror.amaze.com.au/hbase/hbase-1.0.3/hbase-1.0.3-bin.
   tar.gz
   ```

3. Unpack the HBase release:

   ```
   $ tar -xvf hbase-1.0.3-bin.tar.gz
   ```

4. Change directories to the HBase release:

   ```
   $ cd hbase-1.0.3
   ```

5. Open the HBase configuration file (`hbase-site.xml`) using a text editor such as `vi`:

   ```
   $ vi conf/hbase-site.xml
   ```

6. Add the following configuration for running HBase in standalone mode between the `<configuration>` and `</configuration>` XML tags:

   ```
   <property>
       <name>hbase.rootdir</name>
       <value>file:///tmp/hbase_data</value>
   </property>
   <property>
       <name>hbase.zookeeper.property.dataDir</name>
       <value>/tmp/zk_data</value>
   </property>
   ```

7. Start the HBase instance in standalone mode:

```
$ bin/start-hbase.sh
```

8. Open the HBase shell:

```
$ bin/hbase shell
```

9. In the HBase shell, type the following commands to create a table and list all tables:

```
hbase(main):001:0> create 'test', 'cf'
hbase(main):002:0> list
```

You should see output similar to the following:

```
TABLE
1 row(s) in 0.0180 seconds
=> ["test"]
```

10. Put some data into your newly created HBase table:

```
hbase(main):003:0> put 'test', 'row1', 'cf:a', 'value1'
hbase(main):004:0> put 'test', 'row2', 'cf:b', 'value2'
hbase(main):005:0> put 'test', 'row3', 'cf:c', 'value3'
```

11. Scan the data entered into the table:

```
hbase(main):006:0> scan 'test'
```

You should see output similar to the following:

```
ROW    COLUMN+CELL
row1   column=cf:a, timestamp=1421762485768, value=value1
row2   column=cf:b, timestamp=1421762491785, value=value2
row3   column=cf:c, timestamp=1421762496210, value=value3
3 row(s) in 0.0230 seconds
```

12. Get a single row of data from the table:

```
hbase(main):007:0> get 'test', 'row1'
```

13. Disable and drop the table. (NOTE that you need to disable a table prior to dropping the table in HBase):

```
hbase(main):008:0> disable 'test'
hbase(main):009:0> drop 'test'
```

14. Exit the HBase shell by pressing Ctrl-D.

15. Stop HBase:

```
$ bin/stop-hbase.sh
```

HBase is often included in most common Hadoop distributions such as Cloudera and Hortonworks, so in many cases you do not need to install this manually. However, installing HBase in standalone mode is useful for application development using HBase before deploying your application code on a distributed HBase cluster.

Using HBase with Hadoop

HBase is accessible from all of the data analysis tools discussed in this book thus far, including MapReduce, Pig, Hive, Spark, and many of the SQL-on-Hadoop solutions.

Read access to HBase table data is typically facilitated by InputFormats and/or SerDes, and write access is provided through special OutputFormats. These will vary depending upon the project from which you are accessing the data; consult the documentation for the specific project from which you want to access HBase.

Listing 15.4 demonstrates accessing an HBase table from a PySpark program, similar to the programs you looked at in **Hour 13,** "**Introducing Apache Spark.**"

LISTING 15.4   **Accessing HBase from PySpark**

```
conf = {"hbase.zookeeper.quorum": "localhost", \
    "hbase.mapreduce.inputtable": "people"}
keyConv = \
 "org.apache.spark.examples.pythonconverters.
ImmutableBytesWritableToStringConverter"
valueConv = \
 "org.apache.spark.examples.pythonconverters.HBaseResultToStringConverter"
hbase_rdd = sc.newAPIHadoopRDD(
    "org.apache.hadoop.hbase.mapreduce.TableInputFormat",
    "org.apache.hadoop.hbase.io.ImmutableBytesWritable",
    "org.apache.hadoop.hbase.client.Result",
    keyConverter=keyConv,
    valueConverter=valueConv,
    conf=conf)
hbase_rdd.collect()
```

More information on the installation and configuration of HBase and the use of HBase with any of the various ecosystem projects such as Hive, Pig, Spark, and others can be found at http://hbase.apache.org/.

Introducing Apache Cassandra

Another notable project emanating from the Bigtable paper is Apache Cassandra. Cassandra was initially developed at Facebook and later released as an open source project under the Apache software licensing scheme.

DataStax, the commercial entity often associated with the Cassandra project, was formed in 2010 by ex-employees of Rackspace to provide an enterprise distribution and support for the open source project, in a similar vein to Cloudera's and Hortonworks' relationships with the Hadoop project.

Conceptually, Cassandra is similar to HBase in its application of the core NoSQL principles, such as not requiring a predefined schema (although Cassandra lets you define one), no referential integrity, and so on. However, there are some differences in its physical implementation, predominantly the fact that HBase has many Hadoop ecosystem dependencies, such as HDFS, ZooKeeper, and more, whereas Cassandra is more monolithic in its implementation, having fewer external dependencies. They also have some differences in their cluster architecture; where HBase is a master-slave architecture, Cassandra is a symmetric architecture using a "gossip" protocol to pass messages and govern cluster processes. There are many other differences, including the way each system manages consistency, but for the purposes of this discussion, I'll leave it there.

Cassandra Data Model

Similar to HBase, Cassandra is a multidimensional, distributed map. Cassandra tables are called *keyspaces* and contain *row keys* and *column families* (referred to as *tables*). Columns exist within column families, but are not defined at table design time. Data is located at the intersection of a row key, column family, and column key.

In addition to row keys, Cassandra also supports *primary keys*, which can also contain a partition key and a clustering key in the case of composite primary keys. These directives are used for storage and distribution of data, and service fast lookups by key.

Unlike HBase, Cassandra enables and even encourages you to define structure (a schema) for your data and assign datatypes. Cassandra supports collections within a table used to store nested or complex data structures such as sets, lists, and maps. Furthermore, Cassandra enables you to define secondary indexes to expedite lookups based on non-key values.

Cassandra Query Language (CQL)

The Cassandra Query Language (CQL) is a SQL-like language for interacting with Cassandra. CQL supports the full set of DDL and DML operations for creating, reading, updating, and deleting objects in Cassandra. Because CQL is a SQL-like language, it supports ODBC and JDBC interfaces, enabling access from common SQL and visualization utilities. CQL is also available from an interactive shell environment, `cqlsh`.

Listing 15.5 demonstrates creating a keyspace and table in Cassandra using the `cqlsh` utility.

LISTING 15.5 Creating a Keyspace and Table in Cassandra Using cqlsh

```
cqlsh> CREATE KEYSPACE mykeyspace
          WITH REPLICATION = { 'class' : 'SimpleStrategy',
'replication_factor' : 1 };
cqlsh> USE mykeyspace;
cqlsh> CREATE TABLE users (
       user_id int PRIMARY KEY,
       fname text,
       lname text
       );
cqlsh> INSERT INTO users (user_id,  fname, lname)
       VALUES (1745, 'john', 'smith');
cqlsh> INSERT INTO users (user_id,  fname, lname)
       VALUES (1744, 'john', 'doe');
cqlsh> INSERT INTO users (user_id,  fname, lname)
       VALUES (1746, 'jane', 'smith');

cqlsh> SELECT * FROM users;
 user_id | fname | lname
 --------+-------+-------
    1745 |  john | smith
    1744 |  john |   doe
    1746 |  jane | smith
```

This should look very familiar to you if you come from a background that includes relational databases such as SQL Server, Oracle, or Teradata.

Using Cassandra with Hadoop

Similar to HBase, Cassandra is accessible from all of the data analysis tools in the Hadoop ecosystem including Hive, Pig, and Spark. Read-and-write access is provided via Hadoop InputFormats and OutputFormats built specifically for Cassandra. Consult the documentation for your specific project or the Cassandra project page for excplicit connectivity objects and their usage.

Listing 15.6 demonstrates accessing a Cassandra table from a PySpark program.

LISTING 15.6   Updating Data in a Cassandra Table Using Spark

```
import pyspark_cassandra
rdd = sc.parallelize([{
"user_id": 1747,
"fname": "Jeffrey",
"lname": "Aven"
}])
rdd.saveToCassandra(
"mykeyspace",
"users",
)
```

Other NoSQL Implementations and the Future of NoSQL

Other common or popular NoSQL platforms include document stores such as MongoDB and CouchDB, key value stores such as Couchbase and Riak, and memory-centric key value stores such as Memcached and Redis. There are also the full text search and indexing platforms that have been adapted to become general-purpose NoSQL platforms. These include Apache Solr and ElasticSearch, which were both based upon the early search engine processing project, Lucene.

Like the HBase and Cassandra solutions described in this hour, many of the other available NoSQL solutions have specific InputFormat and OutputFormat classes in Hadoop that enable them to be used to read and write data in MapReduce, Hive, Pig, or Spark. Check the project or vendor's website or GitHub for your selected NoSQL platform's integration.

If an integration does not exist, you could always develop your own. Documentation on building your own custom Hadoop input and output format classes is available at http://hadoop.apache.org/.

The Future for NoSQL

As you can see, NoSQL is a fast-moving area. There are new market entrants all the time, from novel solutions to the evolution and adaptation of existing solutions. Even the established vendors such as Microsoft, Oracle, and Teradata, traditionally the proponents of conventional relational database technologies, are expanding into this area.

NoSQL platforms provide the unique combination of massive scalability and fine-grained, as well as coarse-grained, accessibility, servicing both low-latency operational patterns as well as batch analytic patterns. These characteristics make NoSQL an ideal companion to Hadoop and the Hadoop ecosystem.

Summary

Since the Google Bigtable whitepaper in 2006, the database landscape has been irrevocably altered. NoSQL databases have become a viable alternative to traditional SQL systems, offering Internet scale storage capabilities and query boundaries, as well as fast read-and-write access to support distributed device and mobile application interactions.

NoSQL concepts and implementations have emerged in parallel to the evolution of Hadoop and the Hadoop ecosystem because all of these projects emanated from early Google and Yahoo! work.

In this hour, I have introduced you to NoSQL concepts and looked at some practical applications of key value and document stores: Apache HBase, the NoSQL platform which runs directly on top of HDFS, Apache Cassandra, and other NoSQL implementations. I have also discussed the high-level cluster architecture as well as the conceptual and physical data models of HBase and Cassandra.

Additionally, I have discussed how Hadoop ecosystem technologies such as Hive and Spark can interact with various NoSQL platforms as both a consumer and producer of data. Hopefully, I've inspired you to explore this area further. Happy NoSQL-ing!

Q&A

Q. What are the key functional characteristics of a NoSQL database?

A. NoSQL systems are schemaless at design time and schema-on-read at runtime, meaning they do not have predefined columns. Columns are created with each PUT (INSERT) operation, and each record, document, or data instance can have a different schema than the previous instance. Also, data objects typically have no predefined relationship to any other object, meaning there is no concept of foreign keys or referential integrity, and joins are not natively implemented.

Q. What are the various types of NoSQL stores?

A. Key value stores, document stores, and graph stores.

Q. What are the primary differences between HBase's and Cassandra's implementation of Bigtable?

A. HBase relies on many other independent Hadoop ecosystem components such as HDFS and ZooKeeper, whereas Cassandra has a monolithic implementation. HBase clusters implement a master-slave architecture, whereas Cassandra has a peer-to-peer symmetric distributed architecture. HBase data is entirely untyped (uninterpreted arrays of bytes), whereas Cassandra supports schemas and datatype definitions as an option.

Workshop

The workshop contains quiz questions to help you solidify your understanding of the material covered. Try to answer all questions before looking at the "Answers" section that follows.

Quiz

1. What is the query language used by Cassandra?

2. The `put` method in HBase is used to do which of the following?

   A. Insert a new row key along with a data cell into a table

   B. Insert a new cell (column key and value) into an existing row

   C. Update the value for an existing cell

   D. All of the above

3. What Cassandra data construct is used to represent complex objects such as sets, lists, or maps?

4. A physical storage group for columns in HBase is called a _____.

Answers

1. CQL (Cassandra Query Language).

2. D.

3. collection.

4. column family.

HOUR 16
Managing YARN

What You'll Learn in This Hour:

- ▶ Running applications on YARN
- ▶ Administering YARN clusters and applications
- ▶ Queues, users, and application priority in YARN
- ▶ Application and resource scheduling in YARN

YARN is the central component in Hadoop for managing and governing distributed applications such as MapReduce, Spark, Tez, and more, running on the Hadoop platform. In this hour I will deep-dive into YARN, exploring cluster and application management, configuration, fault tolerance, and more. You will also be introduced to some important application scheduling tools, techniques, and approaches for managing multi-user and mission critical Hadoop clusters.

YARN Revisited

You were first introduced to the YARN cluster architecture in **Hour 2, "Understanding the Hadoop Cluster Architecture,"** and then to application management using YARN in **Hour 6, "Understanding Data Processing in Hadoop."** In this hour I will dig deeper into how YARN works and how to effectively schedule concurrent, SLA (Service-Level Agreement) bound applications using YARN. But first, let's revisit some central YARN concepts.

YARN Cluster Architecture

A recap of the YARN cluster architecture detailed in **Hour 2** is pictured in Figure 16.1.

The components, daemons, roles, and processes in a YARN cluster are summarized in the sections that follow.

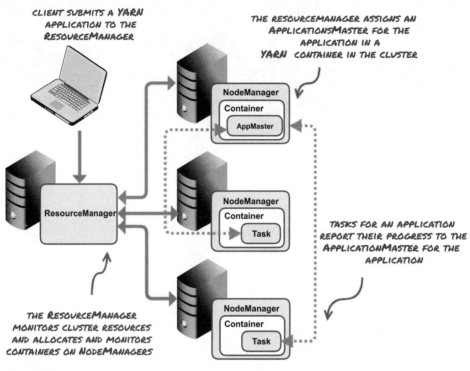

CLIENT SUBMITS A YARN APPLICATION TO THE RESOURCEMANAGER

THE RESOURCEMANAGER ASSIGNS AN APPLICATIONSMASTER FOR THE APPLICATION IN A YARN CONTAINER IN THE CLUSTER

TASKS FOR AN APPLICATION REPORT THEIR PROGRESS TO THE APPLICATIONMASTER FOR THE APPLICATION

THE RESOURCEMANAGER MONITORS CLUSTER RESOURCES AND ALLOCATES AND MONITORS CONTAINERS ON NODEMANAGERS

FIGURE 16.1
YARN Revisited.

ResourceManager

The ResourceManager is the YARN master node daemon which is responsible for granting resources to applications in the form of containers, which are predefined compute units consisting of memory and virtual CPU cores. The ResourceManager receives heartbeats and status reports from slave nodes (NodeManagers) in the YARN cluster to monitor availability of cluster resources. The ResourceManager is also responsible for cluster scheduling and managing concurrency (I will discuss scheduling later this hour).

TIP

Implement High Availability for the YARN ResourceManager on Production Systems

High Availability (HA) can be configured and deployed for the ResourceManager process in YARN clusters. If HA is not enabled for the ResourceManager, the ResourceManager becomes a single point of failure (SPOF) for YARN, much like the NameNode is a SPOF for HDFS if HA is not enabled. ResourceManager HA requires a ZooKeeper ensemble to be deployed. This is the same ZooKeeper project that was introduced in the previous hour as a requirement for a distributed HBase cluster. More information about deploying the ResourceManager in HA mode is available at: http://hadoop. apache.org/docs/current/hadoop-yarn/hadoop-yarn-site/ResourceManagerHA.html.

NodeManager

The NodeManager is the slave node YARN daemon responsible for managing YARN containers running on cluster nodes. The YARN containers running on NodeManagers orchestrate processing stages and run tasks for distributed applications running on YARN. The NodeManager process also monitors consumption and reports application progress, status and health back to the ResourceManager.

ApplicationMaster

The ApplicationMaster is a process spawned in the first YARN container running on a NodeManager allocated by the ResourceManager for an application. The ApplicationMaster is responsible for negotiating with the ResourceManager for the allocation of containers to run tasks for the application. The ApplicationMaster then presents these containers to the application. The ApplicationMaster is delegated the authority to manage the execution of an application, including the orchestration of processing stages such as the Map and Reduce phases of a MapReduce application.

There are also other processes in YARN used to collect and manage application history that are discussed in more detail later in this hour.

Running Applications on YARN

Let's take a closer look at some of the detailed aspects of applications running on YARN now.

Resource Requests

Applications request cluster resources using the ResourceRequest construct. ResourceRequests are low-level, fine-grained resource requests sent to the ResourceManager on behalf of the application that include the following:

- ▶ The priority of the request

- ▶ The amount of memory and CPU (vcore) resources required (e.g., 4 GB, 2 vcores)

- ▶ The number of containers required

- ▶ Data locality information; for instance, which rack and host preferences to dispatch the containers to

If the request is successful, the requested containers are granted. The Scheduler process of the ResourceManager and the configured scheduler sharing policy, which I will discuss shortly, determine when and how many of the containers to release.

The low-level ResourceRequests are normally a function of configuration parameters supplied by the developer or analyst. The `yarn-site.xml` file contains several parameters that relate to upper and lower boundaries for containers, such as the parameters shown in Listing 16.1.

LISTING 16.1   YARN Container Related Configuration Parameters

```
<configuration>
...
<!--
Number of vcores on a NodeManager that can be allocated for containers
-->
<property>
    <name>yarn.nodemanager.resource.cpu-vcores</name>
    <value>8</value>
</property>
<!--
Amount of physical memory that can be allocated for containers
-->
<property>
    <name>yarn.nodemanager.resource.memory-mb</name>
    <value>8192</value>
</property>
<!--
The minimum allocation for every container request at the RM
-->
<property>
    <name>yarn.scheduler.minimum-allocation-mb</name>
    <value>1024</value>
</property>
<!--
The maximum allocation for every container request at the RM
-->
<property>
    <name>yarn.scheduler.maximum-allocation-mb</name>
    <value>8192</value>
</property>
<!--
The minimum allocation of virtual CPU cores for every container request
-->
<property>
    <name>yarn.scheduler.maximum-allocation-vcores</name>
    <value>1</value>
</property>
<!--
The maximum allocation of virtual CPU cores for every container request
-->
<property>
    <name>yarn.scheduler.maximum-allocation-vcores</name>
    <value>32</value>
</property>
...
</configuration>
```

These resource request parameters, especially the scheduler-related properties, can also be supplied by the application being submitted to YARN.

Fault Tolerance and Failure Recovery

YARN, like HDFS, is designed to be resilient. Recall that the design intention of Hadoop was to deploy and scale on commodity, even cheap, hardware that may be more prone to failure. Let's discuss some of the various types of failures and YARN's ability to recover from them.

Task Failure

Tasks run in YARN containers. If a running task fails, the ApplicationMaster for the application will reschedule the task on another node, adhering to the data locality specifications set out in the resource request. The task will be reattempted four times by default, (although this is configurable). If the task fails four times, the application will fail. In this case, all other tasks running for the application will be killed and the applications status will be set to FAILED, which can be seen in the YARN ResourceManager UI.

NodeManager Failure

NodeManagers send regular heartbeats to the ResourceManager. A NodeManager is considered to have failed if the heartbeat threshold (`yarn.resourcemanager.nm.liveness-monitor. expiryinterval-ms` property in `yarn-site.xml`) is exceeded. In such cases, if the NodeManager was hosting tasks for an application, these tasks will be considered to have failed and will be treated accordingly, as just discussed. If the NodeManager is hosting an ApplicationMaster for an application, the application will be considered to have failed.

Furthermore, the NodeManager is removed from YARN's list of active nodes for the cluster, a process called blacklisting, and will no longer be allocated containers or tasks. When the service is restored, the NodeManager will be considered to be active again, and may then be allocated new tasks.

ApplicationMaster Failure

As just discussed, if a NodeManager hosting an ApplicationMaster fails, the application is treated as a failed application. The same applies if the ApplicationMaster process itself fails. By default, the application will not be retried; however, you can enable this behavior by setting the `yarn.resourcemanager.am.max-retries` property in the `yarn-site.xml` configuration file.

If an application is retried, by default all previously complete tasks for the application will be re-run. This behavior—known as *job recovery*—can be changed by setting the `yarn.app. mapreduce.am.job.recovery.enable` property to `true` in the `yarn-site.xml` file.

ResourceManager Failure

As discussed, the ResourceManager process and its host is a single point of failure for a YARN cluster if high availability (HA) is not enabled. If the ResourceManager fails and a standby is not available, no new applications can be launched. Currently running applications are no longer able to negotiate additional resources they may require and will fail.

If HA is enabled, however, the standby ResourceManager will automatically resume the roles and responsibilities that the previously active ResourceManager was performing, and the YARN cluster will continue to operate unaffected.

Auxiliary Services

NodeManagers in a YARN cluster can also be configured to run auxiliary services, which provide specific services to applications running on YARN. These auxiliary services run within JVMs on the NodeManagers.

The most common example of this is the shuffle service, which orchestrates the Shuffle-and-Sort process (the process that sends intermediate data from mappers to reducers, merges-and-sorts data by its key, and presents this data to the respective `reduce()` functions). An overview of the shuffle service is shown in Figure 16.2.

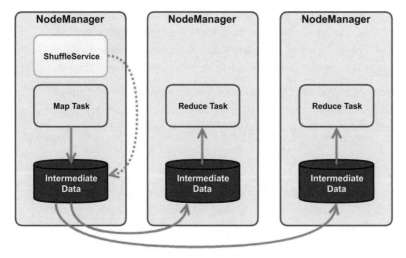

FIGURE 16.2
Shuffle Service in YARN.

Administering YARN

YARN administration encompasses configuration management, application/job management, monitoring and troubleshooting. Let's explore some of the salient points regarding administering a YARN cluster now.

YARN Configuration

You have seen many YARN configuration parameters already, and you will see many more throughout the course of this book. The YARN configuration is located in the `yarn-site.xml` file typically located in the `/etc/hadoop/conf` directory. This file exists on all hosts that assume roles in a YARN cluster, specifically the nodes that are hosting the ResourceManager and NodeManager processes respectively, as shown in Figure 16.3.

ResourceManager

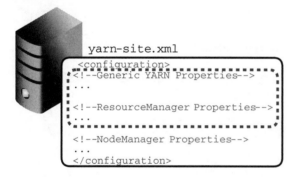

NodeManager

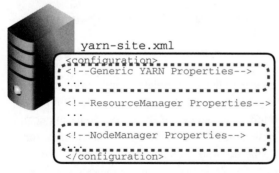

FIGURE 16.3
YARN Configuration on Different Nodes.

As shown in Figure 16.3, each daemon will read the configuration specific to that particular service from their respective `yarn-site.xml` files. However, it is a common convention to keep the configuration file homogeneous across all nodes, as the daemons will ignore configuration properties not relevant to that particular service.

In the vast majority of cases, a change to a configuration property in the `yarn-site.xml` file will require a restart of the daemon or daemons to which the property applies. I will discuss more specific details about configuration and configuration precedence in **Hour 20, "Understanding Cluster Configuration."**

Using the YARN Web Interface

The YARN ResourceManager UI is often your best starting point when managing applications running on YARN. The ResourceManager UI is exposed on port 8088 of the YARN ResourceManager host as shown in Figure 16.4.

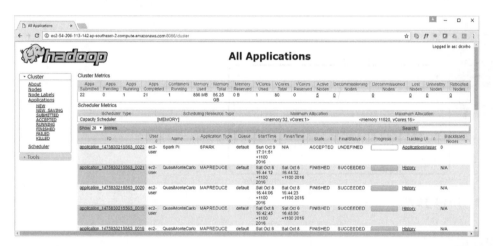

FIGURE 16.4
YARN ResourceManager UI.

The UI can be used to view the status of running, failed, or completed applications running on YARN; to view YARN container logs for a job; or to redirect to the application UI for an application; for instance, the Spark application UI served by the Driver in a Spark application as discussed in **Hour 13, "Introducing Apache Spark."** If a UI is served by the application running on YARN, it is typically accessible using the ApplicationMaster link for the application in the YARN ResourceManager UI. An example of a Spark application UI is shown in Figure 16.5.

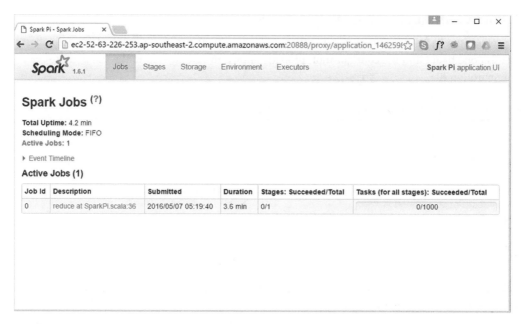

FIGURE 16.5
ApplicationMaster UI for a Spark Application.

SSL Security

Traffic to and from the YARN UI server can be secured using SSL by installing a trusted certificate on the ResourceManager host and adding the configuration property shown in Listing 16.2 to the `yarn-site.xml` configuration file.

LISTING 16.2   Configuring SSL Transport Security for YARN

```
<configuration>
...
<!--the https address of the RM web application-->
<property>
   <name>yarn.resourcemanager.webapp.https.address</name>
   <value>${yarn.resourcemanager.hostname}:8090</value>
</property>
<!--enforces the HTTPS endpoint only for all Yarn Daemons-->
<property>
   <name>yarn.http.policy</name>
   <value>HTTPS_ONLY</value>
</property>
...
</configuration>
```

Killing YARN Applications Using the UI

By default the YARN UI allows read-only access. However, you can configure the UI to kill jobs. This is done by adding the configuration property shown in Listing 16.3 to the `yarn-site.xml` configuration file.

LISTING 16.3   Enabling the Capbility to Kill Running Jobs Using the UI

```
<configuration>
...
<!--enable Kill Application control in the RM web application-->
<property>
    <name>yarn.resourcemanager.webapp.ui-actions.enabled</name>
    <value>true</value>
</property>
...
</configuration>
```

Once enabled, you should now see a Kill Application link for a running application as highlighted in the red box in Figure 16.6.

FIGURE 16.6
Killing an Application Using the UI.

This is generally not recommended for production clusters, however, as this UI is difficult to fully secure.

Using the YARN Command-Line Interface

YARN provides a CLI utility (`yarn`) that can be used to view the status of a job or all jobs running on a YARN cluster. The `yarn` command can be used to launch applications (synonymous to the `hadoop jar` command), view log files, run YARN processes, view information about containers, queues and more. You can see all of the available command-line options for the `yarn` command using `yarn --help` as shown in Listing 16.4.

LISTING 16.4   Using the `yarn` Command

```
$ yarn --help
Usage: yarn [--config confdir] [COMMAND | CLASSNAME]
  CLASSNAME                        run the class named CLASSNAME
 or
  where COMMAND is one of:
  resourcemanager -format-state-store   deletes the RMStateStore
  resourcemanager                  run the ResourceManager
  nodemanager                      run a nodemanager on each slave
  timelineserver                   run the timeline server
  rmadmin                          admin tools
  sharedcachemanager               run the SharedCacheManager daemon
  scmadmin                         SharedCacheManager admin tools
  version                          print the version
  jar <jar>                        run a jar file
  application                      prints application(s)
                                   report/kill application
  applicationattempt               prints applicationattempt(s)
                                   report
  container                        prints container(s) report
  node                             prints node report(s)
  queue                            prints queue information
  logs                             dump container logs
  classpath                        prints the class path needed to
                                   get the Hadoop jar and the
                                   required libraries
  cluster                          prints cluster information
  daemonlog                        get/set the log level for each
                                   daemon
```

As previously discussed, applications running on a YARN cluster in cluster mode cannot be killed simply by exiting the invoking process. The `yarn` command can be used to kill a running application on YARN, as shown in Listing 16.5.

LISTING 16.5   Killing a YARN Application Using the `yarn` Command

```
$ yarn application -list
...
Total number of RUNNING applications : 1
Application-Id                   Application-Name               ...
application_1475830215563_0024  org.apache.spark.examples.SparkPi ...
$ yarn application -kill application_1475830215563_0024
...
Killed application application_1475830215563_0024
```

Log Aggregation in YARN

Logs generated by tasks running on NodeManager's throughout a YARN cluster are an invaluable source of information for debugging and troubleshooting distributed applications. For performance reasons, these logs are generated on the local filesystem of the NodeManager host running the respective tasks.

While tasks are running, logs can be accessed by the ApplicationMaster link for the application in the YARN ResourceManager, which redirects to the relevant NodeManager host for the task (or container) logs. Once the application finishes and the logs are no longer being updated, YARN provides a facility to aggregate the logs by application and move these logs into HDFS for long term storage. This process is known as *log aggregation*. Log aggregation is enabled by setting the `yarn.log-aggregation-enable` property to `true` in the `yarn-site.xml` configuration file. There are also configuration properties that nominate directories and retention policies for aggregated logs as well.

Logs for completed applications are still available through the web UI. Aggregated logs can be accessed using the `yarn` command, as shown in Listing 16.6.

LISTING 16.6   Viewing YARN Logs Using the `yarn` Command

```
$ yarn logs -applicationId application_1475830215563_0024
Container: container_1475830215563_0024_01_000002 on ...
========================================================
LogType:stderr
Log Upload Time:Sun Oct 09 07:02:00 +0000 2016
LogLength:69033
Log Contents:
SLF4J: Actual binding is of type [org.slf4j.impl.Log4jLoggerFactory]
16/10/09 07:01:50 INFO SignalUtils: Registered signal handler for TERM
16/10/09 07:01:50 INFO SignalUtils: Registered signal handler for HUP
16/10/09 07:01:50 INFO SignalUtils: Registered signal handler for INT
16/10/09 07:01:51 INFO SecurityManager: Changing view acls to: yarn,ec2-user
```

```
16/10/09 07:01:51 INFO SecurityManager: Changing modify acls to: yarn,ec2-user
16/10/09 07:01:51 INFO SecurityManager: Changing view acls groups to:
16/10/09 07:01:51 INFO SecurityManager: Changing modify acls groups to:
...
```

I will discuss logging in much more detail in **Hour 23, "Administering and Troubleshooting Hadoop."**

YARN and MapReduce History

Beyond log files, YARN provides multiple interfaces for accessing historical data, such as application metrics, for applications that are running or have run on the cluster. Let's investigate those next.

MRJobHistory Server

As YARN is a generic framework which is extensible beyond MapReduce, application metrics specific to MapReduce such as some of the specific counters used by MapReduce are not captured, stored, or served by YARN natively. The *MRJobHistory* Server (a separate daemon) is responsible for collecting and storing these metrics. The MRJobHistory Server serves a web UI on port 19888 as shown in Figure 16.7.

FIGURE 16.7
MRJobHistory Server UI.

In addition, data from the MRJobHistory Server can be accessed via a REST API. An example of accessing this data using a `curl` command is shown in Listing 16.7.

LISTING 16.7   Accessing the MRJobHistory Server via REST

```
$ curl -XGET http://rmhost:19888/ws/v1/history
{
 "historyInfo":
 {
  "startedOn":1475830220347,
  "hadoopVersion":"2.7.2-amzn-3",
  "hadoopBuildVersion":"2.7.2-amzn-3",
  "hadoopVersionBuiltOn":"2016-07-26T20:15Z"
 }
}
```

Detailed specifications for the MRJobHistory Server REST API are available from the Hadoop project documentation available at **https://hadoop.apache.org**.

Timeline Server

The *YARN Timeline Server* provides generic information about completed applications that is framework-agnostic, such as application attempts, scheduling, resource utilization, and container information. As with the History Server, the Timeline Server is a separate daemon which could run on the same or a different host to the ResourceManager. The Timeline Server uses a *LevelDB* datastore (a key value store) to store its data, and serves a web UI and a REST API. The web UI is available on port 8188 as shown in Figure 16.8.

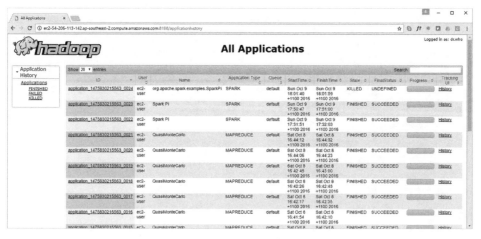

FIGURE 16.8
YARN Timeline Server UI.

An example of a REST API request and response to the Timeline Server is shown in Listing 16.8.

LISTING 16.8   Timeline Server REST API

```
$ curl -XGET http://rmhost:8188/ws/v1/timeline/
{
 "About":"Timeline API"
}
```

As with the History Server REST API, you can find detailed specifications for the Timeline Server API from the Hadoop project web site.

There is activity in the Hadoop project, specifically in the YARN project, to consolidate these services, so watch that space.

Application Scheduling in YARN

Application scheduling in YARN enables multiple applications running concurrently to efficiently and effectively share the cluster's distributed compute and memory resources.

YARN has two primary scheduling policies available to share resources, the *FairScheduler* and the *CapacityScheduler*. In the absence of one of these policies being applied, the default scheduling policy on many clusters is the *FIFOScheduler* (or First-in-First-out scheduler), which allocates resources on a first-come, first-served basis. This is the most primitive approach to scheduling and does not allow long-running applications to coexist with short-running applications or adhere to application SLAs.

Let's discuss the sharing policies, which are a better alternative to the FIFOScheduler for production systems in more detail now.

FairScheduler

The FairScheduler is designed to distribute cluster resources (aggregate memory and CPU) equally or fairly across defined *queues,* or application pools, that have a demand for resources. This concept is pictured in Figure 16.9.

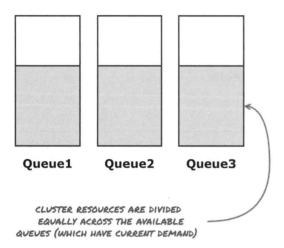

Queue1   Queue2   Queue3

CLUSTER RESOURCES ARE DIVIDED
EQUALLY ACROSS THE AVAILABLE
QUEUES (WHICH HAVE CURRENT DEMAND)

FIGURE 16.9
FairScheduler.

The FairScheduler is enabled by adding the properties shown in Listing 16.9 to the `yarn-site.xml` file on the ResourceManager and all NodeManagers.

LISTING 16.9   Enabling the FairScheduler

```
<configuration>
...
<!--the class to use as the resource scheduler.-->
<property>
<name>yarn.resourcemanager.scheduler.class</name>
<value>org.apache.hadoop.yarn.server.resourcemanager.scheduler.fair.FairScheduler
</value>
</property>
<!--path to allocation file describing queues and their properties-->
<property>
<name>yarn.scheduler.fair.allocation.file</name>
<value>fair-scheduler.xml</value>
</property>
...
</configuration>
```

As shown in Listing 16.9, the specific FairScheduler configuration file is defined in the `yarn.scheduler.fair.allocation.file` property, which defaults to a file named `fair-scheduler.xml` located in the Hadoop configuration directory alongside the `yarn-site.xml` file.

Queues in YARN may be defined with different service-level agreements (SLAs). For instance, you may have a production queue that needs to be guaranteed resources and priority at any given time, and a development queue that takes a lower priority. The FairScheduler enables you to assign minimum guaranteed resources for different queues as well as weighting queues using the FairScheduler configuration file (`fair-scheduler.xml`), as shown in Listing 16.10.

LISTING 16.10 Configuring the FairScheduler

```xml
<?xml version="1.0"?>
<allocations>
 <queue name="Queue1">
  <minResources>10000 mb,0vcores</minResources>
  <maxResources>90000 mb,0vcores</maxResources>
  <maxRunningApps>50</maxRunningApps>
  <maxAMShare>0.1</maxAMShare>
  <weight>2.0</weight>
  <schedulingPolicy>fair</schedulingPolicy>
 </queue>
 <queue name="Queue2">
  <minResources>5000 mb,0vcores</minResources>
  <maxResources>40000 mb,0vcores</maxResources>
  <maxRunningApps>100</maxRunningApps>
  <maxAMShare>0.1</maxAMShare>
  <weight>1.0</weight>
  <schedulingPolicy>fair</schedulingPolicy>
 </queue>
</allocations>
</xml>
```

You can also configure generic scheduling policies such as default queue scheduling and placement policies, as well as policies for all users or specific named users of the cluster. It is also possible to have alternative scheduling policies within a queue. For instance, you could have an application queue which is scheduled by the FairScheduler with applications assigned to the queue scheduled using the FIFOScheduler.

The FairScheduler also has the concept of *preemption*, where containers allocated to low-priority application queues can be effectively annexed by higher-priority applications, such as those running in production queues. The two types of preemption available with the FairScheduler are *minSharePreemption* and *fairSharePreemption*.

The FairScheduler is the default scheduler for Cloudera distributions. You can find more details about the FairScheduler, including detailed configuration information, from https://www. cloudera.com/documentation/enterprise/latest/topics/admin_fair_scheduler.html or http://hadoop.apache.org/docs/stable2/hadoop-yarn/hadoop-yarn-site/FairScheduler.html.

CapacityScheduler

The CapacityScheduler provides limits on application resource use based on users and queues. Similar to the FairScheduler just described, the goal of the CapacityScheduler is to ensure fairness

and stability of the cluster. The CapacityScheduler is a much simpler scheduler than
the FairScheduler, as you simply define your queues, including a default queue, and assign
a percentage of the available cluster resources to the queue as depicted in Figure 16.10.

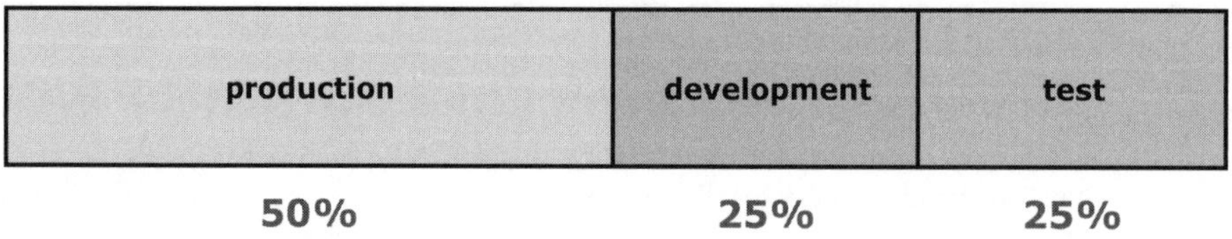

production	development	test
50%	**25%**	**25%**

FIGURE 16.10
CapacityScheduler.

You can also place hard limits on vcore and memory allocated to a queue. Listing 16.11 shows
the configuration required to explicitly enable the CapacityScheduler for a YARN cluster in the
yarn-site.xml configuration file.

LISTING 16.11   Enabling the CapacityScheduler

```
<configuration>
...
<!--the class to use as the resource scheduler.-->
<property>
<name>yarn.resourcemanager.scheduler.class</name>
<value>org.apache.hadoop.yarn.server.resourcemanager.scheduler.capacity.
CapacityScheduler</value>
<property>
...
</configuration>
```

The default CapacityScheduler configuration file, capacity-scheduler.xml, is located
in the Hadoop configuration directory. An example CapacityScheduler configuration is
shown in Listing 16.12.

LISTING 16.12   Configuring the CapacityScheduler

```
<?xml version="1.0"?>
<configuration>
 <property>
  <name>yarn.scheduler.capacity.root.queues</name>
  <value>prod,dev,default</value>
 </property>
 <property>
  <name>yarn.scheduler.capacity.root.prod.capacity</name>
  <value>20</value>
 </property>
```

```
<property>
 <name>yarn.scheduler.capacity.root.dev.capacity</name>
 <value>40</value>
</property>
<property>
 <name>yarn.scheduler.capacity.root.default.capacity</name>
 <value>40</value>
</property>
<property>
 <name>yarn.scheduler.capacity.root.dev.maximum-capacity</name>
 <value>75</value>
</property>
<property>
 <name>yarn.scheduler.capacity.queue-mappings</name>
 <value>u:devuser:dev,u:produser:prod</value>
</property>
</configuration>
```

If you make changes to the `capacity-scheduler.xml` configuration file on a running cluster, you will need to execute the `yarn` command shown in Listing 16.13 to refresh the scheduler information on the ResourceManager.

LISTING 16.13 Refreshing CapacityScheduler Configuration

```
$ yarn rmadmin -refreshQueues
```

YARN schedulers like the FairScheduler and CapacityScheduler can often be configured using your current distribution's management user interface, such as Ambari for Hortonworks platforms or Cloudera Manager for Cloudera systems.

Furthermore, queue and capacity information for schedulers in YARN can be viewed using the `/scheduler` page of the ResourceManager's web UI as shown in Figure 16.11.

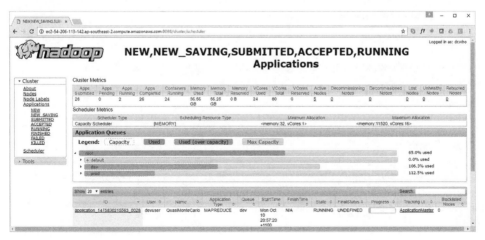

FIGURE 16.11
YARN Scheduler Information Page.

The CapacityScheduler is the default scheduler in YARN and the default scheduler for Hortonworks distributions. You can find more information about configuration and usage of the CapacityScheduler from **http://hadoop.apache.org/docs/stable2/hadoop-yarn/hadoop-yarn-site/CapacityScheduler.html**.

▼ TRY IT YOURSELF

Configuring the YARN Capacity Scheduler

In this exercise you will enable and configure the CapacityScheduler for your YARN cluster.

1. Open the `yarn-site.xml` using a text editor such as `vi`.

2. Add the configuration shown in Listing 16.11 to the `yarn-site.xml` file, save, and exit the text editor.

3. Add the configuration shown in Listing 16.12 to the `capacity-scheduler.xml` located in the Hadoop configuration directory (`/etc/hadoop/conf`) using your preferred text editor, replacing the existing contents of this file.

4. Refresh the queue information in YARN:

   ```
   $ yarn rmadmin -refreshQueues
   ```

5. Add two user accounts:

   ```
   $ sudo useradd -g hadoop devuser
   $ sudo useradd -g hadoop produser
   ```

6. Open two separate terminal windows.

7. In one window, `sudo` as the `devuser`:

   ```
   $ sudo su devuser
   ```

8. In the other window, sudo as the produser:

   ```
   $ sudo su produser
   ```

9. In both windows, execute the following commands, running the two applications simultaneously:

   ```
   $ cd $HADOOP_HOME
   $ bin/hadoop jar \
   share/hadoop/mapreduce/hadoop-mapreduce-examples-2.7.2.jar \
   pi 50 100000
   ```

10. Check the /scheduler page of the ResourceManager UI. You should see usage of both the dev and prod queues by the applications you just submitted. Note how the resources are allocated in accordance with the policies you defined in Step 3.

Summary

YARN is the core subsystem in Hadoop responsible for governing, allocating, and managing the finite distributed processing resources available on a Hadoop cluster. In this hour, you learned about the various practices involved with managing a YARN cluster.

You learned about the resiliency of YARN and how it handles respective failures in its processes, such as task or container failure, ApplicationMaster failure, NodeManager failure, and ResourceManager failure.

You also learned more about YARN configuration, application management, logging, and log file management. Concepts and practices, including YARN configuration, application management, log management, and application history, were covered in more detail as well in this hour.

I will revisit many of the concepts covered in this hour throughout the book.

Q&A

Q. **What is the goal of YARN scheduling? What scheduling policies are available in YARN?**

A. Application scheduling in YARN enables multiple applications running concurrently to efficiently and effectively share the cluster's distributed compute and memory resources. YARN has two primary scheduling policies available that are designed to share resources, the *FairScheduler* and the *CapacityScheduler*. There is also a simple scheduling policy called the *FIFOScheduler* that allocates resources on a first-come, first-served basis.

Q. **How is a NodeManager failure handled on a YARN cluster running an application?**

A. If a NodeManager in a YARN cluster fails or is non-responsive, then tasks hosted by the NodeManager will be treated as failed tasks and will be rescheduled on other nodes by the ResourceManager. If the NodeManager was hosting an ApplicationMaster container or containers, the respective applications will fail by default. The NodeManager will also be blacklisted and will not be assigned additional containers until it becomes responsive again.

Q. **What is the difference between the Timeline Server and MRJobHistory Server in YARN?**

A. The MRJobHistory Server keeps metrics and information about MapReduce applications specifically, such as the number of Map or Map attempt operations, whereas the Timeline Server is generic and keeps more general information about all applications running on the YARN cluster.

Workshop

The workshop contains quiz questions to help you solidify your understanding of the material covered. Try to answer all questions before looking at the "Answers" section that follows.

Quiz

1. Which of the following is included with a YARN resource request?

    A. request priority

    B. container memory and vcores

    C. data locality information

    D. number of containers required

    E. all of the above

2. What are the two types of preemption available with the YARN FairScheduler?

3. **True or False**. It is possible to kill running applications through the YARN ResourceManager UI.

4. What additional Hadoop ecosystem project is required to implement high availability (failover capability) for the YARN ResourceManager?

Answers

1. E.

2. minSharePreemption and fairSharePreemption.

3. True (assuming you have enabled this in the YARN configuration).

4. ZooKeeper.

Working with the Hadoop Ecosystem

What You'll Learn in This Hour:

▶ Using and managing Oozie for workflow coordination
▶ Managing ZooKeeper
▶ Stream processing technologies in the Hadoop ecosystem
▶ Machine learning and data visualization ecosystem utilities

The Hadoop ecosystem has expanded at a rate much faster than the core project itself. In this hour I will revisit some of the notable projects discussed thus far as well as introduce you to some new ecosystem projects, and discuss usage and management considerations for these projects.

Hadoop Ecosystem Overview

You were first introduced to the Hadoop ecosystem way back in **Hour 1, "Introducing Hadoop"** (seems like more than 16 hours ago now!). Recall that the core technologies of Hadoop include HDFS and YARN. Any other project that integrates or interacts with Hadoop is considered to be a Hadoop ecosystem project.

Hadoop ecosystem projects typically fall into one of several broad categories. Let's revisit these categories and some of the notable projects we have discussed thus far before introducing or detailing other projects in the Hadoop landscape.

Data Ingestion Utilities

In **Hour 5, "Getting Data into Hadoop,"** we introduced two of the main data ingestion projects in the Hadoop ecosystem, Flume, and Sqoop. Let's revisit these projects now and discuss their respective management considerations.

Sqoop

Sqoop (SQL-to-Hadoop) is the ecosystem solution for ingesting data into Hadoop from a relational database source such as Oracle, Teradata, SQL Server, and so on. Sqoop can also be used to egest data from Hadoop to external relational database systems. Sqoop can be deployed in two different variants:

▶ *Sqoop client*—All of the Sqoop software resides on clients, which connects directly to a source or destination database system and submit Sqoop jobs directly to YARN

▶ *Sqoop as a Service*—A service is provisioned to connect to remote database systems and submit Sqoop jobs to a Hadoop cluster on a client's behalf

The first release of Sqoop could only be deployed as a client, whereas the subsequent major release—*Sqoop2*—could be deployed as a client or a service.

The advantage to the Sqoop2 server-based implementation is that the connection details, which will include credentials such as usernames and passwords for the target database platform(s), is centrally managed and secure. Furthermore, the Sqoop2 server can be placed so as to act as a firewall for a Hadoop cluster that is isolated from external networks.

Clients connect to the Sqoop2 service using the same `sqoop` binary used to connect directly as a direct client interface. The Sqoop2 client binaries also include an interactive shell that can be used to connect to a Sqoop2 server and submit jobs interactively. Listing 17.1 shows how to get started with the `sqoop2-shell` program.

LISTING 17.1   Sqoop2 Shell

```
$ sqoop2-shell
sqoop:000> set server --host sqoop2server --port 12000 --webapp sqoop
sqoop:000> show version --all
 client version:
  Sqoop 2.0.0-SNAPSHOT source revision 418c5f637c3f09b94ea7fc3b0a4610831373a25f
  Compiled by vbasavaraj on Mon Nov  3 08:18:21 PST 2014
 server version:
  Sqoop 2.0.0-SNAPSHOT source revision 418c5f637c3f09b94ea7fc3b0a4610831373a25f
  Compiled by vbasavaraj on Mon Nov  3 08:18:21 PST 2014
 API versions:
  [v1]
```

More information about Sqoop (including Sqoop2) can be found at http://sqoop.apache.org/.

Flume

Recall that Flume is used to capture data from a source and ultimately route this data into HDFS or another target filesystem such as S3. Flume is deployed as a series of agents that run as background (or foreground) processes with a source, a sink, and a channel.

The source instructs the agent where to source the data from, the sink instructs the agent where to send the data, and the channel defines what to do with the data between the source and sink (e.g., batch, compress, encrypt, transform).

Although channels can be volatile when they are in memory only, it is recommended that you use durable (file-based) channels so that agents can recover from exceptions or outages. Management of agent configuration, which is contained in the `flume.properties` file in the flume agent's `conf` directory), is a key aspect of a Flume deployment. If you are running agents as background processes or services, which is generally recommended, you should monitor these processes to ensure they are running and in a good state.

More information about Flume can be found at **https://flume.apache.org/**.

There are other data ingestion projects that are specifically designed to perform complex event processing on streams of data such as Storm and Spark Streaming. I will discuss these projects in more detail later this hour.

Data Processing and Analysis Utilities

You learned about some of the primary data processing and analysis earlier in this book. Let's recap these now.

Hive

Hive was discussed in **Hour 10, "Analyzing Data Using Apache Hive,"** and **Hour 11, "Using Advanced Hive"** of this book. Like Sqoop, Hive can be deployed as either a client, where all of the libraries, the metastore, and Hadoop connection information reside on the client, or as a service, where the connection information for the metastore and Hadoop is centrally managed. In a server-based installation, clients can use the lightweight interface, Beeline, to access the Hive server, or the Hive server could be accessed via an API, as is the case for web-based applications such as the Hive editor in HUE discussed in **Hour 14, "Using the Hadoop User Environment (HUE)."**

In either type of Hive deployment, client-only or server-based, management of the metastore is essential. Best practice is to set up a shared metastore on a durable, reliable database platform, which could be PostgreSQL or MySQL. Management of this database, including capacity planning, backup and recovery, and business continuity practices, needs to be in place as the Hive or HCatalog metastore database holds the critical link between objects in HDFS and objects used in schema-on-read processing operations such as Hive queries.

In addition to MapReduce, Hive can use Apache Tez as its processing framework without any HiveQL code changes. You simply configure the Hive server or client environment to use Tez as its execution engine using the `hive.execution.engine=tez` property setting in either the Hive interpreter or `hive-site.xml` configuration file. As discussed in **Hour 12, "Using SQL-on-Hadoop Solutions,"** Tez can provide significant performance advantages over MapReduce in many cases, so you might consider this as your default execution engine if it is available on your platform.

More information about Hive, including HiveServer2 and the Hive metastore, can be found at https://hive.apache.org/. More information about Tez can be found at https://tez.apache.org/.

Pig

I covered Pig in **Hour 8, "Analyzing Data in HDFS Using Apache Pig,"** and **Hour 9, "Using Advanced Pig"** of this book. Like Hive, Pig can also be deployed as a server (PigServer) or a client. The same advantages apply to server-based Pig deployments as to HiveServer2, although server-based deployments are less common with Pig. Like Hive, Pig can also leverage Tez as its execution framework, which may be advantageous in some circumstances.

Pig can also leverage object definitions in the Hive metastore using the HCatalog ecosystem project (see https://cwiki.apache.org/confluence/display/Hive/HCatalog). Using HCatalog to share object definitions across projects in the Hadoop ecosystem (such as Pig and Spark) is a good practice.

More information about Pig, including PigServer, can be found at https://pig.apache.org/.

SQL-on-Hadoop Solutions

Back in **Hour 12** we covered some of the ecosystem projects classified as SQL-on-Hadoop solutions, such as Impala, HAWQ, and Drill. These solutions, in most cases, implement their own custom distributed SQL engines that run independently of YARN. The main management consideration when implementing these solutions is their sociability with other workloads such as MapReduce, Pig, Hive, or Spark workloads running on YARN.

These solutions are often part of a commercial application stack such as the Cloudera, MapR, or Pivotal Hadoop application stack. You should consult your platform vendor's documentation for further management considerations if you are using a commercial distribution of Hadoop.

Spark

You were introduced to Apache Spark in **Hour 13, "Introducing Apache Spark,"** as a popular alternative to MapReduce and Hive for data processing and analysis on the Hadoop platform. Spark can be deployed in standalone mode, where it acts as its own cluster manager; in that case it is unaware of any other scheduler such as YARN. The preferred alternative is to deploy Spark on YARN, where Spark Drivers and Executors run on YARN containers and are managed by the YARN framework. This can be done with no additional configuration as the Spark project is built to integrate with YARN and HDFS.

Using Spark on YARN allows Spark workloads to coexist and be scheduled alongside other YARN-managed workloads such as MapReduce. Spark application logs are managed by YARN, and metrics are available using the YARN interfaces discussed in the previous hour.

More information about Spark can be found in **Sams Teach Yourself Apache Spark in 24 Hours**, in the same series as this book.

I will discuss some other emerging projects in the Hadoop ecosystem for data analysis, including Presto and Flink later this hour.

NoSQL Solutions

I introduced you to NoSQL concepts and their primary implementations on the Hadoop platform in **Hour 15, "Introducing NoSQL."** Let's revisit these now.

HBase

HBase is the NoSQL store built on top of HDFS. HBase is essentially a distributed map of keys (row keys) and their associated values that are not defined at design time, unlike a schema in a traditional relational database management platform.

HBase has its own cluster architecture and storage framework designed to efficiently store and distribute data that is stored in tables. Recall that HBase tables are divided into regions which are managed by RegionServers.

The data for HBase tables is ultimately stored in HFile format, which are files in HDFS. The defining difference between HBase and normal data storage in HDFS is that HBase is designed to act as a primary store (or potentially a system of record) of data. HBase circumvents the immutability of HDFS through the creation of new files for inserted or updated data, and then performs a background process called compaction.

The processes of region assignment, the combining and splitting of regions, and data compaction result in HBase clusters being very busy. Depending on how you intend to use HBase, you may need to consider its sociability with other applications running on the platform.

Accumulo

Accumulo is a distributed map built on top of HDFS in exactly the same way as HBase, although the daemon names differ. Regions, as they were referred to in HBase, are called *Tablets* in Accumulo.

Accumulo was designed by the U.S. National Security Agency specifically to be a secure implementation of HBase, and introduces the concept of *cell-level security* or *cell-level visibility*. Cell visibility restricts access or visibility of data contained within a cell in Accumulo (the intersection between a row key and a runtime-defined column) to specific users only, using cell-level *access labels*.

Aside from this key design difference, both projects share the same inspiration from the Google Bigtable white paper, and both projects have the same management and deployment considerations.

CAUTION

Consider Other Workloads when Deploying HBase or Accumulo

HBase and Accumulo clusters are designed to maximize distributed cluster resources. If you intend to deploy HBase or Accumulo in production, you should consider running these platforms on their own dedicated cluster and not mixing these services with general-purpose workloads running on YARN such as MapReduce or Spark.

Others tools such as Druid and Cassandra are not necessarily Hadoop ecosystem projects, but can at least be considered first cousins to Hadoop.

Search Platforms

Search, or more specifically full-text search, was one of the main drivers behind the Hadoop project and subsequent development. In 1999, Doug Cutting, the founder of Hadoop, founded a project called *Lucene* that introduced a Java-based full-text search, indexing framework, and libraries.

In 2004 a new enterprise search platform called *Solr,* based upon the Lucene libraries, was created at CNET Networks, later to become an Apache project. Solr and Lucene have long been closely associated with Hadoop, having a shared lineage. Vendors such as Cloudera have incorporated search (and Solr) into their application stacks through projects such as Cloudera Search. You should consult your vendor's documentation for specific information as to whether these search platforms are part of your Hadoop environment.

There are additional solutions which may not be considered Hadoop ecosystem projects specifically, such as ElasticSearch, which provide search capabilities as well.

Other Ecosystem Projects

Some of the other projects I will discuss include Oozie, which can be used for workflow coordination; streaming and complex event processing systems such as Storm and Spark Streaming; messaging platforms such as Kafka; and additional projects which can be used for data analysis, data visualization, or machine learning.

Additionally, I will cover some notable infrastructure projects in more detail, including ZooKeeper, Thrift, Knox, Sentry, and more.

Introduction to Oozie

Often, problems on the Hadoop platform cannot be solved in one step. Many solutions are implemented using multiple jobs, potentially using different technologies in a workflow.

Oozie Workflows

Apache Oozie is a Hadoop ecosystem project used to orchestrate workflows in Hadoop. These workflows can consist of applications including MapReduce, Pig, Hive, Spark, and more. Workflows can include interactions with a filesystem (HDFS or another), and can also interact with other systems, such as running shell commands or sending email. Workflows can be simple, where steps are run in sequence, or complex, where multiple tasks may be run in parallel and may include conditional logic.

Oozie workflows consist of nodes. Nodes are classified as *control flow nodes* or *action nodes*. Control flow nodes determine the flow of a program; specific control flow nodes include the following:

▶ *Start Control Node*—Starts a workflow. All workflows must start with a Start Control Node.

▶ *End Control Node*—Ends a workflow. All workflows must include an End Control Node used for the successful completion of a workflow.

▶ *Kill Control Node*—Used to abort a workflow, usually based on an exception or a specific condition.

▶ *Decision Control Node*—Used to make a conditional decision for a specific path or action in a workflow.

▶ *Fork and Join Control Nodes*—Used to split or join a workflow path. For instance, to process two nodes in parallel, both the fork and join nodes must be used together.

Action nodes (as the name suggests) perform actions in an Oozie workflow. Examples of action nodes include the following:

▶ Map-Reduce action

▶ Pig action

▶ Hive action

▶ Spark action

▶ Sqoop action

▶ Shell action

▶ Java action

▶ Fs (HDFS) action

▶ Email action

▶ and more.

Workflows are contained in workflow documents, which are XML documents including the control flow and action nodes just mentioned. An example of a simple workflow document to execute a Spark application is shown in Listing 17.2.

LISTING 17.2   Sample Oozie Workflow Document

```
<workflow-app xmlns='uri:oozie:workflow:0.5' name='SparkFileCopy'>
 <start to='spark-node' />
 <action name='spark-node'>
   <spark xmlns="uri:oozie:spark-action:0.1">
   <job-tracker>${jobTracker}</job-tracker>
   <name-node>${nameNode}</name-node>
   <prepare>
     <delete path="${nameNode}/user/${wf:user()}/${examplesRoot}/output-data/
spark"/>
   </prepare>
```

```
  <master>${master}</master>
  <name>Spark-FileCopy</name>
  <class>org.apache.oozie.example.SparkFileCopy</class>
  <jar>${nameNode}/user/${wf:user()}/${examplesRoot}/apps/spark/lib/oozie-
examples.jar</jar>
  <arg>${nameNode}/user/${wf:user()}/${examplesRoot}/input-data/text/data.txt
</arg>
  <arg>${nameNode}/user/${wf:user()}/${examplesRoot}/output-data/spark</arg>
  </spark>
  <ok to="end" />
  <error to="fail" />
 </action>
 <kill name="fail">
  <message>Workflow failed, error
   message[${wf:errorMessage(wf:lastErrorNode())}]
  </message>
 </kill>
 <end name='end' />
</workflow-app>
```

A diagrammatic representation of the workflow provided in Listing 17.2 is shown in Figure 17.1.

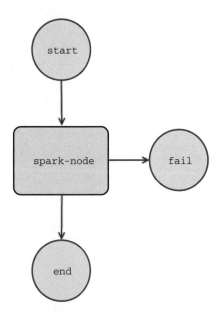

FIGURE 17.1
Oozie Workflow.

Detailed information about workflow documents and node syntax can be found in the "Workflow Functional Specification" link on the Oozie project documentation site, http://oozie.apache.org/.

Oozie Architecture

Oozie is deployed as a service, typically running outside the Hadoop cluster on a non-cluster node, but with network access to the cluster. Clients submit workflow documents to the Oozie service, and the Oozie service then orchestrates the workflow, including executing actions such as submitting jobs to the Hadoop cluster, managing dependencies, and handling exceptions.

An advantage to Oozie, much like the advantages of HUE, Sqoop2 and HiveServer2, is the capability to isolate the Hadoop cluster from external networks and only allow users to access the exposed service—in this case the Oozie service. Figure 17.2 depicts the Oozie architecture.

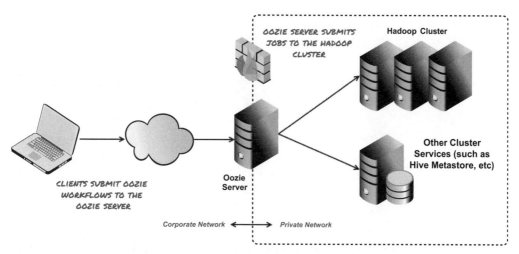

FIGURE 17.2
Oozie Architecture.

The Oozie server maintains the configuration information required to communicate and interact with the Hadoop cluster and any other services required.

Submitting an Oozie Workflow

Oozie workflows are submitted to the Oozie server using the `oozie` client library located in the `bin` directory of an Oozie installation. An example Oozie workflow submission is shown in Listing 17.3.

LISTING 17.3   Submitting an Oozie Workflow Using the Command-Line Client

```
$ bin/oozie job -oozie http://localhost:11000/oozie \
-config examples/apps/map-reduce/job.properties -run
```

There is also a Java API to submit Oozie workflows to an Oozie server that can be incorporated into any Java application by importing the appropriate Oozie libraries.

As discussed in **Hour 14, "Using the Hadoop User Environment (HUE),"** HUE also includes support for Oozie, enabling users to create, edit, manage, and submit workflows using the HUE user interface. An example showing the Oozie Editor interface in HUE is provided in Figure 17.3.

FIGURE 17.3
Oozie Editor in HUE.

There is also a native web UI served on port 11000 of the Oozie server as shown in Figure 17.4.

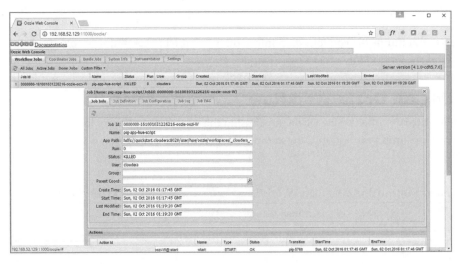

FIGURE 17.4
Oozie Native Web UI.

Getting Oozie

Oozie is often included in commercial Hadoop distributions such as Cloudera, Hortonworks, and others, so in many cases there is no need to install it. If Oozie is not available in your environment, you can obtain the source code from **http://oozie.apache.org/** and build the project yourself. Furthermore, you can extend the code if need be.

Additional Workflow Tools

In addition to Oozie, many organizations have implemented their own workflow orchestration frameworks and scheduling solutions for Hadoop environments, including the *Airflow* project developed by Airbnb, the *Azkeban* project developed by LinkedIn, or the *Luigi* project developed by Spotify. Many of these projects are licensed under the Apache licensing scheme and can be downloaded and deployed from the projects' websites.

Stream Processing and Messaging in Hadoop

The proliferation of devices, sensors, and real-time messaging has accentuated the requirement for streaming data and complex event processing on the Hadoop platform. There are several projects that provide these capabilities and are considered to be first-class citizens in the Hadoop ecosystem. Let's discuss them now.

Storm

Apache Storm is a real-time complex event processing engine. Storm implements a graph (DAG) topology of spouts and bolts. Spouts are data sources like the Flume sources discussed in **Hour 5, "Getting Data into Hadoop."** Spouts acquire data and supply this data to the Storm topology. An example of this could be a spout that reads data from a Twitter data stream. Bolts are processing nodes that process data provided by the spouts. Streams are the primary data abstraction in Storm. Streams consist of tuples, which have defined schemas.

An example Storm topology for processing and ingesting a stream of tweets from Twitter is shown in Figure 17.5.

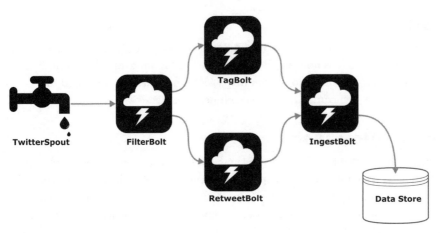

FIGURE 17.5
Storm Topology.

Unlike the DAGs implemented by other projects discussed in this book such as Tez, Oozie workflows, and Spark using its batch processing framework, Storm DAGs are intended to run indefinitely, ingesting, and processing new data as it arrives.

Yahoo! and Hortonworks have invested research and development into the integration of Storm with YARN. Storm is a first-class citizen in the Hortonworks application stack. More information about Storm is available from the Hortonworks website or **https://storm.apache.org/**.

Spark Streaming

Spark Streaming is a sub project of the Apache Spark project discussed in **Hour 13, "Using Apache Spark."**

Spark Streaming introduces the concepts of the StreamingContext and *discretized streams,*or *DStreams*. DStreams are essentially batches of data stored in multiple Spark RDDs (Resilient Distributed Datasets—the distributed in-memory data objects that are the primary processing construct in Spark). Each batch in the DStream represents a time window, typically in seconds. The resultant RDDs can then be processed using the core Spark RDD API transformations that you were introduced to in **Hour 13**.

Figure 17.6 shows a high-level overview of Spark Streaming.

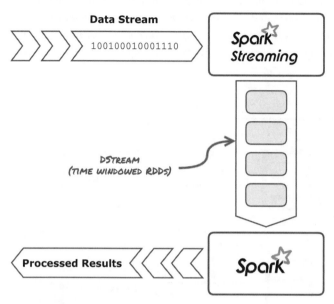

FIGURE 17.6
Spark Streaming.

A Spark Streaming application is essentially no different to any other Spark application running on YARN. However, these are long-lived processes by definition, which needs to be taken into consideration.

More detailed information on Spark Streaming can be found in the **Sams Teach Yourself Apache Spark in 24 Hours** book discussed earlier.

Kafka

Apache Kafka is a popular distributed, reliable, low-latency, pub-sub (publish-subscribe) messaging platform developed at LinkedIn. Conceptually, Kafka acts as a write ahead log (WAL) for messages, much the same way a transaction log or journal functions in an ACID data store. This log-based design provides durability, consistency, and the capability for subscribers to replay messages if required.

Kafka publishers are called producers, and producers write data to topics. Subscribers in Kafka, called consumers, read messages from specified topics. Figure 17.7 summarizes the relationships among producers, topics, and consumers. Messages themselves are uninterpreted byte arrays that can represent any object or primitive data type. Common message content formats include JSON and Avro, (an open source Hadoop ecosystem data serialization project that I will discuss shortly).

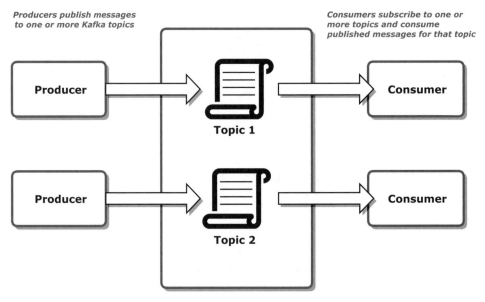

FIGURE 17.7
Kafka Producers, Topics, and Consumers.

Kafka is a distributed system consisting of one or more brokers, typically on separate nodes of a cluster. Brokers manage partitions, which are ordered, immutable sequences of messages for a particular topic. Partitions are replicated across multiple nodes in a cluster to provide fault tolerance. Topics may have many partitions.

Each topic in Kafka is treated as a log (an ordered collection of messages), with a unique offset assigned to each message. Consumers can access messages from a topic based upon these offsets, allowing a consumer to replay previous messages.

Kafka uses Apache ZooKeeper to maintain state between brokers. I will discuss ZooKeeper in the next section. Figure 17.8 shows the Kafka cluster architecture.

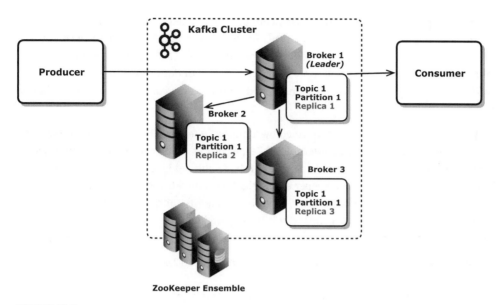

FIGURE 17.8
Kafka Cluster Architecture.

A majority of nodes, or a quorum of nodes, successfully performing an action such as updating a state is required. A quorum is required to "elect" a leader. A leader in a Kafka cluster is the node responsible for all reads and writes for a specific partition; every partition has a leader. Other nodes are considered followers. Followers consume messages and update their partitions. If the leader is unavailable, a new leader will be elected by Kafka.

More detailed information about Kafka is available at http://kafka.apache.org/.

Infrastructure and Security Projects

I have spent considerable time discussing the various ecosystem projects that allow users to access and process data in Hadoop. There are other projects in the Hadoop ecosystem that facilitate key infrastructure requirements such as distributed transaction coordination, object serialization, security and role-based access control, data governance, and more. In this section I will discuss some of the more notable projects in this category.

ZooKeeper

ZooKeeper is an open source, distributed configuration and synchronization service used by many other Hadoop ecosystem projects I have discussed, including HBase and Kafka. ZooKeeper is essentially a helper service for managing concurrency and maintaining state in distributed applications.

ZooKeeper is typically implemented in a cluster configuration called an *ensemble and* deployed in odd numbers such as three or five. A ZooKeeper ensemble maintains a hierarchical collection of *znodes*. Each znode stores data as uninterpreted byte arrays. As ZooKeeper is designed to share state in a distributed system and not to store data, the amount of data stored in each znode is intentionally limited to 1 MB. This collection of znodes presents logically as a directory of files or objects.

Updates (or writes) to ZooKeeper are performed by a master or *leader*. The leader of a ZooKeeper ensemble is chosen by an *election*, an internal ZooKeeper process. Other nodes in the ensemble are referred to as *followers*. Reads from ZooKeeper can be facilitated by any of the followers. Data is replicated across all nodes in a ZooKeeper ensemble. Distributed transactions and consistency are achieved by a two-phase commit process, whereby a majority (or quorum) of nodes acknowledge a successful update, which is why it is suggested to deploy ZooKeeper ensembles in odd numbers: to avoid a tie.

A simple overview of a ZooKeeper ensemble is pictured in Figure 17.9.

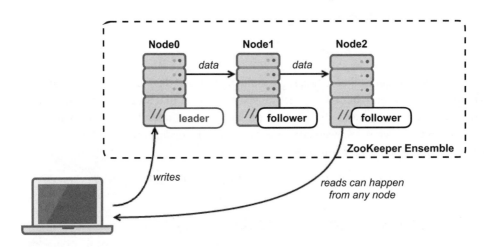

FIGURE 17.9
ZooKeeper Ensemble.

ZooKeeper provides a Java API for programming distributed applications in Java. ZooKeeper also provides a command-line REPL shell (zkCli.sh) that can be used for interacting with a ZooKeeper ensemble. Let's deploy and explore a simple single-node ZooKeeper ensemble now.

Deploying ZooKeeper

In this exercise you will deploy a single node ZooKeeper ensemble and test your deployment using the ZooKeeper command-line interface utility.

1. Download the latest release of ZooKeeper. In our case this is release 3.4.9. Obtain your download link from https://zookeeper.apache.org):

```
$ wget http://apache.mirror.amaze.com.au/zookeeper/current/
zookeeper-3.4.9.tar.gz
```

2. Unpack the release:

```
$ tar xvf zookeeper-3.4.9.tar.gz
```

3. Change directories into your unpacked ZooKeeper release directory:

```
$ cd zookeeper-3.4.9
```

4. Create a simple ZooKeeper config file (zoo.cfg) in the ZooKeeper configuration directory using a text editor such as vi:

```
$ vi conf/zoo.cfg
```

5. Add the following configuration to the zoo.cfg file, save, and then exit the text editor:

```
tickTime=2000
dataDir=/tmp/zookeeper
clientPort=2181
```

Note that you would need to do this for each node if you were deploying a multi-node ensemble.

6. Start the ZooKeeper Server service:

```
$ bin/zkServer.sh start
```

7. Open a ZooKeeper command-line client session:

```
$ bin/zkCli.sh
```

8. In the ZooKeeper client shell, enter the following commands one by one to create, update, read, and delete znodes, noting the return values:

```
create /myFirstZnode "ZooKeeper-Application"
get /myFirstZnode
set /myFirstZnode "Updated-Application"
get /myFirstZnode
```

```
create /myFirstZnode/ChildNode "First-ChildNode"
ls /myFirstZnode
stat /myFirstZnode
rmr /myFirstZnode
quit
```

ZooKeeper is normally included in most commercial Hadoop distributions, so chances are it may already be deployed and usable in your environment.

More information about ZooKeeper is available at **https://zookeeper.apache.org.**

Data Storage and Exchange Formats

Data storage and exchange or interchange projects have evolved with Hadoop as the requirements for integration with other platforms have increased. Let's look at some of the key projects in this category now.

Avro

You learned about SequenceFiles back in **Hour 7, "Programming MapReduce Applications,"** when I discussed programming MapReduce applications in Java. SequenceFiles are pre-serialized files containing binary encoded key value pairs, consisting of Hadoop Writable and WritableComparable objects. SequenceFiles are an optimal format when the output of one Hadoop process becomes the input of another Hadoop process (e.g., in a workflow).

One of the detractions of SequenceFiles was their exclusivity to Java, meaning that these files were not directly accessible to non-Java applications. The Apache Avro project was created by Doug Cutting as an alternative to SequenceFiles. The Avro format is a portable, cross-platform file format that is self-describing, meaning that the schema for the object is included in the file itself.

Avro's compact file format is accessible from C and C++, Python, Ruby, and other programming languages in addition to Java.

Avro files are accessed through special classes such as the AvroMapper and AvroReducer classes. An example of this is shown in Listing 17.4.

LISTING 17.4 AvroMapper

```
...
  public static class ColorCountMapper extends
      Mapper<AvroKey<User>, NullWritable, Text, IntWritable> {
    @Override
    public void map(AvroKey<User> key, NullWritable value, Context context)
        throws IOException, InterruptedException {
      CharSequence color = key.datum().getFavoriteColor();
      if (color == null) {
```

```
      color = "none";
    }
    context.write(new Text(color.toString()), new IntWritable(1));
  }
}
...
```

Thrift

Apache Thrift is a protocol and framework designed to create clients and services in multiple languages using a standard interface definition. Thrift was developed at Facebook to enable rapid and scalable cross-language service and RPC (Remote Procedure Call) development.

Using Thrift, developers can create services and generate language bindings for C, C++, .NET, Go, Erlang, Java, Node.js, Python, and Ruby, among others. The Thrift compiler will map datatypes in an interface definition to their native types in every supported language, and generate server and client code that can be implemented in your application.

Thrift is useful when you have different development teams writing application or system components that need to communicate and exchange state or data with one another over RPC. Many ecosystem and core components leverage Thrift.

Security Solutions

I will discuss the security solutions in the Hadoop ecosystem, including Apache Knox and Apache Sentry, in detail in **Hour 22: "Securing Hadoop"**.

Machine Learning, Visualization, and More Data Analysis Tools

Data analysis, feature engineering, and machine learning were all foundational use cases for Hadoop so it is no surprise that these technologies feature heavily in the Hadoop ecosystem.

Machine Learning in Hadoop

Machine learning is the specific discipline within the field of predictive analytics that refers to programs that leverage the data they collect to influence the program's future behavior. In other words, the program "learns" from the data rather than relying on explicit instructions.

You can see practical examples of machine learning in everyday life in recommendation engines on e-commerce websites, optical character recognition, facial recognition, spam filtering, fraud detection, and so on.

Machine learning is often associated with data at scale. As more data is observed in the learning process, the higher the accuracy of the model, and the better it is at making predictions. This makes machine learning and Hadoop suitable companions to one another.

Mahout

Apache Mahout is a Java-based machine learning library that contains several popular algorithms for classification, clustering, and collaborative filtering, all of which are common machine learning patterns and techniques. Although the Mahout package can be used in standalone Java applications, many of the algorithms included in Mahout are optimized to work with Hadoop.

Mahout has built-in support for common machine learning applications such as recommendation engines or basket analysis. In addition to Mahout's Java libraries, Mahout includes a command-line interface that includes many common applications. A command-line example using Mahout's item-based recommender is shown in Listing 17.5.

LISTING 17.5   Item-Based Recommender in Mahout

```
$ mahout recommenditembased \
-similarityClassname SIMILARITY_LOGLIKELIHOOD \
-input /data/movieratings \
-output /data/output \
—numRecommendations 20
```

Machine Learning in Spark using MLlib

The Spark machine learning solution is Spark MLlib, a Spark subproject providing machine learning functions that can be used with RDDs. MLlib, like Spark Streaming and Spark SQL, is an integral component in the Spark program, and has been included with Spark since the 0.8 release. An example of a machine learning application using the Spark MLlib framework is shown in Listing 17.6.

LISTING 17.6   Spark MLlib

```
from pyspark.mllib.tree import DecisionTree
model = DecisionTree.trainClassifier(data=data,
    numClasses=2,
    categoricalFeaturesInfo={0: 3})
...
print(model.toDebugString())
If (feature 2 <= 80.0)
  If (feature 1 <= 65.0)
    If (feature 1 <= 64.0)
      Predict: 1.0
    Else (feature 1 > 64.0)
      Predict: 0.0
    Else (feature 1 > 65.0)
      Predict: 1.0
Else (feature 2 > 80.0)
  If (feature 0 in {0.0})
    Predict: 0.0
```

```
Else (feature 0 not in {0.0})
  If (feature 1 <= 71.0)
    If (feature 1 <= 70.0)
      Predict: 1.0
    Else (feature 1 > 70.0)
      Predict: 0.0
  Else (feature 1 > 71.0)
      Predict: 1.0
```

In Spark 1.2, an additional library, Spark ML, was introduced to extend MLlib to Spark SQL DataFrames. The APIs, algorithms, and capabilities are based upon MLlib.

Since the MLlib solution is included in the Spark release, there are no additional considerations involved in deploying or using this capability above and beyond the variable or computationally intense workloads it may generate.

H_2O

H_2O is another popular open source machine learning application and in-memory prediction engine which can be deployed on Hadoop leveraging YARN as a resource scheduler. H_2O can also be deployed in standalone mode or using Spark as a processing engine, an implementation known as Sparkling Water. The H_2O web-based interface, Flow, is shown in Figure 17.10.

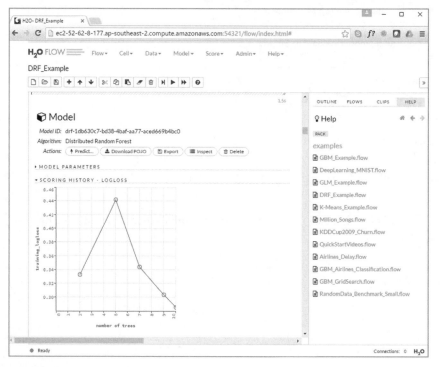

FIGURE 17.10
H_2O Flow.

H_2O's in-memory model building and scoring engine supports most common machine learning algorithms, including clustering, classification, and collaborative filtering algorithms.

The H_2O engine itself is implemented in several layers, which include the following:

▶ In-memory distributed key value (KV) store layer

▶ Lightweight MapReduce layer

▶ "Pre-baked" algorithms layer (H_2O implementations of common machine learning and deep learning algorithms)

▶ API layer (including REST, JSON, R, Python, Excel, and REPL)

All of the layers are orchestrated in a distributed processing framework known as a H_2O Cloud. The high-level overview of the H_2O architecture is shown in Figure 17.11.

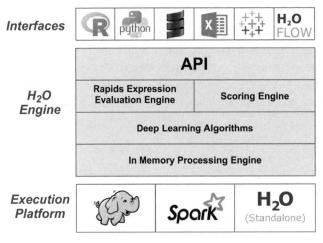

FIGURE 17.11
High-Level Overview of H_2O.

There is much more detailed information about the H_2O architecture available from the H_2O website at **http://www.h2o.ai/**.

Spark MLlib and H_2O are also discussed in more detail in the **Sams Teach Yourself Apache Spark in 24 Hours** book.

Presto

Another emerging platform for data transformation and analysis is Presto, which is an Apache licensed distributed SQL query engine designed for Hadoop. This could also be classified as a SQL-on-Hadoop solution as well. Presto was created at Facebook, notably the same company which originated the Hive project.

Presto leverages the Hive metastore for object definitions like many other data analysis ecosystem projects. Presto can also read data from many other big data/NoSQL ecosystem projects such as Accumulo, Cassandra, Kafka, MongoDB, Redis, and more. Presto includes a command-line shell interface as well as supporting connectivity through JDBC. Presto also includes a connector for Tableau, a popular visualization platform, letting users run queries from Tableau against Presto.

Presto is now included in some commercial distributions and implementations of Hadoop such as Hortonworks and AWS Elastic MapReduce. Presto is gaining momentum, so you should familiarize yourself with this project. More information is available at https://prestodb.io/.

Notebook and Visualization Platforms

Notebooks provide an interactive environment that combines code, markup and media, and visualizations in a single web-based workspace. Notebooks are a popular companion to many of the data analysis and machine learning applications in the Hadoop ecosystem. Let's look at a few of the more popular notebook platforms.

Zeppelin

Apache Zeppelin is a web-based, multi-language, interactive notebook application with native integration into Hive, Spark, and more.

Zeppelin, like other notebook platforms, provides the capability to combine different languages, along with markup facilities. That makes it easy to explore and visualize data in an interactive environment.

Zeppelin provides a query environment for data in Hadoop as well as providing data visualization capabilities that can be combined with rich media in a Zeppelin notebook document. The Zeppelin web UI is shown in Figure 17.12.

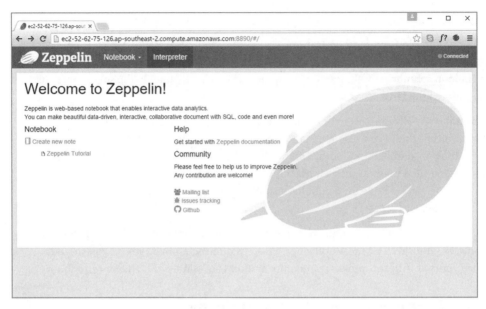

FIGURE 17.12
Apache Zeppelin.

Jupyter

Python is a very popular and useful language that is prolific in the data science community, a major constituency in the Hadoop community. IPython, which is the shortened name for Interactive Python, provides an enhanced interactive development environment for Python. An IPython session is shown in Figure 17.13.

```
ubuntu@ip-172-31-12-111:~$ ipython
Python 2.7.6 (default, Mar 22 2014, 22:59:56)
Type "copyright", "credits" or "license" for more information.

IPython 1.2.1 -- An enhanced Interactive Python.
?         -> Introduction and overview of IPython's features.
%quickref -> Quick reference.
help      -> Python's own help system.
object?   -> Details about 'object', use 'object??' for extra details.

In [1]: def hello_world():
   ...:     """Simple Hello World Python function"""
   ...:     return "hello world"

In [2]: hello_world()
Out[2]: 'hello world'

In [3]: hello_world?
Type:       function
String Form:<function hello_world at 0x7fb2513d9de8>
File:       /home/ubuntu/<ipython-input-1-0770cd529cac>
Definition: hello_world()
Docstring:  Simple Hello World Python function

In [4]:
```

FIGURE 17.13
IPython Session.

Jupyter, the iPython notebook, has become a popular tool, widely in use today in the Hadoop and Spark development communities. Jupyter provides a web-based notebook experience that includes extensions for Ruby, R, and other languages, as well as its native Python bindings. Figure 17.14 shows a sample data visualization using a Jupyter notebook.

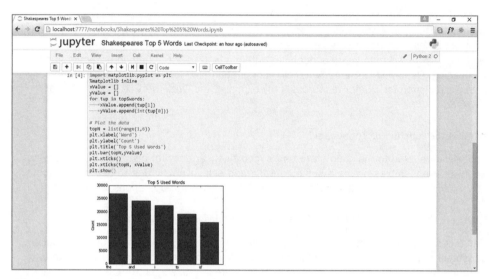

FIGURE 17.14
Jupyter Notebook.

Summary

The Hadoop ecosystem is comprised of the universe of technologies and projects that were designed to integrate or interact with Hadoop. Hadoop ecosystem projects are integral to deploying capabilities on the Hadoop platform.

I could devote an entire book to covering the vast Hadoop ecosystem, so in one hour I can merely scratch the surface, but I have provided a gentle introduction to some of the more significant projects, including deployment and management aspects of key projects such as Oozie and ZooKeeper.

The Hadoop ecosystem is continually evolving and expanding, especially as companies such as Airbnb, LinkedIn, Twitter, and others continue to donate and contribute to new projects they have developed to address a particular business need. As a Hadoop practitioner, you will need to be aware of emerging projects and how they fit into the landscape.

Q&A

Q. What are some of the advantages of using Oozie to orchestrate application workflows in Hadoop, as opposed to building multi-stage workflows in a single application such as a MapReduce application?

A. Oozie workflows are orchestrated by a service so they do not have a reliance on a client, such as a Driver in a MapReduce application. Moreover, Oozie workflows can incorporate different processing frameworks such as Hive, Pig, Spark, and others into a single workflow. Oozie will manage dependencies within a workflow and handle exceptions in processing. Deploying Oozie for workflow coordination also has the advantage of enabling network isolation for cluster resources, only exposing the Oozie service to an external network.

Q. What is the function of ZooKeeper?

A. ZooKeeper is used to maintain state and support concurrency for distributed applications. ZooKeeper ensembles act as a self-organizing and self-governing unit to deliver eventual consistency across all nodes and strong consistency for write operations when needed.

Q. What are the key concepts involved with the Kafka messaging platform?

A. Kafka is a distributed pub-sub (publish-subscribe) messaging platform including producers, consumers, and brokers. Kafka publishers are called producers, and producers write data to topics. Subscribers in Kafka, called consumers, read messages from specified topics. Messages themselves are uninterpreted byte arrays that can represent any object or primitive datatype.

Workshop

The workshop contains quiz questions to help you solidify your understanding of the material covered. Try to answer all questions before looking at the "Answers" section that follows.

Quiz

1. _____ is a Java library containing several popular algorithms for machine learning on the Hadoop platform.

2. A node in an Oozie workflow that executes a Pig program would be classified as what type of node?

   A. Control flow node

   B. Decision control node

   C. Workflow action node

3. Knox and Sentry would fall under what category of ecosystem projects?

4. Which ecosystem project used for streaming data ingestion and complex event processing consists of *streams, spouts,* and *bolts*?

Answers

1. Mahout.

2. C.

3. Security.

4. Apache Storm.

Using Cluster Management Utilities

What You'll Learn in This Hour:

▶ Introduction to Ambari and Cloudera Manager
▶ Deploying clusters and services using management tools
▶ Configuration and service management using management tools
▶ Software management and upgrades using management tools

Deploying and managing clusters and maintaining configuration is a challenging task even for moderately sized clusters, let alone large clusters. In this hour, I will introduce you to Cloudera Manager and Apache Ambari, two utilities designed to make the provisioning and management of Hadoop environments simpler.

Cluster Management Overview

Cluster management tasks span the entire lifecycle of a Hadoop cluster. Management tasks are made more challenging by the scale and distributed nature of Hadoop environments. Cluster management tasks include functions such as

▶ Deployment of new hosts or services, including entire clusters

▶ Service management

▶ Configuration management, including synchronization of changes and change history

▶ Cluster security management

▶ Monitoring and altering

▶ Upgrade capabilities, including rolling upgrades

The two most prolific tools available to manage Hadoop environments are Cloudera Manager for Cloudera Hadoop distributions, and Ambari for Hortonworks and other ODP-based Hadoop distributions.

Cloudera Manager and Ambari are designed to make complex tasks involved with cluster management simple, such as implementing high availability or Kerberos integration. Cluster management tools such as Cloudera Manager or Ambari are often the first port of call for diagnosing cluster, node, or service health, or issues with their monitoring and instrumentation capabilities.

Both popular management tools provide a simple and intuitive web management interface backed by APIs, which enables administrators to accomplish management tasks without writing code. Let's introduce each solution now.

Cloudera Manager

Cloudera Manager (CM) is Cloudera's management solution, designed to manage Hadoop clusters running the Cloudera Distribution of Hadoop (CDH). Cloudera Manager provides cluster and service deployment, configuration and service management, monitoring, and much more. The Cloudera Manager web UI is pictured in Figure 18.1.

FIGURE 18.1
Cloudera Manager.

Cloudera Manager Editions

Cloudera Manager is included in two different editions, *Cloudera Express* and *Cloudera Enterprise*. Cloudera Express is available as a free download and enables you to administer a cluster of any size. Cloudera Enterprise includes all of the features of Cloudera Express, plus some additional features that can be beneficial or even essential for enterprise Hadoop deployments, including:

▶ Configuration history and rollback

▶ Rolling upgrades or updates

▶ LDAP integration for Cloudera Manager

▶ SNMP support

▶ Automated disaster recovery

▶ Additional reporting features

▶ Cloudera support integration

CM Enterprise comes with a commercial support subscription, and can collect and forward cluster logs and configuration to Cloudera's support team, which could be helpful in diagnosing issues or misconfigurations.

Cloudera offers a trial license for Cloudera Enterprise. Cloudera Express can be easily upgraded to Cloudera Enterprise as well. More information is available at http://www.cloudera.com.

Cloudera Manager Architecture

A Cloudera Manager deployment consists of several components including a server, one or more agents, and a database. The server interacts with clients and performs cluster management functions through agents that are installed on cluster nodes, such as master or slave nodes in the cluster. The server stores its configuration and history in a database. MySQL, PostgreSQL, and Oracle are supported.

The Cloudera Manager server can also download software updates for distribution to agents. We will cover CM's software distribution and management capabilities next. Figure 18.2 shows a generic Cloudera Manager topology.

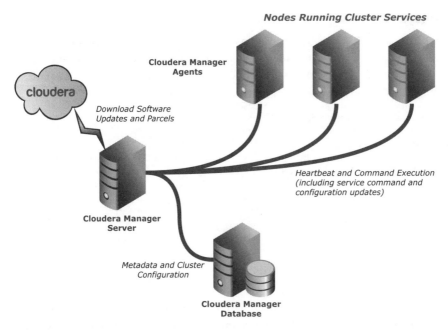

FIGURE 18.2
Cloudera Manager Topology.

The Cloudera Manager Server should run on a system which is not part of the cluster and is often deployed on a DMZ network with secure interfaces to the Hadoop cluster nodes.

The Cloudera Manager Agents start-and-stop Hadoop and Hadoop-related services on agent hosts at the request of the Cloudera Manager Server. The agents also collect statistics and send these to the Cloudera Manager Server, as well as sending regular heartbeats to the server.

Software Distribution Using Cloudera Manager

Cloudera Manager provides a central repository for cluster software, including the software to install or upgrade core or ecosystem components in the CDH application stack. Cloudera Manager coordinates the distribution and installation of software packages on remote agent hosts. Packages can be standard Linux packages such as Ubuntu or Red Hat packages, or *parcels*. Parcels are specific to Cloudera Manager and can assist with upgrading components.

Typically you don't want your cluster nodes to have direct internet access, incoming or outgoing. Using Cloudera Manager, the server can access packages and/or parcels and distribute them to agents.

Installing Cloudera Manager

Cloudera Manager is supported on most common 64-bit Linux operating systems, including Red Hat Enterprise, Linux/CentOS, Ubuntu, SLES, Oracle Enterprise Linux, and more. Cloudera Manager supports most common browsers including Google Chrome, Safari, Firefox, and later versions of Internet Explorer.

As shown in the Cloudera Manager topology in Figure 18.2, Cloudera Manager requires a database in which to store its configuration and history. As mentioned earlier, supported databases for Cloudera Manager include MySQL, PostgreSQL, and Oracle.

Always check the latest documentation for supported operating system versions and service packs, browsers, and database versions before installing.

Cloudera Manager is installed by downloading and executing the Cloudera Manager installation package. The Cloudera Manager installation package is a command-line utility that will install the following components onto the current system:

▶ Oracle Java Development Kit (JDK) 1.7

▶ Cloudera Manager Server

▶ Cloudera package repositories

▶ An embedded PostgreSQL database or existing database from the list of supported databases

The installer can be downloaded from **http://www.cloudera.com/downloads**. More information about Cloudera Manager is available at **http://docs.cloudera.com/**.

Apache Ambari

Apache Ambari is an open source project for management of Hadoop clusters and associated ecosystem technologies. The Ambari web UI is pictured in Figure 18.3.

FIGURE 18.3
Apache Ambari.

Ambari Architecture

Ambari deployments consist of a server (`ambari-server`) and one or more agents (`ambari-agent`). Users interact with the server to make configuration changes or manage services. The server instructs the agents, which are normally co-located with cluster nodes, to execute the resulting operations on its behalf.

The Ambari server process requires a database to store its configuration and history, and Ambari can integrate with corporate directory services and external authentication providers. Ambari can also interface with external monitoring and alerting systems such as Ganglia or Nagios. The Ambari architecture is shown in Figure 18.4.

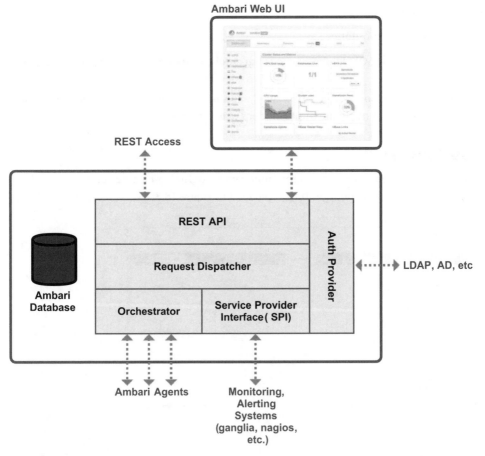

FIGURE 18.4
Ambari Architecture.

Ambari also offers programmatic management interfaces including a shell interface, Python and REST APIs.

Installing Ambari

Ambari is a first-class citizen on the Hortonworks Data Platform (HDP). If you are using a Hortonworks distribution, chances are Ambari is already available to you. Ambari is also typically included on other ODP distributions of Hadoop, such as Pivotal and IBM offerings. You can deploy Ambari on other distributions, however, as this is an open source solution.

Currently, Ambari is only supported on Linux operating systems, including all common distributions such as RHEL, CentOS, and Ubuntu. Deploying Ambari from source can be done by building an installation package for your distribution, such as `yum` packages for RedHat/CentOS-based systems or `apt-get` packages for Debian-based systems. On Red Hat/CentOS systems, the Ambari server package is available in the *Extra Packages for Enterprise Linux (EPEL)* repository. Listing 18.1 demonstrates how to install EPEL and the Ambari server package on a CentOS-based system.

LISTING 18.1   Installing the `ambari-server` Package Using EPEL

```
$ sudo yum install epel-release
$ sudo yum install ambari-server
$ ambari-server setup -j /usr/java/default # path to JAVA_HOME
```

Ambari uses a PostgreSQL database to maintain its own configuration, users, and configuration history. The installation packages created should pull the relevant Postgres packages and create this repository for you. Alternatively, you can obtain installation packages for Ambari from Hortonworks and use these directly to install Ambari servers and agents.

Ambari Views

Ambari Views, a feature of Ambari, can be used to expose user services such as Hive or Pig to users, as well as expose management functions and controls. Figure 18.5 shows a Hive query interface provided using Ambari Views.

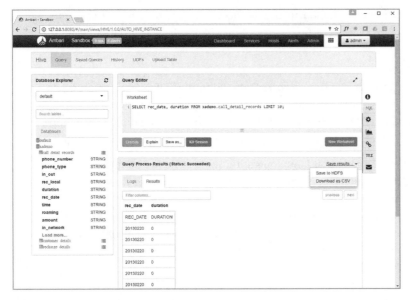

FIGURE 18.5
Accessing Hive Using Ambari Views.

Ambari and Ambari Views can also be used to provide the Zeppelin notebook interface, which provides an interactive programming environment with rich text, markup, and visualizations. This is shown in Figure 18.6.

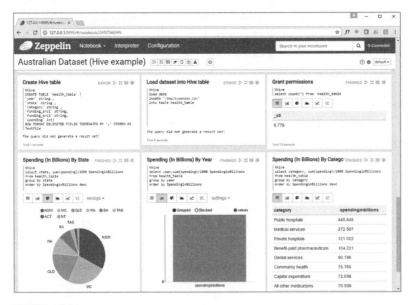

FIGURE 18.6
Zeppelin Notebook.

Deploying Clusters and Services Using Management Tools

Cluster management platforms such as Cloudera Manager and Ambari enable you to easily deploy services such as HUE, Hive, Sqoop, and more to an existing Hadoop cluster. These utilities can also be used to deploy entirely new clusters, including the core Hadoop components, HDFS, and YARN.

Furthermore, as your cluster scales it is often necessary to move services to new hosts due to capacity, hardware upgrades or replacement. This operation is made easier using Cloudera Manager or Ambari.

Deploying Services with Ambari

Clustered services in Ambari, such as HDFS or YARN, consist of roles, which can include master node roles (NameNode, ResourceManager) or slave node roles (DataNode, NodeManager) or other support roles. When used to deploy a new service, Ambari can make intelligent selections as to where to place roles for a given service on the available hosts running the ambari-agent process.

If you are deploying a new cluster or deploying services to new infrastructure, Ambari enables you to add hosts using a simple wizard interface. The new hosts just need to be running the ambari-agent process.

Ambari includes all of the services in the Hortonworks Data Platform (HDP) application stack, including ecosystem solutions such as Accumulo, HBase, Oozie, Spark, and Zeppelin. Figure 18.7 shows some of the services available to deploy using the Add Service wizard.

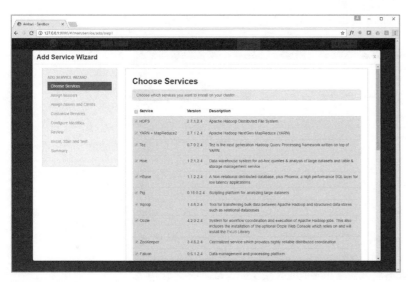

FIGURE 18.7
Adding a Service Using Ambari.

The next step is to assign master and slave roles to specific hosts in the cluster. Ambari will make intelligent recommendations as to which roles are best assigned to which hosts. An example of this is shown in Figure 18.8.

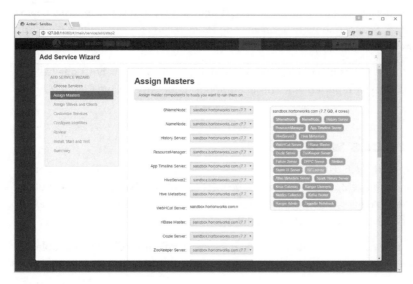

FIGURE 18.8
Service Role Assignment Using Ambari.

Once roles are assigned, you can then customize the service configuration before it is deployed. An example of this is shown in Figure 18.9.

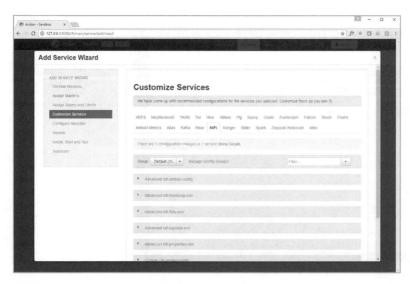

FIGURE 18.9
Customizing Service Configuration Using Ambari.

Once you have assigned service roles to hosts in the cluster and customized the service configuration, you can now install the service across distributed nodes in the cluster with one click and view the status of the installation as shown in Figure 18.10.

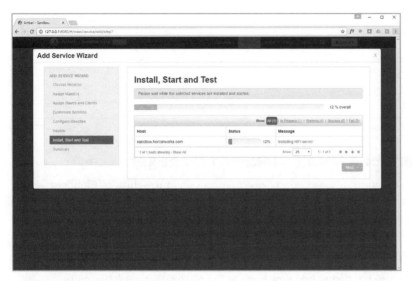

FIGURE 18.10
Service Installation Status in Ambari.

The service and service roles will be installed and configured on each target host. Upon the successful completion of the installation, the service will be up and running.

Ambari Blueprints

Automation and repeatability is often required when provisioning services such as a Hadoop application stack. Many tools offer interfaces to automate the deployment of new services, such as Recipes in Chef. Ambari provides this automation capability through blueprints.

Blueprints are JSON documents that describe a Hadoop cluster that can then be used to automate cluster deployment. An example excerpt from an Ambari blueprint is shown in Listing 18.2.

LISTING 18.2 Ambari Blueprints

```
{
  "blueprint" : "multi-node-cluster",
  "host_groups" :[
    {
      "name" : "master",
      "hosts" : [
```

```
  {
   "fqdn" : "master-node.local"
  }
 ]
 },
 {
  "name" : "slaves",
  "host_count" : 7,
  "host_predicate" : "Hosts/os_type=centos6&Hosts/cpu_count=2"
 }
 ]
}
```

Deploying Services Using Cloudera Manager

Cloudera Manager, like Ambari, is designed to deploy services on entire clusters. Cloudera Manager can add or remove services or reassign service roles to different hosts. Cloudera Manager will make intelligent recommendations as to which hosts are suitable for specific services or service roles. With Cloudera Manager, the entire CDH application stack is made available, so you just need to assign, configure, and start the desired services.

Cloudera Manager can also be used to add new hosts to the cluster, including deploying CDH components to the new hosts.

Configuration and Service Management Using Management Tools

Both the Cloudera Manager and Ambari solutions are designed to manage services and configuration across multiple nodes in a cluster.

Service Management with Cloudera Manager

Cloudera Manager lets you interact with an individual service running on a specific host, such as a NodeManager service running on a slave node host, or all services for an entire cluster, such as all YARN services running on all nodes. This can be useful after changing configuration properties related to a service or upgrading software.

Figures 18.11–18.13 show how you can start all of the services on all nodes of a cluster relating to a particular cluster, in this case HDFS.

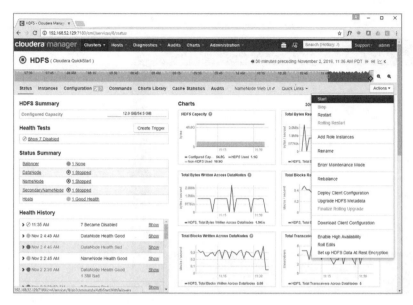

FIGURE 18.11
Starting All HDFS Services Using Cloudera Manager.

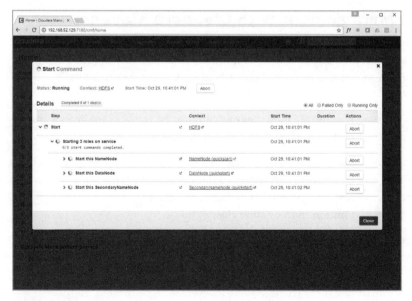

FIGURE 18.12
Starting All HDFS Services Progress Using Cloudera Manager.

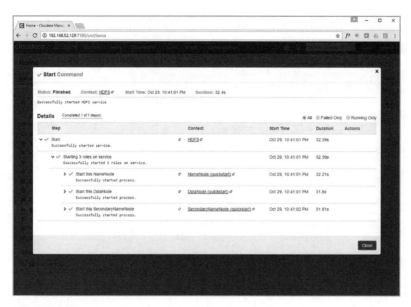

FIGURE 18.13
Starting All HDFS Services Completion Using Cloudera Manager.

Configuration Management with Cloudera Manager

Configuration is integral to Hadoop. Configuration files can become unmanageable after they reach a certain size. Moreover, mistakes in configuration, which are easy to make (such as simple markup errors, incorrectly spelled property names, or erroneous values), can break services.

Cloudera Manager can be used to centrally manage configuration for core and other Hadoop components and will synchronize changes across all hosts in the cluster.

Cloudera Manager also allows you to create role groups, which are groups of machines with homogeneous or similar hardware or operating system configuration. Different configuration settings can be assigned to different role groups. For instance, one class of hosts in your cluster may have a different disk configuration than another class of hosts.

Cloudera Manager presents configuration settings in a format that is easy to understand, with descriptive definitions for each setting, as shown in Figure 18.14.

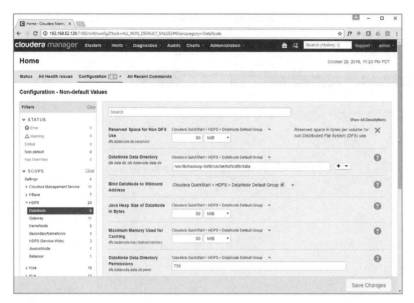

FIGURE 18.14
Cloudera Manager Configuration Settings.

Using Cloudera Manager you can also search for a specific configuration setting, as shown in Figure 18.15.

FIGURE 18.15
Searching for a Configuration Value Using Cloudera Manager.

The property and its current value will then be displayed, as shown in Figure 18.16.

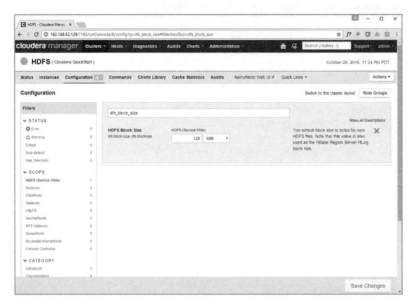

FIGURE 18.16
Configuration Setting in Cloudera Manager.

Cloudera Manager will recommend best practice values for many configuration parameters and will inform you when a service or services need to be restarted after a configuration change. Cloudera Manager will also verify configuration values, such as datatypes, value ranges, or domains.

Cloudera Enterprise keeps track of configuration history, which can be used as an audit trail or to measure the effect of configuration values on cluster performance. Moreover, Cloudera Enterprise can be used to roll back erroneous, detrimental, or unnecessary configuration changes.

Service Management with Ambari

Ambari enables you to start, stop, or restart all services on all hosts related to a particular component such as HDFS or YARN, or a particular service running on a specified host, such as one of the slave node daemons on a cluster node. Ambari will manage the service control operation, providing progress, and error information if required, as shown in Figure 18.17.

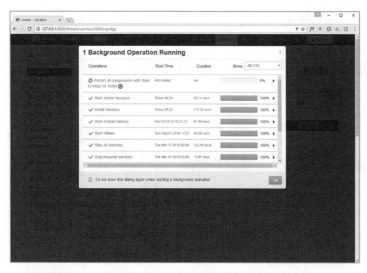

FIGURE 18.17
Starting Services Using Ambari.

Configuration Management with Ambari

A key feature of Ambari, like Cloudera Manager, is its configuration management capabilities. Using Ambari, you can centrally maintain and manage all of the configuration settings for all services in your cluster. Ambari exposes user-friendly widgets and controls to view and update common configuration properties for the various clustered components that it manages, as shown in Figure 18.18.

FIGURE 18.18
User-Friendly Configuration Management Using Ambari.

There are also views for setting more advanced component properties, as shown in Figure 18.19.

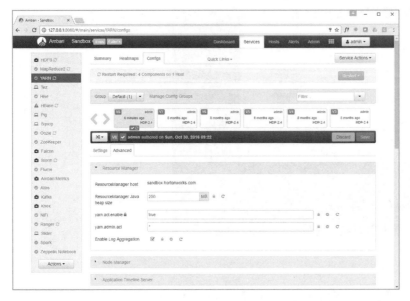

FIGURE 18.19
Advanced Settings in Ambari.

Ambari enables you to view configuration history and revert settings to previously configured values, as shown in Figure 18.20.

FIGURE 18.20
Configuration History and Rollback with Ambari.

Monitoring, Troubleshooting, and Securing Hadoop Clusters Using Cluster Management Utilities

Both the Cloudera Manager and Ambari cluster management solutions provide integrated metrics and events to monitor the health of individual hosts or entire services. Figure 18.21 shows a host view in Cloudera Manager with host-level metrics such as CPU and memory usage.

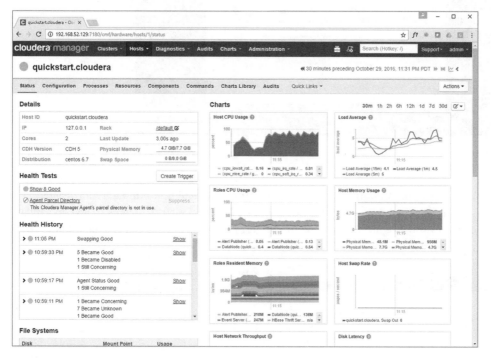

FIGURE 18.21
Host-Level Monitoring with Cloudera Manager.

Similarly, Ambari provides host-level metrics. Figure 18.22 shows a drill down into CPU usage on a particular host using Ambari.

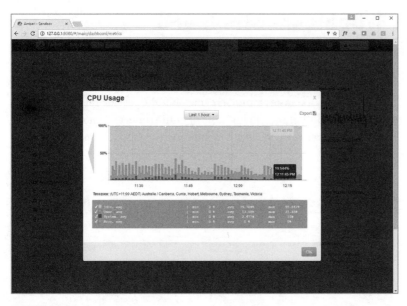

FIGURE 18.22
Host-Level Monitoring Using Ambari.

Cloudera Manager and Ambari can also provide metrics and health information for clustered services such as HDFS, where you are provided with service-level metrics such as HDFS capacity or YARN container usage. Figure 18.23 shows the status of a HDFS cluster using Cloudera Manager.

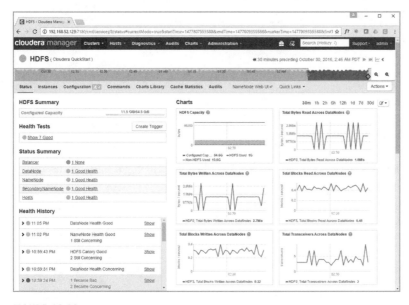

FIGURE 18.23
Service Status Using Cloudera Manager.

Both solutions leverage and extend the Hadoop metrics framework, which I will discuss in **Hour 23, "Administering, Monitoring, and Troubleshooting Hadoop."**

Additionally, both solutions enable Hadoop administrators to manage events on the cluster. An example of viewing events using Cloudera Manager is shown in Figure 18.24.

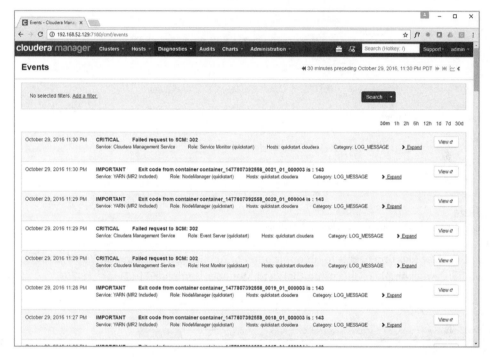

FIGURE 18.24
Viewing Events Using Cloudera Manager.

The capability to view and search log files that may be stored on the local filesystem or on remote nodes in the cluster is a necessary activity when administering a cluster or troubleshooting issues with services or applications. Both solutions provide this capability. Figure 18.25 demonstrates the capability to search and view log records using Cloudera Manager.

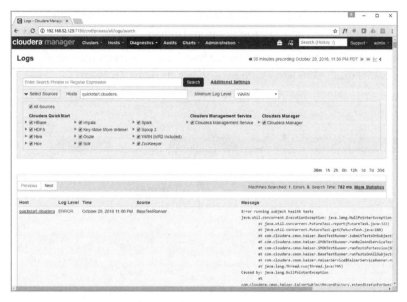

FIGURE 18.25
Searching and Viewing Log Files Using Cloudera Manager.

You can also refine logs and events to an application or applications running on YARN using either solution. An example of this using Cloudera Manager is provided in Figure 18.26.

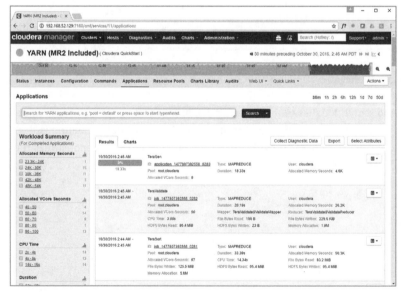

FIGURE 18.26
Viewing Application Logs Using Cloudera Manager.

Cluster Security Using Management Tools

Hadoop clusters are relatively open environments that typically store high volumes of event, transaction, and other important information. With this amount of valuable data stored on the platform, it is important to restrict who has access to the cluster and what resources on the cluster they are allowed to access.

Both cluster management solutions discussed in this hour enable administrators to integrate with corporate directory services such as Microsoft Active Directory, as well as deploying Kerberos to the cluster and all of its services and interfaces.

Additionally, both Cloudera Manager and Ambari enable you to implement role-based access control to management functions, defining which users are allowed to perform specific operations according to their role.

We will discuss specifics around Hadoop security in much more detail in **Hour 22, "Securing Hadoop."** However, you should appreciate that the process of securing a cluster is made easier using one of the cluster management tools.

Getting Started with the Cluster Management Utilities

The easiest way to get started using Cloudera Manager and Ambari, the cluster management utilities discussed this hour, is to download the sandbox or quickstart virtual machines (VMs) available by the major Hadoop distributors, Cloudera, and Hortonworks.

TRY IT YOURSELF ▼

Getting Started with the Cluster Management Utilities

For this exercise, you will require a host capable of virtualization, having Intel VT-x or AMD-V enabled in your systems BIOS. You will also need sufficient memory on your machine to host virtual machines with 8GB of guest memory.

1. Download and install virtualization software. You can use either VMware Player or Oracle Virtual Box. Both are free to use for non-commercial purposes.

   http://www.vmware.com/products/player/playerpro-evaluation.html (**VMware Player**)

   https://www.virtualbox.org/wiki/Downloads (**Virtual Box**)

Getting Started with Ambari

1. Download the Hortonworks Sandbox for your target virtualization platform from https://hortonworks.com/downloads/.

2. Open the guest VM using your selected virtualization system.

3. Once your guest VM running the Hortonworks Sandbox is running, open a browser on the host system and navigate to http://127.0.0.1:8080. This will take you to the Ambari logon screen. Use the credentials `admin`/`admin`.

4. Explore the Ambari user interface, including trying the Ambari Views feature discussed earlier this hour.

Getting Started with Cloudera Manager

1. Download the Cloudera Quickstart VM for your target virtualization platform from http://www.cloudera.com/downloads.html.

2. Open the guest VM using your selected virtualization system.

3. Once your guest VM running Cloudera is running, double-click the *Launch Cloudera Express* icon on the Linux desktop of the guest VM.

4. Once the launch process from Step 3 is complete, open a browser on the host system and navigate to http://*<guestvmipaddress>*:7180. This will take you to the Cloudera Manager logon screen. Use the credentials `admin`/`admin`.

5. Explore the Cloudera Manager user interface, including stopping and starting services such as HDFS or YARN using Cloudera Manager.

Summary

Managing Hadoop clusters of any size presents challenges. Hadoop clusters usually consist of many host systems, each potentially running multiple services. Synchronizing configuration changes, performing software upgrades, managing services, and monitoring service and node health are all tasks made more difficult due to the distributed nature of Hadoop systems.

Apache Ambari and Cloudera Manager are useful tools for managing Hadoop cluster environments and their related core and ecosystem components. Ambari and Cloudera Manager can be used to manage configuration, including synchronizing changes across cluster nodes, keeping track of configuration history, and rolling back erroneous configuration changes. Ambari and Cloudera Manager can also be used to manage distributed services such as starting or stopping services on multiple nodes. Both solutions also provide monitoring capabilities and instrumentation to easily visualize the health of your cluster or of particular services.

Other tasks such as deploying new nodes, decommissioning existing nodes, deploying new services, and more are made easy using the intuitive management interfaces provided by Ambari and Cloudera Manager.

The Cloudera Manager and Ambari solutions are worth exploring as they make complex tasks involved with managing Hadoop clusters simple.

Q&A

Q. What are the advantages of using cluster management tools such as Ambari or Cloudera Manager for configuration management on a fully distributed Hadoop cluster?

A. Using a cluster management tool such as Ambari or Cloudera Manager to manage Hadoop configuration settings ensures that configuration settings are replicated to each required node, maintaining consistency across distributed servers or hosts. Moreover, if the configuration changes require the restart of one or more services, the Ambari or Cloudera Manager UI will alert you to this. You can also track configuration history and roll back changes as required using these tools.

Q. What is a rolling upgrade? How does this work with the cluster management tools?

A. Rolling upgrades are a common administrative task used in maintaining a Hadoop cluster. A rolling upgrade enables services in a Hadoop cluster (such as HDFS) to be upgraded one node at a time with no system downtime. For instance, a HDFS NameNode in a HA configuration could be upgraded one node at a time, with no disruption to the HDFS service. Ambari and Cloudera Manager can both perform rolling upgrades for services in a Hadoop cluster using a guided user interface.

Q. What are the advantages of using Cloudera Manager or Ambari for service management on a fully distributed Hadoop cluster?

A. Many services in a Hadoop cluster need to be controlled simultaneously, such as restarting each DataNode in a HDFS cluster after making a change to a `hdfs-site.xml` property. Both Ambari and Cloudera Manager use agents deployed on distributed cluster nodes to execute service control operations (starting, stopping, restarting) upon request.

Workshop

The workshop contains quiz questions to help you solidify your understanding of the material covered. Try to answer all questions before looking at the "Answers" section that follows.

Quiz

1. What components must be deployed on one or more hosts to use Ambari?

2. True or False. Ambari Views can be used to provide user interfaces to Hadoop.

3. Groups of machines with homogeneous or similar hardware or operating system configuration and which share Hadoop configuration on a cluster managed by Cloudera Manager are called _____.

4. What are the two editions Cloudera Manager is available in?

Answers

1. `ambari-server` and `ambari-agent`

2. True

3. role groups

4. Cloudera Express and Cloudera Enterprise.

HOUR 19
Scaling Hadoop

What You'll Learn in This Hour:

▶ Linear scalability in Hadoop
▶ Adding and removing nodes in a Hadoop cluster
▶ Rebalancing Hadoop
▶ Benchmarking Hadoop

One of the principal design goals of Hadoop was its capability to scale. In this hour, we will explore the elastic properties of the Hadoop platform. Specifically, we look at the processes involved in adding and removing nodes from a cluster, as well as understanding relative performance increases and decreases over time using benchmarks.

Linear Scalability with Hadoop

As discussed in our introduction to Hadoop, Hadoop was designed to circumnavigate the limitations of distributed systems available at the time. The distributed systems in the late 1990s and early 2000s often involved synchronization and shared state, which ultimately meant there was a limit to how much they could scale. Beyond this limit, performance returns would diminish. Hadoop, on the other hand, was designed to scale linearly to a practically infinite number of nodes using its true shared nothing approach. This is illustrated in Figure 19.1.

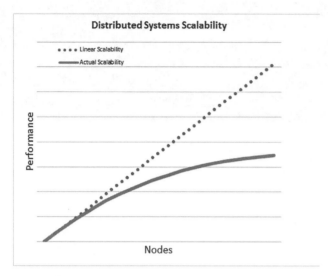

FIGURE 19.1
Linear Scalability with Hadoop.

Recall that Hadoop, as the combination of HDFS and YARN subsystems, co-locates storage and processing resources on cluster slave or worker nodes. As nodes are added to a Hadoop cluster, you get additional HDFS block storage and additional compute capacity in the form of additional vcores and memory to allocate to YARN containers.

Choosing When to Scale

There is no hard and fast rule as to when to add capacity to your Hadoop cluster. Generally speaking, you should monitor your cluster for both available storage capacity and application throughput. One method I will discuss later this hour to measure relative performance of your cluster is to run benchmarks periodically. You could also use monitoring, such as the metrics visible through Ambari. I will discuss some additional methods to collect metrics in **Hour 23, "Administering, Monitoring, and Troubleshooting Hadoop."**

Conversely, as Hadoop is an elastic system, you can also remove nodes when there is a significant reduction in demand, provided there is adequate storage available in the remaining nodes. This may be done to reduce infrastructure costs if necessary, or re-purpose Hadoop slave nodes for other services. I will discuss and demonstrate the process of both adding and removing nodes from a Hadoop cluster in this hour.

Adding Nodes to your Hadoop Cluster

Adding nodes to a Hadoop cluster is very straightforward. Security permitting, in many cases you can just install and start the slave node services, DataNode and NodeManager, on a new host on the same network as the NameNode and ResourceManager. You just need to configure the new host to specify the correct NameNode and ResourceManager hosts in their respective Hadoop configuration files, as shown in Listing 19.1.

LISTING 19.1   Hadoop Configuration Needed to Join a Cluster

```
# core-site.xml configuration
...
<property>
   <name>fs.defaultFS</name>
   <value>hdfs://yournamenodehost:8020</value>
</property>
...
# yarn-site.xml configuration
...
<property>
   <name>yarn.resourcemanager.hostname</name>
   <value>yourresourcemanagerhost</value>
</property>
...
```

Additional configuration may be required if you are running a highly available or secure cluster. We will cover this in **Hour 21, "Understanding Advanced HDFS,"** and **Hour 22, "Securing Hadoop,"** respectively.

Recall from our earlier discussions about HDFS and YARN, that the DataNode service will start sending block reports (even if these block reports are empty) to the NameNode, and the NodeManager service will start heartbeating and updating its configured ResourceManager with its available compute capacity. Both subsystems will then start leveraging this new node, the NameNode will start allocating blocks or block replicas to the new node, and the ResourceManager will start assigning containers to this node, including delegating ApplicationMaster duties to the new instance.

`include` **File**

Having a system in which any host can join the cluster, which is the default behavior of Hadoop, is often not desired. Hadoop provides a way to restrict the hosts that are allowed to join a Hadoop cluster (either a HDFS cluster and/or a YARN cluster). This mechanism is referred to as an `include` file. An `include` file is a file located on the master node that is read by the NameNode and ResourceManager daemons, which defines hosts that are explicitly allowed to act as nodes in the cluster. If you are using this file, only hosts that are listed in this file are allowed to join the cluster, any attempts by hosts not in this file to send heartbeats or block reports will fail—and ultimately their services will fail

To configure an `include` file to govern which hosts are allowed to participate in HDFS and YARN, you need to perform the following steps:

1. Create a text file in your `/etc/hadoop/conf` directory, named `include`, with a new line terminated list of hosts allowed to participate in the Hadoop cluster. The file can have a different name if you wish.

2. Update the `hdfs-site.xml` configuration file (on the NameNode(s) specifically, but you can update all cluster nodes), adding the following property:

```
<property>
    <name>dfs.hosts</name>
    <value>/etc/hadoop/conf/include</value>
</property>
```

3. If you have rack awareness configured, which I will discuss in **Hour 21, "Understanding Advanced HDFS,"** you will need to update your rack topology script as well.

4. Update the `yarn-site.xml` configuration file (on the ResourceManager host specifically, but this property can be set on all nodes) to add the following property:

```
<property>
    <name>yarn.resourcemanager.nodes.include-path</name>
    <value>/etc/hadoop/conf/include</value>
</property>
```

5. Run the following command to instruct the NameNode daemon to read (or re-read) the include file:

```
$ hdfs dfsadmin -refreshNodes
```

Note that you may need to `sudo` as the `hdfs` user to run this command.

6. Run the following command to instruct the ResourceManager daemon to read (or re-read) the `include` file:

```
$ yarn rmadmin -refreshNodes
```

Note that you may need to `sudo` as the `yarn` user to run this command.

The `include` file will normally be read by the master node daemons at startup, so steps 5 and 6 would not be necessary if you started the NameNode and ResourceManager after creating this file and making the configuration changes.

At this stage, you should see the new nodes appear in the NameNode and ResourceManager web UIs.

New DataNodes Added to the Cluster Will Not Be Favored

New nodes added to the cluster as DataNodes will not be treated any differently than existing DataNodes during normal HDFS operations. That is, the NameNode would not specifically instruct clients to write blocks or block replicas to this new node. Over the course of time, block distribution will normalize across all nodes; however, you can preempt this process by rebalancing the cluster, as I will discuss later this hour.

Decommissioning Nodes from your Cluster

Removing nodes from a cluster is sometimes required. This could be done for any number of reasons including a node being faulty or the need to re-purpose hardware. The process of removing nodes gracefully from a Hadoop cluster is referred to as decommissioning. Decommissioning is also used as a common strategy for hardware upgrades or node replacements.

Decommissioning a node enables the system to proactively adapt to the change in the cluster. All HDFS blocks that were stored on the decommissioned node are replicated to other nodes. Moreover, any tasks running on the node will complete, but no new tasks will be scheduled on the decommissioned node.

`exclude` **File**

Decommissioning a node can be accomplished using an `exclude` file. Like the `include` files you learned about, the `exclude` file contains a new line terminated list of hosts. However, this list of hosts is made up of hosts to be removed or explicitly not allowed to join the cluster. The process is similar to the include process I discussed earlier and can be accomplished by following these steps:

1. Create a text file, `exclude`, with a new line terminated list of hosts that are to be *removed* from or *not allowed* to participate in the Hadoop cluster.

2. Update the `hdfs-site.xml` configuration file (on the NameNode(s) specifically, but you can update all cluster nodes), adding the following property:

```
<property>
   <name>dfs.hosts.exclude</name>
   <value>/etc/hadoop/conf/exclude</value>
</property>
```

3. If you have rack awareness configured, which I will discuss in **Hour 21, "Understanding Advanced HDFS,"** you will need to update your rack topology script as well.

4. Update the `yarn-site.xml` configuration file (on the ResourceManager host specifically, but this property can be set on all nodes) to add the following property:

```
<property>
    <name>yarn.resourcemanager.nodes.exclude-path</name>
    <value>/etc/hadoop/conf/exclude</value>
</property>
```

5. Run the following command to instruct the NameNode daemon to read (or re-read) the exclude file:

```
$ hdfs dfsadmin -refreshNodes
```

6. Run the following command to instruct the ResourceManager daemon to read (or re-read) the exclude file:

```
$ yarn rmadmin -refreshNodes
```

As mentioned in the previous section you may need to `sudo` as the `hdfs` and `yarn` users, respectively, to run the admin commands.

The NameNode web UI will show that the DataNode(s) in your exclude files are in a decommissioning state, as shown in Figure 19.2.

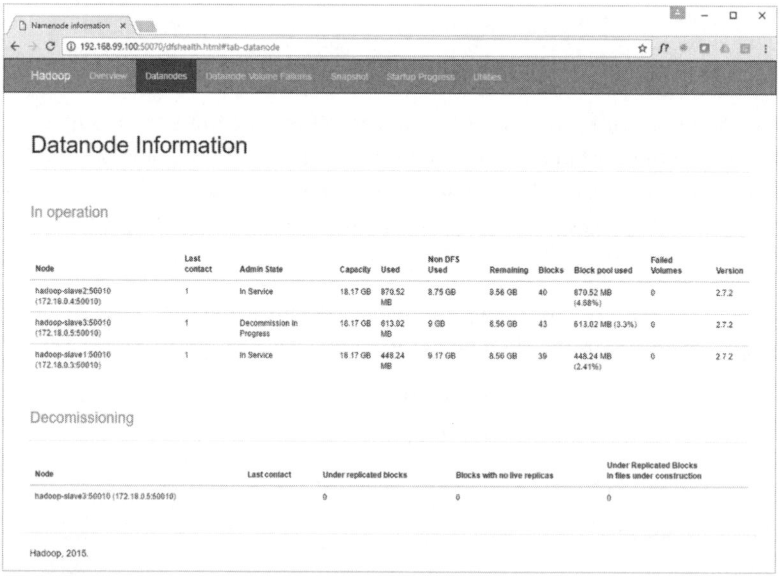

FIGURE 19.2
Decommissioning Nodes in the NameNode Web UI.

At this stage the NameNode is orchestrating the movement of blocks off the decommissioning nodes to other nodes in the cluster. When all the HDFS blocks and the correct number of replicas for these block exist on other non-decommissioned nodes, the state changes to Decommissioned, as shown in Figure 19.3.

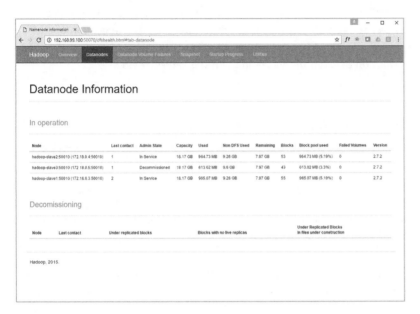

FIGURE 19.3
Decommissioned Nodes in the NameNode Web UI.

At this stage, it is safe to stop the DataNode services on the decommissioned nodes. They will then ultimately be removed from the list of nodes in the NameNode's web UI.

Rebalancing a Hadoop Cluster

Adding new nodes to an existing cluster, especially one which has been running for some time, will naturally cause the cluster to become unbalanced, where the existing nodes contain more blocks than the new nodes. This can occur for other reasons as well during the lifetime of a Hadoop cluster

Uneven block distribution will affect data locality and parallelism. This may degrade performance. In such cases you may need to rebalance the cluster. This can be done using the `balancer` utility.

`balancer` Utility

The `balancer` utility is a tool used with the `hdfs` command-line utility. The `balancer` utility reviews the block placement across all nodes of the cluster and makes adjustments to rebalance the cluster. This is done by moving blocks from over-utilized nodes onto other nodes that store fewer blocks, ensuring that all nodes are within a user-specified percentage tolerance of each other. This tolerance is referred to as a threshold.

A node is considered over-utilized if it is over the defined threshold and under-utilized if it is under the threshold. The `balancer` utility only looks at the aggregate block allocation to each node and does not consider the block placement on the disks of a slave node. That is, it does not try to balance block distribution across multiple spindles on a given slave node.

CAUTION

You Should Rebalance During Off Peak Usage Times

As you could imagine, the `balancer` utility could result in an excessive amount of data transferred across the network. You can govern (or throttle) the amount of data transferred during node rebalancing using the `dfs.datanode.balance.bandwidthPerSec` property in the `hdfs-site.xml` configuration file, or alternatively you can use the `hdfs dfsadmin -setBalancerBandwidth` command to govern the balancing process. Caution should be used however in choosing when to rebalance the cluster as this activity could impact other processes such as block replication and Shuffle processes in applications.

Listing 19.2 shows an example `balancer` command. Note that the `balancer` utility can be cancelled at any time when used interactively by pressing Ctrl-C.

LISTING 19.2 `balancer` **Utility**

```
$ hdfs balancer -threshold 10
# or
$ sudo -u hdfs hdfs balancer -threshold 10
```

Benchmarking Hadoop

As an administrator of a Hadoop platform, before you can begin the task of tuning, optimizing, or planning capacity for your platform, you must first establish a performance baseline. Without one, you have no empirical way to assess whether performance is degrading or whether any changes you make to the system have a positive effect on overall performance. In this section, I will cover some methods that provide this baseline and ongoing measurement.

Benchmarks

Benchmarks are a common approach to establishing a baseline and assessing performance relative to results at future points in time. Benchmarks should be performed either on a recurring basis (once a month, once a year, and so on), or after any significant changes to the processing environment (when a new node or nodes are added to the cluster, for instance).

Benchmarks are typically designed to perform workloads similar to those that would occur under normal operations. Additionally, benchmarks are designed not to be influenced by factors such as statistics or caching. This makes the benchmark results more meaningful as they cannot be biased or influenced by any specific system optimizations.

Much of the basis for data processing benchmarks stems from database and business intelligence (BI) vendors requiring a tool or framework by which to measure themselves against their competitors; for example, Oracle database versus SQL Server database query performance.

Transaction Processing Performance Council

The Transaction Processing Performance Council (TPC) is an organization founded in the late 1980s to establish industry standards for database performance benchmarks. The TPC has published several benchmark standards for various database workloads, including TPC-C, which is a benchmarking standard for OLTP (Online Transaction Processing) systems, and TPC-H, which is a standard for DSS (Decision Support Systems).

The TPC has recently introduced new benchmarks to include the emergent big data platforms in addition to their established set of benchmarks for relational database systems. New standards that have emerged include the following:

▶ *TPCx-HS*—The first published standard for benchmarking Hadoop systems

▶ *TPC-DS*—A recent standard established for benchmarking big data SQL engines in the Hadoop ecosystem (such as Impala and SparkSQL)

Terasort

Terasort is a longstanding Hadoop benchmark. Terasort exercises the MapReduce framework in Hadoop and provides a meaningful benchmark for the system. Terasort is actually comprised of three components:

▶ `teragen`—Generates a terabyte or other configurable amount of random data

▶ `terasort`—Sorts the random data set generated by the `teragen` utility

▶ `teravalidate`—Validates that the resultant dataset from the `terasort` utility has been correctly sorted

Because the Terasort suite of utilities generates random data, each successive test cannot be influenced, coerced, or advantaged in any way.

▼ TRY IT YOURSELF

Running the Terasort Benchmark

In this exercise you will run the Terasort benchmark. You can use any Hadoop cluster you have available.

1. Run the `teragen` program to generate the random input:

```
$ hadoop jar \
$HADOOP_HOME/share/hadoop/mapreduce/hadoop-mapreduce-examples-*.jar \
teragen 1000000000 /teraInput
```

Note that you may need to find the directory containing the `hadoop-mapreduce-examples` jar file as your jar file may be in a different directory.

The first argument to the `teragen` program is the number of 100-byte records to generate. In our case we are generating 1,000,000,000 records, or 100GB. You can make your value less or more, depending upon the cluster you are running the benchmark on.

The second argument is the directory in HDFS in which to store the output of the `teragen` operation.

2. Run the `terasort` program to sort the random data you created using the `teragen` program:

```
$ hadoop jar \
$HADOOP_HOME/share/hadoop/mapreduce/hadoop-mapreduce-examples-*.jar \
terasort /teraInput /teraOutput
```

Note the elapsed time for this operation as this is your benchmark.

3. Run the `teravalidate` program to validate the results of the `terasort` benchmark:

```
$ hadoop jar \
$HADOOP_HOME/share/hadoop/mapreduce/hadoop-mapreduce-examples-*.jar \
teravalidate -D mapred.reduce.tasks=8 \
/teraOutput /teraValidate
```

Note that we supplied generic options using ToolRunner to specify the number of Reduce tasks to run. You can adjust this as necessary for your environment.

If the operation succeeds, you will get output file(s) in the `teravalidate` output directory containing a checksum value.

4. Delete the output directories and random data created by the `teragen`, `terasort` and `teravalidate` operations.

```
$ hadoop fs -rm -r -skipTrash /tera*
```

`terasort` in its Hadoop MapReduce implementation is commonly run to benchmark Hadoop clusters, testing the HDFS, YARN, and MapReduce subsystems. There are many derivatives of `terasort` that have been independently developed, including variants that use Spark (`map` and `sortByKey` or `reduceByKey`) instead of MapReduce.

`terasort` is also useful for "smoke testing" or "shakeout testing" a newly commissioned Hadoop cluster.

Other Testing Suites

There are many more benchmarks available specifically targeting HFDS and YARN, including TestDFSIO, NNBench, MRBench, and others. These utilities are typically included with each Hadoop release. Consult the latest Hadoop project documentation or documentation on the Cloudera or Hortonworks sites for more information about using these test utilities.

Summary

Scaling a Hadoop cluster up or down is a normal function in the management lifecycle of Hadoop. This can be necessary for many reasons including scale, cost, or performance. In this hour, you learned about the processes involved with scaling Hadoop. Specifically, you learned how to add nodes to a fully distributed cluster. You learned about the process of rebalancing a cluster after adding new nodes using the `balancer` utility. Conversely, you also learned how to remove nodes from a cluster using the decommissioning process.

You could also use the cluster management tools such as Ambari or Cloudera Manager to add and remove nodes, but it is worthwhile knowing how this works at a detail level.

Finally, you learned about common benchmarks used to profile performance and throughput on a Hadoop cluster, including `teragen`, `terasort`, and `teravalidate`. Benchmarks are useful at various points in time such as anniversaries of deployment, or after significant events such as the adding or removing of nodes.

Q&A

Q. Why is it sometimes necessary to decommission nodes in a Hadoop cluster? What is the process for doing so?

A. Removing nodes from a Hadoop cluster may be necessary due to node failure or infrastructure repurposing. You may also need to upgrade the hardware for one or more nodes. Decommissioning is the graceful way to remove a node from a Hadoop cluster, allowing all blocks stored on the node to be moved to another node in the cluster. Decommissioning is triggered by adding a host to an exclude file configured in the `hdfs-site.xml` and `yarn-site.xml` configuration files and refreshing the node configuration on the NameNode and ResourceManager. After all blocks have been migrated off of the decommissioned node, you can simply stop the DataNode and NodeManager services on the host and remove it from the cluster.

Q. What is the `balancer` utility? Why is it sometimes necessary to use this?

A. The `balancer` utility is used to re-assign blocks from over-utilized nodes (that is, nodes with a greater percentage of blocks stored relative to other nodes) to under-utilized nodes. It is often necessary to run the `balancer` utility after adding new nodes to the cluster.

Q. Why should you run benchmarks on a Hadoop cluster? When should you run benchmarks on your Hadoop system?

A. Benchmarks establish a baseline for assessing performance relative to readings at future points in time. Benchmarks should be performed either on a recurring basis (once a month, once a year, and so on), or after any significant changes to the processing environment (when a new node or nodes are added to the cluster, for instance).

Workshop

The workshop contains quiz questions to help you solidify your understanding of the material covered. Try to answer all questions before looking at the "Answers" section that follows.

Quiz

1. **True or False.** You should avoid using the `balancer` utility during peak usage times.

2. Which Hadoop benchmarking utilities can be used to generate a random dataset, sort the dataset, and validate the results of the test?

3. What commands should be run after updating include or exclude files for a Hadoop cluster?

4. **True or False.** The `balancer` utility will adjust block placement across the local disks of each individual slave node.

Answers

1. True.

2. `teragen`, `terasort`, and `teravalidate`.

3. `hdfs dfsadmin -refreshNodes` and `yarn rmadmin -refreshNodes`

4. False.

Understanding Cluster Configuration

What You'll Learn in This Hour:

▶ Configuration and default values in Hadoop
▶ Configuration precedence
▶ HDFS and YARN configuration
▶ Ecosystem component configuration

You have already seen firsthand how important configuration is to Hadoop core and ecosystem components. In this hour, we take a closer look at configuration in Hadoop, including configuration defaults and order of precedence for configuration in Hadoop, as well as understanding some more about key Hadoop configuration properties.

Configuration in Hadoop

Everything in Hadoop is configurable and everything has a default value (maybe not everything, but nearly everything!). Let's look closer at configuration in Hadoop and how it is applied.

Hadoop Configuration Basics Revisited

Every host participating in a Hadoop cluster, including clients and servers, has its own local set of configuration files, typically stored in /etc/hadoop/conf (often a symbolic link to a physical directory in $HADOOP_HOME). As you have seen throughout this book, most of the configuration files for core components are written in XML, with <property>, <name> and <value> tags for individual configuration properties.

Many of the configuration properties are specific to a process such as the DataNode process but can exist on other nodes that are not running that particular process and are simply ignored. Often changes to configuration specific to a particular daemon such as the DataNode daemon will require a restart of that specific service to be read and take effect.

CAUTION

Misconfiguration is the Most Common Cause of Daemon Failure

Errors in configuration, such as XML markup errors, for instance, missing closing tags, misspelled property names, or incorrect values are the most common cause of Hadoop daemons failing to start.

NOTE

Property Names Are Commonly Deprecated in New Releases

As Hadoop is still a relatively young project, configuration properties are routinely added and removed in new releases. Properties can also be deprecated in some cases. Often, but not always, the older analogous property names are still acceptable. For instance, the `core-site.xml` property `fs.default.name` changed to `fs.defaultFS` in release 2.x of Hadoop. However, the `fs.default.name` property is still accepted. Moreover, some property names have even been misspelled, such as `dfs.datanode.max.xcievers` (remember, i before e…). The bottom line is to keep current with the Hadoop documentation for your release.

Configuration Defaults

There are literally thousands of configuration parameters available in Hadoop. As mentioned before, "everything is configurable." Each configuration property (in the overwhelming majority of cases) has a default value. You can find the default values in the `*-default.xml` documentation for the specific configuration file and specific release you are interested in. For example, defaults for `hdfs-site.xml` properties for the latest stable Hadoop release can be found at **https://hadoop.apache.org/docs/stable/hadoop-project-dist/hadoop-hdfs/hdfs-default.xml**, as shown in Figure 20.1.

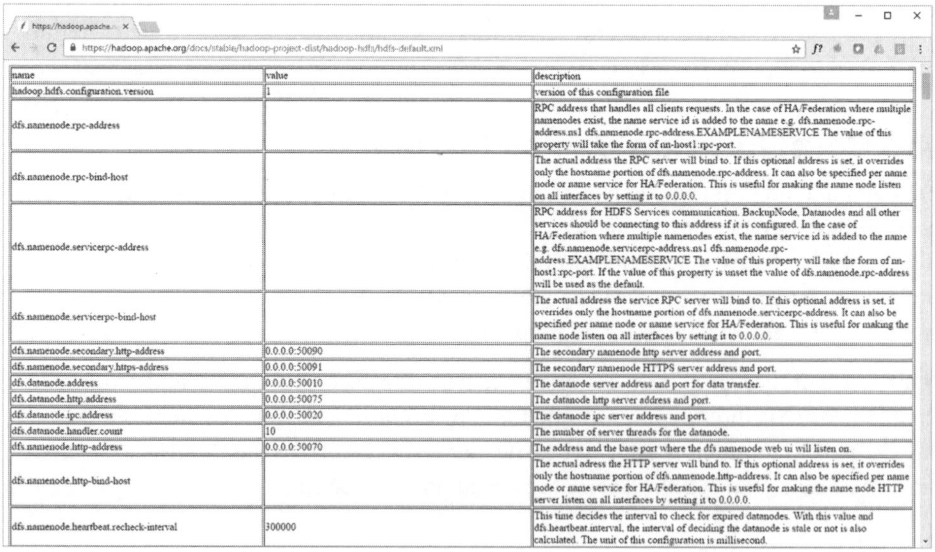

https://hadoop.apache.org/docs/stable/hadoop-project-dist/hadoop-hdfs/hdfs-default.xml

name	value	description
hadoop.hdfs.configuration.version	1	version of this configuration file
dfs.namenode.rpc-address		RPC address that handles all clients requests. In the case of HA/Federation where multiple namenodes exist, the name service id is added to the name e.g. dfs.namenode.rpc-address.ns1 dfs.namenode.rpc-address.EXAMPLENAMESERVICE The value of this property will take the form of nn-host1:rpc-port.
dfs.namenode.rpc-bind-host		The actual address the RPC server will bind to. If this optional address is set, it overrides only the hostname portion of dfs.namenode.rpc-address. It can also be specified per name node or name service for HA/Federation. This is useful for making the name node listen on all interfaces by setting it to 0.0.0.0.
dfs.namenode.servicerpc-address		RPC address for HDFS Services communication. BackupNode, Datanodes and all other services should be connecting to this address if it is configured. In the case of HA/Federation where multiple namenodes exist, the name service id is added to the name e.g. dfs.namenode.servicerpc-address.ns1 dfs.namenode.rpc-address.EXAMPLENAMESERVICE The value of this property will take the form of nn-host1:rpc-port. If the value of this property is unset the value of dfs.namenode.rpc-address will be used as the default.
dfs.namenode.servicerpc-bind-host		The actual address the service RPC server will bind to. If this optional address is set, it overrides only the hostname portion of dfs.namenode.servicerpc-address. It can also be specified per name node or name service for HA/Federation. This is useful for making the name node listen on all interfaces by setting it to 0.0.0.0.
dfs.namenode.secondary.http-address	0.0.0.0:50090	The secondary namenode http server address and port.
dfs.namenode.secondary.https-address	0.0.0.0:50091	The secondary namenode HTTPS server address and port.
dfs.datanode.address	0.0.0.0:50010	The datanode server address and port for data transfer.
dfs.datanode.http.address	0.0.0.0:50075	The datanode http server address and port.
dfs.datanode.ipc.address	0.0.0.0:50020	The datanode ipc server address and port.
dfs.datanode.handler.count	10	The number of server threads for the datanode.
dfs.namenode.http-address	0.0.0.0:50070	The address and the base port where the dfs namenode web ui will listen on.
dfs.namenode.http-bind-host		The actual adress the HTTP server will bind to. If this optional address is set, it overrides only the hostname portion of dfs.namenode.http-address. It can also be specified per name node or name service for HA/Federation. This is useful for making the name node HTTP server listen on all interfaces by setting it to 0.0.0.0.
dfs.namenode.heartbeat.recheck-interval	300000	This time decides the interval to check for expired datanodes. With this value and dfs.heartbeat.interval, the interval of deciding the datanode is stale or not is also calculated. The unit of this configuration is millisecond.

FIGURE 20.1
hdfs-default.xml.

Similarly, defaults for `core-site.xml` for the same release can be found at **https:// hadoop.apache.org/docs/stable/hadoop-project-dist/hadoop-common/core-default.xml** and defaults for `yarn-site.xml` at **https://hadoop.apache.org/docs/stable/hadoop-yarn/ hadoop-yarn-common/yarn-default.xml**. Any defaults for any release are a simple Google search away!

For any particular application, such as a MapReduce application, you can often find the complete set of configuration properties submitted with the application, including defaults and user-defined settings, using the Configuration link in the ApplicationMaster UI (accessible from the YARN ResourceManager UI). This is shown in Figure 20.2.

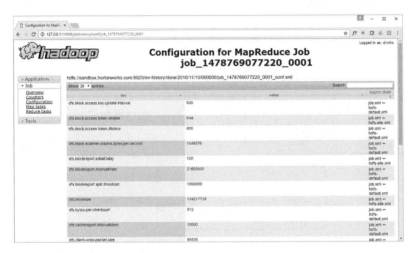

FIGURE 20.2
Configuration Submitted with a MapReduce Application.

Configuration Precedence

You have seen that Hadoop configuration properties can be set on master nodes, slave nodes, and even clients. In addition, if a property is not set, a default value for that property will often be used. So, what happens when a property is set to different values in more than one location? This is where configuration precedence rules come into play.

Every application in Hadoop will at some point engage with a slave node in the cluster, for the purpose of interacting with a YARN NodeManager hosting an ApplicationMaster, or interacting with a DataNode while reading or writing data in HDFS. The first order of precedence for a configuration setting (beyond the defaults) is the `*-site.xml` file on the slave node or nodes that an application interacts with during the submission process.

The next higher order of precedence is the `*-site.xml` file(s) on the client machine. Any property values supplied here will supersede values set on the equivalent files on the slave node host(s).

The highest precedence for a given configuration property value is assigned to the application being submitted. That is either in the Job object or using command-line arguments such as -D dfs.replication=4. Yes, that's right, the developer submitting the application has the highest precedence when it comes to configuration. I will show you how to govern this shortly.

Configuration precedence is summarized in Figure 20.3.

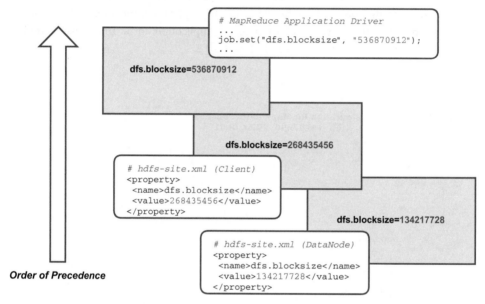

FIGURE 20.3
Configuration Precedence in Hadoop.

As mentioned, it is possible for developers to override configuration values set by administrators. For obvious reasons this may not be desired. For instance, it would be possible for a developer to request different block sizes or replication factors, which could negatively impact other users of the cluster. Fortunately, Hadoop provides a mechanism to address this.

Use a <final> tag in the configuration on your cluster (server) nodes to ensure that a particular configuration value cannot be overridden, irrespective of the order of precedence. Listing 20.1 demonstrates the use of the <final> tag.

LISTING 20.1 <final> **Tag**

```
...
<property>
  <name>dfs.blocksize</name>
  <value>134217728</value>
  <final>true</final>
</property>
...
```

Other Hadoop Environment Scripts and Configuration Files

You may have noticed that there are other scripts in the Hadoop configuration directory besides `core-site.xml`, `yarn-site.xml`, `mapred-site.xml`, and `hdfs-site.xml`. Let's quickly look at some of these other files now.

hadoop-env.sh

The `hadoop-env.sh` file is used to source environment variables for Hadoop daemons and processes. This can include daemon JVM settings such as heap size or Java options, as well as basic variables required by many processes such as `HADOOP_LOG_DIR` or `JAVA_HOME`, for example.

If you need to pass any environment variables to any Hadoop process, the `hadoop-env.sh` file is the file to do this in, as it is sourced by all Hadoop control scripts.

Similarly, there may be other environment shell scripts such as `yarn-env.sh` and `mapred-env.sh` that are used by these specific processes to source necessary environment variables.

For Windows-based clusters, there are equivalent Windows batch scripts to source environment variables including `hadoop-env.cmd`, `yarn-env.cmd` and `mapred-env.cmd`.

log4j.properties

Hadoop uses *Log4J* (the Java logging framework) to store and manage its log files. Log files are produced by nearly every process in Hadoop, including daemons, applications, and tasks. The `log4j.properties` file provides configuration for log file management, including how to write log records, where to write them, and how to manage rotation and retention of log files. We will cover logging in more detail in **Hour 23, "Administering, Monitoring, and Troubleshooting Hadoop,"** but Listing 20.2 shows an example excerpt from a `log4j.properties` file.

LISTING 20.2   `log4j.properties` **File**

```
. . .
log4j.appender.DRFA=org.apache.log4j.DailyRollingFileAppender
log4j.appender.DRFA.File=${hadoop.log.dir}/${hadoop.log.file}
log4j.appender.DRFA.DatePattern=.yyyy-MM-dd
log4j.appender.DRFA.MaxBackupIndex=30
log4j.appender.DRFA.layout=org.apache.log4j.PatternLayout
. . .
```

In some cases different components may have their own specific `log4j.properties` file, which may be located in the Hadoop configuration directory, such as `kms-log4j.properties` and `httpfs-log4j.properties`.

hadoop-metrics.properties

There may be `hadoop-metrics.properties` and/or `hadoop-metrics2.properties` files in your Hadoop configuration directory as well. These are used to define application and platform metrics to collect. I will cover Hadoop metrics collection and monitoring further in **Hour 23.**

Other Files

There may be other files in your configuration directory as well, including the `include` and `exclude` files discussed in **Hour 19, "Scaling Hadoop,"** or the various scheduler xml configuration files discussed in **Hour 16, "Managing YARN."** There are other files such as the `slaves` file, which is used by the cluster startup scripts in the Hadoop `sbin` directory.

Additionally, there are several configuration files related to security or access control policies, SSL configuration, or key management such as `hadoop-policy.xml`, `kms-site.xml`, or `ssl-server.xml`. We will cover some of these in **Hour 22, "Securing Hadoop."**

HDFS Configuration Parameters

So far we have learned about some of the basic HDFS properties. Let's look closer at some of these HDFS configuration properties as well as some new properties and understand how they work.

Common Properties (`core-site.xml`)

The `core-site.xml` file is used to store many properties that are required by different processes in a cluster, including client processes, master node processes, and slave node processes, the most important of which is `fs.defaultFS`.

`fs.defaultFS` is the property that specifies the filesystem to be used by the cluster. More often than not, this is HDFS. However, the filesystem used by the cluster could be an object store, such as S3 or Ceph, or a local or network filesystem. Listing 20.3 demonstrates some various filesystem settings for `fs.defaultFS`. Note that the value specifies the filesystem scheme as well as hostname and port information for the filesystem.

LISTING 20.3 `fs.defaultFS` **Setting**

```
<property>
  <name>fs.defaultFS</name>
  <value>hdfs://mynamenode:8020</value>
</property>
```

NOTE

You May Need to Specify Additional Authentication Credentials for Non-HDFS Filesystems

When using filesystems such as S3, you will need to provide additional AWS authentication parameters, including `fs.s3.awsAccessKeyId` and `fs.s3.awsSecretAccessKey`, to supply your credentials to the remote platform. This may also be the case with other remote filesystems or object stores. Consult the security documentation for your desired filesystem.

When I discuss HDFS high availability and federation in **Hour 21, "Understanding Advanced HDFS,"** you will learn a different approach to specifying the value for this property, using a construct called *nameservices* instead of specifying hosts explicitly.

NameNode Properties

Possibly the most important setting on a NameNode host is the `dfs.namenode.name.dir` property set in the `hdfs-site.xml` file. This property specifies the location on the filesystem where the NameNode stores its on-disk metadata, specifically the `fsimage` file(s) discussed in **Hour 4, "Understanding the Hadoop Distributed File System (HDFS)."**

This value is also used as the default directory for the `edits` files used for the NameNodes journalling function. However, this location can be set to a different directory using the `dfs.namenode.edits.dir` property.

As you learned in **Hour 4**, a loss of the NameNode's metadata would result in the loss of all of the data stored in the cluster's distributed filesystem—potentially petabytes of data. The on-disk metadata structures are there to provide durability and crash consistency for the NameNode's metadata, which is otherwise stored in volatile memory on the NameNode host.

The value for the `dfs.namenode.name.dir` property is a comma-separated list of directories (on a local or network file system—not on HDFS) where the `fsimage` files and `edits` files by default discussed in **Hour 4** will be stored by default. The default value for `dfs.namenode.name.dir` is `file://${hadoop.tmp.dir}/dfs/name`. This should be changed on a production system.

The NameNodes metadata is written to each directory in the comma-separated list of directories specified by `dfs.namenode.name.dir` synchronously—that is, at the same time. If any directory or volume specified in the list is unavailable, it will be removed from the cached list of directories and no further attempts will be made to write to this directory until the NameNode is restarted.

The parallel write operations to multiple directories provide additional fault tolerance to the NameNode's critical metadata functions. For this reason, you should always provide more than one directory, residing on a different physical disk, volume, or disk controller to minimize the risk of outages if one volume or channel fails.

Furthermore, you can, and in some cases such as non-HA deployments should, specify an NFS mount point in the list of directories in `dfs.namenode.name.dir`, which will then store a copy of the metadata on another host, providing further fault tolerance and recovery options. Note that if you do this, you should soft mount and configure retries for the NFS mount point; otherwise the NameNode process may hang if the mount is temporarily unavailable for whatever reason.

Listing 20.4 shows an example of a configuration value for the `dfs.namenode.name.dir` property. Note that there are no spaces between the comma-delimited values.

LISTING 20.4   `dfs.namenode.name.dir` **Configuration Property**

```
<property>
  <name>dfs.namenode.name.dir</name>
  <value>file:///disk1/dfs/nn,file:///disk2/dfs/nn</value>
</property>
```

The `dfs.namenode.name.dir` and `dfs.namenode.edits.dir` properties are read by the NameNode daemon upon startup. Any changes to these properties will require a NameNode restart to take effect.

TIP

You Can Usually Tell which File a Given Property is in by Its Prefix

The hierarchical naming format for Hadoop configuration properties is generally consistent. If you see a property prefaced by `dfs`, for instance `dfs.namenode.name.dir`, this will be located in the `hdfs-site.xml` file. Likewise, properties prefaced with `yarn`, for instance `yarn.resourcemanager.webapp`, will be located in `yarn-site.xml`. The naming format will also indicate where this property is required or read, or if it is specific to a service such as `namenode` or `resourcemanager` in the aforementioned properties.

SecondaryNameNode Properties

In **Hour 4** you learned about the role of the SecondaryNameNode and the checkpointing function it performs. There are three significant configuration properties that relate to the checkpointing function. These are

▶ `dfs.namenode.checkpoint.dir`

▶ `dfs.namenode.checkpoint.period`

▶ `dfs.namenode.checkpoint.txns`

The `dfs.namenode.checkpoint.dir` property is a comma-separated list of directories, analogous to the `dfs.namenode.name.dir` property discussed earlier, used to store the temporary `edits` to merge during the checkpointing process.

The `dfs.namenode.checkpoint.period` property specifies the maximum delay between two consecutive checkpoints with a default value of one hour. The `dfs.namenode.checkpoint.txns` property specifies the number of transactions at which the NameNode will force a checkpoint. Checkpointing will occur when either threshold is met (time interval or transactions).

DataNode Properties

One of the most important properties used by DataNodes in a HDFS cluster is the `dfs.datanode.data.dir` property located in the `hdfs-site.xml` file. The `dfs.datanode.data.dir` is the property that specifies where the DataNode will store the physical HDFS blocks. Like the `dfs.namenode.name.dir` property I discussed earlier, it too is a comma-separated list of directories with no spaces between. However, unlike the `dfs.namenode.name.dir` setting, writes to the directories specified in the `dfs.datanode.data.dir` property are performed in a round-robin fashion (i.e., the first block on one directory, the next block on the next, and so on).

The configuration for each DataNode may differ; just as with the potential for different generation hardware or configuration for different slave nodes, the volumes and directories may differ. However, when planning your cluster, it is best to try to homogenize as many configuration settings as possible, making the cluster easier to manage.

Listing 20.5 shows an example `dfs.datanode.data.dir` setting.

LISTING 20.5   `dfs.datanode.data.dir` **Configuration Property**

```
<property>
  <name>dfs.datanode.data.dir</name>
  <value>file:///disk1/dfs/dn,file:///disk2/dfs/dn</value>
</property>
```

HDFS is a "greedy" file system. Volumes associated with directories on the DataNodes specified by `dfs.datanode.data.dir` will be 100% filled with HDFS block data if left unmanaged. This is problematic because, as you recall from our discussions about MapReduce, slave nodes require working space for intermediate data storage. If available disk storage is completely consumed by HDFS block storage, data locality suffers as processing activities may not be possible on the node.

The `dfs.datanode.du.reserved` configuration property in `hdfs-site.xml` specifies the amount of space in bytes on each volume that must be reserved, and thus cannot be used for HDFS block storage. It is generally recommended to set this value to 25% of the available space or at least 1 GB, depending upon the local storage on each DataNode. Listing 20.6 demonstrates the use of the `dfs.datanode.du.reserved` property.

LISTING 20.6 `dfs.datanode.du.reserved` **Configuration Property**

```
<property>
  <name>dfs.datanode.du.reserved</name>
  <value>1073741824</value>
</property>
```

HDFS Client Properties

Aside from `fs.defaultFS`, which is used by clients and servers alike to identify the entry point for the filesystem to be used (the NameNode in the case of HDFS), there are some other client properties to understand.

The `dfs.blocksize` property located in the `hdfs-site.xml` configuration file specifies the block size in bytes for new files written by clients, including files produced as the result of an application or job run by the client. The default is 134217728, or 128MB. Although commonly thought of as a cluster- or server-based setting, `dfs.blocksize` is actually a client setting, but can be influenced by administrators using the `<final>` tag on a server node as discussed earlier. Listing 20.7 shows the `dfs.blocksize` property.

LISTING 20.7 `dfs.blocksize` **Configuration Property**

```
<property>
  <name>dfs.blocksize</name>
  <value>134217728</value>
</property>
```

The `dfs.replication` property located in the `hdfs-site.xml` file determines the number of block replicas created when a file is written to HDFS. The default is 3, which is also the recommended value. As with the `dfs.blocksize` property, the `dfs.replication` property is a client-side setting. Listing 20.8 shows the `dfs.replication` property.

LISTING 20.8 `dfs.replication` **Configuration Property**

```
<property>
  <name>dfs.replication</name>
  <value>3</value>
</property>
```

The `hadoop.tmp.dir` property located in the `core-site.xml` file specifies a temporary directory located both in HDFS and on local disk. The default value for this property is `/tmp/hadoop-${user.name}` (usually `/tmp/hadoop-hdfs`). Several other Hadoop configuration values include this property. Listing 20.9 shows the `hadoop.tmp.dir` property.

LISTING 20.9 `hadoop.tmp.dir` **Configuration Property**

```
<property>
  <name>hadoop.tmp.dir</name>
  <value>/tmp/hadoop-${user.name}</value>
</property>
```

YARN Configuration Parameters

Let's look at some of the important YARN configuration properties as they apply to each role in a YARN cluster.

Common Properties

The most important YARN configuration property is the `yarn.resourcemanager.hostname` located in the `yarn-site.xml` configuration file. This property is used by clients and NodeManagers to locate the ResourceManager for the cluster. Moreover, several other configuration values are based upon this property, such as `yarn.resourcemanager.webapp.address`, which defaults to `${yarn.resourcemanager.hostname}:8088`.

NOTE

Hadoop Variable Expansion

It is common for default values in Hadoop to be expressed using the `${}` notation as shown previously with `${yarn.resourcemanager.hostname}:8088`. This is a common method used to express a configuration value using the value of another configuration property. This expression is expanded when it is read by the respective Hadoop process.

NodeManager Properties

There are several significant properties used by NodeManagers that affect or assist processing in Hadoop. One such example is the `yarn.nodemanager.local-dirs` property located in the `yarn-site.xml` configuration file. This property specifies a comma-separated list of the local directories used for intermediate data storage, distributed cache, and other storage required during application processing. Listing 20.10 demonstrates the use of the `yarn.nodemanager.local-dirs` property.

LISTING 20.10   `yarn.nodemanager.local-dirs` **Configuration Property**

```
<property>
  <name>yarn.nodemanager.local-dirs</name>
  <value>/hadoop/yarn/local</value>
</property>
```

Some operations, including MapReduce (or MRv2 on YARN, to be specific) or Spark, require auxiliary services to support their specific application framework. An example of this is the the `mapreduce_shuffle` service. The `yarn.nodemanager.aux-services` configuration property located in `yarn-site.xml` is used along with the `yarn.nodemanager.aux-services.<service>.class` property to specify auxiliary services and the corresponding Java classes for the particular services. Listing 20.11 demonstrates the use of the `yarn.nodemanager.aux-services` property. Note that more than one service can be specified.

LISTING 20.11   `yarn.nodemanager.aux-services` **Configuration Property**

```
<property>
  <name>yarn.nodemanager.aux-services</name>
  <value>mapreduce_shuffle,spark_shuffle</value>
</property>
<property>
  <name>yarn.nodemanager.aux-services.mapreduce_shuffle.class</name>
  <value>org.apache.hadoop.mapred.ShuffleHandler</value>
</property>
<property>
  <name>yarn.nodemanager.aux-services.spark_shuffle.class</name>
  <value>org.apache.spark.network.yarn.YarnShuffleService</value>
</property>
```

Logging is integral to Hadoop and YARN, particularly application, container, and task logging, and several properties govern how and where the YARN applications log is generated. This is more about application logging and log aggregation as part of the YARN framework, whereas the `log4j.properties` configuration discussed previously relates to how logs stored locally are managed, rotated, and retained.

The `yarn.nodemanager.log-dirs` configuration property in `yarn-site.xml` specifies the local directories where YARN container and task log files are written to. This property defaults to `${yarn.log.dir}/userlogs`. Listing 20.12 shows the use of the `yarn.nodemanager.log-dirs` configuration property.

LISTING 20.12 `yarn.nodemanager.log-dirs` **Configuration Property**

```
<property>
  <name>yarn.nodemanager.log-dirs</name>
  <value>/hadoop/yarn/log</value>
</property>
```

Log aggregation is the process of moving local YARN application logs into HDFS for long-term storage. Log aggregation in YARN is enabled by setting the `yarn.log-aggregation-enable` property to `true` in the `yarn-site.xml` configuration file, which is strongly recommended.

Once log aggregation is enabled, you will need to specify the target directory in HDFS to store the aggregated logs. This is configured using the `yarn.nodemanager.remote-app-log-dir` property in `yarn-site.xml`. Listing 20.13 demonstrates configuration of the YARN log aggregation used in both of the aforementioned properties.

LISTING 20.13 Enabling Log Aggregation

```
<property>
  <name>yarn.log-aggregation-enable</name>
  <value>true</value>
</property>
<property>
  <name>yarn.nodemanager.remote-app-log-dir</name>
  <value>/app-logs</value>
</property>
```

Note that once log aggregation is enabled, local log files stored in the directories specified by the `yarn.nodemanager.log-dirs` configuration property are deleted, the application completes and log aggregation has been successful.

MapReduce Properties

As you are aware, MapReduce is a foundational processing framework on the Hadoop platform. Prior to Hadoop 2.x, MapReduce had its own dedicated cluster framework, including MapReduce-specific daemons such as the JobTracker and TaskTracker. This is referred to as MR1 or classic MapReduce, as opposed to MR2 or contemporary MapReduce. The original MapReduce cluster framework has its own dedicated configuration file called `mapred-site.xml`. At one stage, this held all of the application processing- and scheduling-related configuration properties. With the inception of the YARN framework, much of this configuration was no longer necessary in the `mapred-site.xml` file. However, the `mapred-site.xml` file remains as part of the project to store properties specific to MapReduce processing.

One such property stored in the `mapred-site.xml` file is the `mapreduce.framework.name` property. It is used to specify the execution framework for MapReduce. The default value is `local`, which is not scalable and not optimal in most cases. It is recommended that you set this value to `yarn` as shown in Listing 20.14.

LISTING 20.14 `mapreduce.framework.name` **Configuration Property**

```
<property>
  <name>mapreduce.framework.name</name>
  <value>yarn</value>
</property>
```

Other acceptable values for this property include `classic` (which refers to MR1). You may still see the `classic` or `mr1` value present on some releases, which include both the MR1 and YARN cluster frameworks.

ApplicationMasters for MapReduce applications need to stage Java packages (`jar` files), job configuration, counters, and distributed cache objects. The directory in HDFS used to stage these objects on the ApplicationMaster host is configured using the `yarn.app.mapreduce.am.staging-dir` property located in the `mapred-site.xml` configuration file. An example setting for the `yarn.app.mapreduce.am.staging-dir` property is shown in Listing 20.15.

LISTING 20.15 `yarn.app.mapreduce.am.staging-dir` **Configuration Property**

```
<property>
  <name>yarn.app.mapreduce.am.staging-dir</name>
  <value>/user</value>
</property>
```

MapReduce applications store their specific history, including MapReduce-specific application metrics and counters, to a JobHistoryServer accessible by all nodes of the cluster. The JobHistoryServer IPC connection information is configured using the `mapreduce.jobhistory.address` property in `mapred-site.xml`. The default value for this setting is `0.0.0.0:10020`, which assumes you are running this process on the local node. This value should be changed to the hostname and port your JobHistoryServer is running on as shown in Listing 20.16.

LISTING 20.16 `mapreduce.jobhistory.address` **Configuration Property**

```
<property>
  <name>mapreduce.jobhistory.address</name>
  <value>myjobhistoryserver:10020</value>
</property>
```

The JobHistorySever itself hosts a web application on port 19888 of the node running the daemon.

Ecosystem Component Configuration

We've spoken a lot about ecosystem projects throughout this book. Let's look at how configuration applies to some of these projects.

Hive

Configuration for Hive deployments is typically available in `/etc/hive/conf`. As with Hadoop, this is usually a symbolic link to the actual physical address of the Hive configuration directory. Hive will usually inherit its HDFS and YARN configuration from the Hadoop configuration files just spoken about (`core-site.xml`, `hdfs-site.xml`, `yarn-site.xml`, and `mapred-site.xml`). However, many other properties specific to Hive are maintained in the `hive-site.xml` configuration file, typically located in `/etc/hive/conf`.

The most significant settings in `hive-site.xml` are the connection details to a shared Hive metastore. Listing 20.17 shows an example excerpt from a `hive-site.xml` file specifying a connection to a shared metastore using MySQL.

LISTING 20.17 Configuring a Connection to a Shared Hive Metastore

```
<property>
  <name>javax.jdo.option.ConnectionURL</name>
  <value>jdbc:mysql://myhost/metastore</value>
</property>
<property>
  <name>javax.jdo.option.ConnectionDriverName</name>
  <value>com.mysql.jdbc.Driver</value>
</property>
<property>
  <name>javax.jdo.option.ConnectionUserName</name>
  <value>hive</value>
</property>
<property>
  <name>javax.jdo.option.ConnectionPassword</name>
  <value>mypassword</value>
</property>
```

Pig

As with Hive, most HDFS- and YARN-specific configuration details are sourced from the Hadoop configuration on the host, typically a client including the Pig and Hadoop client libraries. Additional Pig-specific properties are located in the `pig.properties` file, which is in `/etc/pig/conf` on most distributions. An example `pig.properties` file is shown in Listing 20.18.

LISTING 20.18 `Pig Properties` **File**

```
...
pig.logfile=/tmp/pig-err.log
pig.pretty.print.schema=false
exectype=mapreduce
log4jconf=./conf/log4j.properties
verbose=false
debug=INFO
...
```

Note that the `pig.properties` file, unlike many of the other Hadoop configuration files, is not an XML document.

Spark

Spark configuration properties are set through the `spark-defaults.conf` file located in $SPARK_HOME/conf. This configuration file is read by Spark applications and daemons upon startup. An excerpt from a typical `spark-defaults.conf` file is shown in Listing 20.19.

LISTING 20.19 **Spark Configuration Properties**

```
spark.master                    yarn
spark.eventLog.enabled          true
spark.eventLog.dir              hdfs:///var/log/spark/apps
spark.history.fs.logDirectory   hdfs:///var/log/spark/apps
spark.executor.memory           2176M
spark.executor.cores            4
```

The `spark-defaults.conf` file, like `pig.properties`, is also not in the standard Hadoop XML configuration format.

Spark configuration properties can also be set programmatically in your driver code using the `SparkConf` object; an example of this is shown in Listing 20.20.

LISTING 20.20 **Setting Spark Configuration Properties Programmatically**

```
from pyspark.context import SparkContext
from pyspark.conf import SparkConf
conf = SparkConf()
conf.setAppName("MySparkApp")
conf.setMaster("yarn")
conf.setSparkHome("/usr/lib/spark")
```

HBase

HBase configuration is typically stored in `/etc/hbase/conf`, the primary configuration file being the `hbase-site.xml` file. This will govern the behavior of HBase and will be used by the HMaster and RegionServers alike. If you are managing a HBase cluster you are advised to use the cluster management utilities discussed in **Hour 18, "Using Cluster Management Utilities."** An excerpt from a typical `hbase-site.xml` file is shown in Listing 20.21.

LISTING 20.21 `hbase-site.xml` **Configuration File**

```
...
<property>
  <name>hbase.client.keyvalue.maxsize</name>
  <value>1048576</value>
</property>
<property>
  <name>hbase.cluster.distributed</name>
  <value>true</value>
</property>
<property>
  <name>hbase.hregion.majorcompaction</name>
  <value>604800000</value>
</property>
<property>
  <name>hbase.local.dir</name>
  <value>${hbase.tmp.dir}/local</value>
</property>
<property>
  <name>zookeeper.session.timeout</name>
  <value>60000</value>
</property>
<property>
  <name>zookeeper.znode.parent</name>
  <value>/hbase-unsecure</value>
</property>
...
```

Summary

Configuration is integral to Hadoop. All components—core and non-core—are governed by configuration. In this hour, you learned about the order of precedence in which configuration settings are applied, including how to override this behavior for specific values as an administrator. You also learned about the various Hadoop defaults, namely `hdfs-default.xml`, `yarn-default.xml`, and `core-default.xml`, as well as some of the other environment scripts such as `hadoop-env.sh`, `log4j.properties`, and others.

Additionally, you learned more about important configuration settings for HDFS and YARN, as well as ecosystem projects such as Hive, Pig, Spark, and HBase.

Managing configuration settings is a major part of managing Hadoop systems, so it is worthwhile familiarizing yourself with some of the many configuration properties at your disposal. Also, you will need to stay current with configuration properties, as these have been known to be deprecated or change their name from release to release. Happy configuring!

Q&A

Q. **What is the order of precedence by which configuration properties set in a Hadoop environment are applied? How can this be influenced by administrators?**

A. The order of precedence for configuration properties in Hadoop (from lowest to highest) is: `*-default.xml` values -> `*-site.xml` values on a slave node or nodes -> settings defined by the developer either in a Job object or using command-line arguments to an application (such as `-D` arguments supplied to a `hadoop jar` command). Use a `<final>` tag on one or more configuration properties on your cluster (server) nodes to ensure that the particular values set by the administrator for these properties cannot be overridden, irrespective of the order of precedence.

Q. **Explain the `dfs.namenode.name.dir` and `dfs.datanode.data.dir` properties located in `hdfs-site.xml`. What are these properties used for? How are the values for these properties used?**

A. The `dfs.namenode.name.dir` property specifies a list of directories on the NameNode that are used to store the on-disk metadata structures (`fsimage` and `edits` files). Writes to `edits` files in the directories specified in the list are performed synchronously. The `dfs.datanode.data.dir` property is used by the DataNode process to specify a list of directories used to store HDFS blocks. Block write operations to directories specified in the list are performed in a round robin fashion.

Q. **Briefly explain the `dfs.datanode.du.reserved` property in `hdfs-site.xml`. Why is this property important to configure on cluster slave nodes?**

A. The `dfs.datanode.du.reserved` property is used to specify a percentage of space to be reserved on DataNodes that cannot be used for HDFS block storage. If you do not set this value it defaults to 0, meaning that HDFS will completely consume all available capacity on all volumes configured in `dfs.datanode.data.dir`, leaving no available space for intermediate data, which will compromise data locality.

Workshop

The workshop contains quiz questions to help you solidify your understanding of the material covered. Try to answer all questions before looking at the "Answers" section that follows.

Quiz

1. Which configuration file contains the `fs.defaultFS` property?

   A. `hdfs-site.xml`

   B. `yarn-site.xml`

   C. `core-site.xml`

   D. `httpfs-site.xml`

2. **True or False**. The configuration setting for the HDFS block size (`dfs.blocksize`) is by default a client setting.

3. What is the name of the file located in the Hadoop configuration directory used to source environment variables for all Hadoop processes?

4. What is the name of the configuration property located in `core-site.xml` that defines a temporary directory in HDFS and in the local filesystem to be used by Hadoop processes?

Answers

1. C.

2. True.

3. `hadoop-env.sh`.

4. `hadoop.tmp.dir`.

Understanding Advanced HDFS

What You'll Learn in This Hour:

▶ Understanding NameNode high availability
▶ HDFS rack awareness and rack topology scripts
▶ Understanding HDFS federation
▶ HDFS snapshots, caching, and archiving

HDFS is at the core of the Hadoop platform, literally and figuratively. In this hour you learn about extensions to HDFS to enable high availability, scalability, additional reliability, and performance.

HDFS Rack Awareness

Data locality, fault tolerance, and resiliency are core tenets of Hadoop and remain so to this day. These design goals are further exemplified in Hadoop's support for rack awareness. Rack awareness enables HDFS to understand a cluster topology that may include multiple racks of servers or multiple data centers, and to orchestrate its block placement accordingly.

Implementing a rack topology and using rack awareness in HDFS, data can be dispersed across racks or data centers to provide further fault tolerance in the event of a rack failure, switch or network failure, or even a data center outage. Of course, this is premised upon proper management of the filesystem's metadata, discussed in **Hour 4, "Understanding the Hadoop Distributed File System (HDFS),"** and the implementation of high availability, which we will discuss more in this hour.

With a rack topology defined, Hadoop will place blocks on nodes according to the following strategy:

1. The first replica of a block is placed on a node in the cluster. This is the same node as the Hadoop client if the client is running within the cluster.

2. The second replica of a block is placed on a node residing on a different rack from the first replica.

3. The third replica, assuming a default replication factor of 3, is placed on a different node on the same rack as the second replica.

The block placement strategy for a cluster with two racks and a replication factor of three is shown in Figure 21.1.

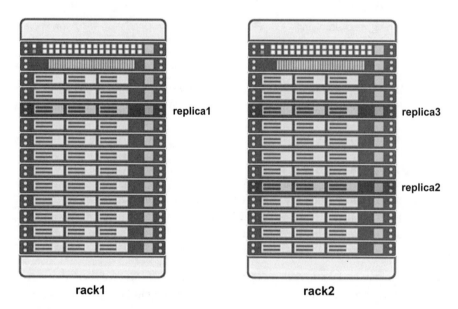

rack1   rack2

FIGURE 21.1
Block Placement Strategy.

Rack awareness is implemented using a user-supplied script, which could be in any scripting language available on the cluster. Common scripting languages used include Python, Ruby, or BASH. The script, called a rack topology script, provides Hadoop with an identifier for any given node, telling Hadoop to which rack that particular node belongs. A rack could be a physical rack (e.g., a 19" server rack) or a particular subnet, or even an abstraction representing a data center.

The script needs to return a hierarchical location ID for a host passed in as a script argument. This can be pseudo-coded as follows:

```
topology_script([datanode_hosts]) -> [rackids]
```

The hierarchical location ID is in the form /datacenter/rack. Rack awareness is still implemented if a rack topology script is not supplied. In that case, all nodes have a default location ID of /default-rack.

The script can be implemented in several different ways with no strict definition of how to accomplish this. For instance, you could embed the location ID in the hostname itself and use simple string manipulation to determine the location, as in the following example:

dc01rack01node02

You could also create a lookup table or map and store this in a file or in a database.

Rack awareness is implemented on the HDFS client or client application, so the script, its chosen interpreter, and any supporting data such as lookup files need to be available on the client.

A sample rack topology script is provided in Listing 21.1.

LISTING 21.1   Rack Topology Script

```
#!/usr/bin/env python
# input: hostname or ipaddress of a node or nodes
# output: rack id for each node
# example:
#    input of dc01rack01node02
#    outputs /dc01/rack01
import sys
DEFAULT_RACK = "/dc01/default-rack"
for host in sys.argv[1:]:
  if len(host) == 16:
    dcid = host[:4]
    rackid = host[4:10]
    print "/" + dcid + "/" + rackid
  else:
    print DEFAULT_RACK
```

This script is enabled using the net.topology.script.file.name configuration property in the core-site.xml configuration file as shown in Listing 21.2.

LISTING 21.2   Enabling a Rack Topology Script

```
<property>
  <name>net.topology.script.file.name</name>
  <value>/etc/hadoop/conf/rack-topology-script.py</value>
</property>
```

HDFS High Availability

As discussed in **Hour 4, "Understanding the Hadoop Distributed File System (HDFS),"** in the absence of high availability implemented on the HDFS NameNode, the NameNode is a single point of failure for the entire filesystem. A SecondaryNameNode, while helpful in reducing recovery times and providing an alternate storage location for the NameNode's metadata, is not a high availability or hot standby solution.

A NameNode may become unavailable for many unplanned reasons; for instance, hardware or software failure. A NameNode may also need to be restarted for other planned reasons such as a software upgrade or configuration change.

Using NameNode high availability (HA), two NameNodes are deployed managing the same HDFS namespace: one active and one standby NameNode. The Standby NameNode takes control of the filesystem, managing client read-and-write requests and metadata updates, if the active NameNode fails. Moreover, the Standby NameNode performs the checkpointing functions normally provided by the SecondaryNameNode, so in a HA configuration the SecondaryNameNode is no longer required.

How HDFS High Availability Works

As mentioned earlier, HDFS HA is implemented by deploying two NameNodes, one active and one standby. Clients only ever connect to the active NameNode. The active NameNode writes its metadata to a quorum of *JournalNodes*, managed by the *QuorumJournalManager* (QJM) process, which is built into the NameNode. Quorums are deployed in odd numbers greater than one (3 or 5 for example). Metadata updates (edits) written to a majority of JournalNodes (a quorum) are considered to be consistent. The Standby NameNode reads consistent updates from the JournalNodes to apply changes to its in-memory metadata representation.

DataNodes in the cluster send their heartbeats and block reports to both NameNodes using an abstraction called a *nameservice*. The nameservice is the same method used by clients to connect to the "active" NameNode.

Using HA, the Standby NameNode is transactionally consistent with the active NameNode, so a failure and subsequent failover will not result in a loss of data or significant disruption.

Figure 21.2 shows a conceptual view of a cluster running HDFS in High Availability mode.

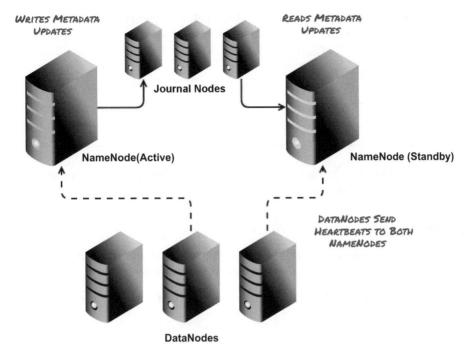

FIGURE 21.2
HDFS High Availability.

Fencing

Clients connect to an active NameNode in a high availability HDFS cluster. As such, only one NameNode can be active in the cluster at any given time. If more than one NameNode were active it could lead to inconsistencies or corruption of the filesystem.

For this reason, *fencing* is a technique employed by the QJM to ensure that clients are not able to access a NameNode that is in standby mode due to a failover. Fencing isolates a NameNode, preventing further requests from being accepted, which may cause issues. Fencing methods include:

▶ `sshfence`—Connects to the active NameNode using SSH, and uses `fuser` to kill the process listening on the service's TCP port (requires additional configuration to specify a private key used to connect)

▶ `shell`—Runs an arbitrary shell command to fence the Active NameNode

Fencing method are implemented using the `dfs.ha.fencing.methods` property in the `hdfs-site.xml` configuration file as shown in Listing 21.3.

LISTING 21.3   Configuring HA Fencing

```
<property>
  <name>dfs.ha.fencing.methods</name>
  <value>sshfence</value>
</property>
```

The QJM does not allow the active NameNode to take further metadata update requests until the previously active NameNode has been fenced.

Types of Failover

Failover of a NameNode, or changing the state of a NameNode from standby to active, can be either *automatic* (system-detected and initiated) or *manual* (user-initiated).

Manual failover can be accomplished using the `hdfs haadmin` command as shown in Listing 21.4.

LISTING 21.4   Manual Failover

```
# failover from nn1 to nn2; you may need to sudo as the hdfs user
$ hdfs haadmin -failover nn1 nn2
```

Automatic failover is implemented using an external service called the *ZooKeeper Failover Controller* (ZKFC) using (you guessed it) the ZooKeeper project discussed in **Hour 17, "Working with the Hadoop Ecosystem."** The ZKFC process runs on each NameNode and uses a quorum of ZooKeeper nodes to maintain the state of the active node and automatically initiate a failover in the event of unavailability of the active NameNode.

A conceptual diagram of a cluster implementing HDFS HA with automatic failover is shown in Figure 21.3.

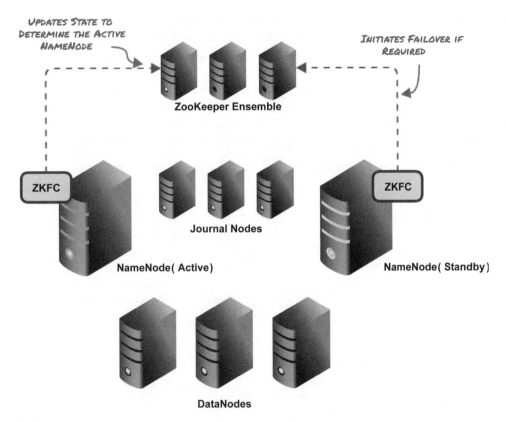

FIGURE 21.3
HDFS High Availability with Automatic Failover.

Deploying HA

To deploy NameNode High Availability, there are several steps you need to take. This is a disruptive exercise as you will need to stop and reconfigure HDFS services. Of course, you will need a second host to act in the NameNode HA pair. This host will ideally have the same configuration and specifications as the existing NameNode as it will need to perform all of the functions of the primary NameNode.

Before deploying HA in our next Try it Yourself exercise, let's briefly discuss the concept of nameservices and the client and server configurations required in a HA cluster.

A *nameservice* provides an abstraction for cluster clients and services to connect to one of the two available NameNodes. This is done through configuration, whereby the `fs.defaultFS` refers to a nameservice ID as opposed to a NameNode host. Nameservices available are defined in the `dfs.nameservices` property in the `hdfs-site.xml` file. References to the hosts involved in the particular nameservice are configured using the `dfs.ha.namenodes.<nameservice_id>` property in the `hdfs-site.xml` configuration file. The hosts themselves are then defined in `dfs.namenode.rpc-address` and `dfs.namenode.http-address` properties, which provide specific connection details to the RPC, and web services respectively for each NameNode.

Figure 21.4 provides a pictorial explanation of the configuration of name services in a HA cluster.

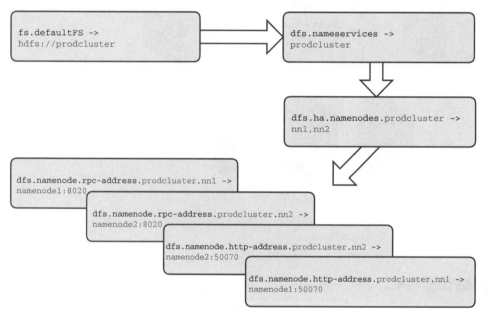

FIGURE 21.4
HA Nameservices Configuration.

▼ TRY IT YOURSELF

Deploying NameNode High Availability

For this exercise, you will need three hosts: two hosts to serve as NameNodes in a HA configuration, and a separate JournalNode. Use the base Hadoop installation performed in **Hour 3, "Depoloying Hadoop,"** for all three hosts, but do not start any of the services.

The HA instance and service topology deployed in this exercise is represented in Figure 21.5.

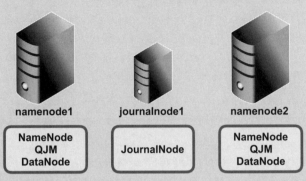

FIGURE 21.5
HA Topology for this Exercise.

For a production deployment, you would have at least three JournalNodes. These can be, and often are, co-located with DataNodes in the cluster.

Each node will need to be able to resolve hostnames for every other host in the cluster before starting the exercise.

1. On **all three hosts** update the `fs.defaultFS` property in `core-site.xml` to the following:

```
hdfs://testhacluster
```

2. Add the following configuration to the `hdfs-site.xml` file on **all three hosts**:

```
<property>
  <name>dfs.nameservices</name>
  <value>testhacluster</value>
</property>

<property>
  <name>dfs.ha.namenodes.testhacluster</name>
  <value>nn1,nn2</value>
</property>

<property>
  <name>dfs.namenode.rpc-address.testhacluster.nn1</name>
  <value>namenode1:8020</value>
</property>

<property>
  <name>dfs.namenode.rpc-address.testhacluster.nn2</name>
  <value>namenode2:8020</value>
</property>
```

```
<property>
  <name>dfs.namenode.http-address.testhacluster.nn1</name>
  <value>namenode1:50070</value>
</property>

<property>
  <name>dfs.namenode.http-address.testhacluster.nn2</name>
  <value>namenode2:50070</value>
</property>

<property>
  <name>dfs.namenode.shared.edits.dir</name>
  <value>qjournal://journalnode1:8485/testhacluster</value>
</property>

<property>
  <name>dfs.journalnode.edits.dir</name>
  <value>/tmp/dfs/jn</value>
</property>

<property>
  <name>dfs.client.failover.proxy.provider.testhacluster</name>
  <value>org.apache.hadoop.hdfs.server.namenode.ha.Configured
FailoverProxyProvider</value>
</property>

<property>
  <name>dfs.ha.fencing.methods</name>
  <value>shell(/bin/true)</value>
</property>

<property>
  <name>dfs.ha.automatic-failover.enabled</name>
  <value>false</value>
</property>
```

Note that this particular fencing method would not be suited for production systems.

3. On **journalnode1** make a directory in which to store shared `edits` files:

   ```
   $ mkdir -p /tmp/dfs/jn
   ```

4. Change the permissions of the shared `edits` directory on **journalnode1**:

   ```
   $ sudo chmod 777 /tmp/dfs/jn
   ```

In production you would change the ownership of this directory to the `hdfs` user.

5. Start the `journalnode` daemon on **journalnode1:**

```
$HADOOP_HOME/sbin/hadoop-daemon.sh start journalnode
```

6. Run the following command on **namenode1:**

```
$ sudo -u hdfs $HADOOP_HOME/bin/hdfs namenode -initializeSharedEdits
```

7. Format HDFS on **namenode1:**

```
$ sudo -u hdfs $HADOOP_HOME/bin/hdfs namenode -format
```

8. Start the NameNode on **namenode1:**

```
$ sudo -u hdfs $HADOOP_HOME/sbin/hadoop-daemon.sh start namenode
```

9. Use the `haadmin` command to check the NameNode's service state on **namenode1** (this should return `standby` as shown):

```
$ sudo -u hdfs $HADOOP_HOME/bin/hdfs haadmin -getServiceState nn1 standby
```

10. "Bootstrap" the Standby NameNode by running the following command on **namenode2:**

```
$ sudo -u hdfs $HADOOP_HOME/bin/hdfs namenode -bootstrapStandby
```

When prompted to Re-Format, select **Y.**

11. Start the NameNode on **namenode2:**

```
$ sudo -u hdfs $HADOOP_HOME/sbin/hadoop-daemon.sh start namenode
```

12 From **either node** run the following commands:

```
$ sudo -u hdfs $HADOOP_HOME/bin/hdfs haadmin -getServiceState nn1
$ sudo -u hdfs $HADOOP_HOME/bin/hdfs haadmin -getServiceState nn2
```

Notice that both NameNodes are in a `standby` state.

13. On **either host**, run the following command to set **namenode1** to be the active NameNode:

```
$ sudo -u hdfs $HADOOP_HOME/bin/hdfs haadmin -transitionToActive nn1
```

14. Re-check the service states from **either node:**

```
$ sudo -u hdfs $HADOOP_HOME/bin/hdfs haadmin -getServiceState nn1
$ sudo -u hdfs $HADOOP_HOME/bin/hdfs haadmin -getServiceState nn2
```

You should see that nn1 (**namenode1**) is now `active` and nn2 (**namenode2**) is in the `standby` state.

15. Failover from **namenode1** to **namenode2** by running the following command from **either host:**

```
$ sudo -u hdfs $HADOOP_HOME/bin/hdfs haadmin -failover nn1 nn2
```

You should see the following output:

```
Failover from nn1 to nn2 successful
```

16. Check the service states again from **either host.** You should see that the states have been inverted:

```
$ sudo -u hdfs $HADOOP_HOME/bin/hdfs haadmin -getServiceState nn1
$ sudo -u hdfs $HADOOP_HOME/bin/hdfs haadmin -getServiceState nn2
```

17. Check the web UI of either NameNode host on port 50070. You should clearly see what state the particular NameNode is in.

Of course, deploying and configuring advanced features with lots of dependent operations, such as the implementation of NameNode high availability, is generally much easier using a cluster management tool. I discussed the two main cluster management tools **Hour 18, "Using Cluster Management Utilities,"** namely Cloudera Manager or Ambari, depending upon your chosen Hadoop distribution.

HDFS Federation

A HDFS filesystem is ultimately limited by the amount of memory in a NameNode, or the lesser of the two NameNodes in the case of a HA cluster. This is because the filesystem's metadata, including all objects in the filesystem, must fit into memory on the NameNode. In large-scale deployments, Yahoo! for example, this was a limit to the scalability of the distributed filesystem. Enter HDFS Federation.

So far we have only discussed having one active (and possibly one standby) NameNode in a given HDFS cluster. NameNode federation enables a HDFS cluster to have many active NameNodes, each managing a different part of the filesystem's namespace. An example of different managed namespaces is shown in Figure 21.6.

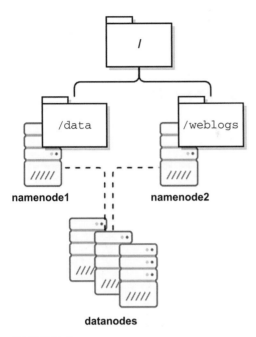

FIGURE 21.6
Namespaces.

The NameNodes managing the different namespaces (or namespace volumes) are completely independent of one another to the extent that they are actually unaware of each other. Each namespace volume manages the metadata for its respective portion of the namespace, as well as managing a block pool or blocks assigned to files in a particular namespace volume. The DataNodes, however, store blocks from all block pools covering all namespace volumes.

Note that there is no inherent hierarchy to namespaces. In other words, they are all treated equally.

Federation uses the same concept of nameservices employed by NameNode high availability. However, in the case of federation, `dfs.nameservices` contains multiple values—one distinct nameservice for each NameNode managing a separate namespace volume. In fact, much of the configuration you learned about in the section on HA is used in deploying HDFS federation, including `dfs.namenode.rpc-address`, `dfs.namenode.http-address`, and more.

A Cluster ID is assigned to each NameNode involved in the cluster. This is typically done when you format the NameNode as shown in Listing 21.5.

LISTING 21.5 Assigning a Cluster ID when Formatting a NameNode

```
$ sudo -u hdfs hdfs namenode -format -clusterId prodcluster
```

You can see the assigned Cluster ID for any given NameNode using the Overview page of the NameNode web UI as shown in Figure 21.7.

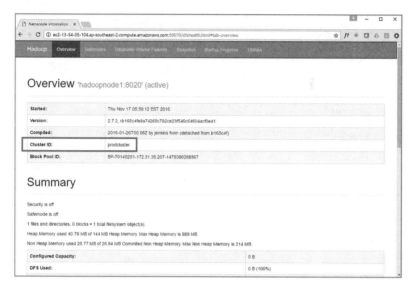

FIGURE 21.7
Viewing the Cluster ID for a NameNode.

Clients use *ViewFS*, a client-side mount table, to connect to a cluster by its Cluster ID. This is defined in the `fs.defaultFS` property in `core-site.xml` as shown in Listing 21.6.

LISTING 21.6 ViewFS

```
<property>
  <name>fs.defaultFS</name>
  <value>viewfs://prodcluster</value>
</property>
```

Each mount point for each namespace volume is defined in `core-site.xml` using the configuration properties shown in Listing 21.7.

LISTING 21.7 Configuring Client Side Mount Points for HDFS Federation

```
<property>
  <name>fs.viewfs.mounttable.prodcluster.link./data</name>
  <value>hdfs://namenode1:8020/data</value>
</property>
<property>
  <name>fs.viewfs.mounttable.prodcluster.link./weblogs</name>
  <value>hdfs://namenode2:8020/weblogs</value>
</property>
```

HDFS High Availability and Federation are Independent Options

HDFS HA and Federation are exclusive functions to one another, but can be combined in the same cluster. For instance, you can have a federated HDFS namespace with two namespace volumes along with a HA configuration. In that case you would need four NameNodes: a HA pair for each namespace volume.

HDFS Caching, Snapshotting, and Archiving

HDFS includes several features that can improve performance or provide additional data protection. Let's discuss some of these now.

Caching

HDFS caching enables you to store frequently accessed data in off-heap memory cache on the DataNodes. Off-heap refers to objects that are not managed as part of a Java heap. Off-heap memory access will generally be faster than disk access by orders of magnitude.

HDFS caching can allow users to do the following:

▶ cache pinned datasets, such as the defined group of HDFS files represented by a Hive table or dataset to be loaded with Pig

▶ cache specific files and directories

▶ cache HBase table data

Caching introduces a new locality option called memory-local, whereby Hadoop applications can query the locations of cached blocks and place their tasks accordingly. The distributed processes can then use the zero-copy read API to read cached data, improving access times significantly.

Obviously, this will require sufficient memory be available on the DataNodes, and you may also need to increase some operating system limits for locked memory to use caching.

In addition, Hadoop 2.3 has introduced support for heterogeneous storage in HDFS. This enables managing of storage costs and latency requirements using different storage classes, including memory and SSD, along with traditional commodity spinning disks.

Snapshots

Directories in HDFS can be snapshotted, which means creating one or more point-in-time images, or snapshots, of the directory. Snapshots include subdirectories, and can even include the entire filesystem (be careful with this for obvious reasons). Snapshots can be used as backups or for auditing purposes.

For a directory to be snapshotted, it must be created as snapshottable. This can be done using the command shown in Listing 21.8.

LISTING 21.8   Creating a Snapshottable Directory in HDFS

```
$ hdfs dfsadmin -allowSnapshot /data
```

Similarly, snapshotting can be disallowed as well. Note that you will probably need to `sudo` as the `hdfs` user, depending upon your level of access. Once snapshotting is allowed, you can use the command shown in Listing 21.9 to create a snapshot.

LISTING 21.9   Creating a Directory Snapshot

```
$ hdfs dfs -createSnapshot /data snapshot_on_20161117
Created snapshot /data/.snapshot/snapshot_on_20161117
```

The process of creating a snapshot is instantaneous as blocks themselves are not copied. There are similar commands for renaming or deleting snapshots.

The snapshots themselves are stored in a `.snapshot` directory under the snapshotted directory. Snapshots can be compared against one another to track changes between snapshots. This is done using the command shown in Listing 21.10.

LISTING 21.10   Performing a Snapshot Diff

```
$ hdfs snapshotDiff /data snapshot_on_20161117 snapshot_on_20161118
Difference between snapshot snapshot_on_20161117 and snapshot snapshot_on_20161118
under directory /data:
M        .
+        ./stop-word-list.csv
```

Archiving

Hadoop can create archive files, similar to `tar` files, for a particular filesystem directory. Hadoop archives are created as `har` files, and contain both metadata and data files. Unlike snapshots, archiving will create entire physical replicas of desired portions of the filesystem. To create a Hadoop archive you can execute the `hadoop archive` command as shown in Listing 21.11.

LISTING 21.11   Creating a Hadoop Archive

```
$ hadoop archive -archiveName data.har -p /data /backups
```

Summary

In this hour, you learned about some of the advanced features of HDFS, many of which—such as high availability, federation, and caching—are considered part of contemporary HDFS, or the HDFS project included in the Hadoop 2.x release, the second generation of the filesystem.

Using High Availability, a given NameNode is not a single point of failure for a Hadoop cluster as it otherwise would be in the original implementation of HDFS (or classic HDFS). High Availability (HA) can be implemented with manual failover (user-initiated) and/or automatic failover (system-initiated). Using a HA deployment, clients connect to a nameservice, as opposed to a specific NameNode host. Metadata updates from the active NameNode are written to shared Journal Nodes and are read by the Standby NameNode to maintain transactional consistency.

Federation enables a filesystem to be managed by multiple NameNodes, each managing a different namespace volume. This enables the filesystem metadata to scale beyond the limits of the finite memory available in one NameNode.

You also learned about rack awareness in HDFS and how this is used to distribute block replicas across different racks or data centers, providing additional resiliency, fault tolerance, and data locality opportunities.

Finally, you learned about caching, snapshots, and archiving with HDFS. Caching uses off-heap memory on DataNodes to provide additional read performance for frequently accessed datasets. Snapshots and archiving provide extended data recovery options for HDFS.

Q&A

Q. Explain the block placement strategy in a cluster with a rack topology including two racks.

A. With a rack topology of two racks defined, Hadoop will place the first replica of a block on an arbitrary node in the cluster. The second replica of a block is placed on a node residing on a different rack than the first replica. The third replica (assuming a default replication factor of 3) is placed on a different node on the same rack as the second replica.

Q. What are the two types of failover in a HA implementation of HDFS? What could either type be used for?

A. The two types of failover available in a HA HDFS cluster are manual and automatic. Manual failover is performed by a cluster administrator using the `haadmin` command. This is useful for routine maintenance and upgrades where administrators can use manual failover for planned outages. Automatic failover is implemented using an external service called the ZooKeeper Failover Controller (ZKFC). The ZKFC determines which NameNode is active and will failover in the event that the active NameNode becomes unavailable or unresponsive. Automatic failover should be implemented for production systems to manage unplanned outages or NameNode issues.

Q. **Briefly explain HDFS federation.**

A. HDFS federation enables one distributed filesystem to be managed by multiple NameNodes, with each NameNode responsible for managing a specific namespace volume. Clients connect to the relevant NameNode for metadata operations relating to the namespace they are querying. DataNodes in the cluster send a heartbeat into both NameNodes and store blocks from all namespaces in the cluster.

Workshop

The workshop contains quiz questions to help you solidify your understanding of the material covered. Try to answer all questions before looking at the "Answers" section that follows.

Quiz

1. What is the default location ID of a node if a rack topology script is not supplied?

2. **True or False.** The `fs.defaultFS` configuration property in a HA cluster refers to a nameservice ID as opposed to a NameNode host.

3. Clients use _____ in the `fs.defaultFS` setting to connect to a cluster implementing HDFS federation.

4. What type of memory is used for HDFS caching?

Answers

1. `/default-rack.`

2. True.

3. `viewfs.`

4. off-heap.

HOUR 22
Securing Hadoop

What You'll Learn in This Hour:

▶ HDFS security and authorization
▶ Securing Hadoop with Kerberos
▶ Perimeter security using Apache Knox
▶ Role-based access control using Ranger or Sentry

As Hadoop has matured, it has gone from being predominantly a research and discovery platform to being a critical data platform in many environments, often storing large volumes of sensitive data. In this hour, we look at ways to secure Hadoop and protect this sensitive information.

Hadoop Security Basics

Security, and securing Hadoop and other big data platforms, covers a broad set of topics, which include but are not limited to the following:

▶ File system security and access control lists (ACLs)

▶ Authentication

▶ Perimeter security and network isolation

▶ Policies and role-based access control (RBAC)

▶ Transport security (SSL and TLS)

▶ Data encryption

I will cover authentication using Kerberos, perimeter security using Apache Knox, and role-based access control using Ranger in subsequent sections this hour. In the meantime, let's look at some of the basics involved in securing Hadoop.

HDFS File System Security

Objects in HDFS, files and directories, have owners and permissions assigned to them. Permissions for HDFS objects are similar to POSIX-based object permissions, which include the access for the object owner, a specified group, and others not in the first two categories.

The permissions mask consists of three permission *triads*, each defining what the owner, group, or others can do with the object. This is referred to as an ACL (or Access Control list). An example of this is shown in Listing 22.1.

LISTING 22.1   File System ACLs

```
$ hadoop fs -ls /data/shakespeare
-rwxr----- 1 jeff analysts 0 2016-11-25 20:43 /data/shakespeare/shakespeare.txt
```

The authenticated user (usually the Linux user account you logged on to the Hadoop client with) is used along with the object's ACL to determine the level of access the particular user has to the object.

Permissions are displayed in symbolic format and set using numeric or octal format. Table 22.1 summarizes the various access permissions and their symbolic and octal notation.

TABLE 22.1   Symbolic Notation

Symbol	Octal	Permission
r	4	Allows the user to read the file or files in the directory
w	2	Allows the user to create (write) a file in the specified directory
x	1	Allows the user to list the contents of a directory. Ignored for file objects.

Permissions are cumulative, so the octal notation of 777, for instance (represented as rwxrwxrwx), is the equivalent of (4+2+1=7)(4+2+1=7)(4+2+1=7).

In the case of the ACLs defined in Listing 22.1, the specific access is broken down in Table 22.2.

TABLE 22.2   Example Permissions

User or Group	Has rights to..
jeff user	Read the file, write to, and list files in the directory
Members of the analysts group	Read the file only
Anyone else	No access

CAUTION

Basic File System Authorization in Hadoop is Not Secure

The built-in file system security in HDFS is designed to stop honest people from inadvertently making mistakes, such as mistakenly deleting a directory or files. In the absence of a strong authentication mechanism, such as Kerberos, which I will discuss next, Hadoop's authentication can easily be defeated, which can circumvent any authorization or file system ACLs in place.

Permissions for an object can be set using the chmod command in the Hadoop filesystem client, as shown in Listing 22.2.

LISTING 22.2   Changing Object Permissions

```
$ hadoop fs -chmod 777 /data/shakespeare
# will make the directory "world writable"
```

Ownership for an object in HDFS can be changed using the chown command as shown in Listing 22.3.

LISTING 22.3   Changing Ownership of an Object in HDFS

```
$ hadoop fs -chown william /data/shakespeare
# will make the user william the owner of the shakespeare directory...
```

Securing Hadoop's Web UIs

As you have seen throughout this book, almost all of the Hadoop server processes, including core and ecosystem services, serve embedded web user interfaces. Additionally, client interfaces such as Hue and Zeppelin, and management interfaces such as Cloudera Manager and Ambari, serve web UIs as well.

All of the Hadoop and Hadoop ecosystem web UIs are served via HTTP, which means the traffic to and from these interfaces is not encrypted. In a secure environment, this is not recommended. Instead HTTPS (or HTTP over SSL—secure sockets layer) should be used to encrypt all traffic between clients and services. All of the web interfaces provide a straightforward mechanism to enable serving their respective web UIs over HTTPS.

A prerequisite to enabling HTTPS is to install a trusted certificate onto the server hosting the web UI. Trusted certificates can be purchased from *Certificate Authorities* (CAs) such as VeriSign or Thwaite. These CAs provide instructions for requesting and installing certificates onto servers.

With a trusted certificate installed, instructions for configuring HTTPS for the project's web UI that you are securing will be available in your project's documentation. Examples of configuration settings for securing the NameNode's web UI using HTTPS are provided in Listing 22.4.

LISTING 22.4   Securing the NameNode's Web UI Using HTTPS

```
<property>
  <name>dfs.https.address</name>
  <value>namenodehost:50470</value>
</property>
```

Furthermore, many of the UIs do not require authentication, such as the NameNode's web UI. Although the majority of these UIs are read-only (as they do not give the user control of altering the cluster), for additional security it is often desirable to password-protect these interfaces, at a minimum. Many of the web interfaces are hosted by *Jetty* (a Java-based embedded HTTP service). Basic or Kerberos-based authentication can be easily integrated into the Jetty framework to password-protect the otherwise open Hadoop web UIs. Let's do this now in our Try it Yourself exercise.

▼ TRY IT YOURSELF

Requiring Basic Authentication for Hadoop Web UIs

In this exercise, we will enable and require basic authentication for one of the built-in Hadoop web UIs, the NameNode UI.

1. On your NameNode host or hosts, open a terminal session and change directories to the following:

   `$HADOOP_HOME/share/hadoop/hdfs/webapps/hdfs/WEB-INF`

2. Using a text editor such as `vi`, open the `web.xml` file.

3. Under the `<webapp>` XML tag, add the following configuration block:

```
<security-constraint>
  <web-resource-collection>
    <web-resource-name>Protected</web-resource-name>
    <url-pattern>/*</url-pattern>
  </web-resource-collection>
  <auth-constraint>
    <role-name>admin</role-name>
  </auth-constraint>
</security-constraint>
<login-config>
  <auth-method>BASIC</auth-method>
  <realm-name>namenodeRealm</realm-name>
</login-config>
```

Exit and save the `web.xml` file.

4. In the same directory, create a new file called `jetty-web.xml` and add the following configuration to this file:

```
<Configure class="org.mortbay.jetty.webapp.WebAppContext">
<Get name="securityHandler">
  <Set name="userRealm">
   <New class="org.mortbay.jetty.security.HashUserRealm">
    <Set name="name">namenodeRealm</Set>
    <Set name="config">
     <SystemProperty name="hadoop.home.dir"/>/jetty/etc/realm.properties
    </Set>
   </New>
  </Set>
</Get>
</Configure>
```

`jetty-web.xml` is an additional Jetty configuration file that you can include with a web application. Jetty will look for this file when initializing the application (in this case the NameNode web application).

5. Make a directory on the local filesystem to store a credentials file:

```
$ mkdir -p $HADOOP_HOME/jetty/etc
```

6. Create a new file called `$HADOOP_HOME/jetty/etc/realm.properties` in the directory created in **Step 5** and add your credentials to the file as follows:

```
<your_username>: <your_password>,admin
```

User credentials are added in each line in the following format:

```
username: password,group
```

7. Restart the NameNode daemon.

8. Open a browser and go to *http://<your_namenode>:50070*. You should immediately be prompted to enter your credentials. Enter the credentials created in **Step 6**.

This is just a basic security mechanism you can put in place. Stronger authentication can be enabled for web UIs using Kerberos and Simple and Protected GSSAPI Negotiation Mechanism (SPNEGO), which can be LDAP-integrated as well. Information on how to do this is available on the Jetty and Hadoop project web sites.

Data Transport Encryption

In addition to the web traffic just discussed, processes and daemons in a Hadoop cluster routinely exchange data over remote procedure call (RPC). This can include control messages, state messages, or data, as is the case with the intermediate data transferred between hosts in a Shuffle and Sort operation.

Although the best practice of network isolation that we will discuss later this hour is the best approach to mitigating the risk of in-flight data being "sniffed" or compromised, RPC traffic can be encrypted using SSL as well.

With the appropriate certificates installed and configured on all slave nodes in a cluster, an encrypted shuffle can be configured to secure intermediate data transfers as shown in Listing 22.5.

LISTING 22.5 Transport Security for Intermediate Data

```
# core-site.xml
<property>
  <name>hadoop.ssl.require.client.cert</name>
  <value>false</value>
  <final>true</final>
</property>
<property>
  <name>hadoop.ssl.hostname.verifier</name>
  <value>DEFAULT</value>
  <final>true</final>
</property>
<property>
  <name>hadoop.ssl.keystores.factory.class</name>
  <value>org.apache.hadoop.security.ssl.FileBasedKeyStoresFactory</value>
  <final>true</final>
</property>
<property>
  <name>hadoop.ssl.server.conf</name>
  <value>ssl-server.xml</value>
  <final>true</final>
</property>
<property>
  <name>hadoop.ssl.client.conf</name>
  <value>ssl-client.xml</value>
  <final>true</final>
</property>

# mapred-site.xml
<property>
  <name>mapreduce.shuffle.ssl.enabled</name>
  <value>true</value>
  <final>true</final>
</property>
```

Encryption for Data at Rest

For some specific implementations, transport encryption alone may not be sufficient. Some statutory regulations require that certain data must be encrypted at rest, such as the PCI-DSS, FISMA, or HIPAA regulations.

HDFS provides support for encryption of data at rest using *Transparent Encryption*. Transparent Encryption uses a *key management server* (KMS) to provide access to encryption keys used to seamlessly encrypt and decrypt data as it is written to or read from disk on Hadoop DataNodes.

More information on Transparent Encryption is available at **http://hadoop.apache.org/docs/current/hadoop-project-dist/hadoop-hdfs/TransparentEncryption.html**.

Securing Hadoop with Kerberos

Before discussing Kerberos, let's recap some fundamental principles regarding security.

Authentication and Authorization

Authentication is the process of confirming the identity of a user or host, also known as a principal. This is typically done by checking credentials such as a username and password. Authorization is the process of determining whether a principal can perform an action such as reading a file or writing to a directory. This is typically accomplished by checking an access control list (ACL). ACLs for HDFS, for example, determine what access levels the owner of an object, members of a group, and other users have to an object (directory or file) in the filesystem.

Kerberos is a network authentication protocol that has become the de facto standard in distributed computing environments. It is the principal authentication mechanism for secure Hadoop clusters.

Kerberos Overview

Kerberos involves negotiations between several independent participants that coordinate with one another to authenticate and authorize a host or user, known as a principal.

Kerberos requires messages to be exchanged between three parties. Kerberos message exchange participants include:

- ▶ The client requesting a service
- ▶ The server providing the requested service
- ▶ A Kerberos Key Distribution Center (KDC)

The KDC is responsible for authenticating and authorizing a client. The KDC is an independent component not provided by Hadoop. Most Linux distributions include the MIT KDC. For Windows systems, a KDC is provided by the Active Directory Domain Controller(s).

The three-way exchange between the client, KDC, and service is pictured in Figure 22.1.

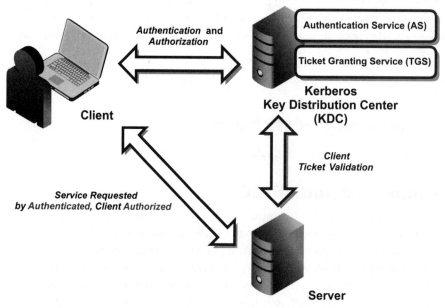

FIGURE 22.1
Kerberos Exchange Participants.

Some Kerberos concepts and terminology you should be familiar with include:

▶ *Principal*—A unique entity (host or user) that can be authenticated. In a secure "Kerberized" cluster, all host, user, and service accounts must have a Kerberos principal.

▶ `keytab` *file*—A file storing Kerberos principals and their associated keys. `keytab` files enable service accounts and batch users or other non-interactive processes to be authenticated by Kerberos.

▶ *Realm*—A group of users and hosts participating in a Kerberos secured network, analogous to a domain in Microsoft Active Directory parlance.

▶ *Authentication service (AS)*—A service that accepts user access credentials and verifies these with the KDC database. If the credentials are verified, the KDC issues a Ticket Granting Ticket (TGT) to the client.

▶ *Ticket Granting Ticket (TGT)*—A ticket used to request a service ticket from the Ticket Granting Server. Ticket Granting Tickets are issued as part of the logon process with an expiry time.

▶ *Service ticket*—A ticket that validates that a principal can access a service.

▶ *Ticket Granting Service (TGS)*—A service that issues a service ticket to an authenticated and authorized principal.

After it's authenticated and authorized with a valid service ticket, the client can access the desired service. Credentials do not need to be submitted with each subsequent request because the authenticated status of a principal is cached.

NOTE

Passwords Are Not Exchanged between Participants

It is important to note that passwords are not exchanged between participants. Instead, passwords are used to compute encryption keys in a Kerberos authentication system. Encryption is used extensively in the Kerberos protocol.

A few Kerberos client commands you should be familiar with are listed in Table 22.3.

TABLE 22.3   Kerberos Client Commands Command Description

Command	Description
`kinit`	Used to request a TGT, often as part of the logon process
`klist`	Used to list your current tickets
`kdestroy`	Used to delete your tickets

Kerberos with Hadoop

Most Hadoop vendors recommend implementing Kerberos to secure a Hadoop cluster. Some general steps to "Kerberize" a Hadoop cluster include the following:

1. Install and configure a Kerberos KDC.

2. Install Kerberos client libraries on all cluster nodes.

3. Synchronize clocks across all cluster nodes (timestamps are integral to Kerberos). Using NTP is recommended.

4. Ensure reverse domain name lookups work correctly.

5. Create `keytab` files for all service principals (such as `hdfs`, `yarn`).

6. Make necessary configuration changes to Hadoop configuration files.

7. Restart Hadoop services.

Kerberos is an "all in" protocol. After you implement Kerberos, all components in the cluster must be Kerberos-aware, Kerberos-enabled, and configured correctly for your Kerberos Environment.

NOTE

Kerberos is a Highly Specialized Topic

If you are responsible for installing, configuring, and managing Kerberos, you should refer to the security guides provided for your Linux or Hadoop distribution.

Perimeter Security Using Apache Knox

Big data platforms (including Hadoop) provide low-friction access to high fidelity data and extensive history. It is important to remember that this set of technologies originated in start-ups, social networking, search companies, and research laboratories, far from mainstream enterprises like banking institutions, retailers, and telecommunications companies in which this technology is proliferating today. Security was not the primary consideration, if it was any real consideration at all, in the early beginnings of the big data and open source software movement. As the technology was increasingly used to process more valuable and sensitive information, the need for security and solutions for information security and governance started to emerge.

With this in mind, and putting additional security measures aside, the establishment of network isolation and strong perimeter security should be your first step in securing a Hadoop cluster wherever possible. Let's look closer at what this means and tools you can use to assist you with this.

Perimeter Security

The first security model to be introduced into big data platforms such as Hadoop was perimeter security. Perimeter security is the practice of placing storage and processing assets in a private network that is not directly addressable from outside networks such as enterprise networks or the public Internet.

Specific user access and management interfaces are exposed through an edge node, which is placed on the perimeter with access to both the private and public networks. Open ports are minimized on the edge node to expose only required services.

These techniques effectively reduce the attack surface area of the system and provide a control point that can also act as a kill switch if required, isolating the cluster from any external access. This approach can be used with on-premise bare metal systems or virtualized private or public clouds with software-defined networks, such as AWS. Figure 22.2 depicts a high-level architecture employing perimeter security.

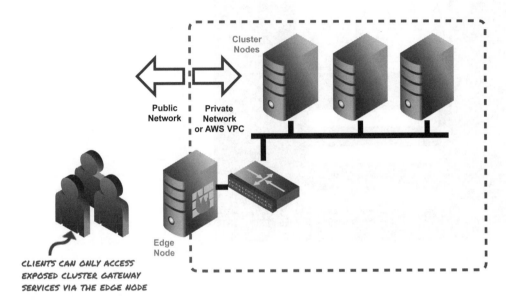

CLIENTS CAN ONLY ACCESS EXPOSED CLUSTER GATEWAY SERVICES VIA THE EDGE NODE

FIGURE 22.2
Perimeter Security.

Often, the edge node is used for proxy access to applications and interfaces that may not be routable from the outside network. The edge node may also be used to establish an SSH tunnel to access services inside the perimeter, or be used as a jump host to directly access cluster nodes.

Perimeter security remains the most common and best practice approach to security for big data systems, although it is typically used in combination with other techniques, such as the ones discussed in this hour.

Apache Knox

Apache Knox is a service that can be used to provide perimeter security for Hadoop. Knox can be deployed on a cluster edge node to provide a reverse proxy to Hadoop cluster services, interfaces, and applications. Although other reverse proxy projects exist, such as NGINX and HAProxy, Knox is specifically designed to proxy Hadoop services. Knox supports both REST and Websockets interfaces.

Knox has out-of-the box integration with HDFS, YARN, HCatalog and Hive, HBase, Oozie, Storm, Ambari, and more. Knox also enables *single sign-on* (SSO), and can integrate with corporate directory services using LDAP as shown in Figure 22.3.

FIGURE 22.3
Apache Knox.

More information on Knox is available at **https://knox.apache.org/**.

Role-Based Access Control Using Ranger and Sentry

Before discussing role-based access control using the Ranger or Sentry Apache projects, lets briefly discuss policies.

Policies

Policies are similar to ACLs and are used for resource authorization. However, policies tend to be more fine-grained, or involve a series of actions that often require the implementation of multiple ACLs. Policies are often more granular than users and groups and are applied to roles. Roles tend to be more functional, such as "reporting user" or "support engineer," and users may enter and leave groups routinely as their job requirements dictate. This approach to authorization is known as *role-based access control* (RBAC).

Ranger and Sentry are two separate Apache projects that are used to create, administer, and enforce policies, and to implement RBAC on Hadoop platforms.

Apache Ranger

Apache Ranger is an authorization solution for centralizing and managing fine-grained access control policies for Hadoop projects including the following:

- ▶ HDFS
- ▶ YARN
- ▶ Hive
- ▶ HBase
- ▶ Storm
- ▶ Solr
- ▶ Kafka
- ▶ NiFi
- ▶ and more...

Ranger and Knox can be implemented together to provide integrated authentication and authorization for Hadoop services. A screenshot of the Ranger management interface is shown in Figure 22.4.

FIGURE 22.4
Apache Ranger.

Ranger is a first-class citizen on the Hortonworks Data Platform and is deployable and configurable using Apache Ambari on Hortonworks platforms.

Apache Sentry

Apache Sentry is a role-based access control module used to implement fine-grained policies within Hadoop. Sentry supports policy definition and enforcement for Hive and Impala, and filesystem ACLs and extends to search platforms and indexes. Sentry is a first-class citizen in the Cloudera application stack and is deployable and configurable using Cloudera Manager. Sentry also has user interface integration to HUE, as shown in Figure 22.5.

FIGURE 22.5
Apache Sentry Configuration using HUE.

Visit the projects' websites, **http://ranger.apache.org/** and **http://sentry.apache.org/**, for more detailed information about policies and RBAC on Hadoop.

Summary

Security for Hadoop and other Big Data platforms is a complex and broad topic. I have discussed many approaches to cluster security in this hour that can be employed individually or collectively to secure a Hadoop environment.

Hadoop has some basic filesystem authorization and access control mechanisms built into the platform, but generally these alone cannot be relied upon to secure a cluster. Instead, cluster security can be achieved by implementing various techniques detailed in this hour including network isolation using Apache Knox, policy-based, role-based access control using Ranger, as well as securing data in transit and securing the various web interfaces available on the platform using SSL certificates. Ultimately, if you want a strong and secure authentication mechanism for your Hadoop environment, Kerberos would be required, and Kerberos was introduced in this hour.

Security is itself a specialized topic. There are experts who dedicate their professional lives to this topic. By default, Hadoop is an open platform that has many known vulnerabilities. For this reason, you should seek counsel from security experts, review your environment with them, and identify weaknesses or security vulnerabilities—after all, it's your data!

Q&A

Q. What should be your first step in securing a Hadoop cluster? Why?

A. Your first step in securing Hadoop wherever possible is to isolate the cluster by placing it on a secure subnet not directly accessible from outside networks. This network isolation enables you to implement perimeter security and control what traffic gets into the cluster environment, effectively reducing the attack surface area of your cluster. Implementing Hadoop in this way will often minimize or negate the requirement to take other steps such as encrypting RPC traffic.

Q. What is the difference between *authentication* and *authorization*?

A. Authentication is the process of confirming the identity of a user or host (a principal). This is typically done by checking credentials such as a username and password. Authorization is the process of determining whether a principal can perform an action such as reading a file or writing to a directory. This is typically accomplished by checking an Access Control List (ACL). ACLs for HDFS, for example, determine what access levels the owner of an object, members of a group, and other users have to an object (directory or file) in the filesystem.

Q. What are the differences between the Apache Knox and Apache Ranger projects?

A. Apache Knox is a reverse proxy designed specifically for Hadoop and Hadoop-related services. Knox can restrict network access and require authentication to access selected services on a Hadoop cluster, providing strong perimeter security for your Hadoop environment. Ranger is an authorization project that enables you to define and enforce granular access policies and role-based access control (RBAC) for various Hadoop services. The two projects are often deployed in tandem to secure a Hadoop environment.

Workshop

The workshop contains quiz questions to help you solidify your understanding of the material covered. Try to answer all questions before looking at the "Answers" section that follows.

Quiz

1. **True or False.** Hadoop's built-in filesystem authorization and security is designed to stop bad (nefarious) people from doing bad (malicious) things.

2. What encryption method should be used to secure web UIs served by Hadoop processes?

3. A file used by Kerberos for storing principals and their associated keys is called a _____ file.

4. **True or False.** You can selectively implement Kerberos for specific components on a Hadoop cluster.

Answers

1. False. Built-in security in Hadoop is designed to stop decent people from making honest mistakes.

2. SSL.

3. `keytab`.

4. False. Kerberos is an "all in" protocol. After you implement Kerberos, all components in the cluster must be Kerberos-aware, Kerberos-enabled, and configured correctly for your Kerberos environment.

HOUR 23

Administering, Monitoring, and Troubleshooting Hadoop

What You'll Learn in This Hour:

▶ Hadoop administration commands and utilities
▶ Logging and log file management in Hadoop
▶ Hadoop Metrics Framework
▶ Best practices for exception handling and application debugging

Along with Hadoop's flexibility and extensibility come many management and administration challenges. Security is one challenge I discussed last hour. In this hour I discuss some of the other challenges associated with administering a Hadoop environment, which include monitoring and managing the state and health of Hadoop services and applications.

Administering Hadoop

Administering Hadoop involves the management and administration of core and ecosystem components. Many of the concepts, utilities, and practices covered in this hour will have been introduced or discussed earlier in the book in various chapters. However, this hour will be helpful in distilling this information before you set off on your Hadoop journey. Let's look at some of the activities and commands involved with administering a Hadoop cluster.

Starting and Stopping Services

You have already seen many examples in which we had to (and did) start-and-stop daemons or services for various reasons, including configuration changes, implementing HA, or bringing up a cluster after a server restart.

Many of the scripts used to start or stop services on a Hadoop cluster are located in the host's $HADOOP_HOME/sbin directory. Table 23.1 provides a brief description of some of the scripts in this directory.

TABLE 23.1 Hadoop `sbin` Directory Scripts

Script(s)	Description
`hadoop-daemon.sh`	Used to start-and-stop individual HDFS daemons on the local machine
`start-dfs.sh,` `stop-dfs.sh`	Used to start-and-stop all master and slave node HDFS daemons on all nodes
`yarn-daemon.sh`	Used to start-and-stop individual HDFS daemons on the local machine
`start-yarn.sh,` `stop-yarn.sh`	Used to start-and-stop all master and slave node YARN daemons on all nodes
`mr-jobhistory-` `daemon.sh`	Used to start-and-stop the MapReduce History daemon on the local machine
`start-all.sh,` `stop-all.sh`	Used to start-and-stop all daemons associated with a Hadoop cluster (Deprecated—instead use the `start-dfs.sh, start-yarn.sh,` etc. commands)

Often, to start-and-stop services you will need to `sudo` as the appropriate user for that particular service, e.g. the `hdfs` or `yarn` user. Some sample usage of these scripts is provided in Listing 23.1.

LISTING 23.1 Starting Services in Hadoop

```
$ sudo -u hdfs $HADOOP_HOME/sbin/hadoop-daemon.sh start namenode
$ sudo -u hdfs $HADOOP_HOME/sbin/hadoop-daemon.sh start datanode
$ sudo -u yarn $HADOOP_HOME/sbin/yarn-daemon.sh start resourcemanager
$ sudo -u yarn $HADOOP_HOME/sbin/yarn-daemon.sh start nodemanager
$ sudo -u mapred $HADOOP_HOME/sbin/mr-jobhistory-daemon.sh start historyserver
```

HDFS Administration

There are many useful tools designed to help with routine HDFS administration tasks. One of these tools is the `hdfs dfsadmin` command. Some of the significant tools available with the `hdfs dfsadmin` command are shown in Table 23.2. Typically, these commands can only be run as the HDFS superuser (`hdfs`).

TABLE 23.2 `dfsadmin` Commands

Command	Description
`-report`	Reports basic filesystem information and statistics.
`-safemode`	Used to manually enter or leave safe mode.
`-saveNamespace`	Saves current namespace into storage directories and reset edits log. Requires the filesystem to be in safe mode.

Command	Description
`-rollEdits`	Rolls the edit log on the active NameNode.
`-fetchImage`	Downloads the most recent `fsimage` from the NameNode and saves it in the specified local directory.
`-metasave`	Saves NameNode's primary data structures to a file.
`-triggerBlockReport`	Triggers a block report for the given DataNode.

As discussed in **Hour 4, "Understanding the Hadoop Distributed File System (HDFS),"** the Hadoop filesystem is in safe mode while the NameNode is in the recovery process. One of the main HDFS administration tasks you may be required to perform is to manually leave safe mode for a NameNode. This can be done using the `hdfs dfsadmin` command, as shown in Listing 23.2.

LISTING 23.2   Leaving Safemode

```
$ sudo -u hdfs $HADOOP_HOME/bin/hdfs dfsadmin -safemode leave
```

In **Hour 21, "Understanding Advanced HDFS,"** you also saw the examples of the `hdfs haadmin` command used to get the service state for a particular NameNode or to initiate a failover of the NameNodes. These are just two examples of the various commands and tools you may be required to use from time to time.

Management of the HDFS metadata is a critical activity when managing Hadoop, as discussed in **Hour 4.**

Management of the metadata involves monitoring of the NameNode's memory usage as well as monitoring of the disk structures associated with the metadata, mainly the disk volumes and partitions specified for the `fsimage` and `edits` files of the JournalNodes involved with a HA configuration. You can use any of the monitoring techniques introduced in this hour, such as collecting host metrics and creating alerts if critical thresholds are met or exceeded. You could also use the cluster management utilities discussed in **Hour 18, "Using Cluster Management Utilities."**

Backup of the NameNode is another important HDFS administration task. Tools such as `hdfs dfsadmin` are available to manually back up the on-disk metadata, specifically `fsimage`. An example of using the `hdfs dfsadmin` command to back up the NameNode's lastest `fsimage` file is shown in Listing 23.3.

LISTING 23.3   Backing up the NameNode's fsimage File

```
$ sudo -u hdfs $HADOOP_HOME/bin/hdfs dfsadmin -fetchImage fsimage.backup
```

YARN Administration

The yarn rmadmin commands are helpful and are often required for administering a YARN cluster. Some of the administrative functions included with the yarn rmadmin utility are described in Table 23.3.

TABLE 23.3   yarn rmadmin Commands

Command	Description
-checkHealth	Performs a health check of the YARN services.
-refreshNodes	Refreshes the hosts' information at the ResourceManager.
-transitionToActive	Used in a HA configuration to transition a ResourceManager to an active state.
-transitionToStandby	Used in a HA configuration to transition a ResourceManager to a standby state.
-failover	Used in a HA configuration to failover the ResourceManager.
-getServiceState	Used in a HA configuration to check the service state of a ResourceManager (returns active or standby).

Managing jobs or applications is a major component of administering a YARN cluster. The yarn application command includes many commands that enable you to view, manage, and even kill jobs running in YARN given the appropriate permissions. Table 23.4 shows some of the utilities available in the yarn application command.

TABLE 23.4   yarn application Commands

Command	Description
-list	Lists all applications or applications in a specific state (e.g., RUNNING).
-kill	Kills a specific running application by *ApplicationId*.
-status	Prints the status of an application.

An example of using the yarn application command to list jobs running and to kill a running job in YARN is provided in Listing 23.4.

LISTING 23.4 Using the yarn Command to Control YARN Applications

```
$ yarn application -list
...
Total number of RUNNING applications : 1
Application-Id                  Application-Name              ...
application_1475830215563_0024  org.apache.spark.examples.SparkPi ...
$ yarn application -kill application_1475830215563_0024
...
Killed application application_1475830215563_0024
```

Hive Administration

A major part of administering a Hive environment is managing the Hive metastore. You will recall that the Hive metastore contains all of the object definitions linking tables in Hive or HCatalog to directories in HDFS.

Recall that the Hive metastore can be local or shared. In most cases, a shared metastore is recommended where the metastore database is available to multiple users from a central location. Hive can be provisioned as a service, rather than a local, single user implementation as well, which is recommended for enterprise deployments.

Administration of Hive can include the service provisioning and activation, which includes the following steps:

1. Create the database for the metastore.

2. Set the appropriate permissions.

3. Initialize the schema for the metastore using the schematool utility. An example of this is provided in Listing 23.5.

4. Start the metastore service, which is implemented using Thrift when using HiveServer2 or Hive-as-a-Service.

LISTING 23.5 Using the schematool to Initialize the Metastore Schema

```
$ sudo /usr/lib/hive/bin/schematool -dbType mysql -initSchema
```

You will need to manage the database server hosting the metastore as well as manage the metastore database itself. This can include the following:

▶ Performing a regular backup of the metastore database

▶ Managing the metastore database's transaction logs

▶ Establishing a disaster recovery or business continuity plan (DR/BCP) for the metastore database and service

▶ Establishing high availability for the metastore database server if required

Troubleshooting Hadoop

Things can and often will fail in a busy, distributed environment. When they inevitably do, you will need to know how to find the root cause of the issue.

Logging and Log File Management in Hadoop

Your first port of call when troubleshooting any issue in Hadoop is the log files. Hadoop uses *Log4j* as its logging framework. Let's discuss Log4j and logging in Hadoop now.

Log4j

Log4j is a Java-based logging library commonly used by Java applications, processes, and daemons. Log4j enables developers to implement loggers (objects that represent a log file output) and to log various events according to specific criteria and severity levels.

Severity levels defined in the Log4j specification are summarized in Table 23.5 ordered by their verbosity, from the least verbose to the most.

TABLE 23.5   Log4j Severity Levels

Log Level	Description
OFF	Used to turn off all logging.
FATAL	Severe errors that typically cause premature termination of the application.
ERROR	Runtime errors. These are often followed by a Java stack trace.
WARN	Warnings. Typically these are not necessarily errors, but they may lead to issues (such as the use of deprecated APIs).
INFO	Informational and status messages implemented by the developer.
DEBUG	Include additional detailed information about the process or application as implemented by the developer.
TRACE	More detailed logging level than DEBUG, including lower-level process information.
ALL	Log everything (TRACE through to FATAL).

Log4j also includes log management capability with its *appenders*, classes that manage where log events are sent to and how logs are stored, rotated, and managed. Some of the common Log4j appenders available are listed in Table 23.6.

TABLE 23.6   Log4j Appenders

Log4j Appender	Description
ConsoleAppender	Logs events to the console stderr (by default).
FileAppender	Logs events to a file.
RollingFileAppender	Extends FileAppender to back up the log files when they reach a certain size.
SyslogAppender	Logs events to a remote syslog daemon.
JDBCAppender	Logs events to a database via JDBC.

There are also appenders available for popular messaging platforms such as Kafka, JMS (Java Message Service), and ZeroMQ.

The log4j.properties File

The `log4j.properties` file is used to specify the default logging configuration for applications and processes using Log4j. In the case of Hadoop, this file is located in the Hadoop configuration directory, `/etc/hadoop/conf` by convention. Listing 23.6 shows an example excerpt from a `log4j.properties` file.

LISTING 23.6   The log4j.properties File

```
. . .
# Set everything to be logged to the console
log4j.rootCategory=INFO,console
log4j.appender.console=org.apache.log4j.ConsoleAppender
log4j.appender.console.target=System.err
log4j.appender.console.layout=org.apache.log4j.PatternLayout
log4j.appender.console.layout.ConversionPattern=%d{yy/MM/dd HH:mm:ss} %p %c{1}:
%m%n
. . .
```

As you can see from Listing 23.6, the `log4j.properties` file sets the default configuration for what gets logged (in this case, INFO messages and above), how it gets logged (the log file layout), where it gets logged, and how logs are managed (using the *ConsoleAppender*, in this case). Example log events from a Spark application using this configuration are shown in Listing 23.7.

LISTING 23.7   **Example Log Events**

```
16/05/14 07:01:34 INFO SparkContext: Running Spark version 1.6.1
16/05/14 07:01:36 INFO SecurityManager: Changing view acls to: hadoop
16/05/14 07:01:36 INFO SecurityManager: Changing modify acls to: hadoop
16/05/14 07:01:37 INFO Utils: Successfully started service 'sparkDriver' on port
40806.
16/05/14 07:01:38 INFO Slf4jLogger: Slf4jLogger started
16/05/14 07:01:38 INFO Remoting: Starting remoting
16/05/14 07:01:39 INFO SparkEnv: Registering MapOutputTracker
16/05/14 07:01:39 INFO SparkEnv: Registering BlockManagerMaster
16/05/14 07:01:39 INFO SparkEnv: Registering OutputCommitCoordinator
16/05/14 07:01:39 INFO Utils: Successfully started service 'SparkUI'
16/05/14 07:01:39 INFO HttpServer: Starting HTTP Server
...
```

If the `log4j.properties` file is not available in the Hadoop configuration directory, Hadoop will use the first `log4j.properties` file found in the Java classpath for the process. You can also specify the `log4j.properties` file by specifying a JVM by using the `-D` option when submitting a Java MapReduce application or a Spark application. An example of specifying the `log4j.properties` file for a Spark application running on YARN is shown in Listing 23.8.

LISTING 23.8   **Specifying the log4j.properties File for an Application**

```
$SPARK_HOME/bin/spark-submit  \
    --class org.apache.spark.examples.SparkPi \
    --master yarn-cluster \
    --driver-java-options \
        "-Dlog4j.configuration=log4j.properties.erroronly" \
    $SPARK_HOME/lib/spark-examples-*.jar 1000
```

Much more information about Log4j configuration settings can be found at http://logging.apache.org/log4j.

Hadoop Daemon Logging

Hadoop daemons such as the NameNode and ResourceManager typically write their log files to `/var/log/hadoop-*` directories. For instance, a NameNode's daemon log file would be written to `/var/log/hadoop-hdfs/hadoop-hdfs-namenode-<hostname>.log`. The log level can be changed using the `log4j.properties` file in the Hadoop configuration directory as discussed.

TIP

Check the Daemon Logs to Troubleshoot Failed Master or Slave Node Processes

Checking the daemon log files (`.out`, `.log`, and `.err` files) should be your first step in troubleshooting Hadoop daemons that terminate unexpectedly or fail to start.

You can adjust the log level for a running daemon from the command line using the `hadoop daemonlog` utility, as shown in Listing 23.9.

LISTING 23.9   Adjusting the Daemon Log Level

```
$ hadoop daemonlog \
-setlevel localhost:50070 \
org.apache.hadoop.hdfs.server.datanode.NameNode \
WARN
Connecting to http://localhost:50070/logLevel?log=org.apache.hadoop.hdfs.server.
datanode.NameNode&level=WARN
Submitted Log Name: org.apache.hadoop.hdfs.server.datanode.NameNode
Log Class: org.apache.commons.logging.impl.SLF4JLocationAwareLog
Submitted Level: WARN
```

The daemon log level will revert to the level originally configured by the setting specified in the `log4j.properties` file after the daemon is restarted.

The log level can also be adjusted using the `/logLevel` page of the daemon web UI, as shown in Figure 23.1.

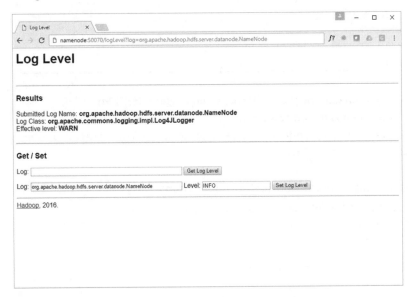

FIGURE 23.1
Changing a Daemon Log Level Using the Web UI.

TIP

Watch Out for Misconfiguration Issues

Recall that misconfiguration is one of the main causes of issues in Hadoop. Often the stack traces and messages in the log file(s) will help to identify where you have a misconfiguration or a configuration error.

Logging within an Application

Developers often require detailed information about applications or processes. This is necessary to troubleshoot failed processes as well as to analyze performance. A common approach is to add print statements to your code, although this is not very scalable and is difficult to implement when running in a distributed system (print to where?).

A better, more extensible, and more scalable alternative is the effective use of logging within an application, which provides the application developer with control and granularity over what gets logged and how it gets logged.

Although log levels can be set in the `log4j.properties` file, as you have seen, this often does not provide the flexibility needed during the application development process. A better solution may be to set or adjust the log level within your program. An example of setting the log level programatically in a MapReduce application is shown in Listing 23.10.

LISTING 23.10   Adjusting the Log Level Programmatically

```
public static Logger LOGGER =
           Logger.getLogger(My.class);
LOGGER.setLevel(Level.DEBUG);
LOGGER.debug("Log Level changed to DEBUG");
...
```

I discussed YARN log aggregation and the yarn logs command in **Hour 16, "Managing YARN."** To recap, log aggregation is the process by which application logs for completed applications are moved into HDFS for long-term storage. Aggregated logs can be accessed using the yarn command as shown in Listing 23.11.

LISTING 23.11   Accessing Logs for Completed Applications

```
$ yarn logs -applicationId application_1475830215563_0024
Container: container_1475830215563_0024_01_000002 on ...
========================================================
LogType:stderr
Log Upload Time:Sun Oct 09 07:02:00 +0000 2016
LogLength:69033
Log Contents:
```

```
SLF4J: Actual binding is of type [org.slf4j.impl.Log4jLoggerFactory]
16/10/09 07:01:50 INFO SignalUtils: Registered signal handler for TERM
16/10/09 07:01:50 INFO SignalUtils: Registered signal handler for HUP
16/10/09 07:01:50 INFO SignalUtils: Registered signal handler for INT
16/10/09 07:01:51 INFO SecurityManager: Changing view acls to: yarn,ec2-user
16/10/09 07:01:51 INFO SecurityManager: Changing modify acls to: yarn,ec2-user
16/10/09 07:01:51 INFO SecurityManager: Changing view acls groups to:
16/10/09 07:01:51 INFO SecurityManager: Changing modify acls groups to:
...
```

Using the Hadoop Web UIs for Troubleshooting

You have seen many of the embedded web UIs available in the Hadoop project, such as the NameNode web UI or the YARN ResourceManager web UI. These can often be a quick and easy way to diagnose issues on your cluster. Most service UIs include the facility to drill down into daemon or application log files without needing to SSH into remote master or slave nodes. An example of using the NameNode UI to view its daemon logs is shown in Figure 23.2.

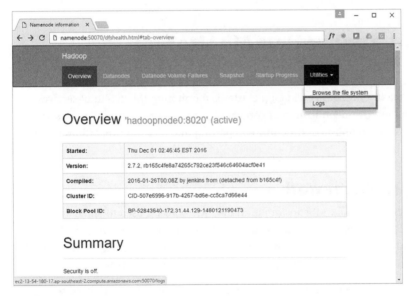

FIGURE 23.2
Viewing Daemon Logs Using Hadoop Web UIs.

Logs for completed and running applications or containers are seamlessly available through the YARN ResourceManager web UI as well. An example of this is shown in Figure 23.3.

FIGURE 23.3
Accessing Application Logs Using the YARN ResourceManager UI.

System and Application Monitoring in Hadoop

Another activity required in managing a Hadoop cluster is monitoring the health of services and applications, including the identification of capacity issues, resource contention, or service degradation. This is often accomplished through the reporting and alerting capabilities provided through the collection of metrics.

Hadoop Metrics Framework

Hadoop exposes metrics via *MBeans*. MBeans are managed Java objects used to emit notifications that consist of events and metrics within the *Java Management Extensions (JMX)* framework. The JMX specification provides lightweight interfaces that enable clients to connect remotely to a JVM, and manage and monitor processes running within the JVM.

MBeans can emit metrics via broadcast messages (JMX broadcasts), which can be accessed through JMX Ports for JMX monitoring solutions such as JConsole, Nagios, or Zabbix.

Hadoop metrics sources can include metrics from HDFS, YARN, MapReduce, and more. Hadoop metrics can also be integrated as metrics sinks, exposing data that can be integrated into common cluster monitoring solutions and metrics visualization platforms such as Ganglia and Graphite.

The Hadoop metrics framework is depicted in Figure 23.4.

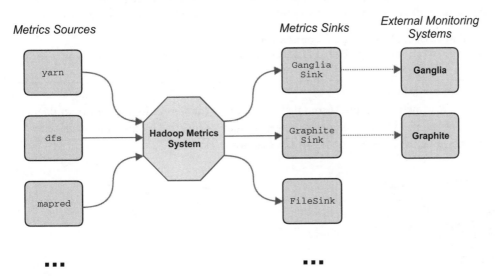

FIGURE 23.4
Hadoop Metrics Framework.

Hadoop metrics are configured using the `hadoop-metrics2.properties` file located in the Hadoop configuration directory. An example of this file is provided in Listing 23.12.

LISTING 23.12 `hadoop-metrics2.properties` **File**

```
# syntax: [prefix].[source|sink].[instance].[options]
# See javadoc of package-info.java for org.apache.hadoop.metrics2 for
details
*.sink.file.class=org.apache.hadoop.metrics2.sink.FileSink
# default sampling period, in seconds
*.period=10
# The namenode-metrics.out will contain metrics from all context
namenode.sink.file.filename=namenode-metrics.out
# Specifying a special sampling period for namenode:
namenode.sink.*.period=8
datanode.sink.file.filename=datanode-metrics.out
resourcemanager.sink.file.filename=resourcemanager-metrics.out
nodemanager.sink.file.filename=nodemanager-metrics.out
mrappmaster.sink.file.filename=mrappmaster-metrics.out
jobhistoryserver.sink.file.filename=jobhistoryserver-metrics.out
# the following example split metrics of different
# context to different sinks (in this case files)
nodemanager.sink.file_jvm.class=org.apache.hadoop.metrics2.sink.FileSink
```

```
nodemanager.sink.file_jvm.context=jvm
nodemanager.sink.file_jvm.filename=nodemanager-jvm-metrics.out
nodemanager.sink.file_mapred.class=org.apache.hadoop.metrics2.sink.
FileSink
nodemanager.sink.file_mapred.context=mapred
nodemanager.sink.file_mapred.filename=nodemanager-mapred-metrics.out
...
```

You can also view metrics captured using the /jmx page of the web UI for the particular daemon you are interested in. For instance, to view the HDFS metrics collected by the NameNode, you would go to <namenode-host>:50070/jmx as shown in Figure 23.5.

FIGURE 23.5
Viewing JMX Metrics from the Web UIs.

Understanding Application Counters in Hadoop

Counters are a construct available to programmers to define custom metrics and aggregate values for these metrics during the processing of a distributed application. The values for the metrics defined by the developer are typically read by the application driver after the completion of the application. Counters can be used to count occurrences of an event seen while processing the data, or for operational purposes such as the number of malformed records in a dataset.

Counters are very simple name value pairs that belong to user-defined groups for logical groupings of related counters. Counters are created when they are first accessed or updated. For instance, if you were processing a dataset and wanted to capture the various types of malformed records encountered during processing, you could create and increment counters in the Java MapReduce application as shown in Listing 23.13.

LISTING 23.13 Creating and Updating Java MapReduce Counters

```
// context is the context object created in a MapReduce application
// available to the Driver, Mappers, and Reducers at runtime
context.getCounter("BadRecords","incorrect_fields").increment(1);
context.getCounter("BadRecords","datatype_errors").increment(1);
```

The counters can be accessed from your MapReduce driver application using the code provided in Listing 23.14.

LISTING 23.14 Reading MapReduce Counters

```
// always use a long datatype to accommodate
// potentially extremely large values
long BadFields =
job.getCounters().findCounter("BadRecords","incorrect_fields").getValue();
long CastErrors =
job.getCounters().findCounter("BadRecords","datatype_errors").getValue();
```

The counters are also visible in the console output after running the job, as shown in Figure 23.6.

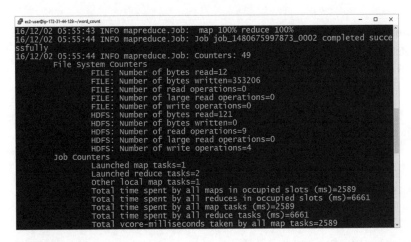

FIGURE 23.6
Viewing Counters in the Console.

Counters are also visible using the JobHistoryServer UI accessible through the YARN ResourceManager UI, as shown in Figure 23.7.

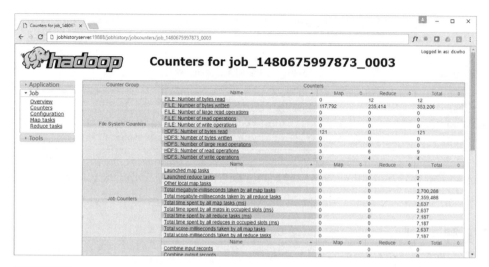

FIGURE 23.7
Viewing Counters through the JobHistoryServer UI.

Spark includes a similar construct called accumulators. As we will discuss in the next section, counters and accumulators provide part of a best practice approach to exception handling in a distributed application, in addition to their other uses.

CAUTION

Don't Overuse Counters

Counters are very useful, but they should be used in moderation. Excessive use of counters (hundreds or thousands) can affect system performance.

▼ TRY IT YOURSELF

Using Counters in a MapReduce Application

In this exercise we will extend the Java MapReduce WordCount application written back in **Hour 7, "Programming MapReduce Applications,"** to add counters. In this case we will create a counter for each word based upon its first letter.

Note that we will still perform WordCount; the counters are incidental to the output and could represent anything—bad or escaped records, for example.

You can run this example on your pseudo-distributed Hadoop cluster.

1. Create a directory that will be used for your source code.

2. Create a `WordCountDriver.java` file, and add the following code using a text editor.

```
import org.apache.hadoop.fs.Path;
import org.apache.hadoop.io.IntWritable;
import org.apache.hadoop.io.Text;
import org.apache.hadoop.mapreduce.lib.input.FileInputFormat;
import org.apache.hadoop.mapreduce.lib.output.FileOutputFormat;
import org.apache.hadoop.mapreduce.Job;
import org.apache.hadoop.conf.Configured;
import org.apache.hadoop.conf.Configuration;
import org.apache.hadoop.util.Tool;
import org.apache.hadoop.util.ToolRunner;

public class WordCountDriver extends Configured implements Tool {
  public int run(String[] args) throws Exception {
    if (args.length != 2) {
      System.out.printf("Usage: %s [generic options] <input dir data-
uuid="3cb3cc2a13e14a969ae2e4a9bd789952"> <output dir>\n", getClass().
getSimpleName());
      return -1;
    }
    Job job = new Job(getConf());
    job.setJarByClass(WordCountDriver.class);
        job.setJobName("Word Count");
    FileInputFormat.setInputPaths(job, new Path(args[0]));
    FileOutputFormat.setOutputPath(job, new Path(args[1]));
    job.setMapperClass(WordCountMapper.class);
    job.setReducerClass(WordCountReducer.class);
    job.setMapOutputKeyClass(Text.class);
    job.setMapOutputValueClass(IntWritable.class);
    job.setOutputKeyClass(Text.class);
    job.setOutputValueClass(IntWritable.class);
    boolean success = job.waitForCompletion(true);
    // Retrieve and Print Counters
    long a_count = job.getCounters().findCounter("FirstLetterCounter", "a")
      .getValue();
    long b_count = job.getCounters().findCounter("FirstLetterCounter", "b")
      .getValue();
    long c_count = job.getCounters().findCounter("FirstLetterCounter", "c")
      .getValue();
    System.out.println("Words starting with a : " + a_count);
    System.out.println("Words starting with b : " + b_count);
    System.out.println("Words starting with c : " + c_count);
    return success ? 0 : 1;
  }
```

```
public static void main(String[] args) throws Exception {
    int exitCode = ToolRunner.run(new Configuration(), new WordCountDriver(),
args);
    System.exit(exitCode);
  }
}
```

3. Create a `WordCountMapper.java` file and add the following code:

```java
import java.io.IOException;
import org.apache.hadoop.io.IntWritable;
import org.apache.hadoop.io.LongWritable;
import org.apache.hadoop.io.Text;
import org.apache.hadoop.mapreduce.Mapper;

public class WordCountMapper extends Mapper<LongWritable, Text, Text,
IntWritable> {
  private final static IntWritable one = new IntWritable(1);
  private Text wordObject = new Text();

  @Override
  public void map(LongWritable key, Text value, Context context)
      throws IOException, InterruptedException {

    String line = value.toString();
    for (String word : line.split("\\W+")) {
      if (word.length() > 0) {
        String firstLetter = word.substring(0,1).toLowerCase();
        context.getCounter("FirstLetterCounter", firstLetter).increment(1);
        wordObject.set(word);
        context.write(wordObject, one);
      }
    }
  }
}
```

Note that we will be incrementing the counter(s) here.

4. Create a `WordCountReducer.java` file and add the following code:

```java
import java.io.IOException;
import org.apache.hadoop.io.IntWritable;
import org.apache.hadoop.io.Text;
import org.apache.hadoop.mapreduce.Reducer;
```

```
public class WordCountReducer extends Reducer<Text, IntWritable, Text,
IntWritable> {
    private IntWritable wordCountWritable = new IntWritable();
    @Override
        public void reduce(Text key, Iterable<IntWritable> values, Context
context)
                        throws IOException, InterruptedException {
                int wordCount = 0;
                for (IntWritable value : values) {
                        wordCount += value.get();
                }
                wordCountWritable.set(wordCount);
                context.write(key, wordCountWritable);
            }
    }
```

5. Compile the application:

```
$ javac -classpath `$HADOOP_HOME/bin/hadoop classpath` *.java
```

6. Package the application:

```
$ jar cvf wc.jar *.class
```

7. Submit the application:

```
$HADOOP_HOME/bin/hadoop jar wc.jar WordCountDriver shakespeare wordcount
```

You should see output similar to the following upon completion of the WordCount application, including the counter values you printed in your driver.

```
...
Words starting with a : 76066
Words starting with b : 40929
Words starting with c : 28061
```

These could also be collected and monitored using any of the metrics sinks discussed earlier.

Best Practices and Other Information Sources

Whether you are a developer or an administrator of a Hadoop environment, you should be aware of good and bad practices for exception handling in Hadoop applications or functions, as these can have a profound impact on applications or the entire system.

Exception Handling and Debugging in Hadoop

When developing applications in Hadoop, there are a few principles you should adhere to that will help you greatly with debugging issues. Those principles include the following:

▶ *Program defensively*—Always expect the unexpected. Unlike a relational database where the data and datatypes are well known, data can be malformed or differ from what you may think it is. Common issues included type casting errors, divide by zero errors, or array index out of bounds errors—all of which come from making assumptions about data and not practicing defensive coding. You should always use try catch blocks for any and all data operations.

▶ *Don't log key value pairs*—The temptation may be to log the offending data record when you catch an exception, but don't do this. If you were analyzing 1TB worth of data, and made the same assumptions causing the same error on every record, you would end up with 1TB worth of log files! Instead, use the counters we spoke about in the previous section or accumulators, a similar concept for Spark applications.

▶ *Don't throw exceptions*—Unless you really want to abort processing altogether. Throwing an exception will cause the given task to re-execute. If the new task performs the same function on the same data as the failed task, it too will fail. After four failed task attempts the entire application will fail, eliminating all other tasks which had completed successfully. Instead, use logging (or messages, not data) or counters.

These are just some general guidelines. You will likely develop some of your own practices as you develop more applications.

Other Information Sources

As the big data and Hadoop movements have grown, there are many additional resources available to you to assist you with troubleshooting issues you may have with Hadoop. Some of these resources include the following:

▶ The Hadoop project site: http://hadoop.apache.org/

▶ Commercial vendors' websites such as http://www.cloudera.com/ or http://hortonworks.com/

▶ Blogs and wikis (a decent Google search should direct you to some of these)

▶ Community support forums such as Stack Overflow at http://stackoverflow.com/

▶ Conferences such as *Strata + Hadoop World* and the *Hadoop Summit,* sponsored by Cloudera and Hortonworks respectively

▶ Books such as this one! (or others such as **Expert Hadoop Administration: Managing, Tuning, and Securing Spark, YARN, and HDFS)**

Summary

In this hour, you learned about some of the various commands used for administration of HDFS and YARN, such as `dfsadmin`, `haadmin`, and `yarnadmin`. You also learned about logging in Hadoop and log file management using Log4J, as well as best practices for application logging and exception handling. Log files serve as a key troubleshooting tool, whether you are debugging services that don't start or crash, or debugging application issues—in most cases, log files are your first port of call. We also looked at metrics in Hadoop for both processes and applications, and the use of counters as a mechanism to count events or exceptions in Hadoop applications.

You may perform many of these administration and troubleshooting activities routinely, depending upon your role. Fortunately, in most cases, there are resources and documentation to help you with many of these functions, so don't be afraid to use them.

Q&A

Q. What steps would you take to troubleshoot a Hadoop daemon that fails to start? What is a common cause of issues with Hadoop processes?

A. You should first check the daemon log files for the failing daemon, checking both the latest `.log`, `.err`, and `.out` files. The last entries in the log file should give you an indication as to why the service will not start. Misconfiguration or configuration errors are among the most common causes of issues in Hadoop, such as daemons not starting.

Q. What sort of host-level metrics should you monitor on nodes in a Hadoop cluster?

A. You should monitor disks and partitions and set warning and alert thresholds when disk space utilization is at 80% or more. Recall that slave nodes require available disk space for staging and processing intermediate data. You should also monitor for excess CPU usage and memory usage, such as the NameNode heap usage. Also, you should monitor and alert if you see excess swapping on any nodes as this is an indication that you may be over-committed.

Q. What are good practices for debugging and exception handling when developing applications for Hadoop?

A. You should always program defensively, using try catch blocks around all of your data operations. When you encounter errors, you should never log key value pairs as you may create an excessively large amount of log data unnecessarily. Instead, you should use counters or log simple messages. You should also avoid throwing exceptions as this will cause tasks to re-evaluate, failing multiple times before the entire application inevitably fails.

Workshop

The workshop contains quiz questions to help you solidify your understanding of the material covered. Try to answer all questions before looking at the "Answers" section that follows.

Quiz

1. Which utility would you use to take a NameNode out of safe mode?

2. Which directory on a Hadoop node contains scripts used to start or stop Hadoop daemons?

3. What file contains information about log file rotation and retention?

4. Which log4j appender can be used by Hadoop to rotate log files on a given interval, such as a daily rotation?

Answers

1. `dfsadmin`.

2. `$HADOOP_HOME/sbin`.

3. `log4j.properties`.

4. DailyRollingFileAppender.

Integrating Hadoop into the Enterprise

What You'll Learn in This Hour:

► Hadoop and the data center
► Using Hadoop for data warehouse/ETL offload
► Complex event processing using Hadoop
► Predictive analytics using Hadoop

Hadoop has moved well beyond its roots as a platform for Silicon Valley tech startups or a university research platform, and is now a mainstream enterprise technology that is prevalent in many corporate and government data centers. In this hour, we wrap up our Hadoop journey together by looking at some of the ways Hadoop is used by organizations today.

Hadoop and the Data Center

As Hadoop has matured and more and more organizations have benefited from the scalable storage and processing capabilities of the platform, Hadoop has become an accepted part of the enterprise data center. In fact, some pundits have estimated that 50% or more of enterprise data will reside on Hadoop by 2020.

Commercial vendors such as Hortonworks and Cloudera have worked to harden the platform and have been significant contributors, along with others in the Hadoop community, to enterprise integration features. Hadoop now takes its place alongside operational systems and data warehouse platforms, providing deep storage and scalable, extensible distributed processing capabilities, as well as enabling real-time event processing.

We look at three specific use cases for Hadoop in the next three sections, including data warehouse offload, complex event processing and predictive analytics, but first let's look at how Hadoop fits into the enterprise data center to provide deep, scalable storage.

Deep Storage using Hadoop

You have seen throughout this book how Hadoop provides reliable, resilient distributed storage using economical, commodity infrastructure. Hadoop's storage, along with other cloud, object, or block storage platforms such as S3, Ceph, or Gluster, can complement other enterprise storage platforms such as SAN, NAS, or NFS.

Hadoop's storage can be used for economical long-term archival purposes, along with the other uses I will discuss later this hour, forming part of a tiered storage strategy where hot, or frequently accessed, data is served from high-end storage systems such as SAN, and less-frequently accessed historical data can be served from Hadoop.

Tiered Storage in Hadoop

Hadoop itself has introduced its own internal support for tiered storage. Hadoop's implementation of tiered storage supports heterogeneous storage media such as disk, SSD, RAM disk, memory, and archival. Hadoop lets you configure storage policies to define different storage levels depending upon the frequency of access (hot, cold, warm). You could combine Hadoop's heterogeneous tiered storage with external, in-memory data grid technologies such as Alluxio or Hazelcast, as shown in Figure 24.1. Hadoop's tiered storage helps you optimize the balance between cost and performance.

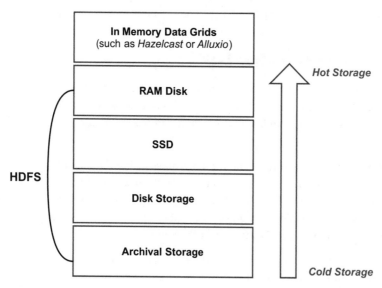

FIGURE 24.1
Tiered Storage.

Use Case: Data Warehouse/ETL Offload

One of the first commercial use cases established for Hadoop was to offload storage and processing from relatively higher cost, massively parallel processing (MPP) platforms. Relational data warehouses on MPP platforms became popular in the mid-2000s and usually conform to the three-tier information model, with staging, integration, and semantic tiers.

The typical processing pattern is to load structured data from operational sources (such as ERP, CRM, or others) into tables in a staging tier, sometimes referred to as tier 1. The staging tables are then conformed to a data model in the integration tier, sometimes referred to as tier 2, using SQL-based ETL routines. Further processing then occurs to create reporting performance objects in the semantic tier (tier 3), including data marts, OLAP structures, and pre-materialized aggregates fit for reporting and business intelligence (BI) systems.

Storage on MPP platforms is expensive and these systems are typically not easily scalable—it's not as simple as adding commodity nodes, as with a Hadoop cluster. Hadoop and HDFS is a low-cost alternative for storing data associated with your enterprise data warehouse where applicable.

Two such common adoptions of this approach are *Aged History Offload* and *Persistent Staging Offload*.

Aged History Offload

While organizations are required to (and want to) store historical data for as long as possible—indefinitely in many cases—this data does not need to be stored at a premium after a designated period of time. Most organizations have a threshold beyond which they are not reasonably expected to produce reports for (e.g., one or two years). An obvious use case is to move aged history beyond the designated threshold to a much lower-cost storage medium—HDFS.

Persistent Staging Offload

Often in an MPP relational warehouse environment, data is not only staged on the platform but staged data is retained on the platform for a period of time, in many cases to support restart/recovery operations or for data lineage purposes. This can contribute to much higher costs. Using Hadoop for some or all of your tier 1 storage can significantly reduce the operating costs of your data warehouse and avert or defer costly hardware upgrades. This use case is especially relevant for the storage of transactional or event data, which usually requires minimal transformation and is usually the most voluminous source of data in a warehouse environment.

Figure 24.2 depicts a typical data warehouse offload pattern using Hadoop.

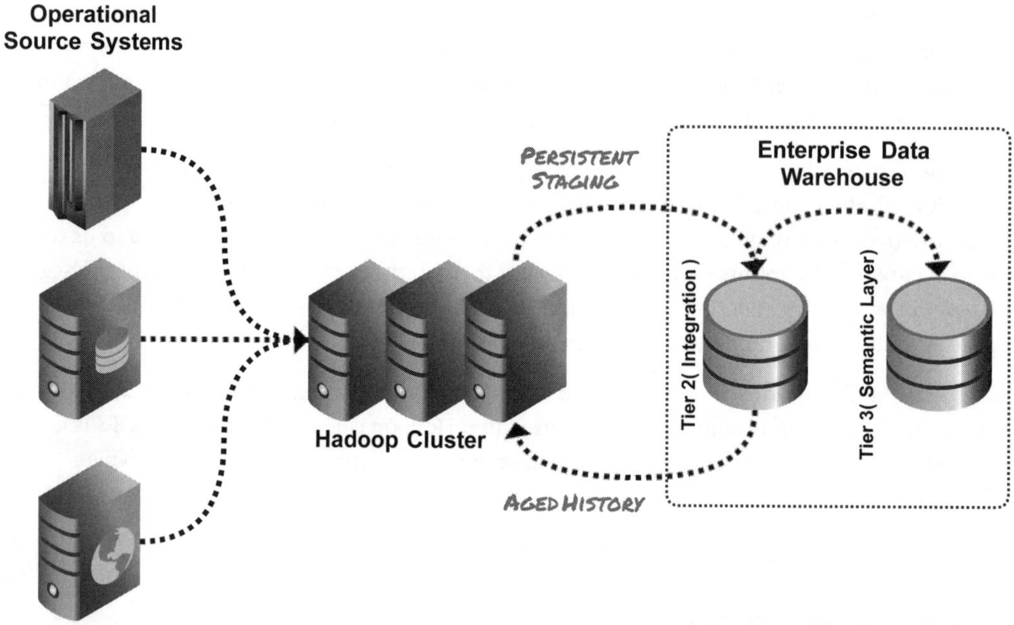

FIGURE 24.2
Data Warehouse Offload.

CAUTION

Consider SLAs and Non-Functional Requirements When Using Hadoop

Accessing and transforming data on Hadoop for data warehouse integration can be much slower than the equivalent ETL routines using a relational MPP platform such as Teradata. You should test integration patterns on Hadoop before implementing to ensure that your batch processing SLAs and NFRs are met.

Hadoop—Data Warehouse Query Integration

In both of the data warehouse offload use cases discussed, the data stored in HDFS is accessible in most cases using the same ETL or BI tools used in your environment. Moreover, many data warehouse vendors offer integrated solutions where the warehouse platform and a Hadoop cluster are combined in an appliance or a unified architecture such as the Teradata Unified Data Architecture (UDA) or the Oracle Big Data Appliance (BDA). In these cases, the vendors often provide an integrated query solution that enables users to seamlessly query (including JOIN and UNION) data from multiple sources, which could include both the relational warehouse and HDFS using Hive/HCatalog. An example of this is Teradata's Query Grid technology.

Use Case: Event Storage and Processing

The storage and processing of events or signals is a common use case for big data platforms such as Hadoop and related ecosystem technologies. Let's discuss this use case and understand the components required to implement it.

Apache Kafka

In **Hour 17, "Working with the Hadoop Ecosystem,"** you were introduced to Apache Kafka. Recall that Apache Kafka is a popular distributed, reliable, low-latency, pub-sub (publish-subscribe) messaging platform designed for message brokering and queuing between various Hadoop ecosystem projects. Although it is a monolithic messaging platform, Kafka is closely related to Hadoop in the big data/open source software ecosystem, and is often used in conjunction with Hadoop and Spark to broker messages from external systems for consumption by Hadoop-based applications.

Kafka is commonly the entry point for messages and events to be processed in Hadoop.

Complex Event Processing in Hadoop

Complex Event Processing (CEP) involves consuming and processing streams of data, potentially enriching or combining this data with batch-processed data, such as master data from a customer or account management system. The combination and integration of both real-time and batch processes in a single architecture is referred to as the lambda architecture.

CEP can also involve triggering other events or processes based upon observed events, such as in the case of fraud detection systems.

CEP can be implemented in many ways. Two common approaches to processing events are Spark Streaming (introduced in **Hour 13, "Introducing Apache Spark"**) and Apache Storm (introduced in **Hour 17, "Working with the Hadoop Ecosystem"**). Spark Streaming uses the Spark runtime processing architecture to process events using Discretized Streams (DStreams), while Apache Storm uses the Hadoop processing platform to process events using a network of spouts and bolts.

Figure 24.3 depicts a high-level event processing architecture involving Kafka for message brokering, Spark Streaming or Apache Storm for event processing, and Hadoop for event storage.

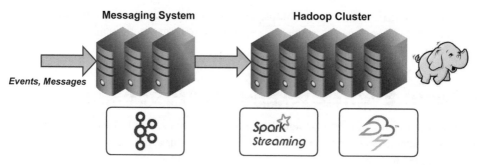

FIGURE 24.3
Event Processing.

The Event Lake

Events have many uses in analytics, from building predictive models to path analysis to mapping customer journeys and more. *Event lakes* are an extension of the *Data Lake* concept, which is a central raw data store on Hadoop. Event lakes can be implemented on HDFS to extract and store events in a customer or operational process journey. These events can then be aggregated into features that can be used for machine learning, predictive modeling, or descriptive analytics. This data can also be useful for operational purposes, such as presenting contact center agents or retail staff with a cross-channel understanding of the customers' interactions.

Hadoop and the Internet of Things (IoT)

IoT (or the *"Internet of Things"*) is a popular term encompassing the universe of connected devices, such as sensors, monitors, components, RFID tags, smart devices, and others, communicating with each other, control systems, and monitoring systems over the Internet. From concepts such as smart homes and smart cities to asset tracking, air quality monitors, and wearables, advancements in low-power wireless technology, the seemingly infinite IPv6 address space, and the ubiquitous Internet have enabled countless IoT device applications and billions of devices.

Distributed messaging platforms such as Apache Kafka, along with distributed storage and processing platforms such as Spark and Hadoop, have become common receivers for events and signals from IoT devices.

Use Case: Predictive Analytics

Hadoop and predictive analytics and machine learning have been intrinsically linked together since Hadoop's early beginnings at Yahoo!. From text mining and sentiment analysis to image recognition to recommendation engines and more, Hadoop has long been a platform conducive to performing advanced analytics.

One of the primary reasons Hadoop is an ideal platform for analytics is its deep and infinitely scalable storage. This enables Hadoop to store historical data for an indefinite period, providing analytic algorithms with massive datasets to use for model training and machine learning.

> "It's not who has the best algorithm that wins. It's who has the most data."
>
> Andrew Ng, co-founder of Coursera and machine learning expert

Feature Engineering on Hadoop

Features are attributes of an entity you are trying to model the behavior of, usually for the purposes of predicting a target attribute or variable, or producing a score—such as a propensity score (a score indicting the likelihood of an event or a condition, e.g., a propensity for a customer to buy a specific product).

Features are often derived from events or transactions; for example, the spend on a product category over the last 52 weeks or a significant change in customer spending patterns. In our previous use case on complex event processing I introduced you to the concept of an event lake where events extracted from raw data could be stored. This event lake could be used to extract features, a process referred to as feature extraction. This event lake could be used to extract features. The features could then be used to train models.

There are many workflow utilities in the immediate and extended Hadoop ecosystem, such as Oozie, Airflow, Azkaban, Luigi, and others, which can be used to orchestrate feature extraction on the Hadoop platform. Furthermore, Hadoop's massively scalable distributed processing framework is well suited to executing feature extraction tasks performed on nodes in a workflow DAG.

Not only can workflows help to orchestrate the discovery process, but workflows can be used to deploy features and models into production as well. These workflows can be easily integrated with your DevOps environment to perform continuous integration or continuous deployment, shortening the cycle between awareness to action.

Flexibility is paramount with event libraries and feature libraries. They need to be able to adapt to new data structures and events over time. Flexibility is a key characteristic of Hadoop, with its schema-on-read architecture. This makes Hadoop and Hadoop-related technologies such as HBase a suitable on-platform store for features. This is often referred to as a feature store. A feature store enables you to re-use historical features without requiring re-computation as well as adding additional features that may be significant variables for a predictive model.

Figure 24.4 shows a conceptual predictive analytic pipeline that involves the training and deployment of a model using the various components and constructs discussed.

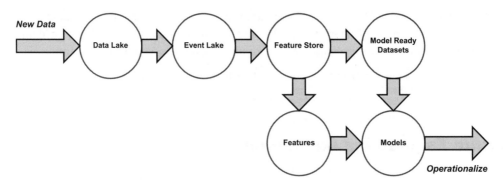

FIGURE 24.4
Predictive Analytics.

On-Platform Analytics

In addition to Hadoop's ability to extract and store features using its integrated distributed storage and processing capabilities, there are many integrated machine learning and predictive modeling utilities available in the Hadoop ecosystem as well.

One such utility is Mahout, which was introduced in **Hour 17, "Working with the Hadoop Ecosystem."** Recall that Apache Mahout is a Java-based machine learning library that contains several popular algorithms for classification, clustering, and collaborative filtering, all common machine learning patterns and techniques. Mahout's algorithms are optimized to run on the Hadoop platform and include built-in support for common machine learning applications such as recommendation engines or basket analysis.

Spark ML and MLlib are Spark's machine learning solutions providing machine learning functions that can be used with Spark RDDs and DataFrames. These are included with each Spark release and can be used for feature extraction, machine learning, and model deployment on the Hadoop platform. H_2O is another popular open source machine learning application and in-memory prediction engine that can be deployed on Hadoop (YARN). H_2O can be deployed using Spark as a processing engine as well, an implementation known as Sparkling Water. R, a popular statistical modeling language, is also available on Spark using the SparkR API.

SparkR, MLlib, and H_2O are discussed at more length in *SAMS Teach Yourself Apache Spark in 24 Hours*.

Summary

Hadoop has become an integral part of the processing fabric of many organizations, public and private. Many mainstream enterprise use cases for Hadoop have emerged that leverage Hadoop's massive scalability. Common use cases for Hadoop discussed this hour include ETL or data warehouse offload, in which Hadoop is used for aged history or persistent staging offload, reducing costs for tier 1 and tier 2 data warehouse storage and processing. Other use cases discussed include complex event processing and predictive analytics, both of which benefit from Hadoop's economical parallel processing capabilities. Furthermore, the economics of storing and processing data on Hadoop have become compelling drivers for the platform, where Hadoop can be used for long-term storage or to form part of a tiered storage strategy.

Well, this brings us to the end of our journey together, but hopefully this is just the beginning for you in your Big Data journey!

Q&A

Q. What are two common patterns for data warehouse offload using Hadoop? What are the benefits of data warehouse offload?

A. Two common implementation forms of data warehouse offload include aged history offload and persistent staging offload. Aged history offload is the process of moving historical data beyond the scope of reporting to HDFS as a lower-cost storage medium. Persistent staging offload is the process of moving some or all of your tier 1 storage and processing from the data warehouse to Hadoop. In both cases, Hadoop's lower-cost storage and scalable processing can be used to minimize data warehouse operating costs or defer costly upgrades.

Q. What is complex event processing? How can this be implemented using Hadoop?

A. Complex Event Processing (CEP) involves consuming and processing streams of data in real time or near real time, potentially enriching or combining this data with other data, such as batch-processed data. CEP can be implemented in Hadoop using distributed stream processing technologies such as Apache Storm or Spark Streaming.

Q. How can Hadoop be used for predictive analytics?

A. Hadoop can be used to complement existing predictive analytic patterns and tools by providing access to massive amounts of historical data as well as pre-calculated features or variables that can be used in predictive models. Furthermore, there are many on-platform machine learning solutions such as Spark MLlib and Mahout that can be implemented to perform distributed machine learning on Hadoop.

Workshop

The workshop contains quiz questions to help you solidify your understanding of the material covered. Try to answer all questions before looking at the "Answers" section that follows.

Quiz

1. What is the method of stratifying Hadoop storage based on its frequency of use, to optimize costs and performance?

2. What is the primary motivator for implementing data warehouse offload using Hadoop?

    A. Increased query performance

    B. Lower operating costs for the data warehouse

    C. Increased reliability

    D. Increased security

3. _____ is a popular distributed, reliable, low latency, pub-sub (publish-subscribe) messaging platform.

4. Which Apache project implements a set of machine learning libraries in Java designed to be used with Hadoop?

Answers

1. Tiered storage.

2. B.

3. Apache Kafka.

4. Mahout.

Index

B

C